COLORADO WOMEN

TIMBERLINE BOOKS

STEPHEN J. LEONARD and THOMAS J. NOEL, editors

COLORADO WOMEN
A HISTORY

GAIL M. BEATON

UNIVERSITY PRESS OF COLORADO

Published by University Press of Colorado
5589 Arapahoe Avenue, Suite 206C
Boulder, Colorado 80303

The University Press of Colorado is a proud member of
the Association of American University Presses.

AAUP 1937 2012

The University Press of Colorado is a cooperative publishing enterprise supported, in part, by Adams State University, Colorado State University, Fort Lewis College, Metropolitan State University of Denver, Regis University, University of Colorado, University of Northern Colorado, Utah State University, and Western State Colorado University.

∞ This paper meets the requirements of the ANSI/NISO Z39.48-1992 (Permanence of Paper).

Library of Congress Cataloging-in-Publication Data

Beaton, Gail Marjorie.
  Colorado women : a history / Gail M. Beaton.
    p. cm. — (Timberline books)
  Includes bibliographical references and index.
  ISBN 978-1-60732-195-8 (cloth : alk. paper) — ISBN 978-1-60732-207-8 (ebook)
  1. Women—Colorado—Biography. 2. Women—Colorado—History. 3. Colorado—Biography. I. Title.
  CT3262.C6B43 2012
  920.72—dc23
  [B]
                            2012024898

Design by Daniel Pratt

21 20 19 18 17 16 15 14 13 12   10 9 8 7 6 5 4 3 2 1

To my mother,
Alice K. Beaton,
and in memory of my father,
Arthur P. Beaton,

who instilled in me a deep
appreciation for history

and to
my nieces and nephews,
Brian, Anna, Alice, Caroline, Matt, and Abbey Beaton
May you embrace life's opportunities
and challenges

CONTENTS

FOREWORD

Colorado history has been mostly his story. Her story has been seldom told. Bohdan Wynar's exhaustive 1980 *Colorado Bibliography* lists 9,181 publications on Colorado, only 10 of which focus on women. Perhaps 25 other general works published since then concentrate on women. A third of those are devoted to Colorado prostitution—the only women's field that seems to titillate authors and publishers.

The official state website, Colorado.com, covers "Outstanding Women in Colorado History" in a paragraph that is less than 200 words long. Yet Colorado way back in 1893 became a global pacesetter by being the first state where men voting solely on the issue of women's suffrage fully approved that then-radical idea (Wyoming men had earlier approved women's suffrage but only as part of a much larger constitutional package on which they were voting). Colorado became the first state in the union to elect women to its legislature and as of 2011 led the United States in the percentage (41%) of female legislators. In 1894 Clara Cressingham, Carrie Clyde Holly, and Frances Klock were elected to the Colorado House of Representatives. Helen Ring Robinson became Colorado's first female state senator in 1913.

Oddly, Colorado has never had a female governor or US senator and has had only four US representatives.

Nevertheless, women have come a long way since the male mining frontier days and an 1860 census count of 32,654 males and 1,577 females. The Colorado Women's Hall of Fame, founded in 1985, has inducted more than 200 ladies and thus introduced the public to worthy but little-known heroines in various fields.

Architects drew up grandiose plans for a Women in the West Museum in Boulder during the 1980s—it never happened because of a lack of funding and interest. Of 1,900 Colorado sites listed on the National and State Register of Historic Places, only a handful commemorate women. Residences, ranches, farms, even mausoleums are nearly always named for the male with little, if any, mention of his female partner. Although women typically took the leading role in establishing churches, hospitals, libraries, and schools, these institutions are generally named after or associated with a male clergyman, head librarian, or school principal.

This book is a pioneering attempt to cover a broad spectrum of women and women's roles in a statewide perspective. Chronologically, it stretches from prehistoric Native Americans to today's immigrant and refugee women.

Author Gail M. Beaton is a teacher, scholar, and re-enactor—her favorite role is Rosie the Riveter, and she wears a T-shirt with Rosie's World War II slogan for women: "We Can Do It." Gail does it with this book. She completed two MA theses, one in history and another in public history, at the University of Colorado at Denver: "The Literary Study and Philanthropic Work of Six Women's Clubs in Denver" and "Making Visible the Invisible: Her Story in Colorado's Queen City." Gail has since broadened her horizons to explore the statewide role of women and has written various articles and given many talks.

A Boston Marathon runner, she has the stamina and courage to finish this monumental task. As a teacher at the high school and college levels, she is experienced and knowledgeable about how to make history appealing, as you will discover in these pages.

The Timberline Series of the University Press of Colorado, which takes pride in publishing the best new scholarship on Colorado as well as classic reprints, proudly adds this candidate to the shelf of important books on the Highest State.

Thomas J. Noel, professor of history and director of
Colorado studies, University of Colorado at Denver

Co-editor with Prof. Stephen J. Leonard of
the Timberline Series, University Press of Colorado

PREFACE

Colorado Women: A History is a history of women's lives in, and contributions to, Colorado. At the beginning of each chapter, an essay places Colorado women in historical context. In ten of the twelve chapters, vignettes on individual women or organizations follow the narrative.

As with any major undertaking, there were challenges in the preparation of this book. One was deciding where to divide the chapters. Because the usual historical divisions are not necessarily appropriate for women's history, I chose to delineate the chapters at important crossroads for women in Colorado.[1] Chapter 1 begins with the lives of Paleoindians and ends at 1858 when the discovery of gold lured scores of Anglo men and women who disrupted the lives of Native American, Spanish, and New Mexican peoples. Chapters 2 and 3 conclude in 1877, the year the first suffrage campaign ended in defeat. Chapter 4 discusses the lives of working women in towns, mining communities, and rural settlements. The significant strides Colorado women made in winning the right to vote and in occupations, club work, and philanthropic efforts are chronicled in chapter 5. The first two decades of the twentieth century, discussed in chapters 6 and 7, mark an era of new occupations, expanded educational opportunities, and Progressive Era reforms. In chapter 8, the dichotomous decade of the 1920s collapsed into the 1930s' Great Depression (chapter 9). Chapter 10 chronicles the significant impacts of World War II on women's personal, domestic, and occupational lives. Chapter 11 depicts the postwar period, while Chapter 12 addresses women in the modern era.

A recurring challenge was what—and whom—to include. Given the constraints of space, neither everything nor everyone could complete the trek from research to written page. Throughout history, migrating women chose what to include on their journeys. At times the piano or grandma's rocking chair was packed, only to be discarded along the trail as too cumbersome or heavy. There it remained to suffer the vagaries of weather or perhaps to be adopted by another pioneer family to complete the journey westward. I view this book in much the same way. While I gleaned and edited, it was consoling to know that other historians will find different avenues of research to explore.

On any given late evening as the sun sets behind the Rocky Mountains, one can look west and see layers of mountains, their colors a gradation of whites, grays, mauves, and blues. They evoke in me a sense of the layers of Colorado women's history. Layers through time. Layers differentiating the experiences of Native American, Hispanic, African American, and Anglo women. Layers of stories sweeping from the eastern plains to the Western Slope. Layers of stories affected by economic and social class. Layers, even, in individual women's stories. Amache Ochinee Prowers was born and raised an American Indian but wed into Anglo society. Maggie "Molly" Brown, best known as a survivor of the *Titanic*, was also a suffragist, philanthropist, wife, mother, and club woman. As historians sift through the layers of the lives and experiences of Colorado women, a more complete picture of Colorado history will emerge.

ACKNOWLEDGMENTS

When one arrives at the end of a journey, it is humbling to look back and see who and what guided you to your destination. The idea to do this book originated nearly thirty years ago when I was a first-time graduate student and grew as I finished a second MA. Both times I was fortunate to work with top-notch professors. I would like to thank Dr. Mark Foster, Thomas J. Noel, Myra Rich, Pamela Laird, and Marjorie Levine-Clark for their pertinent comments on writing style and content. Dr. Noel has seen this book since its infancy. It was from his prompting that I expanded an initial study of Denver women to a book on women throughout the state. Although this undertaking often appeared to be a foolhardy attempt, his encouragement over the years helped sustain my efforts.

Numerous authors and historians have sequestered themselves in libraries and searched archival records to write books and articles on Colorado women that proved helpful to me. I am also indebted to the staffs at the

Western History Collection of the Denver Public Library and the Colorado Historical Society/History Colorado who aided me in following leads and finding material. Equally helpful were the staffs at the Carnegie Branch Library for Public History (Boulder), Penrose Library's Special Collections (Colorado Springs), Fort Collins Museum and Local History Archives, and the City of Greeley Museums.

I would like to thank the Coulter Family Foundation for monetary support when I was a graduate student and the Ward Family Prize in Public History Scholarship Foundation for a thesis award that helped fund research trips. Those trips were productive because of the staffs at the Aspen Historical Society, Big Timbers Museum (Lamar), Cozens Ranch Museum (Fraser Park), Fort Morgan Museum, History Colorado museums, Koshare Indian Kiva and Museum and Otero Museum (La Junta), Museum of Western Colorado (Grand Junction), and Tread of Pioneers Museum (Steamboat Springs). The Center of Southwest Studies (Fort Lewis College), Tutt Library at Colorado College, Norlin Library at the University of Colorado–Boulder, University of Colorado Heritage Center, Auraria Library Archives, Penrose Library at the University of Denver, the National Archives and Records Administration, and Colorado State Archives were also valuable repositories of archival collections. Joining me on a research foray or two were Alice Beaton, Sherrie Langston, Jo Grasso, and Anna Beaton. Their pleasant company and diligent efforts are appreciated.

The process of writing, editing, and rewriting was strengthened through the careful reading and cogent comments offered by a number of people. I am especially grateful to Sherrie Langston, who heard and read many of the chapters in all states of readiness. When it all seemed too overwhelming, she encouraged me to go forward while also exhorting me to enjoy the rigorous process. Jo Grasso, with her English teacher's red pen handy, read early chapters with a keen eye for errors. Alice Beaton, Colleen Nunn, Nancy Speck, and Tamela Cash gave thoughtful feedback on various chapters. I am also indebted to my running friend, Paula Engel, whose company on long runs provided a captive audience with whom I could discuss ideas.

A heartfelt thank you to my brother, Stuart P. Beaton, and his wife, Sheryl. They came to my rescue numerous times to solve computer issues that threatened to derail my mental state, if not the manuscript itself. Stuart also spent many hours with me working on the illustrations and taking the photograph of me as the book's author.

I would like to thank José Aguayo, Linda Alvarado, and Stella Rodgers who graciously permitted me to use family photographs.

As the entire manuscript was brought together, it was greatly enhanced by the staff at the University Press of Colorado. Director Darrin Pratt wisely warned me of potential difficulties but also encouraged me to pursue my idea of a book on Colorado women. Timberline editors Thomas J. Noel and Stephen J. Leonard corrected many of my mistakes, offered suggestions, and led me to numerous sources. As this project proceeded from its first draft to the book you hold in your hands, Jessica d'Arbonne and Laura Furney patiently guided me through the process, diligently answering my questions and calming my apprehensions. Cheryl Carnahan's extraordinary job as copyeditor has given me a deep appreciation for her craft. Daniel Pratt succinctly captured the essence of *Colorado Women* with his cover design, and Beth Svinarich worked diligently to bring this book to the attention of a wide audience.

In sum, it took an army of women—and several men—to bring forth *Colorado Women: A History.* I am profoundly grateful to all of them. Any errors that remain are mine and mine alone.

COLORADO WOMEN

ONE

EARLY WOMEN

(Pre-History—1858)

In the southwest corner of Colorado lies Mesa Verde National Park. For centuries, its cliff dwellings lay silent and empty until a rancher stumbled upon the site. Even then, it was years before the place buzzed once again with human noise and activity.[1] In centuries past, the dwellings snuggled beneath the overhang of cliffs were bustling with activity. Archaeological excavation and studies have helped to paint a picture of the lives of ancient cliff dwellers. Living high above the canyon floor, they threw what they did not want down the slope. Their garbage pits have provided scientists with an array of artifacts to study.[2]

Stone *metates, manos,* and remnants of corn, beans, squash, and cotton indicate the existence of agriculture. Crops were planted on the flat mesas above the cliff dwellings. In front of the homes, kiva roofs created open courtyards where daily routines took place. Ancient Puebloans wove yucca plant fibers into sandals and mats for sitting, kneeling, or sleeping. In the

DOI: 10.5876/9781607322078.c01

FIGURE 1.1 *Ancient Puebloans of Mesa Verde produced baskets and pottery. Awls, axes, and scrapers were forged from bone and stone. Courtesy, History Colorado, (William Henry Jackson Collection, scan #20100739), Denver.*

hands of a skilled basket weaver, strands of yucca formed an airtight basket.[3] Pottery was also made. Over the years, quality improved and pottery designs changed. The most recently found shard is of a distinctive black-on-white design. Long strands of clay were circled from bottom to top on a stone slab to form the sides of a pot. A woman used a stone tool to scrape the inside and outside of the clay vessel. Every so often she dipped the stone scraper into a small bowl of water. With the moistened scraper, she smoothed, shaped, and thinned her creation. She inspected, polished, and painted the pot before placing it in a campfire.[4]

PALEOINDIANS

Living in the southwestern corner of the state, the Ancient Puebloans of the twelfth and thirteenth centuries were only the latest people to occupy the region later known as Colorado. The first people to arrive came from the north and west, moving south and eastward, approximately 12,000 years ago. They hunted herds of Columbian mammoths and mastodons for food, clothing, and shelter. Using stone-tipped spears, Paleoindians also competed with and hunted carnivorous saber-toothed cats, lions, bears, and wolves who feasted on plant-eating giant ground sloths, camels, mastodons, and mammoths. For thousands of years, the people followed the migrating herds. Perhaps a change in climate altered their habitat, resulting in extinction, or Paleoindians themselves brought about their demise through over-hunting.[5]

Whatever the reason, by the time of the Folsom peoples—so named because of their distinctive tools discovered at Folsom, New Mexico—the mastodons and mammoths had given way to *Bison antiquus*, giant buffalo standing nine feet tall at the shoulders, as well as deer, antelope, bighorn sheep, and elk. Rabbits, prairie dogs, and rodents were also hunted. Although several hunters in extended family groups could fell most animals, it took a communal effort to dispatch enough bison to provide plenty of food and skins to last through the winter months. In the fall, bands of Paleoindian hunters gathered together at one site to kill dozens and even hundreds of bison at a time. Hunters stampeded the animals into a ravine or over cliffs, forcing the panicked bison to fall on top of one another. Next came the grueling work of butchering and processing tons of meat, fat, bone, and hide for food, tools, clothing, and shelter. Paleoindian women used stone tools to scrape, cut, and soften hides. They fashioned bone awls to pierce leather and sewed with thread of animal sinew.

After the butchering and processing of hides, the large group split up, spending most of the year in small bands of family members (mother, father, children, grandparents, perhaps aunts, uncles, and cousins). In this way they could forage for other foods to supplement their meat supply. Women and young children gathered chokecherries, raspberries, and wild cherries that were combined with meat paste and fat to form pemmican, an ancient portable "energy bar." Dandelions, prickly pear cactus, wild rose, and cattails were gathered and eaten, as well as piñon pine seeds and juniper berries. For medicine, Paleoindians gathered sagebrush and sweet grass that grew abundantly on the high plains.

Foraging for wild plant leaves, roots, and fruits; hunting; and food processing and cooking consumed the lives of Paleoindians. They traveled by foot and outfitted their domesticated dogs with a wood-framed travois to carry heavier items. Woven baskets of native grasses and reeds were used as storage containers, carrying vessels, and pots. For cooking, fire-heated stones were placed in water in a basket.

By around AD 1000, the Apishapa culture developed in today's southeastern Colorado and northeastern New Mexico. Modern man, zipping through this region in an automobile, scarcely notices the Arkansas River and its tributaries carving wide arroyos and deep, rock-lined canyons into the prairie grasslands. But for the Apishapa people this was home. Like earlier

Paleoindians, the Apishapa traveled with the seasons, returning to certain camps over and over again. Extended families hunkered down under rock overhangs and between outcrops formed by the rivers and streams. Using rocks to create round enclosures, they added posts, brush, and mud to build shelters. They gathered wild plants and hunted small and large game using projectile points and bows and arrows. The Apishapa chiseled or carved petroglyphs and painted pictographs on canyon walls. Around AD 1400 the Apishapa disappeared from southeastern Colorado. Theories abound, including the idea that they and their unique culture were simply assimilated into other tribes.[6]

ANCIENT PUEBLOANS

Agriculture in the Western Hemisphere developed in Central America before spreading north and south into the rest of the Americas. People in the Southwest farmed as early as AD 500.[7] In the valleys of the South Platte, Arkansas, Purgatoire, and Republican Rivers, people built earth-lodge villages and planted gardens in the bottomlands along the streams. They wandered in search of game and wild plants during the summer, returning to harvest their crops in the fall. In the Southwest, the Ancestral Puebloans slowly exchanged their nomadic life for an agricultural one with the planting of corn and squash. For the next twelve or thirteen centuries, their civilization advanced through four stages. During the first era, the Basket Maker Period (approximately AD 1–450), they lived in caves. The men hunted deer, mountain sheep, and mountain lions aided by an *atlatl*, an arm extender, to help them throw the spear farther. They also hunted rabbits, mice, gophers, badgers, and birds. Women farmed with wooden planting sticks and processed animal hides. The Basket Makers built pit houses as they made the transition from large animal hunting to agriculture. With only primitive tools, the Basket Makers laid the foundation for future civilizations, using "their own ingenuity to wrest the necessities of life from a none too favorable environment."[8]

The Ancient Puebloans of the Southwest were short people with coarse black hair and brown skin. They usually wore little clothing; however, the cool evenings and winter months required fur blankets. Another important item they wore were sandals, woven of yucca fiber cord, double-soled, with heel and toe loops of human hair to attach them to the foot. Women hacked off their hair for these sandals. Burial sites yielding remains of Basket Maker men with ornaments in their hair elicited this observation from

Hannah Marie Wormington, one of Colorado's earliest and most respected anthropologists:

> This preoccupation with ornamentation might suggest some degree of vanity, and it is probably true that Basketmaker men gave a good bit of time and thought to their personal appearance. Basketmaker women, however, seem to have been a practical lot, far more concerned with material for their weaving than with their own appearance. The hair of female mummies is hacked off to a length of two or three inches. Of course cutting with a stone knife could hardly be expected to provide a particularly glamorous hair-do, and the fact that strands of hair seem to have been cut off at different times, presumably as the need for weaving material rose, added nothing to the general effect. While Basketmaker women would hardly furnish "pin up" material according to our standards, they presumably seemed attractive to Basketmaker men which, after all, was far more to the point.[9]

Women carried their young in cradleboards they made by creating a frame of sticks, padding the frame with juniper bark, and covering the frame with fur-cloth blankets. A mother tied her baby to the cradle with a soft fur cord. In this way she could carry the cradle on her back, hang it on a branch, prop it against a tree or rock, or lay it on the ground as she worked.

Following the first Basket Maker Period was the Modified Basket Maker Period (AD 450–750), characterized by a more sedentary life and the establishment of regular communities. They began making rudimentary pots in addition to their woven baskets. The following Developmental-Pueblo Period (AD 750–1100) was a transitional period. Pit houses evolved from dwellings to specialized ceremonial structures. Cotton was grown; axes and hoes were developed. Women also changed the cradles they used for their young. Instead of a wooden frame covered in juniper bark, the new cradle was a wooden slab that flattened the infant's soft skull, giving earlier scholars the mistaken idea that these were an entirely new people and not a group descended from the earlier Basket Makers.

During the Great Pueblo Period of the twelfth and thirteen centuries, Ancient Puebloans built terraced communal houses in open areas and in caves. Cliff Palace at Mesa Verde, one of the best-known examples, is tangible evidence of a civilization at its peak. Clay or packed earth was laid upon the stone floors to make them warmer; doorways were T-shaped to allow a person with a load on his or her back to enter. Openings were cut to ventilate the space and allow smoke to escape. Niches and shelves were cut to store things. Dry farming and crude irrigation were used to grow beans, corn, squash, and cotton. Turkeys were raised for food. Their feathers were used for ornamentation and their bones for tools. The cliff dwelling settlements grew and prospered until the mid-1200s when, for reasons still unclear to archaeologists, the Ancient Ones abandoned the sites, perhaps to establish settlements in Arizona and the Rio Grande Valley of New Mexico.[10]

UTE INDIANS

Sometime after the Ancestral Puebloans deserted southwestern Colorado, bands of Ute Indians from the Great Basin migrated east and south into Colorado. Having acquired horses by the late 1600s, the Utes lived off the bounty of the forests, killing elk and deer during the summer and fall. Originally limited to the Western Slope, mounted Utes were able to conduct large bison-hunting expeditions on the eastern high plains where they competed with Plains Indians. With the acquisition of horses, the Utes came to resemble their enemies in many ways while still retaining some aspects of their Great Basin culture. Their clothing was similar to that of the Plains Indians, except that they also wore woven blankets of rabbit-skin strips. Women, who made most of the tribe's clothing, wore short skirts of shredded bark as they had done in the Great Basin. Men made some of their own ceremonial and hunting clothing and accessories. Vegetable fibers were used for clothing, shelter, blankets, basketry, and footwear. Women made sandals of yucca fiber, sagebrush bark, or muskrat hides tied together at the toes and heels and lined with softened sagebrush bark. In winter, leggings provided warmth.

A woman's most laborious chore was tanning hides. To do that, she scraped the inner surface clean of fat and flesh with a chisel-shaped flesher of antler or bone. Then she hung the hide on a slant pole frame to continue scraping. She stretched heavier buffalo hides on the ground. Working together, several women washed, soaked, rinsed, and wrung out the hide and then thoroughly rubbed boiled animal brains into it. After drying the hide in the sun for a few days, they again soaked, rinsed, and wrung it out by twisting it with a stick before hanging it out to dry. The long, tedious process of stretching by holding the hide with the feet and pulling it toward the body took half a day or more. Heavy hides might be further softened by rubbing them with a stone or pulling sinew rope back and forth over the surface, while lighter hides might be chewed. A woman left hides for her clothing white, but she smoked the hides used for men's clothing, tepees, and various bags. She hung the hides by a tripod over a fire for fifteen to thirty minutes.

This was done early in the morning when the air was still, and different types of wood were burned. Greasewood turned skins yellow, willow dyed them brown, and pine resulted in a light yellow coloring.

Originally, Utes lived in wickiups—small, round shelters of poles and brush—like their Great Basin kin, but after acquiring the horse they adopted the tepees of the Plains Indians. The tepee was the woman's responsibility. She made it, put it up, took it down, and moved it from camp to camp. Dogs and, later, horses that were owned by women were used for riding, packing, and dragging the travois that carried the heavy tepees when camp was moved.

To make a tepee, a woman sewed together a dozen elk or fewer buffalo hides. Twelve tall poles from lodgepole pine were preferred, but Utes also used aspen and cedar poles. Four poles were bound together with a rawhide rope. Three women usually set up a tepee. Two women raised four poles to a vertical position and separated them to form an inverted cone. Slowly, one woman opened them out to full diameter, with the exception of two poles that were left about two feet apart to form the entrance. Directly opposite these, a pole on which the top of the canvas had been firmly fashioned was raised. The rest of the poles were then placed in position, supported by the crotches of the tied poles. A hide was stretched over the poles. Just above the entrance, two triangular-shaped flaps were used for ventilation and as a smoke hole. At this point, one woman would go inside the tepee and move the poles outward until the hide was tautly stretched over them. The lower edge was securely fastened to the ground with wooden pegs.

When breaking camp, women dismantled the tepees. They tied six poles on each side of a horse, laid the folded cover over the extension of the poles that dragged on the ground behind the horse, and then stacked their belongings on top of the extension. The dragging of the poles on the ground made a very broad track that was used year after year until the path became a well-worn "road." These "lodgepole trails" became wilderness highways followed by later explorers, prospectors, and freight wagons. Many of these old Ute trails—like Ute Pass, which runs from the plains through the Rockies near Colorado Springs—evolved into the routes of present-day roads and highways.

In the winter, fortified by the bounty of bison, Utes returned to the western river valleys to avoid harsh alpine conditions. Women and children gathered roots, pine nuts, acorns from dwarf oaks, and different kinds of berries. Some were eaten immediately; others were mashed with or without their seeds, dried in the sun, and stored. Women and young children

FIGURE 1.2 *The introduction of horses significantly changed the lives of Native Americans. Horses that dragged the tepee-laden travois were the property of Ute women. Courtesy, Special Collections, Pikes Peak Library District, 001–295, Colorado Springs.*

gathered seeds of grasses and flowers by brushing the seeds into baskets or onto pieces of buckskin with willow branches or small woven fans. Seeds were parched on flat basketry trays by placing a handful or two of powdered charcoal or ash over them. The ashes and seed were then tossed in the air so the chaff was carried away by the wind or blown away by the mouth. A day's labor could result in about a quarter of a bushel of clean seeds, which were roasted in a tray.

Utes used a variety of methods to preserve food. Buffalo, deer, and elk meat were cut into thin strips and hung on racks to dry. Small fires under the racks kept insects away, added flavor, and hastened the drying process. Strips of dried meat were stored in *parfleches*, an Indian rawhide "suitcase." Doing double-duty, *parfleches* were also used to store clothing. Utes ate piñon nuts raw or parched over hot coals to remove the shells. What was not immediately eaten was ground into meal for later use. Women added water before baking the mixture in ashes or on hot rocks.

In addition to making and setting up tepees and gathering, processing, and cooking food, Ute women made basketry items. They coiled willow twigs to form baskets used for collecting, processing, and storing food;

added pine sap to make baskets watertight; and constructed sleeping mats of willows laid in rows and twined together. Although baskets were an integral part of Ute life, pottery was rare, consisting mostly of water cups and cooking utensils.

While Ute women were occupied with their own chores, the men of the tribe spent the majority of their time hunting, fishing, and making the tools necessary to pursue and capture game. Rabbits, antelope, deer, and elk were stalked or ambushed by an individual hunter. Men, like women, made their own tools and weapons for hunting: bows and arrows, arrowheads, knives of obsidian or flint, quivers, and shields.

Although everyone had a general knowledge of plants used for cures, medicine women were the tribe's pharmacists. They gathered as many as 300 plants with therapeutic properties. Sage leaves were used for colds, split cactus or pine pitch for wounds and sores, powdered obsidian and sage tea mixture for sore eyes, grass to stop bleeding, and teas from various plants to treat stomachaches.

PLAINS INDIANS

Nomadic Plains Indians—Apache, Kiowa-Apache, Comanche, and Cheyenne tribes—depended on the buffalo for most of their basic needs. Men wore shirts, leggings, aprons, and breechcloths of buffalo hide. Women wore long one-piece dresses that stretched from their necks to their ankles. The dresses covered their upper arms but had no sleeves. Both men's and women's clothing was decorated with elk's teeth, paintings, porcupine quills, and trade beads. Buffalo bones were used to fashion tools, while buffalo dung provided fuel for warmth and cooking. Surplus hides and meat were traded with the Pueblo Indians for maize and cotton cloth.

As the Utes moved eastward into the region, bands of Athabascan-speaking Indians moved south from Canada into present-day Colorado. Moving along the base of the Rockies, Apache tribes reached the plains of Colorado, Kansas, and New Mexico by the early 1500s. The Navajos settled into southern Colorado and northern New Mexico, encountering the descendants of the Ancient Ones. The relationship among the three groups ranged from trade to raids. By 1720 the Utes roamed much of the region, having driven the Navajo and Apache tribes into New Mexico. By 1820 the Shoshone hunted in the far northwest while the Arapaho, Kiowa, and Cheyenne roamed the northeast. Utes claimed the west, and the Comanche controlled the lower southeastern corner along the Arkansas River.

THREE CULTURES MEET

Meanwhile, cataclysmic changes were occurring far south of the Arkansas River. In the 1500s Spanish conquistadors stormed the beaches of Central America. Hernando Cortés, with the help of superior weaponry, horses, and native allies resentful of Aztec subjugation, defeated this great civilization. Other Spanish explorers and conquistadors defeated indigent tribes in the southern part of the Western Hemisphere. Within a short time, Spanish invaders had conquered and enslaved the native populace on plantations and in silver mines, built cities, and established Catholic missions. Explorers journeyed as far north as present-day Colorado and Kansas. In their wake came settlers who faced a number of obstacles in forming successful villages, mainly the dry climate and native tribes who refused to be Christianized. Although New Spain (basically present-day Mexico) thrived, the northern provinces suffered from governmental neglect and Indian attacks. Periodically, Spanish troops swept into the region to root out the American or French presence but did little to bring in more settlers from the south. When Mexico won its independence from Spain in 1821, the new government encouraged populating these provinces to bolster their claims as a new danger arose from the north and east. But while Americans from the southern states eagerly joined Stephen Austin in Texas, the land of New Mexico continued to languish. Villages remained small agricultural communities far removed from the rest of the Mexican nation. However, trade with American cities along the Missouri, Arkansas, and Mississippi Rivers would soon affect Mexico's northern provinces in the Southwest.

William Becknell, a Missourian, was the first American trader to realize the change in Mexico's attitude toward American trade goods and influence. In 1821 he traveled the overland trail to Santa Fe, sold his goods, and returned to Missouri five months later laden with Mexican silver. Within three years, caravans had replaced Becknell's small pack train; four years later, 100 wagons completed the journey. With the market for beaver pelts on the rise, mountain men and trappers established themselves in the southern Rockies. Ceran St. Vrain and Charles Bent formed Bent, St. Vrain and Company. With Charles's brother William, they built Bent's Old Fort to take advantage of the trade among Santa Fe merchants, mountain men, and Indian tribes. Located between present-day La Junta and Las Animas on the north side of the Arkansas River, the fort was constructed of adobe bricks made by Mexican workers brought in from Taos. Adobe walls three feet thick and fourteen feet high formed the back walls of a ring of dormitories, workrooms, and storerooms surrounded by a large courtyard. The slightly slanted roofs were made of poles covered with a foot of mud. As many as 100 employees worked at the fort. Some lived there; others camped outside the adobe walls.

One such resident was Owl Woman. The oldest daughter of Tail Woman and White Thunder, a Cheyenne sub-chief, Owl Woman had caught Bent's eye. Marriages between European or American traders and native women were nothing new. French trappers had cemented business relations with many Canadian tribes in the same way. We may not know for certain the advantages for the women involved, but for the men, it was a very fortuitous relationship.

The rising trade in buffalo robes had drastic social and economic consequences for American Indians, especially the women. Trading posts such as Bent's Fort on the Arkansas and Fort Union on the Missouri River offered the men of buffalo-hunting tribes a variety of goods paid for with tanned hides. As the demand for hides increased, a man needed more wives to prepare them. The average number of wives per lodge rose from three to five. Because tribes were unable to provide enough women, intertribal warfare increased in an effort to acquire more women. The power, prestige, and wealth from the robe trade flowed to the men of the tribe, eroding women's social position. For some Native American women, an alternative was marriage to a white man, who usually took only one wife and lavished attention and baubles on her. The disadvantage was the loss of the company of her tribal sisters. Some white trappers and traders abandoned their Indian wives and children after years together. Still, some native women freely married or shared their lives with these men.

Along with Owl Woman, her sister came with the marriage to Bent, following Cheyenne custom. Although Bent was reluctant to agree to that part of the arrangement, he compromised by accepting Yellow Woman into his family, although not as a second wife. Owl Woman sometimes stayed within the fort confines overnight, but she generally stayed outside the fort walls with her Indian kin. Accustomed to a tepee, when she did stay in Bent's quarters, she slept on the floor.[11] Owl Woman and Bent had four children—Mary, Robert, George, and Julia—all named after Bent's siblings. As was customary for Cheyenne mothers-to-be, when it came time for her to give birth, Owl Woman stacked skins on the ground, knelt or squatted between the stacks, and grasped them. Either an Indian midwife or a female relative—in Owl Woman's case, probably her sister, Yellow Woman—assisted with the birth. In 1847 Owl Woman died following the birth of her third child. Within two years, Bent married Yellow Woman; they had one son, Charley.

In addition to the Indian wives of Anglo traders and trappers, other women lived at Bent's Fort. Some were the wives of the Mexican laborers brought in to make the original adobe bricks, who stayed on as livestock hands and maintenance crew members. Today, at the reconstructed fort, one can see their quarters on the lower level. Religious art and crosses adorn the thick walls, while chilis hang near the fireplaces. One carpenter's wife, Rosalie, of French and Indian heritage, is remembered for her dancing. Another woman received more praise and notice than most because of her race and her position at the fort.

Charlotte Green, her husband, Dick, and his brother, Andrew, were slaves of Charles Bent, who had brought them to the fort from Missouri. "Black Charlotte," as she was known, was the fort's cook. Her pies and holiday feasts were widely praised by many who dined at the fort. She also reputedly loved *fandagoes* on nights when the fort was celebrating.[12] For army officers, trappers, and traders accustomed to lonely nights on the trail or in the mountains hunting, the opportunity to partake of Green's culinary productions and to be her or Rosalie's dance partner was especially memorable. For her meals, Green relied on buffalo, venison, and other meats provided at the fort. She spiced her dishes with herbs such as citron and sage, as well as chili peppers and fresh vegetables from the garden. Fort visitors quaffed "hailstorms" at dinner and in the billiards room while enjoying a post-dinner cigar. A mixture of whiskey, sugar, mint, and "something special," the drink sounds suspiciously like a mint julep. Considering Bent's Missouri heritage, that seems likely.

SUSAN SHELBY MAGOFFIN

As more Anglo-American men traded at Bent's Fort and further south at the Mexican settlements of Taos and Santa Fe, it was only a matter of time before the fort would welcome female Anglo-Americans. Well-known because she left behind a diary of her travels is Susan Shelby Magoffin, the nineteen-year-old bride of trader Samuel Magoffin. Shelby was born near Danbury, Kentucky. She spent her childhood on the family plantation in a sheltered upbringing. Although Samuel was twenty-seven years older than she, the two fell in love and were married in November 1845. In June 1846 they began their journey westward to Santa Fe. Magoffin's wealth provided his wife with a journey less arduous, but no less an eye-opener, than the one thousands of women would experience along the overland trails beginning in the 1840s. With Jane, her personal attendant, a dog, "grand accommodations," and plentiful provisions, it is no wonder the bride found camp life "a good deal."[13]

Magoffin spent time when the wagons were stopped for the noon meal ("nooning it" in trail parlance) collecting pebbles, roses, and other flowers to keep as souvenirs. She delighted in many of the new sights, such as the way the prairie dogs resembled humans in the manner in which they "ran to their doors to see the passing crowds."[14] "Millions upon millions" of mosquitoes swarming about her drew her to compare the experience as "equal to any of the plagues of Egypt."[15]

In spite of the pests, Magoffin was usually content with trail life, but illness altered her view.[16] As the days passed, their party was overtaken by two other companies, one of which included a doctor. By the end of the week, Magoffin was so sick that her husband sent a man ahead to bring the doctor back to their wagon train. Dr. Mesure, a Frenchman from St. Louis, was reputed to be an excellent physician *"especially in female cases."*[17] Magoffin was pregnant, and her "sickness" worsened as they drew closer to Bent's Fort. Suffering from morning sickness, Magoffin neglected her diary. When she returned to it, she likened the fort to an ancient castle, albeit one of adobe with high, thick walls. The twenty-five rooms had dirt floors that were sprinkled with water several times a day to prevent dust from accumulating. In addition to bedchambers, there was a dining room, kitchen, store, blacksmith's shop, barbershop, and icehouse. On the south side was an enclosure for stock. Their room had two windows, a bed, chairs, washbasin, and table furniture. While waiting for their room to be ready, Magoffin met *las senoritas*, the wife of George Bent, and other women of the fort. One woman's dressing of her hair surprised Magoffin when "she paid her devoirs to a crock of oil or greese [*sic*] of some kind, and it is not exaggeration to say it almost *driped* [*sic*] from her hair to the floor. If I had not seen her at it, I never would have believed it greese [*sic*], but that she had been washing her head."[18]

Although Magoffin liked the fort well enough, her sickness continued to plague her, and she began to regret having made the journey west. Perhaps if she had been in her hometown with her mother or had another American woman to talk to on the Santa Fe Trail and at Bent's Fort, she may have been more informed about her plight and symptoms. After a week's break from her diary, she wrote that what should have been a joyful event—her pregnancy—had tragically resulted in a miscarriage.[19]

On the evening of August 7, 1846, the couple left Bent's Fort, bound for Santa Fe. Their departure was a mixed blessing. Magoffin was anxious to be away from the fort, the site of the loss of her baby, but she left the fetus

Bent's Old Fort - Colorado   (From an old sketch by Le Roy Boyd)

FIGURE 1.3 *Bent's Old Fort, founded in the 1830s, was an important trading post along the Santa Fe Trail for Americans, Indians, and Mexicans. Courtesy, Special Collections, Pikes Peak Library District, 208-9283, Colorado Springs.*

behind in a grave.[20] Devastated, she waited a month before writing to her mother about the miscarriage. Even then she could not bear to be blunt, simply calling it her "sickness."[21] The Magoffins stayed in Santa Fe for six weeks, then continued on to other destinations.

Although her diary ended on September 7, 1847, it is known that Magoffin again became pregnant but lost a son. When her husband retired from the Santa Fe trade, they returned to the United States. She gave birth to a daughter in 1851. However, her ill health continued, and after the birth of their second daughter in 1855, Susan Shelby Magoffin died. She had not lived to her thirtieth birthday.

EL PUEBLO

Bent's Fort, although famous and successful, was not the only settlement in the southeastern region. Five years before the Magoffins' journey, an eclectic group of farmers and traders moved north to found El Pueblo, at the confluence of Fountain Creek and the Arkansas River. It is now the site of the city of Pueblo. Teresita Sandoval was among the group. Born in Taos, New Mexico, she married Manuel Suaso at age seventeen. Known for her stubbornness and hot temper, Sandoval was also intelligent and courageous. She eagerly embraced new challenges and worked hard to help support her family. She also was not hesitant to leave her husband for another man. The couple had four children before moving to Mora, New Mexico, in the 1830s to settle a land grant. There she met Mathew Kinkead from Kentucky. Kinkead had become a Mexican citizen to avoid the Spanish colonial government's law forbidding foreigners from establishing businesses in Mexico and New Mexico. In 1835 Sandoval gave birth to a baby boy who was baptized Juan Andres Suaso, although the baby's real father was Kinkead. Sandoval left her husband to live with Kinkead, with whom she had a daughter, Rafaela. Between 1841 and 1843, Kinkead and Sandoval ran a buffalo farm. Every April or May the two went out to the plains with a few milk cows to lure newborn buffalo calves away from their mothers. When they were a year old, the calves were sold to frontier settlers in Missouri for $100. In 1842 the family moved to the American side of the Arkansas River, where they joined others and founded El Pueblo. The settlement survived until 1854, when Ute and Jicarilla Apache Indians massacred or kidnapped all of the settlers in desperate retaliation for the loss of their land.

Later, when gold was discovered in the Rocky Mountains of Colorado, a new Fort Pueblo was constructed. In the meantime, British trader Alexander Barclay, who had served as a sutler at Bent's Old Fort, saw Sandoval one day as she returned from the river with a bucket of laundry on her head. Years later, still haunted by that image, he drew the only known portrait of her. It shows her in traditional Mexican clothing—ankle-high moccasins, a bright red skirt, a white off-the-shoulder chemise, white stockings, and a long blue *reboso* that covers her shoulders and reaches nearly to the ground. Her dark hair is parted in the center, looped behind her ears, and secured with ribbons. Two years after Barclay first saw her, Sandoval left Kinkead for him. In 1844 the two moved to Hardscrabble. Sandoval was thirty-three years old and a grandmother. When Barclay learned that the US government was planning to build a fort in the region, he figured he would build one first and then sell it to the United States. But the climate in the place he chose (east of present-day Pueblo) was extremely harsh, making farming and the raising of livestock practically impossible. The failed endeavor increased the strain between Sandoval and Barclay. After ten tumultuous years together, the two separated. It was then, in 1853, that he sent a copy of the portrait to his brother, George.[22] Once again unmarried, Sandoval went to live with her daughter and son-in-law, who supported her until her death in 1894 at age eighty-three, by which time she had witnessed Colorado's gold rush, statehood, and even woman's suffrage.

T W O

PIONEERING WOMEN

(1859–1877)

In 1858 prospectors panned out small pockets of gold from the banks of Little Dry Creek, a few miles up the South Platte from its confluence with Cherry Creek. News of the find spread quickly. By early September, would-be miners from Lawrence, Kansas, who had spent the previous two months unsuccessfully mining the streams of South Park and the San Luis Valley, arrived at Clear Creek. One of the original members of this group was Julia Archibald Holmes, who had walked from the eastern part of the Kansas Territory (which included portions of present-day Colorado) to the western part to build up her endurance. She was determined to climb Pikes Peak, which she did in the summer of 1858, clad in the "American costume" (a calico dress over calico bloomers named after Amelia Bloomer who, like Holmes, was an advocate of women's rights). From the top of the peak she wrote a letter to her mother in which she described her feelings: "I have accomplished the task which I marked out for myself, and now I feel

DOI: 10.5876/9781607322078.c02

amply repaid for all my toil and fatigue. Nearly everyone tried to discourage me from attempting it, but I believed that I should succeed; and now, here I am, and I feel that I would not have missed this glorious sight."[1] Years later another American woman, Katherine Lee Bates, who was teaching at Colorado College in Colorado Springs, was so moved by the vista that she wrote the poem "America the Beautiful."

No one knows if Holmes was indeed the first woman to have stood on the summit of Pikes Peak, although she was probably correct in assuming that she was the first white woman to do so. Perhaps a Native American woman—or many of them—had sat on one of the summit's rocks and gazed out over the land of their ancestors. It would soon be a land native women would have difficulty recognizing as thousands of Americans followed the Holmes party into the Rocky Mountains.

LIFE ON THE OVERLAND TRAIL

While Holmes and her husband went on to New Mexico, the rest of the party stayed in Colorado to search for gold. The discovery in Little Dry Creek and Clear Creek set off a gold rush similar to California's a decade earlier. In towns along the Missouri and Mississippi Rivers, the news of gold was electrifying. In November 1858, William Larimer's party set up along the right bank of the South Platte opposite the town of Auraria on the left bank. During the winter the rush to the goldfields was a mere trickle compared to the onslaught that began in the spring of 1859. Of those spring arrivals, one couple would make their mark on the new city of Denver, a consolidation of Auraria and Larimer's Denver City. William N. and Elizabeth Byers settled in the fledging town. On April 23, 1859, he published the first newspaper in the Pikes Peak region. While Byers used the *Rocky Mountain News* to extol the region's potential riches and healthy climate, his wife busied herself with taking care of their young children and providing aid to wives and children abandoned or left behind in Denver while their men traipsed up to the goldfields with dreams of becoming rich.

Between 1858 and 1870, thousands of Americans journeyed from the States to the western territories. Many were single men or husbands who left their families behind in hopes of striking it rich in the area's goldfields. Some also traveled as families. Others emigrated for farming and ranching opportunities—"to mine the miners"—or to improve their health. For both men and women the decision to journey west was a momentous one. Dangers lay along the trail, and uncertainty awaited them at trail's end. Some couples made this decision jointly; for others, the decision was made by the husband. Some women eagerly embraced the opportunity; others dreaded it and found leaving family and friends heart-wrenching. For all, it usually meant a permanent break from those loved ones.

Emigrants who started far east of the Mississippi and Missouri Rivers often began their journey by rail. At the "jumping-off" places of Council Bluffs, Kansas City, St. Louis, and Omaha, emigrant families bought a covered wagon, a team of oxen, and provisions. Joining a caravan meant shared troubles, companionship, and a united front against the many obstacles along the way. It could also mean disease, minor disagreements, and violent arguments. Women whose husbands were already in the Colorado Territory boarded a stagecoach to traverse the plains. For all travelers, leaving the States meant leaving behind family heirlooms, furniture, and clothing. A covered wagon held approximately forty square feet of storage. Provisions included flour, bacon, coffee, sugar, salt, tea, dried fruit, dried beans, and chipped beef. Basic kitchenware was a fry pan, kettle, coffeepot, tin plates, cups, and utensils. Families needed a supply of powder, lead, and shot for their rifles. Because enough food had to be carried to sustain the emigrants for a five- to eight-week journey, little room was left for sentimental possessions. Emma Doud's stepfather forbade her and her three sisters to bring their dolls, stating that there was no room for them after the family packed the necessities.[2] Chickens were caged and attached to the back of the wagon to provide eggs and meat along the trail. Perhaps the family dog was included; other times it, too, was left behind, howling as the family rode away. Emigrants who could not part with a large item, such as the family piano or hope chest, later abandoned it along the trail when the load was too heavy for the team to pull through deep sand or muddy ruts.

Depending on the weather and trail conditions, a caravan could make as many as twenty miles a day or as little as one mile. Some wagon trains traveled every day; others stopped on Sundays. Hattie L. Hedges's family and Susan Riley Ashley came to Colorado by horse-drawn coach. They traveled twenty-four hours straight, with horses changed every ten to twenty miles. The stage driver bugled as soon as he was within earshot of a station so horses were ready when he pulled in. Within five minutes, the stagecoach was on its way.[3] For Hedges, it took seven days and nights to travel from Quincy, Illinois, to Denver. Ashley spent eight days and nights traveling from Omaha, Nebraska, to Denver, after having endured three days by rail from Ohio to Iowa and another three-and-a-half days by hack from there to Omaha. Stagecoach passengers bought stage station meals at exorbitantly high prices. A cup of tea or coffee sold for one dollar.[4]

On the trail, women performed the same duties they had back home, but conditions were much more primitive than in the States. There was limited water for cleaning and cooking, the latter over an open fire amid dust and insects. Meals became monotonous over the course of the journey. As one woman noted, "The only change we have from bread and bacon is to bacon and bread."[5] Antelope or buffalo supplemented the emigrants' diet. While wives prepared and broke camp, drew water, cooked, washed, and took care of the children, husbands drove teams and took turns with other men guarding them at night. For emigrants who did not travel on Sundays, it was a rest day for men, but, as Agnes Miner recalled, for women it was a day to catch up on washing and baking.[6] There were also the endless duties of child care, aggravated by sick and cranky little ones. Individual families adapted to these issues differently, often working out gender roles in relatively novel ways. As wives fell sick or died, husbands picked up the domestic chores; with an injured or deceased husband, a widow managed the oxen team and drove the wagon. Orphaned children joined other families or pulled together, with the oldest leading the way as a surrogate "parent."

For nearly all the emigrants, the novelty of trail life faded as the trip wore on. Weeks of scarce water, dust, disease, water crossings, uncertainty, and monotony wore down the strongest emigrants. After six weeks of trail life with three weeks to go, Sarah Hively was "tired of traveling."[7] In late April Andrew Hively was not well, but his wife would not let him sleep "for I will get so lonesome setting [sic] here all alone."[8] Two weeks later she entertained the two of them as best she could, reading old letters to him.[9] While loneliness was sometimes a problem during the long hours of travel, when the caravans stopped for the night, other females provided companionship. Women sat around campfires, cooked and washed together, knitted, and talked over the day's events. Some women formed close friendships that lasted beyond the journey; others found that the end of the trail ended those friendships.

The real fear on the trail was death, with disease the most voracious killer. The overland trail was an ideal breeding ground for contact illnesses. As they moved across the sweeping plains, emigrants, paradoxically, suffered from overcrowding. Never before or after would they be pressed together so closely with so many other people. Garbage and human waste from thousands of previous travelers littered the campsites. Typhus, measles, scarlet fever, and diphtheria struck early in the trip. During the second half of the journey, hundreds died from "mountain fever," a term that probably described a variety of infections, including one carried by ticks indigenous to the Rockies. Dysentery plagued emigrants from start to finish. The great-

FIGURE 2.1 *While many emigrants started west filled with optimistic anticipation, as the days and weeks dragged by, trail life wore down their spirits. Weary pioneers, such as this family, grew tired of dust, disease, inclement weather, and monotonous meals. Courtesy, Denver Public Library Western History Collection, X-11929.*

est scourge was Asiatic cholera. Travelers grew familiar with its terrifying symptoms—high fever, diarrhea, swelling of the tongue, delirium, and hallucinations.[10] Within the first week of travel, Mary Elizabeth Kellogg Hunt, wife of Alexander Cameron (Cam) Hunt, was stricken with cholera morbus. Continuing to travel, she was very sick all day every day for nearly a week. By the eighth day of her illness, her limbs were covered with "large purple blotches."[11]

Hunt and Susan Shelby Magoffin, of Santa Fe Trail fame, recovered from their illnesses, but their health was ruined, and they died at a young age. For others, the trail became their gravesite. It has been estimated that 5 or 6 percent of the emigrants died.[12] With little time to stop and prepare a proper gravesite, no wood to spare for a coffin, and often hard frozen ground in which to dig, the deceased was wrapped in cloth, placed in a shallow grave, and covered with stones to prevent wolves from digging up the body. If possible, a small cross or headstone with a brief description marked the end of the trail for someone's child, mother, father, or sibling.

The overland trail challenged emigrants. Water was often a problem—too much, too little, or badly polluted, the carrier of deadly diseases. River crossings never ceased to be adventurous at best, treacherous at worst. In

Missouri and eastern Kansas, ferries took wagons across. Further west, wagons often had to be unloaded so the oxen could successfully fight the river current and steep banks. Rain poured into tents at night and drenched travelers during the day. Storms overturned wagons and scattered stock. Scouts often had to search off-trail to find water. Too little rainfall and the trail was dusty, making travel uncomfortable. At other times, emigrants suffered through violent hailstorms. During the day, swarms of gnats and horseflies attacked people and animals. At night, clouds of mosquitoes invaded campsites. Prairie fires stampeded animals and burned wagons. The deep sand of the high plains brought caravans to a halt. Wind added to the misery.

Although emigrants feared Indian attacks, Lillian Schlissel found that most wagons and stagecoaches were not attacked by Native Americans as whites invaded their hunting grounds.[13] In fact, in the earliest years of travel, Indians aided whites with gifts of buffalo robes and meat. If anything, the Indians were as mystified by the whites' culture as whites were of the Indians'. Women wrote of Indians wanting to touch their blond curls and finger their clothing. It was customary among tribes to offer strangers a token of hospitality, so Indians often expected such tokens from Anglo travelers. Ignorant of this custom, whites repeatedly complained of Indians "begging." But even after having positive, or nonviolent, interactions with various Indians, many whites remained fearful. Early in their journey, the Hivelys were robbed by an Indian man. Days later another Indian approached their wagon and asked to ride; when refused, he asked for bread. Although this incident did not scare them, several days later they had another encounter during which 200 Indians arrived at their campsite. This time, perhaps because of the large number of Indians, the Hivelys promptly moved another twelve miles further west to camp.[14]

Other women were in the Colorado Territory in the early 1860s with their husbands who were army officers stationed in the region. Shortly after their wedding in 1860, Byron Sanford and his wife, Mollie Dorsey, emigrated to the Pikes Peak area. While mining at Gold Hill, he received his commission as first lieutenant in the Colorado Regiment of Volunteers. His first station was at Camp Weld, in present-day Denver. Although enlisted men seldom had wives or families with them in the forts, it was not uncommon for officers' wives to join their husbands. Wives often found themselves to be unpaid military "servants." Sanford discovered that the rather limited hospital accommodations at Camp Weld provided insufficient green cloth shades for men suffering from snow blindness. When she could not obtain the fabric from the town's stores, she cut up her green satin parasol to make shades for the afflicted soldiers.[15] In early January the regiment was assigned to Fort Lyon, where the Sanfords occupied Captain Martin's quarters. The treeless plain evoked loneliness for Sanford; she knew, however, as military wives throughout the years have known, that she should reconcile herself to her situation, as she had little choice.[16] In March, the Colorado Regiment was on the move to thwart the Confederate march on Fort Union in New Mexico. With a battle impending, Sanford was sent back to Denver where, with no money or relatives, she boarded with Elizabeth Allen Sopris who kept the officers' mess.[17]

SOUTHERN SETTLEMENTS

In the 1860s and 1870s, New Mexican settlers followed kin northward into the San Luis Valley and surrounding areas. Their settlements reached as far north as Saguache, as the demand for wool uniforms for Civil War soldiers drew shepherds to southern Colorado. By the droves, sheepherders along with their wives and children journeyed north and established villages. By 1870, 90 percent of the 6,400 residents of Las Animas and Huerfano Counties were either New Mexican natives or children of New Mexicans. Early settlements were built in the form of a plaza (*placita*), or enclosed square, for protection. The earliest homes were of three types. A *jacal* was made of logs placed in an upright position. A *fuerte* was a cabin built of horizontal logs; while adobe homes were constructed by pouring clay, sand, and straw into molds that were then baked or sun-dried.[18] Low adobe sheds, workshops, and houses were built with common walls to encircle an open plaza. The backs of the buildings were left without windows or doors, making the complex a small fortress that could shelter livestock as well as people. Residents grazed herds of sheep on higher land and dug short ditches to cultivate farms on river bottomlands.

As was true in other agricultural communities, women and women's work occupied a central place in the Hispanic villages of southern Colorado. While pastureland and water resources belonged to the community, most families owned their own small agricultural lot, a house, and the land surrounding it. Communally, women plastered houses, baked bread, and spun wool. Men—together and sometimes in concert with women and children— plowed, hoed, and harvested the fields. They herded the family's sheep on the open range.[19] In their absence, women handled the men's farming duties in addition to tending the family garden. The plot was usually located close to the home; women planted, weeded, and harvested sweet corn, green beans,

FIGURE 2.2 *Settlers from New Mexico built adobe homes in the southern and south-eastern regions of present-day Colorado. Every fall, women plastered them inside and out. Photograph by Myron Wood, © Pikes Peak Library District, 002-1477, Colorado Springs.*

melons, chili peppers, onions, pumpkins, and radishes. If a family owned goats or chickens, they, too, were a woman's responsibility.[20]

In addition to small settlements, southern Colorado was home to larger communities. In 1860 Felipe Baca, a New Mexican, cleared land along the Purgatoire River and started the permanent settlement of Trinidad, a few miles north of Ratón Pass, two years later. Both Anglos and New Mexicans settled the town, although the population was predominantly New Mexican. Trinidad developed into an important point on the stage and telegraph lines between Denver and Santa Fe.

NORTHERN SETTLEMENTS

Farther north, for Anglo emigrants their arrival in Denver or one of the other towns meant a continuation of struggles against the elements and loneliness. For shelter, the wagon was exchanged for a tent, crude cabin, or boardinghouse. Early arrivals found Denver quite unsettled. Katrina Murat, a German married to a Frenchman who claimed to be a count, was one of the first white women, arriving on November 3, 1858. Their first cabin was by the river and was later rebuilt on what is now Tenth Street east of Larimer.[21] Within fourteen months, Mr. and Mrs. Samuel Dalman arrived. In a letter written many years later, Mrs. Dalman stated that, when they put up their tent on Blake Street, there were two sod and log houses—one each on Blake Street and McGaa (changed to Holladay Street in 1866 and to Market Street in 1877). Soon, her husband constructed a house of lumber, which they called the Kansas House.[22] In 1859 the extended family of Mr. and Mrs. Alexander Cameron Hunt arrived from the South. Cameron secured a cabin for them on the outskirts of Auraria. Built of logs and mud, it had no windows or floor. Mary Elizabeth Hunt noted that although the cabin was much better than most of its neighbors, she still felt blue at the prospect of trying to live in such a place.[23] In 1861 when the Ashleys arrived, Denver was still a primitive three-year-old town of mostly unplastered and unpainted log, frame, and adobe buildings housing "about 3,000 souls."[24] The Ashleys lived at the Tremont House for three months until their home was built. Two years later, Sarah and Andrew Hively arrived. Although their first accommodations were not luxurious, to Sarah, weary of living in a wagon, their room for five dollars a night was a welcome change from trail living.[25]

The earliest female emigrants found themselves in the minority, as the town was mainly populated by men. Mrs. Dalman lamented that there were "onley two woman bysides my selfe that could associate together."[26] Susan Ashley remembered that the sidewalks, on which few women were seen, "seemed always covered with men."[27] Fortunately for Ashley, she was quickly invited to a social function at which she met other women who became her lifelong friends. Because of the large male population, single or widowed women were in high demand. In 1866 Elizabeth Parks Keays, a thirty-six-year-old widow with a ten-year-old son, accepted her aunt's invitation to join her in Fort Collins at the site of a recently abandoned military fort, Camp Collins. She arrived on a Friday, and her aunt introduced her and her traveling companions to several of her friends. On Sunday more men came calling, interrupting her letter writing. In contrast, Keays did not receive her first female caller until she had been in town for four days. In late December Keays became a bride for the second time when she married Harris Stratton, a dairy farmer. She had lived in Fort Collins unattached for a mere seven months.[28]

In addition to being aware of the large number of men, newly arrived women also noted the presence of Cheyenne and Arapaho Indians. Dalman commented that 200 wigwams of "very peacible and friendly" Indians were camped at the confluence of Cherry Creek and the South Platte River.[29] Ashley, on the other hand, stated that it was "deemed advisable in these earlier years for all women living on this frontier to know how to load and use both revolver and rifle. Target practice was one of the amusements in which both men and women participated in the early '60s, and many women became expert markswomen."[30]

Once accommodations were secured, either temporarily in a boarding-house or in their own homes, women's housekeeping tasks continued. Many early arrivals—such as the Dalmans who opened the Kansas House—took in boarders because housing was at a premium. Hunt spent the rest of June 1863 baking, washing, stewing peaches, making loaves of bread and Dutch cheese, and taking care of her two young children. Her son Bertie's teeth made him exceedingly fretful, adding to her daily burdens. But things turned even worse for Hunt. In the first week of July, her husband and his brother, John, bought an eating house. Hunt abandoned daily recounting in her diary, as her long waking hours were spent running a boardinghouse. She did not mention whether she had been consulted about this new endeavor, which substantially increased her labor. Over a period of three weeks she baked nearly 200 loaves of bread and 450 pies, which left her "weak and trembling and far from cheerful." What probably made her particularly cheerless was the fact that the men's Fourth of July celebration included "plenty of squaws and one white woman from Missouri."[31] Hunt herself was too busy—and weary—to attend.

Hunt was not the only woman thrust into additional duties as a cook, laundress, and boardinghouse proprietor. Agnes Miner's father operated the post office in Breckenridge in the early 1860s. Her mother baked pies, bread, and cakes to sell to the miners who came in for their mail. Baking thirty to forty pies a day emptied a 100-pound sack of flour.[32] In 1864 Levi Booth and his wife, Millie, bought land from Mary Cawker, a squatter, soon after the Denver flood. There they ran the Four Mile House for several years until the establishment of railroad tracks into Denver cut into their business. They stayed, received proof of their homestead in 1872, and eventually enlarged their ranch to over 600 acres.[33]

Another family who came west in the 1860s were the Douds. In 1866 Emma Doud, her parents, and four sisters traveled to Colorado. In Golden, loggers convinced her mother to cook for them in exchange for boarding the family. She did so for two months until the family once again packed up and moved to Fort Lupton. Her father was hired on as a ranch hand

and soon was able to rent the place. By the end of the third year acquired eighteen cows and mules. He traded the latter for a road present-day Parker, where his wife served meals to traders, freighters, gold seekers, Indians, and preachers.[34] The family ran the Twenty Mile House for four years before selling it. Doud ran a blacksmith shop and stable, conveniently located near Cherry Creek on Smoky Hill Trail, for the horses of the stage lines. The surrounding area was becoming more settled, so much of the trade was with folks going back and forth to Denver from Bijou Basin, Kiowa, Running Creek, and Cherry Creek. After selling the place, her husband wanted to go to Michigan; her health was better in Colorado's climate, though, so she bought a house three miles away and operated it as the Seventeen Mile House. Mr. Doud elected to remain with his wife rather than return to Michigan alone.[35]

Although very few blacks emigrated to the Colorado Territory during the gold rush era, one black woman gained notoriety. Clara Brown, a former slave, settled in Denver and Central City where she took in laundry. For a black woman whose choices were limited, this was one of only a few available options. Brown, although typical in her choice of occupations, was a most atypical woman. She parlayed her earnings into real estate and mining claims, amassing a small fortune that she used to help individuals, churches, and other charities.[36]

In addition to running a boardinghouse or selling eggs, butter, pies, and bread to supplement the family income, women in frontier towns found work outside the home. On the seedier side, prostitutes plied their trade in the red light districts of the mining towns Cripple Creek, Leadville, and Central City and in the towns along the Front Range. A more "upstanding" choice was teaching school. In the spring of 1860 Captain Richard Sopris brought his wife and eight children to a two-story log house in Auraria. His eldest daughter, Indiana, began teaching two weeks after their arrival in a frame house she rented from the town's blacksmith. Students sat on wooden benches and used "a variety of text books such as had been brought by the parents from widely scattered sections of the country."[37] On the eastern plains, fifteen-year-old Carrie Ayres, who had accompanied her mother in homesteading in Sterling, opened the first school in that area. Her salary was $25 a month, from which $10 paid her rent for a fourteen-by-sixteen-foot soddy with dirt floors. She paid $38 for furniture and supplies, for a total cost of under $160 for the first year. The fact that students brought their own seats helped keep costs down.[38]

COLORADO WOMEN BY THE NUMBERS

In 1860 there were 34,277 persons living in the Colorado Territory (American Indians were not recorded in the census taking). Of this total, less than 5 percent of the population was women. Most men and women were white native-born Americans. Only forty-six were "free colored" persons (the term used by the Census Bureau), half of whom resided in Denver. Only South Park, with seven men, had more than a handful of African Americans. The majority of Colorado men and women were between the ages of fifteen and fifty; over half of the men and a third of the women were between ages twenty and thirty.[39]

Female totals had risen to nearly 38 percent by the 1870 census and 45 percent in 1880, while "coloreds" increased to 456 in 1870 and 2,435 in 1880. In the 1870 census, 7 Chinese were recorded along with 180 Indians. The 1880 census recorded 593 Chinese and 19 Japanese persons. Indians numbered 154. Women were concentrated in Denver, indicating the presence of families there versus the heavily male population of the mining regions. Between 1870 and 1880, Colorado's population exploded by nearly 400 percent, from 39,864 to 194,327, with the largest increase coming in urban areas.[40]

The 1860 census table of occupations in Colorado Territory did not differentiate between men and women; but from a survey of records left behind by Coloradans and a comparison of national records for the same year, one can surmise that women in Colorado made up the vast majority—if not all—of the servants, milliners, seamstresses, and laundresses. Men were miners, laborers, carpenters, teamsters, traders, merchants, farmers, and saloon-keepers.[41] The 1870 census delineated occupations by sex, age, and nativity. Over 99 percent of all employed females age ten and older were in the professional and personal services (87 percent) or manufacturing and mining (12.4 percent) categories. Within the former, domestic service accounted for over 70 percent, with hotel and restaurant keepers and employees, launderers and laundresses, and teachers making up the remainder. Within manufacturing and mining, 69 percent of the females were employed as milliners and dress and mantua makers. Of note, in 1870 not one female was listed as employed in agriculture, although numerous diaries and receipts show that women ran farms, sold agricultural products, and raised animals for income.[42] In 1880 women employed outside the home remained in similar categories; however, 77 females were now listed as employed in agriculture.[43]

AGRICULTURAL COMMUNITIES

Mining and "mining the miners" in mountain and Front Range towns were not the only reasons emigrants made the treacherous journey to Colorado in the 1860s and 1870s. At least two agricultural colonies were founded in the northern part of the region in the 1870s. The most successful was the Union Colony at Greeley. Nathan Meeker and his wife, Arvilla, were veterans of communal living. During the 1840s they were part of the Trumbull Phalanx, an Ohio community organized on the principles of Charles Fourier. Fourier believed that an individual's unique needs and contributions would best be realized if people lived and worked in "phalanxes" of 1,600 to 1,800 people.[44] Participation in the Ohio experiment taught Meeker the value of communal living; it also reinforced his beliefs that a common religion and an autocratic leader were vital to the community's success. In the 1860s Meeker visited Colorado on assignment from the *New York Tribune,* run by Horace Greeley. It was then that he saw the potential for an agricultural community in Colorado. In 1869 Meeker and Greeley drew up a charter for the colony and invited people of "good temperance and character" to join their enterprise.[45] The colony owned the grazing land and financed the irrigation systems, while colonists received both a farm and a town lot. The response from the first meeting was overwhelming, and by the spring of 1870 the first settlers were in Union Colony, soon renamed Greeley. Debt, grasshoppers, and clashes over religion marked the settlement's early years; but the town also met its high-minded standards through its support of lyceums, a library, and a school. The colonists built a giant fence around their land in an attempt to keep neighbors' cattle out of their crops. The fence, along with the Union Colony's ban on alcohol and gambling, led outsiders to deride Greeley's residents as self-righteous "saints."[46] When the colony charter expired in 1880, Greeley was a tidy, efficient city.

One Union Colony family was the Greens. Annie Green was less than enthusiastic about the new settlement: "After securing several lots in the new town, we pitched our tent, which was almost daily blown to the ground. To say that I was homesick, discouraged and lonely, is but a faint description of my feelings."[47] The Greens, with their two young children, lived in the tent for two weeks before moving into a small cottage abandoned by a Minnesota man who had returned "to his wife who had wisely remained in her happy home."[48] Other settlers found life a daily struggle against the harsh elements of the eastern plains. In 1869 Ella Bailey, recently married to a rancher and sheepherder in Weld County, kept a diary of her experiences in Latham. Because of their livestock, the Baileys had a number of hired help. Ella, of course, fed the men. On the first day of 1869 she wrote of having "nine for breakfast, six for dinner, five for supper. Washed, scrubbed, and baked two loaves of light bread. Tired as a hungry wolf."[49] When the men moved cattle or sheep, she baked food for them to take on their trip. She also tended to the hens and turkeys, skimmed milk, and churned butter. Twice during the year commissioners descended upon the Bailey ranch to hold court and settle business. Their visits were particularly stressful for the sole woman in the household. In early March she prepared for their arrival by baking 92 pies, 3,000 cookies and gingersnaps, 4 cakes, and 15 loaves of bread. After hosting seven men for breakfast and another thirteen for supper during the week, Bailey was "tired as a beggar" and "too near worn out to do anything."[50] Ever resilient, as most women on the plains proved to be, she recovered from her exhaustion, regained her sense of humor, and spent a March day "in the stable rolling in the hay and listening to the hens sing."[51]

While male settlers worked alongside other men or traveled into town to buy supplies, their wives remained isolated. Bailey was often lonesome for her husband, especially with the lack of female companionship. In her diary, she frequently mentioned that her husband had gone into town.[52] She, however, made the twelve-hour journey only twice in 1869. After months of enduring pain, she went to town to have seven teeth pulled, which cost the young couple fifteen dollars. Taking advantage of her rare sojourn, she bought herself a new pair of shoes.[53] On July 8 their house burned to the ground, leaving her "without a bonnet, my good man without a coat."[54] Although neighbors built the Baileys a new sod house, they moved to town where she presumably had fewer ranch chores, although she still baked and cooked for their boarders.[55]

Another group, the Chicago-Colorado Colony, founded Longmont. Part of its success resulted from the support of New Yorker Elizabeth Thompson, who purchased memberships for poor settlers.[56] Further north, memberships were offered for sale in Fort Collins to persons of good moral character, entitling them to city lots, farming land, or both. Elizabeth Hickok Robbins Stone had pioneered in Missouri, Illinois, and Minnesota before becoming the first white woman settler at Camp Collins in 1862. She and her second husband, Judge Lewis Stone, built and ran a mess hall for the men stationed at the military outpost. Four years later her husband died, leaving her a widow for the second time. Faced with the decision to move again, "Auntie" Stone, as the officers and soldiers called her, chose to stay. She partnered with H. C. Peterson to build a flour mill, only the second such mill in northern Colorado. They also built the region's first kiln, from which came the building blocks for the first brick house in Fort Collins.[57] She expanded the use of her mess house to that of a hotel, the first to be opened and operated in Fort Collins.[58]

MORMON SETTLEMENTS

Later colonies in Colorado were closely tied to religious groups. Members of the Church of Latter-Day Saints (LDS) from Alabama, Georgia, and Tennessee founded Manassa, south of Alamosa, in 1878. Two years later Mormons from Salt Lake City founded Ephraim until unhealthful marshes forced a move to Sanford, which also received displaced Mormon settlers from Richfield. Within the next five years, Mormon settlements were founded at Morgan and Eastdale. Although southern Colorado newspapers printed editorials against them, the Mormons stayed, enlarging the two San Luis Valley towns. Part of Manassa's growth was a result of the arrival of Mormon "widows," or exiles from Utah. In 1882 the US Congress had passed the Edmunds Act, which subjected men convicted of plural marriage or living polygamously (defined as "cohabitation") to fines and imprisonment. If captured with their offspring, plural wives were considered sufficient evidence to convict their husbands. In the late 1880s plural wives went into exile after the election of Benjamin Harrison and the Republicans on an anti-LDS platform brought fear of even more drastic measures against Mormons.

One woman who went "underground" was Emily Wells Grant, the third wife of Mormon apostle Heber J. Grant of Salt Lake City.[59] To conceal the birth of her first child, Grant took refuge in England and then hid in various residences in northern Utah and southern Idaho. In November 1889 her husband sent her to Manassa accompanied by his mother. Situated on a treeless flatland 500 miles from the center of Mormon headquarters in Salt Lake City, Manassa became a haven for polygamist families who figured that territorial marshals would not hunt that far for them and, if they did, they could be forewarned. Among Grant's neighbors were the wives of five general authorities. Another dozen were plurally married to prominent Utah businessmen and bishops. With their children, the "widows" constituted less than 10 percent of the population of Manassa.[60]

Grant's two-room home was one of the most comfortable in the town, with sawdust for insulation against the winds and bitter cold of the high-altitude settlement. Her husband visited five times during her sixteen months of exile, and they regularly exchanged letters. In addition to Emily, he had a wife, Lucy, in Salt Lake City; a wife, Augusta, sequestered in New York City; and a half dozen church-business enterprises that required his attention. Although his visits and those of the husbands of other "widows" temporarily eased her loneliness, Grant grew increasingly despondent after her mother-in-law returned to Utah. To compensate for that loss, Heber Grant sent her brother and sister to Manassa, but their companionship and church activities did not fill the void of her husband's absence. An outbreak of measles, diphtheria, and smallpox in the Mormon settlements also strained the wives' fortitude. The arrest of General Authority John Morgan, who was visiting his plural wife in Manassa, heightened everyone's fears.[61]

When Grant wrote that she was desperate, her husband offered New York City, Mexico, or Salt Lake City as a release from Manassa. Without hesitation she chose her home and left Colorado in 1890. Pressure from the US government eased after LDS president Wilford Woodruff's 1890 Manifesto banned plural marriages in the future. Emily Grant and other "widows" gradually emerged from the "underground" and their lives of exile in other communities and states.[62]

INDIAN AND ANGLO RELATIONS

As white women slowly emigrated to Colorado, they brought their "eastern" middle-class values of white superiority and Protestantism. The onslaught of hundreds and then thousands of Anglo-Americans disrupted the lives of American Indians. In 1851, in response to emigrants on the Oregon Trail, the Arapaho and Cheyenne tribes signed an agreement at Fort Laramie that allowed passage through the area. The federal government promised the Native Americans annuities, but they were generally late and of poor quality. Ten years later the Treaty of Fort Wise offered the Sand Creek area in southeastern Colorado as a sanctuary, but that reservation was insufficient for the nomadic Cheyenne and Arapaho. In 1863 the Utes signed a treaty with Territorial Governor John Evans to vacate the San Luis Valley. But troubles continued to dog Indian and Anglo relations. In 1864 Cheyenne chief Lean Bear was murdered and Cheyenne camps were burned by Colorado cavalrymen near the South Platte. In June Indians attacked and killed the Hungate family thirty miles southeast of Denver. The mutilated bodies were brought to Denver for all to see. Sarah Hively chose not to view the bodies but reported that those who did "said that they was [sic] a sight to behold."[63]

The incident scared Denver citizens, and many prepared to defend themselves against an Indian attack. Governor Evans met with a group of chiefs, but little was accomplished. Volunteers rushed to form the First Regiment of Colorado. One recruit was Hively's husband. Although his regiment left town in September, he stayed behind for two months. On November 26 he was at last forced to go to Fort Lyon because they were "expecting a large battle there with the Indians."[64] It wasn't until December 8 that the citizens of Denver heard the news about this large "battle," later known as the Sand Creek Massacre. Hively missed the massacre because he departed from Denver only three days before the incident.

On November 24, 1864, a force of 700 soldiers, under the command of Colonel John M. Chivington, rode toward Fort Lyon. On the evening of November 28, the soldiers arrived at a ridge above Sand Creek. Here, in the stillness before dawn, the troops caught their first sight of the sleeping camps of Black Kettle, White Antelope, and other leaders. Within moments, the troops bombarded the Indians with a barrage of small arms fire and howitzers. The Indians used driftwood, clumps of sage, and underbrush as defense, while women and children dug hiding pits along the banks of the stream. Throughout the day, members of the First Regiment, many in undisciplined groups, continued to pursue Indians up Sand Creek. By late afternoon about 160 Cheyenne and Arapaho lay dead, the majority women and children. Before departing, the regiment ransacked and burned the village. Three hundred surviving Indians fled north. About sixty wounded and dead troopers were taken to Fort Lyon.[65]

The returning Colorado volunteers were hailed as heroes in Denver. Sarah Hively was amused by their physical appearance: "they were perfectly black, they was [sic] so dusty."[66] For Indian survivors, the event was tragic. Amache Ochinee, a Cheyenne woman married to the trader John Prowers, lost her father and other relatives in the massacre, although her mother survived. Most whites reacted favorably, at least initially. But once contradictory reports surfaced, some viewed the "battle" as a heinous massacre of a peaceful encampment of Indians who had thought they were protected and safe. At Sand Creek, Captain Silas Soule refused to participate in the attack and restrained his troops. In court, he eloquently recounted the attack on the Indians and criticized Chivington's actions. Because of his testimony, he was assassinated on the streets of Denver on April 24, 1865.

In a futile effort to maintain peace between Native Americans and Anglo-Americans, the US government formulated agreements with the various tribes inhabiting Colorado. The 1867 Medicine Lodge Treaty called for the permanent removal of the Southern Arapaho and Southern Cheyenne to the Indian Territory. The next two years witnessed the last major plains battles in Colorado (at Beecher Island and Summit Springs) between whites and Plains Indians.[67] In 1868 Ute chiefs were persuaded to abandon much of central Colorado. Their "reward" was 16 million acres in western Colorado and a promise of $60,000 a year for thirty years from the US government. But white miners again encroached on Indian land. Five years after signing the treaty, the Utes signed the Brunot Agreement, which effectively removed them from the San Juan Mountains. The agreement established an agency on the Gunnison River to distribute food and annuities to the Southern and Tabeguache bands of Ute Indians.

Assigned to the White River Reservation, Northern Utes were administered by Indian Agent Nathan Meeker, who had left his Union Colony after personal and financial difficulties. On the reservation, his wife, Arvilla, and daughter, Josephine, lived among the Ute Indians. Josephine taught Ute children at the reservation school. Adamant that the nomadic Utes become God-fearing farmers, Meeker instituted religious and farming reforms. Although warned that his policies angered the Utes, he ordered that their horse racetrack and pastureland be plowed up. After years of shoddy treatment and broken promises, this was the final straw for the Utes. Concerned about the safety of his family and that of other whites on the reservation, Meeker asked for the protection of federal troops from Fort Steele, Wyoming. Led by Major Thomas Thornburgh, the approaching soldiers alarmed the Indians, who believed they would be forced onto a reservation in Utah. In the chaos that followed, Utes attacked the troops at Mill Creek fifteen miles from the agency.

When they heard about the battle, another group of Utes attacked the White River agency, killing Meeker and eleven other white men. They captured Arvilla and Josephine Meeker, Flora Ellen Price, and her two young children. Although the agency women at first reported no abuse, they later stated that they had been "violated" by their captors.[68] True or not, Coloradans demanded that the Utes be punished; in Congress, the Colorado delegation lobbied for complete removal of the tribe from Colorado. An arrangement signed by Ute chiefs in 1880 provided new lands in Utah for the White River bands and offered a Utah reservation for the Uncompahgre Utes if no suitable location could be found in Colorado; of course, none was found. Members of the Capote, Mouache, and Weeminuche bands were relegated to a reservation 15 miles wide and 110 miles long in southwestern Colorado. Land developers waited impatiently for the last of the Utes to vacate their land. By September 1881, white settlers were madly platting the new towns of Delta and Montrose on old Ute lands. As the towns grew in population, a new federal law set up the Southern Ute Reservation for the Capote and Mouache bands; the Ute Mountain Reservation became the property of the Weeminuche band.[69]

CHIPETA: QUEEN OF THE UTES

Chipeta, wife of the Ute chief Ouray, was born a Kiowa Apache. At a young age her family was killed, and she was found and adopted by members of the Tabeguache Ute tribe. When she was fifteen years old, she began taking care of Ouray's baby son after his wife died. A year later she and Ouray became a couple. Although they never had children of their own, Chipeta warmly embraced all children, and the couple later adopted other Indian children, a common custom among the Utes.[70]

For several years life was fairly peaceful for Chipeta and Ouray, but once silver was found in the San Juan Mountains, whites clamored for the Utes to be displaced. Tensions also broke out among different factions within the Ute tribes. Chipeta once bravely intervened and stopped Ouray from killing her stepbrother Sapovanero, who had ambushed her husband over matters dealing with white encroachment on Ute lands. A council was later held on the reservation in hopes of convincing the Utes to leave the San Juans. When this failed, agents again invited Ute leaders to Washington, DC, to discuss the issue. Leaving Chipeta in Colorado, Ouray and others journeyed to the nation's capital. A few years after their return, the Los Pinos Agency was moved from its original location on Chochetopa Pass in Gunnison County to a place ten miles south of what is now Montrose. Following the 1873 Brunot Agreement, Ouray and Chipeta settled on a farm and moved into a government-provided house at the southern agency. Although not comfortable in a white man's house, Ouray and Chipeta felt it was important to set an example for the rest of the tribe. Chipeta also sent their "adopted" children to the agency school taught by Margaret Adams, the daughter of Indian Agent Charles Adams.

In 1880 Ouray was called to Washington, DC, to negotiate an agreement. Ailing, he asked Chipeta to accompany him. During their visit, she was given gifts, and photographs were taken. Chipeta gave testimony at the hearings, something unusual for a woman, white or native. Back in Colorado, they tried to convince the Southern Utes to accept the negotiated terms. By this time, Ouray was deathly ill. Despite the efforts of Ute medicine men and

FIGURE 2.3 *Chipeta, respected wife and confidant of Chief Ouray, testified at hearings on Indian–US government relations in Washington, DC. Photograph by Tod Powell. Courtesy, Special Collections, Pikes Peak Library District, 001-4149, Colorado Springs.*

Anglo doctors, he died in August 1880. Per Ute custom, Chipeta hacked off her hair, burned all possessions in the tepee where he died, and had him buried under a rock ledge. Several of his horses were killed and placed at the foot of the ledge.[71]

Within the year, the Utes were forced onto a reservation in Utah. Although Chipeta could have stayed in Colorado, she chose to go with her tribe. Promised a house as nice as the one she had in Colorado, Chipeta found that federal agents also broke that promise. The new reservation was very different for the Utes than their home in Colorado. Accustomed to forests, abundant snow and rainfall for crops, and Colorado's temperate climate, the Utes found the desert land of eastern Utah a monumental adjustment. Government annuities were never enough to subsist on, and the land was ill-suited for farming or hunting. Many Utes crossed back into Colorado to hunt. Chipeta made do as well as possible. As she grew older she faced a multitude of infirmities, most notably blindness. In August 1924, nearly forty-four years to the day after Ouray's death, Chipeta died at age eighty-one. As they had for Ouray, the Utes buried her according to their customs. However, the Montrose Chapter of the Daughters of the American Revolution, which wanted to build a memorial to her, convinced the Utes to allow her body to be reburied in Montrose, where a tomb was erected in her honor.

Chipeta, the confidant and wife of Ouray, was given only begrudging respect by Anglo-Americans during her lifetime. During the last few years of her life, however, whites on the Western Slope treated Chipeta as a folk hero, and she has been honored in death with a number of places and businesses named after her: Chipeta Falls, Chipeta Park, Chipeta Sun Lodge, and Chipeta Golf Course, to name just a few.

THE BELLES OF BOGGSVILLE: RUMALDA JARAMILLO, JOSEFA CARSON, AND AMACHE PROWERS

By the early 1860s Anglo, Spanish, and American Indian cultures were living side by side in relative peace in the Arkansas River Valley. As usual, women were at the heart of this melting pot. John Hough, a resident of Boggsville, wrote that although the wives of Thomas Boggs, Kit Carson, and Charles Ritc were Spanish, John Prowers's wife was a full-blooded Cheyenne Indian, and Hough's wife was the only woman of Anglo-Saxon blood, they "all got along very pleasantly."[72]

The Jaramillos

Boggsville was founded by Thomas Oliver Boggs and his wife, Rumalda Luna Boggs. Rumalda was born into the Jaramillo family of Taos. Her grandparents were landowners and merchants. Her great uncle, Cornelio Vigil, was mayor of Taos. Shortly after Rumalda's birth, her father died and left her mother, Ignacia Jaramillo, a widow. A few years later, Ignacia remarried. Rumalda's new father was Charles Bent, of Bent, St. Vrain and Company.

In 1846 Charles Bent was named the new American governor of New Mexico, but on January 19, 1847, an angry mob of Hispanics and Taos Indians started the Taos uprising. They stormed Bent's home and shot and scalped him. By this time, Rumalda had married Tom Boggs, and she and her aunt, Josefa Jaramillo Carson (wife of Kit Carson), were caught as they tried to escape.[73]

Before the Americans took over Nuevo Mexico, land grants were given to influential Mexican citizens who promised to colonize the properties. Cornelio Vigil and Ceran St. Vrain (a French Canadian–born trapper, trader, and citizen of Mexico) were awarded the Vigil–St. Vrain Land Grant, 4 million acres spread across southeastern Colorado. After Vigil was killed in the Taos uprising, his part of the land grant was portioned out to his heirs. Boggsville was built on Rumalda's two-acre share of that grant. The Boggs's first home was an L-shaped six-room house along the west bank of the Purgatoire River. In 1866, with the start of construction of Fort Lyon on the north bank of the Arkansas River, Thomas Boggs began construction on a nine-room adobe home that blended a Greek Revival (or Territorial) architectural style with a Spanish Colonial style to form a unique structure.

In 1867 Rumalda was joined at Boggsville by her aunt, Josefa Jaramillo Carson, Josefa's husband, Kit, and their family. Josefa was only three years older than Rumalda, and the two women had been known as "the Belles of Taos" when they were younger. Josefa also had a claim to the Vigil–St. Vrain Land Grant on which the Carsons had been running cattle for years. Josefa's father, Don Francisco Jaramillo, did not approve of Carson and allowed the couple to marry only after Carson converted to Catholicism. Josefa was not quite fifteen at the time; Carson was thirty-three. In 1850 their first son, Carlos Adolfo, was born. Carson then left for the next two months on a trading trip to Fort Laramie. Their son died a year later while Carson was away on another trip. Over the next fourteen years, Josefa gave birth to six children: sons Julian, Cristobal, and Charles and daughters Teresina, Rebecca, and Estefana.

When Carson's health began to fail, the couple moved to Boggsville to be near friends and extended family. On April 27, 1868, only months after their arrival, forty-year-old Josefa died of complications related to childbirth. A heartbroken Carson could scarcely bring himself to see his newborn daughter or to give her a name. Finally, he named her Josefita, or Little Josefa, in his wife's honor. Ailing from old injuries and grieving the loss of his third wife, Carson died a month later. Tom and Rumalda Boggs raised si: the Carson children to adulthood, including the newborn Josefita.

By 1880 Boggsville was being abandoned. The Boggs family moved to Clayton, New Mexico. Rumalda had five children, three of whom lived to adulthood. When she died at age seventy-five, Rumalda's obituary called her "one of New Mexico's most respected women."[74]

Amache Ochinee Prowers

In about 1846, Amache was born to Ochinee (Lone Bear), a Southern Cheyenne sub-chief, and his wife. As she was growing up, her mother passed down to Amache the knowledge and skills of Cheyenne women. She was taught how to turn buffalo hides into clothing and tepees; gather wild plants for food, medicine, and dyes; and decorate hides with beads and animal teeth. When her tribe set up camp outside Bent's New Fort (Bent's Old Fort was abandoned in 1840 and destroyed in 1849; his new fort was established on the north bank of the Arkansas River in the Big Timbers area) and bartered buffalo robes for American goods, she came into contact with the diverse people populating the fort. While still in her teens, she met John Wesley Prowers. As a trader for Bent, St. Vrain and Company, Prowers drove a wagon loaded with trade goods from Westport, Missouri, to Bent's New Fort. Prowers began courting Amache, and they exchanged gifts. The couple married in 1861, and Amache was quickly immersed in Anglo life. She gave birth to their first daughter, Susan, that same year. In the winter of 1862, Prowers, accompanied by Amache and Susan, made his usual trading trip to Westport. When Prowers returned to Colorado months later, he left Amache and Susan in Missouri with his aunt. There she gave birth to daughter Mary. Through the years, the Prowers added Katie, Inez, John, Frank, Leorea, Amy, Hope, and Charles to their household. Susan, the oldest daughter, died in 1868. In 1883 Frank, the second son, died before his twelfth birthday.[75]

Amache's mother survived the Sand Creek Massacre, but her father and many other relatives did not. To atone for their losses, the US government gave a 640-acre parcel of land to each of the survivors. Amache, her mother, and two of the Prowers's oldest daughters were each given tracts along the Arkansas River, on which, along with other Cheyenne lands, Prowers largely ran his cattle. For several years after the Sand Creek Massacre, young Cheyenne dog soldiers terrorized the countryside, killing and looting American settlers in retaliation for the massacre. Amache's presence at Boggsville, coupled with the common knowledge that Native Americans were treated fairly and as equals there, left Boggsville untouched by the war-ring dog soldiers.[76]

Amache was born a Cheyenne but married into the Anglo-Victorian world. She dressed as a proper Victorian—a ruffled shirtwaist and heavy jewelry—but did not wear a constricting corset, as middle-class Anglo-American women did. Her daughters' favorite memories are of her Cheyenne ways. Every Christmas she made buffalo candy by slicing dried buffalo meat very thin, sprinkling it with sugar and cinnamon, and rolling it up like a jelly roll. She often gathered wild herbs and greens from the prairie for medicinal purposes and for teas. She preserved chokecherries, wild plums, and grapes.[77] Amache and her best friend, Mary Bent Moore (daughter of William Bent and Owl Woman), often went buffalo hunting together. In the summer, traveling Cheyenne tribesmen allowed the women to lasso colts from their herd of horses and keep them until fall. Amache spoke fluent Cheyenne and Spanish and understood English, which she spoke only when she chose to do so. Amache did not speak Cheyenne to her children, so her mother tried to teach Mary their native language. She never grasped more than five or six words, though, prompting her grandmother to say, "Oh, you too dumb to learn Cheyenne language."[78]

Amache's children grew up with Mexican, Anglo, and Indian friends. When they were older, their father sent them away to school. Mary, the old-est daughter to survive childhood, was sent to the Rice Institute (Trinidad) when she was six years old. She lived with Uncle John Hough during the school year. She attended Bent County's first subscription school the follow-ing year. The teacher was Hattie Smith, who later became Mary's sister-in-law after marrying her brother, John W. Prowers. Between the ages of twelve and fifteen, Mary was schooled at Denver's Wolfe Hall. In 1879 she gradu-ated from Central (now Bethany) College in Lexington, Missouri. The next year, she married Asa Dickerson Hudnall.[79]

Amache was active in church activities, community work, and the Eastern Star. Her daughter Mary once recounted that her mother attended an Eastern Star meeting in Denver that Colonel John Chivington also attended. A friend brought him over to meet Amache. "Mrs. Prowers, do you know Colonel Chivington?" Amache ignored his outstretched hand and replied, "Know Colonel Chivington? I should. He was my father's mur-derer." No record is given as to Chivington's reply.[80]

It was the women and their land claims that made Boggsville possible. The only woman in Boggsville with no land was Mary Prowers Hough, but her family was there because she was John Prowers's sister. The women of

Boggsville also influenced the settlement through the architecture and artifacts they left behind. The Prowers and Boggs homes were built of adobe in
a U-shape around central courtyards. These were features of New Mexican
hacienda-style architecture. The Prowers's home faced east, greeting the rising sun each morning like a typical Cheyenne encampment. In the Prowers
house, Cheyenne stone tools were found, a testament to Amache's Cheyenne
heritage. Stone tools were also found in remains in Boggsville, evidence of
Hispanic food preparation.[81]

"A SURVIVING VICTIM OF UNION COLONY": MRS. ANNIE M. GREEN

Upon hearing her husband's decision to move west as a member of the
Union Colony, Annie Green "sank upon a chair" and "scores of tears" ran
down her cheeks.[82] He offered to go to Colorado alone, but she would not
hear of it, much to her later regret. The Union Colony was touted by the
New York Tribune as a wonderful opportunity for Americans aching for their
own arable land. For Annie Green, it was hell in a dust bowl of sudden natural calamities, loneliness, and heartache.

But like many other future emigrants, Green was soon caught up in
westward fever, even reading the *Tribune* with unusual interest. Much to her
chagrin, however, she found the articles did nothing to foretell her struggles,
beginning with the journey from their Pennsylvania home. After passing
through Chicago and Omaha, the Greens and their two young children
launched themselves out onto the Great Plains, "those dreadful, hateful,
woeful, fearful, doleful, desolate, distressed, disagreeable, dusty, detestable,
homely and lonely plains, which stretched to the foot of the towering Rocky
Mountains."[83]

For most of her sixteen years on the Great American Desert, Green
was miserable. Like many women in frontier towns and rural communities,
however, she was determined to help her husband in a pecuniary way, so
she decided to open the colony's first school. After two weeks of enjoyable
teaching, she reluctantly gave it up when she was asked to help care for an
ill friend. Despite her best efforts, her patient died.[84] The next day was usually a grand holiday for a native of Pennsylvania, the land of the Liberty Bell
and the Constitutional Convention, but the Fourth of July 1870 was a bleak
day for the former Keystone native. At the end of the day, she received a
letter from a friend back home asking if she, too, should come to Colorado.
Although she was discouraged, disgruntled, and depressed and would have
loved to have had her friend nearby, Green could not cast aside her integrity

FIGURE 2.4 *Annie M. Green, an early—and reluctant—emigrant, found the early settlement of Union Colony (Greeley) woefully desolate and dusty. Courtesy, City of Greeley Museums, Permanent Collection, Greeley, CO.*

and lie to her friend. From the "depth of her soul" she considered the Union Colony "the greatest swindle of the age" and was "praying every day for its dissolution."[85] Knowing how much her unhappiness taxed her husband, she quickly mailed the letter before he arrived home and asked to read it.

Thwarted in her effort to teach, Green's next pecuniary attempt was selling homemade bread, an enterprise she felt she had to hide from her husband. During the week that was easily done, as he spent weekdays five miles from Greeley prospecting for coal. Unfortunately, her two young children were not adept at keeping secrets, and she soon had to 'fess up. After hearing about her bakery business, her husband replied, "Well if you think it best I have nothing to say." Upset, she responded, "You believe in 'Woman's Rights,' and I claim that it is my right and also my duty to aid you when I can, without interfering with my household affairs."[86] Chastised, he let the matter drop.

After one week of living on the ranch, which she called "the longest and most dreary week" of her life, Green was desperate for company.[87] Aware of her unhappiness, her husband sent her to live in Greeley for the summer. He visited her on weekends. One night a thunderstorm roiled through town. Frightened, she awoke her husband, who laughed at her fears until the rain began to fall in torrents. Within an hour their roof was completely demolished, saturating everything inside the house.[88]

Violent thunderstorms were not the only danger settlers on the plains faced. Tornadoes also wreaked havoc. Weeks before the thunderstorm, a tornado had whirled through the settlement. With her children clutched to her side, Green looked out the north window of her home to see a new house, which belonged to "Father" Meeker, lifted from its foundation and hurled to the ground. Paper roofs, pieces of timber, clothes, baskets, and men's hats filled the sky. Miraculously, no one was killed. Green found pieces of coal—weighing several pounds—in her yard, deposited by the tornado.[89] At other times, natural disasters came in the form of drought or heavy rain that destroyed crops. Diseases struck, such as the typhoid fever that left Annie's husband and daughter bedridden. They recovered after several weeks, luckier than some others in Greeley who succumbed to the disease. As Green noted, the *Tribune,* which regularly extolled the healthiness of the region, seldom recorded these deaths.[90]

Although she did not mention it, Green was pregnant with the couple's third child when the family moved from Pennsylvania to Colorado. A daughter, Kate, was born in January 1871 in the middle of a blizzard. A doctor, on hand for the delivery, "placed in my arms (on that terrible night, never to be forgotten) the first production of Colorado I had ever seen which I considered worth raising; the first prairie flower I really loved and admired."[91] Four years later another "prairie flower" was born to the Greens; this one, a son, was "a more hardy variety than the former" and "required less attention and grew more rapidly."[92] In 1876 the Greens moved from the ranch to a home in town so the children could go to school, a fairly common decision for many rural families.

While she was in Colorado, Green's mother, sister, and father-in-law died and her father remarried, compounding her feelings of isolation, loneliness, and homesickness. To give vent to those feelings and to again try to bring in cash to help the family's financial situation, Green wrote plays, songs, and a booklet, *Ten Years on the Great American Desert*. Her older daughter acted in the plays, which were performed in Greeley and Fort Collins. The two of them also wrote poems about their differing views of Colorado. Although Green was never content with her life on the Great American Desert, her children were "natural Coloradoites" who, with their father, preferred to remain in the state.[93]

In 1886, still hoping to return to Pennsylvania, she recounted the family's assets. They had 160 acres of land, 20 acres southeast of Greeley, two lots in the city, and 100 head of stock. They raised 4,000 bushels of potatoes, 1,500 bushels of small grain, and 100 tons of alfalfa that year. Even though they had been "crushed by misfortune, robbed by monopoly and swindled by usury," the family had triumphed over all the adversities the Colorado plains afflicted upon them.[94]

In early 1887, Green exuberantly wrote that the family would leave shortly for her home state after "almost seventeen years on the Great American Desert."[95] Although ecstatic about finally leaving the "lonely plains," she was also very proud of Greeley. She boasted of its real and personal property, including the "best of hotel accommodations" and "the finest opera house outside of Denver."[96] She extolled the city's electric lights, educational and church facilities, and pure artesian water. Her pride in Greeley's growth from the start of the Union Colony to its development as a city with $1 million in real and personal property was obvious. Perhaps, after all those years, Green had grown to admire the plains in much the same way Theodore Roosevelt had, who once observed, "I think it does not come easily to us to love such a land. It is easy to love a mountain, with its inherent grandeur, handsome profile and aristocratic air. But the prairie's charms take more looking. The prairie doesn't run off with your heart the way a mountain does. Its beauties are subtle, rooted in the hues of the grasses, the undulation of the land, the infinite sky. The prairie is a girl whose beauty lies in her smile."[97]

THREE
MAKING A DIFFERENCE
(1859–1877)

In 1864 three nuns who were barely settled into their new home scurried around trying to find desks for the long line of students standing at their doorstep.[1] As days passed into weeks, St. Mary's Academy, founded by Sisters Ignatia Mora, Beatriz Maes, and Joanna Walsh of the Sisters of Loretto, accommodated day and boarding students eager to take advantage of the first private school in Denver. Weeks later, the sisters could relax and laughingly recall their journey from Santa Fe, New Mexico, and their first hectic weeks in Denver. Answering a call for help from Father Joseph P. Machebeuf, the nuns were following a long line of successful Loretto sisters who had founded girls' schools in Kentucky, site of the motherhouse, and in Santa Fe.[2]

After receiving Father Machebeuf's request, the sisters packed their meager belongings and hired a coach to drive them north from Santa Fe to Denver. Their five-day journey took them through Glorieta Pass, site of a 1862 Civil War battle in which Union soldiers defeated Texas troops, thwarting the rebel attempt to reach the rich goldfields of the Rocky Mountains to finance the struggling Confederacy. Although the sisters wanted to stop at the historic site, their driver refused. He did not even slow the horses as they approached the place from which the sisters had once heard war cannons at their convent in Santa Fe.[3] Rushing past Pueblo's adobe homes and the beginnings of Colorado City, the coach's horses galloped to their final reward of oats and flannel blankets in a Denver stable.

The three Sisters of Loretto received less rest. After only a few hours' sleep, they were busy preparing their new school at Fourteenth and California for its first students. Father Machebeuf had promised parents a school that would accommodate day scholars and boarding students. When St. Mary's Academy opened, the sisters were confronted with preparing lessons for students in different grades, finding housing for the boarding students, and doing housework and cooking. Amid all that, they had to find time for their own spiritual exercises.[4] It was a monumental task, but one the sisters handled adroitly. As the school grew steadily in response to its reputation as offering an excellent fine and liberal arts education, the sisters asked for additional help. Answering the call was Sister Mary Pancratia Bonfils, a first cousin of Frederick G. Bonfils, co-publisher of the *Denver Post*. She would soon leave a lasting impression on her adopted city in the fields of education and charity.[5]

EARLY SCHOOLS

As towns and rural settlements took hold in the Colorado Territory, trappings of civilization—schools, churches, community organizations—appeared. Until farmers and townspeople could afford to build a school or a church, they conducted classes and services in their own homes. If the schoolteacher was a young single woman, she may have enjoyed Indiana Sopris's luck in persuading a man to rent her space in a building he owned.[6] Parents paid a "subscription," or tuition, for their children to attend. In the fall of 1863, Irene, Indiana Sopris's younger sister, became the schoolteacher. The first school in Pueblo opened in 1860. Four years later, Clara Weston taught the summer term. She boarded on the east side of the Arkansas River with the school on the west side. There was no bridge, so Weston took off her shoes and waded across the river twice a day for four months.[7] Further north, Elizabeth Parks Keays, the widowed niece of "Auntie" Elizabeth Stone, was the first schoolteacher in Fort Collins. She first taught her own son and then also the son of a laundrywoman. When other children in the valley wished to attend school, Auntie Stone gave up the large bedroom upstairs in her home for a school room. For fifty dollars a month, Keays taught fourteen pupils. After the fort was vacated entirely, her school was moved to a room in the commissary building.[8]

MARY RIPPON

In 1876 the University of Colorado (CU) was formally established in Boulder. Hopes ran high in the lone building near the Flatirons. Mary Rippon, the first woman to be hired as an instructor and one of only three on campus, arrived by train and was met by university president Joseph Sewall. Her tenure at CU included many firsts for the college. Originally hired to teach German language and literature classes, Rippon also taught mathematics in the early years.[9] Outwardly, Rippon led a life similar to the lives of other female professors in the late nineteenth century. She planted flowers with the university president's wife to beautify the new campus. She was a boarder for many years until she bought her own cottage, where her garden was a source of pleasure and creative expression. She co-founded a woman's club, served as a role model for her female students, and was well-respected for her teaching. She acted as a de facto dean of women in the early years of the university and spent her summers and sabbaticals in Europe, returning with treasured mementos to fill her home. She also led "separate lives."[10]

In 1886 twenty-three-year-old Will Housel began a degree program at CU. Rippon was one of his professors. Sometime in early 1888, the two became lovers. Just shy of her thirty-eighth birthday, she became pregnant with his child. Knowing that an illegitimate child would be fodder for gossipers and death to her professorial career, Rippon and Housel secretly married in St. Louis, Missouri. With her sabbatical leave approved, the couple boarded a ship bound for Germany. Rippon gave birth to Miriam Edna Housel on January 19, 1889. Housel missed the birth of his daughter because he was in Boulder finishing his degree. Sheepskin in hand, he returned to Germany to see his wife and daughter. At the end of the summer, Rippon left her husband and daughter to return to CU. Housel began graduate studies, and Miriam was placed in an orphanage.

Over the next several decades, Rippon supported Housel and their daughter, who was brought to the United States. She even supported his family from his second marriage after hers and Will's marriage ended. Years after Housel's death in a motorcycle accident, Miriam finally learned that Rippon, whom she had always thought of as her aunt, was in fact her mother. Rippon

FIGURE 3.1 *The first female instructor and a popular German professor at the University of Colorado, Mary Rippon carried the story of her "other" life to her grave. Courtesy, Carnegie Branch Library for Local History, Boulder Historical Society Collection, Boulder, CO.*

had kept her secret from all but a few close friends. When she retired from CU in 1909 after thirty-one years of teaching, the German professor was fondly remembered. The following year daughter Miriam fell in love with, became pregnant by, and married Rudolph Rieder, her German teacher at the University of Wisconsin. When Rippon died in 1935, Miriam was listed as a "close friend" in the obituary. Rippon's friends convinced the University of Colorado to name its outdoor theater the Mary Rippon Theater in honor of her decades-long contribution as a professor. In 1976 an elderly Wilfred Rieder donated two photographs to the university, identifying himself as a descendant of Rippon's. The announcement stunned Boulder residents and faculty members. A decade later he unveiled the story of Will Housel, Mary Rippon, and Miriam Housel Rieder.[11] As historian Sylvia Pettem points out, the secret lives Rippon and Housel led exacted a toll on their marriage and on Rippon's health, but they do not lessen the positive role she played at the University of Colorado and with her many students.[12]

WOMEN'S CHARITABLE WORKS

Like industrialists in the East and Midwest, the power elites of Colorado's cities did little to ease the burdens of those they had encouraged to immigrate. Intent on profit and growth, the power elite ignored deplorable working and living conditions. It was left to a few individuals—primarily upper-class women, freed by servants from many traditional female duties—to come to the aid of the poor, especially women and children. As early as 1860, William Byers, editor of the *Rocky Mountain News* and one of Denver's chief boosters, persuaded the city government to raise a stipend for the poor. In 1862 the county levied a tax for relief, but it was never enough. City and county authorities tried to push the burden off on each other while many property owners believed indigents were unworthy of any aid, a common belief among people at the time.[13]

In towns where saloons outnumbered churches and schools, the need for charity was profound. During Denver's early years, charitable organizations were spearheaded, led, and supported by women. In 1860 Elizabeth Byers, Susan Ashley, and other Denver women organized the Ladies Union Aid Society. In meetings at the Broadwell House the women—who paid ten dollar monthly membership dues—made underwear, nightshirts, and bandages for Colorado's First Volunteer Regiment. The proprietor of the Broadwell allowed the organization free use of his largest room and chairs and tables for cutting. Byers served as the society's first president. In the

1870s she joined with other women to found the Denver Orphans' Home and the Old Ladies' Home, in response to the plight of the city's deserted children, elderly women, and widows.[14]

In 1872 Byers encouraged Margaret Gray Evans to establish the Denver Orphans' Home (now the Denver Children's Home), to which several other women contributed. Evans made sure the Denver Tramway Company, run by her son William Gray Evans, provided free excursions for the children. In 1883 the first residence, a two-story building at 1600 Race Street, was built. Within days, 40 children filled the Denver Orphans' Home. By 1889 over 1,000 children considered it their home. In 1902 the home moved to its current location at 1501 Albion Street. Renamed the Denver Children's Home in 1962, the facility continues to care for the state's abused and neglected children.[15]

Another project of Byers and her charitable cohorts was the Old Ladies' Home. Ella Vincent, wife of Bethuel Thomas (B.T.) Vincent, the minister of Lawrence Street (now Trinity) Methodist Church, taught a Sunday school class to young women. In 1872 she organized a Christmas social for poor widows. Astonished by the number of attendees, members of her Sunday school class formed the Young Ladies Relief Society. Their fundraising efforts at a bazaar a few evenings before Christmas netted a handsome sum. During the winter, so many residents were found to be extremely needy that the society was taxed to the utmost. It was apparent that a home for those no longer able to care for themselves was greatly needed.

The Young Ladies Relief Society joined forces with the Ladies Union Aid Society to form the Ladies' Relief Society (LRS). At the first meeting of the board of directors, an advisory board of eight men and one woman was appointed. Raising funds for the indigent, the society's 1875 receipts totaled nearly $5,000, all of which was distributed to various charities. Seeing a desperate need for housing for widows and elderly women, the society decided "to establish and maintain a home for destitute and homeless aged and infirm women (and for the care and cure of the sick, so far as practical), to give temporary relief, provide suitable employment, and to encourage and promote industry, thrift, and good morals among such classes of persons as shall come under our charge, care, or influence."[16] Board member Richard E. Whitsitt donated twelve lots at the corner of Eighth and Logan Streets for the proposed building. In early 1876 the Old Ladies' Home was completed. At first the large, $50,000, red brick building was admired, at least by one reporter for the *Denver Republican* who praised its "spacious and comfortably furnished rooms," excellent ventilation, and "creditable appearance."[17]

FIGURE 3.2 *The Ladies' Relief Society founded the Old Ladies' Home in Denver. Women were admitted if they came with "high character" and a black silk dress (which could serve as their burial garb). Courtesy, History Colorado (Scan #10041260), Denver.*

For the next twenty years, the Ladies' Relief Society ran the Old Ladies' Home with generous donations from women's clubs, church auxiliaries, and city residents. By 1900, when the society established a policy of admitting life members upon payment of a life membership fee, forty elderly women lived there. The original life fee was on a sliding scale that ranged from $300 to $600, depending on the woman's age. Fees and monthly board payments increased through the years as the cost of living rose. A constant problem was the fact that the life membership fee was never set on an actuarial basis, leaving the home short of funds.[18]

In addition to the home, the LRS also opened a day nursery and free kindergarten for underprivileged children. By 1885 it had assumed the work of the Home of the Friendless and established a wood yard where needy men and boys exchanged their labor cutting wood for food and shelter in another facility. Three years later the women opened a free dispensary. Prominent women served on the advisory board and held appointed or elected offices at the Old Ladies' Home. By 1889, the year Frances Wisebart Jacobs was elected president, the Ladies' Relief Society was the largest single charity in Colorado, annually raising and spending $10,000 to assist more than 2,000 persons. Its board included Protestants, Jews, and Catholics. Through Jacobs's efforts, charitable work in Denver was consolidated in the new Charity Organization Society.[19]

By the late 1890s the location of the Old Ladies' Home had become a fashionable neighborhood for Denver's wealthy families, who complained that it was a hideous building that blocked their view of the mountains. In 1897 Leadville gold tycoon John F. Campion paid the Ladies' Relief Society $15,000 for the property so he could demolish it. The society used $3,000 from this sale to buy its present site in the 4100 block of West 38th Avenue. By-laws were revised to limit eligibility to women over age sixty-five. The main sections of the new home were completed between 1898 and 1900. Over the next ten years the west and north wings were built, the dining room enlarged, a new kitchen installed, and the Cheever wing built (named after Charles G. Cheever, who gave $25,000 to the home). A first-floor parlor and hospital unit were added. In 1920 the Emeroy S. Sweet Hospital was erected through a gift from Mr. and Mrs. Channing Sweet, enlarged by a gift from Governor William E. Sweet. The last building was completed in 1929, with the addition of a solarium connecting the hospital with the main building. The home supported itself through Christmas bazaars, bake sales, and other activities.

Between 1911 and 1925, internal rifts rocked the LRS regarding administration of the Old Ladies' Home. In March 1911, Mrs. Alfred C. Kerns and Dr. Mary E. Bates, members of the board of county visitors, charged the home's managers with mistreating residents and feeding them poorly. A subsequent hearing before the state board implied that Dr. Bates, chief instigator of the probe, had not visited the institution and that charges were based in part on complaints made by residents who visited her office. The state board dismissed the charges as unwarranted and without foundation.[20]

In 1915 six women ousted from the home because of overcrowding stated that they had been removed for criticizing the house matron. Ten years later, new disagreements led to an investigation that revealed wasteful spending and petty restrictive regulations. Requirements that residents were not allowed to use the front door, that they had to report to their rooms after dinner, and that lights were turned off at 9:00 p.m. caused adult women to be treated like children. Again, the home and the LRS weathered the discord and continued to offer affordable residences and care to elderly women at 4115 West 38th Avenue.[21]

While some women established homes for charity, Helen Hunt Jackson wrote about the beauty of her adopted home, Colorado Springs, and nearby Cheyenne Canyon. Helen was already an accomplished author and poet when she ventured west for her health. She met and married William Sharpless Jackson in 1875. A few years later she learned about the harsh treatment of American Indians by government officials. After extensively studying the US government's history of broken promises and mistreatment of the Indians, Jackson published the tome *A Century of Dishonor* and mailed it to every member of the US Congress. She later wrote *Ramona*, a novel about Indians living on Spanish ranches. The two books sealed her reputation as an American Indian activist.

EARLY SUFFRAGE CAMPAIGNS

In addition to establishing schools and aiding the needy, women were hard at work trying to secure the right to vote in Colorado. In 1870 Territorial Governor Edward M. McCook spoke in favor of women voting, prompting the legislature to debate the issue. Racist arguments were used by both sides. Allison H. DeFrance, chairman of the special house committee, pointed out that it was unfair for an uneducated, non-property-holding Negro to vote on matters of property owned by white women who were themselves not permitted to vote. In opposition, Representative Matthew Taylor argued, "From nature, education and principle I am a Democrat, consequently opposed to negro [sic] suffrage in any shape or form. Are the supporters of this measure aware that in passing this bill as it now reads, they confer upon negro wenches the right to vote?"[22] Taylor suggested that Colorado women did not want the franchise; rather, they were henpecked by national leaders Anna Dickinson, Elizabeth Cady Stanton, and Lucy Stone. Another anti-suffrage argument held that rather than purify politics, the right to vote would sully women's sensitive nature. By February 1870 the Colorado legislature had defeated both the house and council versions of woman's suffrage. Accusatory fingers were pointed at many villains. Some suffrage supporters vilified legislators for lacking backbone or being prejudiced. Others blamed the women themselves as the most ardent opponents of woman's suffrage. Whatever the cause—undoubtedly a combination of many reasons—the suffrage issue was politically dead for several years.[23]

In late 1875 through 1876, as Colorado prepared for its state constitutional convention, the woman's suffrage issue gained new life. Women of Colorado realized the significance of the nation's centennial year. In 1776 "taxation without representation" had been a favorite slogan, and they were prepared to use the slogan for their own campaign for political rights a century later.

Margaret Campbell organized a woman's suffrage association during the state constitutional convention. Dr. Alida C. Avery, chosen the association's president, encouraged convention members and the press to present arguments for and against suffrage. Like Campbell, Dr. Avery had arrived only a year or two before the constitutional convention was held. A New Yorker by birth, she taught at local schools before studying medicine. In 1862 she received her diploma from the New England Medical College in Boston. Three years later she joined the founding faculty at Vassar as professor of physiology and hygiene and resident physician. The only other female original faculty member at Vassar was Maria Mitchell, a self-taught astronomer. As was common, Avery and Mitchell were paid significantly lower salaries than the male instructors. Avery received $1,000 a year plus board, and Mitchell was paid only $800 a year and given an apartment in the Observatory. The men earned $2,500 without the cost of board. In 1870 Avery and Mitchell wrote to President John H. Raymond asking that their salaries be made equal to those of other professors. Following the women's request, the board of trustees raised their salaries.[24] While Mitchell made Vassar her home and passion for the next seventeen years, Avery left Vassar for Colorado in 1874.

Dr. Avery opened a private practice in Colorado and quickly became a leader in the fledgling state's suffrage campaign, serving as president of the Colorado Woman Suffrage Association. Although Denver's most progressive men and women attended the first meeting, the suffragists also had powerful opponents. One of the major opponents was the Right Reverend Joseph P. Machebeuf, Denver's first Catholic bishop. He specifically targeted leaders of women's rights, perhaps especially Dr. Avery, a single woman in her mid-forties. The bishop argued that "the class of women wanting suffrage are battalions of old maids disappointed in love—women separated from their husbands or divorced by men from their sacred obligations—women who, though married, wish to hold the reins of the family government, for there never was a woman happy in her home who wished for female suffrage."[25]

Ultimately, the proposal to grant women the right to vote in the new state constitution failed because members of the convention were unwilling to risk rejection of the entire constitution over the inclusion of female suffrage. As approved, the constitution stated: "Every male person over the age of twenty-one years . . . shall be entitled to vote at all elections."[26] Even though the last part of the section stated that women would be allowed to vote in all elections for district school officers and on issues relating to public schools, it was small consolation to the suffragists.

The Colorado State Constitution granted the general assembly the power to extend suffrage if the people voted to do so in a general election. In fact, the constitution, as approved, made it mandatory that the first legislature provide such an election on the issue. In hopes of winning the right to vote by a mandate of the male voters, the suffrage association brought in Lucy Stone, Henry Blackwell, and Susan B. Anthony to speak throughout the state. Stone and Blackwell traveled through the southern part of the state before campaigning in Boulder, Weld, Gilpin, and Clear Creek Counties. Anthony spent most of her time in the southern part of the state, including the communities of Las Animas, Pueblo, Trinidad, Walsenburg, Del Norte, and Lake City. In that part of the state, Anthony struggled just to reach the towns. Then she was often forced to speak in noisy saloons, crowded hotel dining rooms, and bustling railway stations. A final obstacle was that the vast majority of the townspeople strongly opposed woman's suffrage. As Anthony later reported, she found her audience was made up of a "densely ignorant class of foreigners," almost entirely Mexican. "It was to these men that an American woman [Anthony], her grandfather a soldier in the Revolution, appealed for the right of women to representation in this government."[27]

Newspapers, however, strongly supported woman's suffrage. All of the Denver papers, except the *Tribune,* came out in favor of it, and the *Tribune* was leaning that way. The *Lake City Silver World,* which had previously opposed suffrage, carried an editorial in January stating that it believed the time had come to confer the right of suffrage on women.[28] Elsewhere in the state, the *Ouray Times* devoted several columns to the Wyoming suffrage experiment and denounced Bishop Machebeuf's claims that woman's suffrage in Wyoming was a failure.[29]

On Election Day, October 2, 1877, women spent the day at the polls, hoping to bolster their cause. But as the votes were counted, the measure lost by a substantial margin. The final count showed 6,612 in favor, with 14,053 opposed. Once again, fingers were pointed at various groups. A bitter Susan B. Anthony blamed Mexicans in the southern part of the state. Although the southern counties and mining districts did vote heavily against the measure, these regions were less populated than other parts of the state. For example, in Boulder County, the only county to pass the measure, more people voted against it than was the case in any of the southern counties except one. An editorial in the *Lake City Silver World* blamed the loss on election fraud.[30] Some blamed women themselves, saying they did not want suffrage badly enough. Defeated but undaunted, it would be another sixteen years before Colorado women pushed the suffrage issue again.

CATHOLIC SISTERS, CHRISTIAN CHARITY, AND PRIVATE EDUCATION

St. Mary's Academy, founded by the Sisters of Loretto in 1864, quickly outgrew its original building at Fourteenth and California Streets, prompting the sisters to ask for additional help. A year later a fire destroyed part of the academy, giving the sisters an opportunity to enlarge the school during the rebuilding effort. St. Mary's Academy issued the first high school diploma granted in the Colorado Territory to Jessie Forshee in 1875.[31] An additional building was erected in 1881 to meet the demands of the continually growing school. By 1884 the academy's 25 instructors were teaching 100 boarders from a variety of states and 125 day students from Denver. Within a decade, students again faced crowded facilities. To remain close to the church, the Sisters of Loretto built a large, still-standing edifice at 1370 Pennsylvania in 1911. Classes were initiated for the advanced training of teachers. Within a year, the nuns opened a chemistry and physics laboratory, disregarding the conventional notion that only boys pursued the sciences.

To alleviate the crowding at St. Mary's, the sisters searched for a new site on which to build a boarding school. By this time, Mary Pancratia Bonfils, who had arrived twenty years earlier, was mother superior of the sisters. She, along with Sisters Bartholomew Nooning, Agatha Wall, and Victorini Renshaw, selected a site southwest of downtown Denver at the present location of Federal and Yale Avenues. On a high knoll with a commanding view of Denver and the Rocky Mountains, Mother Bonfils geographically and spiritually elevated her students and the Sisters of Loretto. Located on forty-five acres, the new academy, Loretto Heights, opened with twenty sisters and fifty-one girls. Although she was transferred to Alabama in 1892, Mother Bonfils's influence ran deep. Her dream of a college for young women, Loretto Heights College, was realized in 1918 by Mother Clarasine Walsh, Sister Dolorine Morrison, and Sister Vivian Edelen. Ten years later, ground was broken for Pancratia Hall.

By the middle of the Great Depression, the Sisters of Loretto had established numerous schools along the Front Range, including Holy Family, St. Philomena's, St. Johns, St. Mary's School (Colorado Springs), Sacred Heart (Pueblo), and St. Joseph's (Fort Collins).

In 1951 St. Mary's Academy moved from downtown to 4545 South University Boulevard in the upscale neighborhood of Cherry Hills Village, where it thrives as Denver's oldest private school. Upon the academy's 100th anniversary in 1964, the high school building cornerstone was laid. Helen Bonfils, co-owner of the *Denver Post*, donated $500,000, funding half of the cost of the new building.

One hundred years after its founding, Loretto Heights College, affectionately called "LoHi," was absorbed by Teikyo University and became Teikyo Loretto Heights University (TLHU). The international Japanese university preserved Old Main and the graveyard, the final burying place for Mother Pancratia Bonfils and many other nuns. Old Main, a four-story administration building designed by Frank Edbrooke, has an open bell tower that can be seen for miles. Beginning in 2009, TLHU became Colorado Heights University. Old Main's historic bell tower—a symbol of Mother Pancratia's dream—is still a prominent landmark overlooking the city from the southwest.

BLACK HUMANITARIAN AND ENTREPRENEUR: "AUNT" CLARA BROWN

In the early 1800s Clara was born a slave of Ambrose Smith. In 1809 he moved to Russellville, Kentucky, taking his slaves with him. At age eighteen, Clara married. She and her husband had four children: Margaret, twin daughters, Eliza Jane and Paulina, and a son, Richard. At age eight, Paulina drowned. In 1835, after Smith's death, all his slaves were sold on the auction block. Clara was bought by George Brown, a Kentucky hatter, who separated her from her children.

At age fifty-five, after twenty years of faithful service, Brown was granted her freedom. According to Kentucky law, manumitted slaves were required to leave the state within a year or be re-enslaved, so she moved to Missouri. She found work in St. Louis and soon emigrated to Leavenworth, Kansas, with her employer. Determined to find her daughter Eliza Jane, Brown decided to move to Colorado, hoping her daughter had also found her way west. In Leavenworth, she convinced Colonel Wadsworth to transport her washtubs, washboard, and stoves in exchange for cooking for the twenty-six men heading west.[32]

In Denver, Brown first cooked in a local bakery and then worked as a laundress. She became friends with Reverend Jacob Adriance of the Cherry Creek Methodist Episcopal Mission and opened her cabin for church services. In October 1859 she was one of several adults and a dozen children who attended a meeting to establish the first Sunday school in Denver.

FIGURE 3.3 *"Aunt" Clara Brown, a former slave, worked as a laundress in Central City, where she grubstaked miners and aided those down on their luck. She was the first black inducted into the Society of Colorado Pioneers. Courtesy, History Colorado (Scan #10027902), Denver.*

In the spring of 1860 she joined a party moving to Central City, where she secured a three-room cabin with an attached woodshed. In the main room, she set up a laundry. She used the second room as her bedroom. The shed stored the wood needed for warmth, cooking, and heating water for her laundry work. It also had enough room for anyone needing a t/ place to stay. The laundry room doubled as a church. Brown charged .. cents a garment at a time when miners were lucky to be paid ten dollars a week. She earned that wage with every twenty grimy shirts, overalls, or long johns she laundered. Business boomed. Brown worked hard and was able to buy her foodstuffs, fuel, and soap as well as stash money away. Her savings grubstaked miners, paid their medical bills, and helped others in need. She delivered babies in the mining town and cooked for single miners. Her hard work and willingness to help others won her the respect of miners and town leaders alike. Shortly after the end of the Civil War, the editor of the *Daily Miners' Register* [Central City] received word that "some low-lived fellow" had addressed Brown on the street with "some very indecent, disgraceful and insulting language." Stating that "there is not a more respectable, upright colored woman in the territory than 'Aunt' Clara," the *Register*'s editor asserted that the unnamed slanderer was "no gentleman."[33] Although she may have been insulted, "Aunt" Clara was in no way discouraged. She continued to work long hours laundering filthy overalls and long johns. With the help of Jeremiah Lee, another black, she bought a house and began investing in Central City real estate and mines. Within five years, Brown had saved $10,000. It was time to look in earnest for Eliza Jane.

In 1866 she traveled to Tennessee and Kentucky in the hope of finding her sole remaining daughter. Unsuccessful, she gathered up sixteen freed blacks and paid their way to Central City, where they could embark on a new life. Upon her return to Colorado, the *Rocky Mountain News* praised her humanitarian effort: "We will put 'Aunt' Clara against the world, white or black, for industry, perseverance, energy, and filial love."[34] For the next decade or so, Brown remained a laundress in Central City, stayed active in her church, and helped those in need. Never one to let religious affiliations interfere in her efforts to be a true Christian, she, a member of St. James Methodist Church in Central City, gave a substantial amount of money to Father Machebeuf to help build a Catholic church in the mining town.

In 1879, now nearly eighty years old, Brown traveled to Kansas to help poor black "exodusters."[35] After she returned to Central City, she found that decades of hard work, coupled with the town's high altitude, were taking a toll on her. A doctor advised her to move to a lower elevation, so in 1880 "Aunt" Clara returned to Denver. Her savings depleted (a result of her philanthropic efforts as well as unscrupulous acquaintances), it was time for others to return her past generosity. Charles Cheever, who owned several homes that he rented to newcomers, gave her a house on Arapahoe Street rent-free for the rest of her life. Although ill health temporarily laid her low, her indomitable will soon reemerged. With the help of friends, the illiterate former slave launched a letter-writing campaign to find Eliza Jane. In 1882 a letter arrived from Council Bluffs, Iowa, from a friend stating that she had met a Mrs. Brewer whose story of being separated from her family at the auction block when she was only eleven years old sounded like the story "Aunt" Clara had told. Friends in Denver gave the eighty-year-old Brown a discounted rail pass and food for the train ride to Iowa. Mrs. Brewer, her long-lost Eliza Jane, met her at the station. After a short visit, Brown returned to Denver accompanied by her granddaughter.[36]

Brown's health continued to fail. In 1884 a testimonial dinner was held in her honor to raise funds for her welfare. Within a year, the first black member of the Society of Colorado Pioneers lay dying in her house on Arapahoe Street. The *Rocky Mountain News* lamented her situation, saying she was a remarkable woman "for the many good deeds done to sick and destitute travelers in the early days."[37] Four days later she died in her sleep. The Society of Colorado Pioneers was in charge of her funeral service at Central Presbyterian Church. Reverend E. P. Wells "gave an animated sketch of 'Aunt' Clara's life, mingled with personal reminiscences, he having been acquainted with her for a period of seventeen years. He recounted her many struggles in Colorado, her life of labor and self-denial, and the large amount of money she had saved and expended in bringing to Colorado" other freed blacks. The black choir of Zion Baptist Church provided the music.[38] Beloved and respected by the many people she had helped, Brown was buried at Riverside Cemetery in Denver. The governor and mayor were among the mourners. The former slave, philanthropist, and entrepreneur is commemorated with a stained glass window and a chair at the Central City Opera House. A bronze plaque also honors her at St. James Methodist Church in Central City.

"THE COLORADO HUNTRESS": MARTHA MAXWELL

Martha Ann Dartt was born on July 21, 1831, to Spencer and Amy Sanford Dartt in Dartt's Settlement, Pennsylvania. When she was two-and-a-half years old, her father died. Her mother married Josiah Dartt, her late husband's first cousin, when Martha was ten. Josiah and Amy were stricken with "Oregon fever," so they packed up their three daughters, Martha, Mary Emma, and Sarah Elizabeth, and headed west but got no further than Baraboo, Wisconsin.[39]

A strong believer in women's education—an uncommon stance in the mid-nineteenth century—Josiah encouraged his stepdaughter to attend Oberlin College (Ohio). She thrived in the intellectual atmosphere of college classes and community reform activities. She worked with the Oberlin Female Moral Reform Society, founded to fight against impure thought, dress, and action. When her parents' financial situation worsened, she left Oberlin and returned to Baraboo to teach school.[40] She met James A. Maxwell, a businessman and widower. He offered to pay her tuition and living expenses if she accompanied his two oldest children to Lawrence University (Wisconsin). Thrilled at the opportunity to continue her education, she readily agreed. More reluctantly, she accepted his marriage proposal. Maxwell, twenty years older than she, had four younger children in addition to the two she chaperoned at Lawrence University. Only twenty-two years old, she was now a wife and the stepmother of six children. Although burdened with the responsibilities of a large household, the new Mrs. James Maxwell continued her reform work. She joined other women in raiding town taverns, opening bottles, and pouring liquor onto barroom floors. For their part in the "Whiskey War of 1854," the women were arrested and fined.[41]

On November 17, 1857, she gave birth to Mabel, the couple's only child. Financially struggling, the Maxwells were lured westward by news of Colorado gold. Leaving their young child behind, they arrived in Denver in the spring of 1860 before continuing on to Golden and Central City. Her husband tried mining while she ran a boardinghouse. In early 1861 she bought a ranch claim ten miles downstream from Denver along the Platte River. That fall, after a fire destroyed much of Central City—including her boardinghouse—the couple moved to the ranch. When they arrived, they found squatters living in the cabin. Before they were evicted, Maxwell was able to study the stuffed animals one of the squatters had created. Intrigued, she had serendipitously found her life's work.[42]

Maxwell obtained a gun, practiced her marksmanship, and set off into the mountains. By 1868 she had gathered 600 specimens, which she exhibited at the Third Annual Exposition of the Colorado Agricultural Society. She constructed a natural habitat to display the mounted specimens. Although museum visitors expect this sort of exhibit today, it was unique in the nineteenth century. The *Rocky Mountain News* reported that her exhibit was "probably the greatest attraction in the room."[43] Territorial Governor Alexander Hunt was so impressed that he asked her to represent Colorado at the St. Louis Fair in 1870. She later sold her collection to Shaw's Gardens, which allowed her to buy land at the mouth of Boulder Canyon, where she had a house moved. She had a workshop for taxidermic work separate from the house she shared with her husband and daughter.

Her half-sister, Mary Dartt, later described Martha's mountain of supplies crowding the workshop. There were piles of wire, cotton, and hay; containers of clay, salt, and plaster; mounds of mosses and grasses; blocks of wood; bottles of insects and glass eyes; and collections of animal horns and heads.[44] To prepare an antelope skin she had recently shot, Maxwell skinned the trophy and took measurements. She cleaned the bones, a particularly disagreeable task but vital in allowing her to study the shape and disposition of the animal's muscular system. Rather than sew up the skins and stuff them, Maxwell used molds of plaster of paris or clay. Later, she developed an iron framework that was then covered with hay or various other materials.[45]

Continually strapped for money and with specimens threatening to overtake the house, Maxwell resolved to find a way to bridge finances with her passion. She decided to open a museum where the public could be educated and entertained. She located her Rocky Mountain Museum on the second floor of the Debney-Macky block at the corner of Pearl and 12th Streets in Boulder. Admission was twenty-five cents. Helen Hunt visited the museum in 1875. Her column in the *New York Independent* described how Maxwell arranged Colorado animals in lifelike settings. There was a doe licking two fawns, a bear crawling out of the mouth of a cave, a fox pouncing on a rabbit, and a mountain lion springing through the branches of a tree toward a terrified deer.[46] Although the museum awed Hunt and impressed scholarly critics, it was a financial bust. Thinking there would be more foot traffic in Denver, Maxwell moved the museum to Lawrence Street. There, however, the museum proved no more of a financial success than it had been in Boulder.

For the Centennial Exposition in Philadelphia in 1876, Maxwell created a more sophisticated habitat grouping than what she had displayed at either the Boulder or Denver museum. Housed in the Kansas-Colorado Building erected near the Women's Pavilion, the exhibit earned her national recognition and fame. The public was amazed that a woman had created the comprehensive exhibit of mammals and birds of Colorado's plains and mountains. Arrayed against one wall was a mountain landscape of trees and boulders, down which a stream trickled into a small lake inhabited by fishes, turtles, beavers, muskrats, and waterfowl. Between the stream and the lake was a cave overshadowed by "fierce bears, shy mountain sheep, savage mountain lions or pumas, and a multitude of smaller creatures." Buffalo, elk, and antelope populated the plains. In front of it all, a placard read "Woman's Work."[47]

FIGURE 3.4 *An exhibit of Martha Maxwell's taxidermic work amazed visitors with its lifelike animals shown in their natural environment. Courtesy, Carnegie Branch Library for Local History, Boulder Historical Society Collection, Boulder, CO.*

Visitors in long queues peppered Maxwell and her half-sister with questions about how she acquired and treated the animals. They were equally curious about the "modern Diana" who created the display. Articles about Maxwell appeared in *Harper's Bazaar*, *New Century for Women*, and newspapers from coast to coast. Most were "struck by the disparity between the masculine image they thought her work suggested and the appearance of the woman herself."[48] Expecting to meet "an Amazon in size and strength, clad in a suit of buckskin, with murder in her eye, a Sharp's rifle in her hands, and wearing a belt stuck full of revolvers and knives," reporters instead found "a petite little woman, dressed in a plain dark suit, slight of stature, with pleasant face, dark hair, and the manners of a thorough lady."[49]

The exposition ran from May to November 1876 and attracted nearly 10 million visitors. At its close, Colorado and Kansas commissioners presented Maxwell with an Evans rifle but failed to pay her expenses as agreed upon. Strapped for money, Martha sought ways to exhibit or sell her collection. She also worked with her half-sister, who was writing her story. As was the case with so many of her other attempts to earn money for herself and for Mabel's college education, however, *On the Plains and among the Peaks; or How Mrs. Maxwell Made Her Natural History Collection* was not a financial success.[50]

Estranged from her husband, who remained in Colorado, Maxwell moved from Philadelphia to Rockaway Beach, New York. There she decided to combine a museum with a bathhouse. While preparing her bathhouse-museum for the summer months, the lonely Maxwell began to suffer physically and emotionally. Her health deteriorated over the winter. Mabel, summoned from Colorado, was informed that Maxwell was dying from an ovarian tumor. In the early morning of May 31, 1881, she died in her daughter's arms.[51]

Martha Maxwell was in many ways ahead of her time, both as a woman scientist and as a museum developer. What separated her from other naturalists was that she always placed stuffed animals in natural poses and among natural surroundings. That innovation made her work very popular. In 1877 Smithsonian ornithologist Robert Ridgway named the little screech owl *Scops asio maxwelliae* in honor of her discovery of the subspecies. She was pleased with the suffix "ae," indicative of its female honoree, since most animals had the "i" or "ii" for male discoverers. Its common name, Mrs. Maxwell's owl, prompted her to boast that it gave her "so much to be remembered by hereafter."[52]

FOUR

SETTLING IN

(1878–1900)

As communities developed and residents settled in, opportunities opened for single women. Female teachers in particular knew their services would be welcome. One such woman was Phoebe Fidelia Skinner. Skinner was born in Ohio in 1841, making her of marrying age about the time the nation was torn asunder by the Civil War. As young men joined regiments and marched off to war, Skinner and thousands of other women supported the Union war effort. Following the surrender of General Robert E. Lee in April 1865, the men returned, but they were not the vibrant youth of five years past. War had taken its toll on their bodies and minds. Skinner found no eligible bachelors among the veterans. Restless, she left the Midwest and traveled by train to Boulder. In 1875 she was hired to teach in Crisman, a prosperous mining area at the junction of Sunshine Gulch and Four Mile Creek.[1] Her students were the sons and daughters of miners, merchants, farmers, and ranchers. As a single woman in her early thirties, Skinner was a bit of an anomaly because

DOI: 10.5876/9781607322078.c04

most schoolteachers were ten years younger than she. She boarded with the Simon Davidson family in town.

An impudent student once asked if she had come west to teach or to find a husband. Although there is no record of her response, whatever her original motive, she had proven successful in acquiring both a teaching job and a husband.[2] Two years after arriving in Colorado she married James Andrew Walker, a Civil War veteran from Virginia who had moved to Missouri after the war. Within a few years he was in poor health, suffering from consumption. His life in danger, Walker followed his doctor's orders and moved west. Finding the mountain air restorative, he worked as a farmhand in Left Hand Canyon. He first rented before buying land near Boulder on which to farm and ranch. After spending several summers in the mountains, he bought a homestead relinquishment.[3]

James Walker knew Simon Davidson from his postwar years in Missouri. Although he was seven years younger than Skinner, Walker began courting her. They were married on January 6, 1876. The couple lived in the mountains during the summer and in Boulder during the winter. Walker steadily increased his landholdings on Flagstaff Mountain until he had over 6,000 acres on which he grazed Galloway cattle, imported from Scotland because of their ability to withstand the severe mountain weather.[4] The Walkers grew corn as feed for the cattle and raised pigs for family meals. Phoebe tended to the milk cows and numerous chickens. Boulder's growing population provided a ready market for her eggs and butter.

COLORADO GROWTH

In addition to the Walkers, other ranching and farming families benefited from Colorado's growing population after the 1870s. Booster efforts by Denver's leaders and the building of railroads into the region encouraged this growth. William N. Byers, John Evans, and David H. Moffat constantly publicized the advantages of the Colorado region.[5] At their urging, the state legislature created and funded the Board of Immigration, whose mission was to encourage migration to Colorado. A railroad line from Denver to Cheyenne, Wyoming, which connected Colorado to the transcontinental line, was joined by other rail lines into and out of Denver. By the early 1880s Denver had been transformed from a collection of makeshift shacks into the hub of a rapidly growing region.

Rail lines provided transportation to Colorado for westward-bound women as well as job opportunities for women already in the state. For ten years, Mrs. Nancy Wickham and her three daughters ran the Wickham House. Originally built in Granada in 1873, it was moved by flat car and became the first wood-framed house in La Junta. The Wickham women ran it as a boardinghouse for railroad workers until 1886, when the Fred Harvey House was built at the train station.[6] In 1876 Fred Harvey, an English immigrant, opened his first Harvey House Restaurant in the Santa Fe Depot Station in Topeka, Kansas. He had noticed that, although railroad traffic was slicing across the country, trains typically had few dining cars. Trains usually stopped every 100 miles, but stations often lacked eating establishments or the eating establishments that did exist were of poor quality and took too long to serve famished passengers before the train pulled out. After leasing the lunch counter at a depot, Harvey focused on efficient service, reasonable prices, and good food. His business was an immediate success. The Atchison, Topeka & Santa Fe Railroad turned over control of food service along the rail line to Harvey. The Harvey Houses became the nation's first chain restaurants, and the Topeka depot became the training base for the company. By the late 1880s there was a Harvey establishment every 100 miles along the Santa Fe line.[7]

In Colorado, Harvey Houses were located in La Junta and Trinidad. The restaurants set high standards for efficiency and cleanliness. The food was served on china plates, and male customers were required to wear coats. Harvey soon realized that the men he hired to work in his restaurants were as wild as the West itself. In an effort to attract a more civilized crew, Harvey recruited young women through newspaper ads placed nationwide. To qualify as a "Harvey Girl," women had to have at least an eighth-grade education, strong moral character, proper manners, and be neat and articulate. The girls were subjected to a strict 10:00 p.m. curfew administered by a senior Harvey Girl who assumed the role and responsibilities of house mother. Harvey paid "his girls" as much as $17.50 per month, with free room, board, and uniforms. The official black-and-white starched uniform consisted of a skirt that hung no more than eight inches off the floor, opaque black stockings, and black shoes. A woman's hair was restrained in a net and tied with a regulation white ribbon. Makeup of any sort was prohibited, as was chewing gum while on duty. In return for employment, Harvey Girls accepted a six-month contract, agreed not to marry, and promised to abide by all company rules during their term of employment.[8] In no time, positions with Harvey Houses became prized jobs. When they were hired, women were given a free rail pass to their chosen destination. Many girls worked in more than one Harvey House, wanting to see parts of the United States they would probably never see once they were married and had children (marriage was the most common reason a girl terminated her employment).[9]

During the last quarter of the nineteenth century, although women living in Colorado's major cities experienced a more settled life than women during the early years of settlement had known, their lives were still difficult and physically taxing. Unhealthy water supplies, streets strewn with garbage and livestock manure, and daily chores of shopping, cleaning, and child rearing filled their days. Emily Louisa Rood French was typical of many women struggling in Denver. Born in Michigan in 1843, she had eloped with Marsena French when she was fifteen. He was eleven years her senior. The couple lived in Michigan, Iowa, and Colorado while he tried to establish himself as a physician. The Frenches had eight children between 1860 and 1881. In 1884 they homesteaded three miles east of Elbert.[10]

For ranchers and farmers on the high plains, the mid-1880s were fairly prosperous years, but several years of drought beginning in 1889 forced many to abandon their claims. That same year the Frenches divorced after more than thirty-one years of marriage. She was forty-seven years old, with a daughter (Olive or Ollie, age 13) and a son (Dannie, age 11) living with her. She helped her invalid sister, Annis Rood, with cooking, washing, and cleaning for several Elbert families. As her financial situation worsened, she moved to Denver to find work. As a middle-aged woman, her opportunities were few. Uneducated, she did not qualify for teaching, sales clerking, or office jobs. Domestic work was one of her few available choices. At times, the physically taxing work was bearable; when she worked for particularly demanding women, though, it was especially exhausting and demeaning. Working for a Mrs. Mauck was a particular trial. The "perfect tyrant" found fault with Emily's cooking and was prone to ugly fits and verbal abuse.[11] Unable to eat well, keep a decent roof over her head, or dress warmly enough for the winter cold, French was frequently ill.[12] On January 1, 1890, French started a diary.[13] The diary, while a testament to her tenacity and hard work, is grim and tedious—as was her life. It was a life she shared with other domestics, who did what they could to survive.

PROSTITUTION

Some women—though not French—turned to prostitution. Red light districts—Denver's Market Street, Silverton's Blair Street, Cripple Creek's Myers Avenue, Boulder's Water Street, Aspen's Durant Street, and Leadville's fifth Street—conjure up images of flamboyantly well-dressed parlor house

FIGURE 4.1 *In Cripple Creek brothels on Myers Avenue, customers were entertained with music, gambling, and dancing. Farther down the street, prostitutes plied their trade in crude cribs where the only other amenity for a customer was a twenty-five-cent beer. Courtesy, Special Collections, Pikes Peak Library District, 001-2097, Colorado Springs.*

"ladies of the night," as well as career-worn crib harlots and lowly street-walkers. Some women resorted to prostitution only during particularly lean times. Between 1870 and 1913, approximately 800 women worked in Denver's tenderloin district at one time or another. The majority were in their mid-twenties, white, and single. Approximately 10 percent of Denver's prostitutes were blacks born in this country. "Part-timers" came from all marital status, races, and ethnicities.[14]

Minnie Mundsack, alias Lillian Powers—a Denver "fallen angel" who eventually moved on to Cripple Creek's red light district—first worked as a domestic servant, earning two dollars a week. Next she worked in a laundry. Her coworkers were "out doing business" and encouraged her to do the same. Powers worked briefly in a dance hall but complained that there was "too much booze." She preferred working out of her own crib. She charged a dollar a "date" and sold beer for a dollar a bottle.[15] Other women cited different reasons for their entry into the "underworld" of vice. For some, their men were unemployed or had deserted them; others rationalized that they were getting used by men anyway, so they might as well get paid for it; still others had been falsely promised marriage.[16]

Denver's Holladay (Market) Street became one of the most famous red light districts in the Rockies, housing several hundred "working girls."[17] Prostitutes who worked for famous madams like Mattie Silks and her rival Katie Fulton were at the top of the hierarchy. A drunken brawl between Silks and Fulton along the South Platte River on April 21, 1897, was sensationalized into a tale of a topless duel between two competing madams. As the story goes, neither woman hit her rival, although Silks did manage to wound her lover, Cort Thompson, who was watching on the sidelines. Historian Clark Secrest recently unwound the twists and turns that magnified the story, but the topless duel version will undoubtedly continue to be told and perhaps embellished even further.[18]

Silks first opened a brothel in Springfield, Illinois, at age nineteen. As men were drawn by Colorado gold, she followed, opening brothels in Georgetown, Leadville, and Denver. Silks ran a "high-class place" frequented by many of the city's businessmen. She treated her girls well, providing two meals a day, plush accommodations, and medical care. They were also paid well. She allowed them to keep half of the fee she charged for their favors, which generally ran from $25 to as high as $100 if the gentleman decided to stay the night. In a parlor house, a girl could earn from $100 to over $200 a week. In return, Silks ran a tight ship—her girls could not smoke or curse. Those who broke house rules incurred her wrath. Mattie's friend and rival Jennie Rogers (who also went by the names Leah J. Tehme and Leah Woods) purchased a small parlor house at 1942 Market Street from her soon after Rogers arrived in Denver. Mirrored ceilings, a grand piano, a golden harp, and a wine cellar decorated the luxurious brothel. Being one of Rogers's girls was high-living prostitution at its best.

Other prostitutes fared less well. Undoubtedly, the few Chinese prostitutes endured the worst fate. Sold or tricked into the slave trade, they often found it impossible to escape.[19] Prostitutes in business for themselves were cramped in "cribs," small rented one- or two-room shacks along railroad tracks and near depots. In contrast to rooms in a parlor house, cribs were sparsely furnished, with a bed and perhaps a small bedside table. A prostitute placed an oilcloth at the foot of the bed to protect the bed sheets from a man's boots or shoes. While a customer in a parlor house was wined, dined, and musically entertained before heading upstairs, his counterpart in a crib, who may have only paid between twenty-five cents and two dollars, was "treated" to a speedy encounter. With such low prices, it was imperative that a girl work as many customers as possible, perhaps as fast as five minutes each. The customer did not remove his shoes and often was not allowed the luxury of removing any of his clothing either to speed up the process. The true "ladies of the lamplight" walked the streets, engaged a customer, and completed the transaction in a seedy hotel or back alley. They were usually prostitutes on a part-time basis, moving in and out of the profession as their economic fortunes fell and rose.

Whether they worked in high-class parlor houses, in cramped cribs, or on the streets, all prostitutes faced certain dangers. One was arrest. Prostitution was illegal in Colorado, although it was generally tolerated by law enforcement officials. Working girls periodically faced raids and a general crackdown on their activities when purity reformers became active or city coffers ran low. Fining prostitutes and madams provided lucrative revenue for municipalities. While madams were taken into custody instead of their employees, those in business for themselves dealt with the issue alone. If arrested, a prostitute could incur jail time, fines, and an order to leave town. Fines ranged from twenty-five dollars to fifty dollars. Some prostitutes were released from jail to earn the money to pay their fines—and no doubt went right back to business to do so.[20] Other professional dangers included pregnancy, venereal disease, violence, and robbery. A pregnant prostitute had few available options. She could carry the baby to term and put it in an orphanage to be adopted or relinquish the child to a family member to raise. Abortion was another option. Prostitutes often contracted venereal disease—especially gonorrhea and syphilis—and were sometimes beaten, raped, and murdered. They were known to use opium and alcohol. Although definitive numbers are not available, some prostitutes committed suicide.[21]

SCHOOLS

Wives and daughters of town leaders and businessmen fared substantially better economically and socially than either Emily French or the prostitutes. Some middle- and upper-class women were fortunate to have hired help and comfortable homes. In Denver, their daughters had access to new private schools such as Wolfe Hall, the Wolcott School, and St. Mary's Academy. Wolfe Hall, a preparatory school for girls wishing to attend eastern women's colleges, was first located in a red brick Gothic structure at Seventeenth and Champa before moving to Fourteenth and Clarkson. Each student was required to furnish six table napkins, six toilet towels, three pillowcases, three sheets, one blanket, utensils, a napkin ring, an umbrella, one rug, a waterproof cloak and overshoes, and a Bible and prayer books. Some girls traveled long distances to attend Wolfe Hall. Mary, the daughter of Amache Ochinee and John W. Prowers, attended Wolfe Hall for three years after having begun her education in Boggsville.[22]

Anna Wolcott was the principal at Wolfe Hall until she opened her own day and boarding school in 1893. She was a graduate of Wellesley College and a member of the Denver Fortnightly Club and the Woman's Club of Denver. Miss Wolcott's School had four levels: kindergarten, lower and upper primary, intermediate, and sub-academic. Boys were admitted only to the kindergarten and primary levels. Designed as a "high-class preparatory school," Wolcott's school offered classes in English, mathematics, history, science, foreign languages, art, and literature. The school at the corner of Marion Street and East Fourteenth Avenue averaged 300 students a year. They received a quality academic education and were also exposed to the social issues of the day, including the lecture "Relation of Playgrounds to Child Labor," presented by Jane Addams of Chicago's Hull House.[23]

School conditions were much different in remote areas of Colorado. In 1897 Nellie Carnahan accepted a teaching job in Lavender, in the Disappointment Creek area of Dolores County. Although she expected primitive conditions, Carnahan was appalled by her schoolhouse. If a child dropped a pencil, he or she learned to quickly retrieve it before it rolled through the cracks in the floor. Every so often students lifted the floorboards and reclaimed erasers, pencils, and chalk the resident wood rat had stashed.[24] The only toilet convenience was a deep, crooked arroyo near the back of the schoolhouse. Boys used the lower part of the arroyo, and girls used the upper part. Carnahan taught the settlement's fifteen children for two years before marrying the school board member who had tendered her first teaching contract.

Although many emigrants settled in Colorado for its economic opportunities, others, including Carnahan, moved west for their health. Between 1860 and 1900, hundreds of people who suffered from tuberculosis arrived in towns along the Front Range, hoping the dry air would be a cure or at least the path to improved health. Consumptives were encouraged by the same boosters who lauded the cities' economic advantages. Samuel Bowles wrote that the entire central Rockies region seemed to be "the fountain of health," one that would surely be "a summer resort for the invalid."[25] However, only wealthy consumptives could afford a seasonal migration between Colorado and their hometowns. Others, after their pilgrimage to the state, could only hope for a quick return to health, as no hospitals or sanatoriums were avail-

FIGURE 4.2 *School buildings varied widely from one community to the next. One teacher was thankful that the school board always provided a good axe with which to chop firewood for the school room, while another lamented that cracks in her classroom's floorboards swallowed students' pencils, erasers, and chalk. Courtesy, Denver Public Library Western History Collection, Charles Redmond, Z-152.*

able until the turn of the century. Once in Colorado, many consumptives found they were too sick to be cured and ended up dying hundreds of miles away from family and friends. For others, the elite were unwelcoming, afraid the city would acquire a reputation as a city of the sick. In the meantime, many consumptives gathered in "tent cities" on the outskirts of Colorado Springs and Denver.

LIFE IN MINING COMMUNITIES

Although the gold mines of the 1850s and 1860s had played out, a new, valuable mineral brought a resurgence of settlers to the nation's thirty-eighth state. In the late 1870s, Leadville's population boomed with the discovery of silver. Within two or three years, the town boasted 51 groceries, 17 hardware stores, 12 shoe stores, and 9 book and stationery stores, as well as 4 banks. Thirty-one restaurants, 35 brothels, over 100 gambling houses, and 120 saloons catered to miners.[26] Horace W. Tabor, one of many who abandoned the dying Oro City for Leadville, became one of the richest men in town after he sold his Little Pittsburgh mine and reinvested in another mine. While erstwhile miners dreamed of striking the mother lode, few ever experienced his riches—or his notoriety after he left his first wife, Augusta, to marry the twice-divorced Elizabeth Bonduel McCourt "Baby" Doe.[27] Miners faced exorbitant prices, inflated claims of possibilities, and played-out surface mines. To be a miner soon meant laboring for wages for a large mining company, living in company shacks, and receiving company scrip for pay.

Women in mining communities faced more obstacles than their sisters in other Colorado towns. There were fewer female residents, so social networks were rarer and more precious. Because mining was so dangerous, miners' wives regularly feared losing their loved ones in an accident. Jobs for women were fewer and generally more physically taxing because department store clerking and secretarial jobs were rare in mining camps. Many men had come west for the gold and silver but found themselves broke, with few prospects of getting rich from the mountain ores. Those with families often returned to the "jumping-off" spot of Denver or Colorado Springs seeking other employment. Others left their families in town while they pursued their dreams in the mountains. Still others abandoned their families at the foot of the Rockies. Family members did the best they could as domestic servants, errand boys, and homesteaders.

A few women had talents they could use to supplement the family income. Mary Halleck Foote, a noted illustrator for newspapers and national magazines, followed her mining engineer husband to the bustling town of Leadville. Educated at the Female Seminary in Poughkeepsie, New York, and the Cooper Institute School of Design for Women in New York City, she had married Arthur Foote in 1876. Her artwork and writing helped support their family when her husband was between jobs. She sketched life in Leadville and turned to writing novels that captured the essence of a mining community.[28]

WOMEN MINERS

While Foote observed and wrote about life in a mining camp, a few women mined claims themselves. At age fifty-eight, Caroline Morehouse Mallen left her children in Ohio to prospect in the Twin Lakes area of Colorado.

Living in a log cabin on the crest of a hill, Mallen discovered and sold u.. richest leads in the district. At one time she had fifteen mines recorded in her name. Doing the work alone, she shored up mines with timbers, drilled, blasted, and hauled ore.[29] In 1893 Anna Mau began working in a mine near Breckenridge. A small, slender woman weighing less than 100 pounds, she performed all the tasks of a male miner. She swung hammers, twisted drills, wielded picks, fired dynamite, and wheeled away debris.[30] Thirty-year-old Nettie Hornbeck and her mother, Mrs. P. J. Thomas, prided themselves on their traditional womanly skills of sewing and cooking as much as on their ability to shoot bears, ride horses, and protect their claims with loaded shotguns.[31] Hornbeck quickly developed a passion for her work, believing she could not "live without mining."[32]

Another woman owned but did not work her mine. In September 1891 Mary (Mollie) Kathleen Gortner was living in Colorado Springs with her husband. Her son, Perry, was a surveyor of mining claims in Cripple Creek. Concerned about her son in the raw mining town and curious about the new goldfields, Gortner visited Cripple Creek. An Iowan by birth, she was eager to observe the elk in upper Poverty Gulch. Perry encouraged her to keep a lookout for rock outcroppings that might contain gold. Noticing an intriguing rock formation, Gortner broke off a piece and discovered gold sparkling in the quartz. She hid the rock in her dress and rushed back to find her son, who saddled his pack mule and staked her claim. Gortner took the ore and survey description to the claims clerk. He refused to file her claim, saying that, as a woman, she had no right to file. Angry, she snatched the file papers from the clerk, signed them, and named the claim the Mollie Kathleen. She told the clerk he could argue with her husband, a lawyer, when he came to Cripple Creek. Her claim was never contested.[33]

HISPANIC WOMEN'S LIVES

By the 1880s the arrival of Anglo settlers and coal-mining companies in southern Colorado threatened the Hispanics' varied economy of farming, sheepherding, and trading. They lost grazing lands to railroad and mining companies, Anglo cattle stock growers, and the US government. In response, they turned to seasonal migration. With the aid of women's labor in the villages, Hispanic men took jobs with the railroads as maintenance workers and as coal miners in southern Colorado. By 1905 over 10 percent of the miners employed by the Colorado Fuel and Iron Company (CF&I) were Hispanic males. Railroads also needed timber for ties. Although men of other ethnicities worked in the mines, nearly all of CF&I's timber workers were Hispanic men.[34] For families that moved to new railroad towns, opportunities existed for Hispanic women to work outside the home as seamstresses, cooks, washerwomen, domestic servants, and keepers of boardinghouses. Their husbands were gone for as long as six months at a time as coal miners or timber workers, so the wives who remained in the villages were increasingly alone at the center of village life.[35]

LIFE ON THE EASTERN PLAINS

Changes were also occurring on the eastern plains of Colorado. In 1862 the US Congress passed the Homestead Act, the first of four such acts. Under its provisions, a man or woman age twenty-one and older could file a claim for a homestead of 160 acres. Male homesteaders could be single or married; female homesteaders could not be married (only single, widowed, or divorced). After filing a claim, a homesteader had five years to make improvements on the land. This generally meant building a livable cabin and implementing ranching or farming activities. After the five-year period, a homesteader applied for ownership of the land. If he or she met the provisions of the law, the homesteader had "proved up" and received a patent on the property. Thousands of men and women used the Homestead Acts to acquire land.

In addition, settlement of the eastern plains of Colorado was enhanced by the arrival of railroads, a series of wet years, the opportunity to profit from miners by supplying them with foodstuffs, and the removal of Indian tribes to reservations. In the southern part of the state, Mexican families had settled in the area as early as the 1850s but found life tenuous as Utes and other Indians attacked communities. As treaties moved the Utes further and further into the southwest corner of Colorado, that land became available for permanent settlements. In the northeastern section of the state, railroads offered incentives to prospective settlers and a less arduous journey to the region. For farmers in Kansas and Nebraska, the plains of Colorado seemed like the next likely spot to homestead.

A common homestead dwelling on the plains was a "soddie," constructed of cut "bricks" of prairie sod laid atop one another. Bricks were generally two to three feet long and one to two feet wide. Wood was scarce on the plains, so it was only used for doors, support beams, and window and door frames. The floor was dirt. Problems abounded with these early homes. Bedbugs, fleas, snakes, and rats joined homesteaders in their soddies. Still, it

FIGURE 4.3 *Congressional acts in 1862, 1909, 1912, and 1916 enabled men and single, widowed, or divorced women to file homestead claims. In the absence of trees on the eastern plains, settlers formed dugouts or constructed sod houses for their first homes. Courtesy, Special Collections, Pikes Peak Library District, 001-160, Colorado Springs.*

was an improvement over a dugout, a home cut into a small hill so three sides were earthen. Over time, a sod house was plastered. Later, as the family prospered, a frame house replaced the soddie. Since it was expensive, this type of home created the image that the family was financially stable. Frame houses, however, were vulnerable to fire and strong winds that blew them over. Because sod houses and frame homes were labor-intensive to construct, "sod bees" were held in which neighbors joined together to help a family build their first home. Pieces of furniture were mostly handmade or adapted from orange crates and soapboxes. A comprehensive list of a family's furnishings might be a table, cabinets, chairs, a two-hole sheepherder's stove, one or two kerosene lamps, and a wooden or iron bedstead. Women of the household made bedding, curtains, and rag carpets. Kitchenware consisted of tin cups and pie plates. Other buildings on the homesteaded land were a privy and a barn. As homesteaders "proved up," got married, had children, and increased their livestock holdings or arable land, more outbuildings were added.

Most homesteaders planted gardens of potatoes, tomatoes, lettuce, peas, beans, cabbage, turnips, cucumbers, sweet corn, watermelons, pumpkins, and squash. On the northeastern plains, corn was the principal crop until the 1910s, when wheat, oats, and barley were cultivated. Game was hunted, but, as time went by, domestic stock—chickens, cattle, and hogs—were raised to provide eggs, cheese, milk, and meat. Gathering water was an important daily chore. A mother saved a baby's bathwater to wash clothes, scrub the floor, and pour on the homestead's lone tree. Homesteaders gathered buffalo "chips," an abundant but inefficient source of fuel. Two large washtubs-full were needed for a typical winter night. Families also burned pots of packed trash. More affluent families used coal or kerosene purchased in town. Others scavenged coal from railroad tracks or from coal deposits, such as the one near Deer Trail in eastern Colorado.

Farming the high plains was a risky proposition. Those who chose to ignore Stephen Long's earlier pronouncement of the eastern plains as "wholly inhabitable, a desert" faced tremendous odds in converting the high plains of Colorado into arable land.[36] Dangers, mostly from the hand of nature, plagued settlers. Blizzards, hailstorms, and grasshoppers were common scourges. Many homesteading families saw an entire year's worth of work eliminated by a flash flood, buried under twenty inches of snow, pummeled to shreds by hail, or gobbled up by hordes of grasshoppers. These women understood the plagues of biblical times. Beyond those catastrophes, daily fights against rodents, bedbugs, and mosquitoes were taxing. Rattlesnakes were so abundant that women "bragged to each other about the size and number of snakes they dispatched."[37] Then there was the wind. Howling day and night, this harbinger of winter blizzards and searing heat blew prairie dirt into the tiniest crevice of one's humble abode. Women especially dreaded such blasts. Winds tore freshly washed clothes off the line, woke colicky babies from their naps, and shredded garden plants, greatly magnifying the household burden. They also brought the added danger of prairie fires that were known to suddenly sweep through the open prairies, scorching everything in their paths. And yet homesteaders persevered, improved their crude dwellings, farmed the land, established schools, and started churches.

Amid all the hardship and dangers, women found pleasure on the open plains. Spring blossoms brought renewed hope and the celebration of traditions such as Children's Day, at which community members joined together to decorate the schoolhouse and church. Women exchanged labor and joined to aid one another in childbirth, caring for the sick, and making linings for coffins.

Women's contribution to the westward movement and the settling of the West is commemorated by the Madonna of the Trails memorials placed by the Daughters of the American Revolution in the 1920s. Mary Sullivan Cain was asked to dedicate the Lamar, Colorado, memorial. Sullivan married homesteader Felix Cain in 1885. At the time of her marriage, Sullivan and Mrs. Marsena McMillin were reputedly the only white women between Las Animas, Colorado, and Kansas until more settlers arrived in the late 1880s.[38] The twelve memorials erected between Maryland and California honor not only the women who traversed the overland trails but also their pioneering work once they reached their destination. Although the husband's name might have been on the original homestead claim and the subsequent patent after five years, it was just as much the wife's land. It usually took more than one person and more than one kind of work to succeed as a homesteader. Some women worked alongside their men planting, hoeing, and harvesting crops. They were in charge of the family vegetable garden and orchard, if fortunate enough to have the latter. The chickens they raised not only sat dressed on the family dinner table but were also valuable as a commodity to trade or sell for much-needed cash. The same was true for the family cow. Its milk and butter were consumed on the ranch and sold in town. Wives also boarded and fed ranch hands.

THE COZENS FAMILY

As discussed earlier, some ranching women contributed to the family's economic well-being by providing services at stage and railroad stops. In 1875 William (Billy) and Mary York Cozens moved into the Fraser Valley, where Cozens was appointed postmaster. He opened his ranch house as a stage stop. By 1885 their property included 320 improved acres, land and buildings worth $6,000, $800 in livestock, and $300 in farming equipment.[39] Hired hands aided Cozens and his son, William Zane, with the ranching duties. Mrs. Cozens and her two daughters, Mary Elizabeth and Sarah Agnes (Sadie), provided meals and board for stagecoach travelers going from Georgetown to Hot Sulfur Springs. In 1887 the twenty-two-year-old Mary Elizabeth began a diary that detailed the joys and struggles of living and working in a mountain valley. Particularly irritating to her were travelers who expected round-the-clock attention.[40] The harsh winter months when the road was closed brought loneliness, irregular mail delivery, fewer guests or neighborly visits, and more difficult working conditions. A cold and stormy day made hanging out clothes a "severe penance."[41]

The family dog, Shep, was both a comfort and a trial for Mary, as he repeatedly tried to run away. She swore that "as long as I live I never will own another cat, dog, bird or any live thing to which my heart can become attached. These last two years have taught me the folly of suffering for the sake of owning them—A tender heart is a difficult thing to support."[42] True to her vow to spare her heart, she remained single, as did her younger sister and older brother. In the early 1900s the Cozens, devout Catholics, opened their home to Jesuits from Denver's Sacred Heart College as a summer vacation retreat. After the deaths of their parents, the Cozens siblings began deeding the family property to the Jesuits. Sarah died at the ranch in 1923, Mary in 1928, and brother Will in 1938. The last remaining sections were deeded in 1924. In 1987 the Jesuits deeded the property to the Grand County Historical Association, which began restoration of the building. At present, the Cozens Ranch House, the oldest homestead in Fraser Valley, is on the National Register of Historic Places and operates as the Cozens Ranch House Restoration Museum.

FEMALE HOMESTEADERS

The framers of the homestead laws wanted to encourage settlement of western lands by Anglo families when they gave single women, as well as men, the right to claim government land. Some spinsters, however, found they enjoyed the excitement and adventure of learning to live on their own, removed from close family scrutiny, and they did not rush to marry. Controlling their own real estate for the first time, women discovered that homesteading opened up a new spectrum of choices. As farmers and land speculators, they gained personal and financial independence. In El Paso County, over a dozen women filed homestead claims in the early 1890s, often serving as witnesses for one another. In 1892 Nellie M. Keith filed her final proof for her homestead and served as a witness for Eleanor E. Hook when she filed for her patent.[43] West of Colorado Springs, Adeline Hornbek, whose husband ran out on her, filed on 160 acres near what is now Florissant Fossil Beds National Monument. Over the years she increased her holdings five times over. At one-and-a-half stories, her house was larger than the average cabin. There were three bedrooms upstairs and one bedroom downstairs to accommodate Hornbek and her four children. She owned a barn and wagon shed, milk house, chicken house, and a large corral for the livestock. Her assets included 21 horses, over 100 cows, 3 swine, and 50 poultry.[44]

Another female homesteader who settled in the mountains rather than on the eastern plains of Colorado was Katherine (Kate) Jensen Lindvig. The "Cattle Queen of Snowmass" was born in Jutland, Denmark, in 1865.

FIGURE 4.4 *Kate Lindvig immigrated to the United States from Denmark as a mail-order bride for a farmer. She took one look at her intended and the plains of Nebraska and promptly moved west to Aspen, where she eventually ran cattle on 640 acres. Courtesy, Aspen Historical Society, Aspen, CO.*

At age twenty-five she came to the United States as the mail-order bride of a Nebraska farmer. However, one look at her future husband and the plains of Nebraska convinced Lindvig to continue moving west. She settled in Aspen, where she was hired as a cook. Lindvig diligently saved her wages to open her own boardinghouse. She made up to 400 bag lunches a day for the region's miners. In 1896 she received a homestead in the upper Snowmass Creek Valley when one of her tenants could not pay his bill. She homesteaded an adjacent property and bought two parcels. She named her 640-acre property Snowmass Falls Ranch, on which she raised hay, potatoes, and oats. In exchange for room and board, three older men helped with the ranch work. She ran eighty head of cattle on US Forest Service land. Each week she drove a sled or a wagon (depending on the season) to Aspen loaded with butter, eggs, and the meat from two head of cattle to sell there. Physically strong and an astute businesswoman, Lindvig was charitable—feeding out-of-work miners—and in demand as a potential spouse. However, she spurned all offers of marriage. Over the years she rented horses to sightseers. In 1925 she expanded her ranching operation to include guest cabins, which she rented to fishermen. She packed people into Snowmass Lake, sometimes making three trips a day—a total of fifty-two miles. Later, Lindvig leased her place to her niece and moved in with her nephew. In the 1940s, before Aspen experienced rejuvenation as a ski resort, the Scandinavian native sold the ranch and moved to San Diego, where she died at age ninety-two.[45]

A teaching job provided for little more than life's necessities, so a number of young female teachers made the conscious effort to exploit the economic opportunity homesteading offered. Lucy Bigler Wilson, a rural schoolteacher, recorded how she got the idea to file a claim: "While here in the community I saw that everybody lived on the free land, and I thought 'Why can't I have some, too?'"[46] Lucy's brother helped her locate land and homesteaded with her. Another teacher left New England, determined to make a living as a teacher and homesteader. She contacted several communities and asked if they needed a teacher. Rangley, Colorado, replied that while the town did not presently have a school, residents did want to build one, and they hired her. She made the long journey with her cousin, who later returned to the East having quickly tired of western hardships after the novelty of the adventure had worn off. The schoolteacher remained, taught in a log school building, and moved onto a preemption claim where she lived alone for the required six months, although it was "not half as much" fun as she had anticipated.[47] She persevered, though, in "proving up" her home-

stead claim and married the man who had hired her to be Rangely's teac
so she "acquired a husband and pre-emption claim in one day."[48]

WORKING WOMEN

While female teachers were visible in their communities, most of the work
done by women was not noted by US census takers in 1890. Categories did
not exist for nursing and midwifery. Farmwomen who sold eggs and butter
were not counted as agricultural workers. In fact, no Colorado woman was
recorded as an agricultural worker in the 1870 census. Census takers also did
not note women who took in boarders or laundry. Jobs that helped sustain
a household were simply viewed as women's duties or responsibilities, not
as occupations. By the 1880 and 1890 censuses, however, the demographics of the state showed changes, the result of a number of factors. Mining
had evolved from an individual enterprise to one dominated by large cor-
porations often controlled by absentee owners. This brought more families
into mining areas. As towns were established, more schools were founded.
Although many of the earliest schools were subscription schools (private
schools to which families paid a "subscription," or tuition, to send their children), they soon gave way to public schools.[49]

Between 1870 and 1900 the percentage of women employed as teachers rose from 7 percent to 10 percent of all employed women in Colorado
and 87 percent of the women listed under the census category "Professional
Service." Over three-quarters were single women.[50] Mate Smith came to
Colorado in 1882 because her brother had told her western teachers were
paid as much as $70 a month. He secured her a job at Red Rock, a country
district just west of the present town of Berthoud.[51] Colorado teaching salaries may have been higher than those in the East, but schoolhouse conditions
were usually more primitive. Smith's first classroom was a lean-to bedroom
she shared with a homesteader's daughter. Each school morning she carried
the bed into the yard before the pupils arrived and returned it afterward.
Her next schoolhouse had neither tar-paper siding nor a stove. The children
used soapboxes for desks and a painted wooden board for a blackboard. In
addition to lacking the most basic educational supplies, the community also
lacked irrigation ditches, an agricultural necessity on Colorado's high plains.
When the community was able to pledge only $100 of the required $300 for
the installation of irrigation ditches, a school director asked Smith to loan
three months of her salary to pay the contractor. She agreed and was eventually repaid, with interest.[52]

In Paonia and Hotchkiss, schoolteachers Jessie Yoakum and Mamie Wade taught in a building with a dirt floor and roof. Holes in the sides of the schoolhouse served as windows. Yoakum and Wade solicited money from the "old batches" (bachelors) to buy enough canvas to line the room. The men made seats and desks for the children, a stand for the teacher's desk, and placed a wood stove between two rows of desks for warmth. While Smith was lured westward by a salary of seventy dollars a month, teaching salaries around the state varied widely (as they do today). Yoakum and Wade received only thirty dollars a month plus board.[53] In Montrose, Erena Osborn received fifty dollars a month, only two-thirds of a male teacher's salary.[54]

Twenty percent of Colorado's female teachers were musicians and music teachers and artists and art teachers.[55] In the latter category were Helen Henderson Chain and Emma Richardson Cherry. In 1871 Helen and her husband, James A. Chain, arrived in Denver and opened Chain and Hardy, a bookstore that also sold art supplies. Helen studied art under a number of professionals, including the landscape painter George Innes. In 1877 she opened a studio to students and began painting the majestic Colorado Rockies. She often took her students—including her best-known student, landscape painter Charles Partridge Adams—with her into the mountains on sketching trips. She was equally noted for her mountain climbing, conquering Longs Peak, Grays Peak, Pikes Peak, and Mount Lincoln. She was thought to have been the first woman to have sketched the Mount of the Holy Cross on location. Chain's paintings were praised by Thomas Moran, the landscape artist whose sketches of Yellowstone were instrumental in the US Congress's approval of the region as the nation's first national park. The Chains often opened their home (at the present site of the Daniels and Fisher Tower) to display her art and that of her pupils. The couple drowned in 1892 when they encountered a typhoon in the South China Sea on a journey around the world. In its report of Helen's death, the *Denver Republican* praised her work for its "delicacy of touch and coloring."[56] The year after Chain's death, her contemporary, Emma Richardson Cherry, invited artist friends to organize a club to promote an interest in art in Denver. The Artists Club, with Cherry as its first president, eventually evolved into the Denver Art Museum.[57]

Occupations held by most women in Colorado mirrored those of women in other parts of the United States. In the 1890 census, the top three categories for employed females of all ages who were age ten or older were domestic and personal service (54 percent), manufacturing and mechanical industries (21 percent), and professional service (12 percent). However, the percentages were quite different between whites and "colored" (a US Census Bureau term for "persons of negro descent, Chinese, Japanese"). Of the latter, 90 percent were employed in domestic service; for whites, the percentages ranged from 76 percent (foreign-born whites) to 49 percent (white women with foreign-born parents) to 40 percent (white women with native-born parents). In manufacturing, the vast majority of women in Colorado were employed in garment-making occupations as seamstresses, dressmakers, milliners, and tailoresses. In general, white native women held these jobs; only 7 percent of "colored" women did so.[58] Colorado's black female population was very small and concentrated in urban areas. For this reason, less than 1 percent of black women in Colorado were engaged in agricultural occupations. In contrast, the majority of black women in the United States were agricultural workers in the southern states.[59]

Between 1870 and 1900, as women found job opportunities in other fields, the percentage of women employed as domestics nationwide dropped from 70 percent to 63 percent. New US census categories for clerks and copyists and typists and stenographers meant that the percentage of women employed in the trade and transportation field increased from 3 percent to 14 percent, with nearly all of that increase in the two new occupations. At the national level, the 1890 census noted, "Persons engaged in trade and transportation have increased 78.20 percent since 1880, the percentage of increase for females being especially large, or 263.43 [percent], principally due to the large increase in the number of females employed as bookkeepers, clerks, stenographers, typewriters, and salesclerk[s]."[60]

One Colorado example was Nola G. Kirkpatrick, who grew up and attended schools in the La Junta area before attending business college in Missouri. When she returned home to Colorado in 1890, she secured a job as a court reporter. Later, she worked as a bookkeeper at a grocery store and then as a bookkeeper, stenographer, and saleslady for Buckey and Albera Dry Goods Company.[61] Had Kirkpatrick been born a few years later, she could have remained in southeastern Colorado and attended Commercial College. Its three-year program offered classes in bookkeeping, shorthand, typing, banking, penmanship, spelling, arithmetic, and business English.[62]

NONTRADITIONAL EMPLOYMENT

A small percentage of women took less traditional jobs as lawyers, doctors, scientists, and journalists. A few medical colleges began admitting female students after the Civil War.[63] At its first commencement in 1891, the University of Colorado's School of Medicine graduated Nellie Frances Mayo. But the number of trained female physicians remained low. In Colorado the 1890 census recorded fifty-nine physicians and surgeons. Pueblo County was home to nine of those physicians: Anna Williams, Genevieve Tucker, Carrie Johnson, Josephine Nachtriels, Mary F. Barry, Louise Black, Theresa Black, Ella Finch, and Josephine Myers. Barry, the first female physician in the county, was elected to the Colorado General Assembly in 1898.[64] Another doctor, Dr. Mary Elizabeth Bates, arrived in Denver in 1890 and opened her medical practice the following year in the Kittredge Building. She founded a humane society and campaigned for drinking fountains for humans and animals. Because of her efforts, twenty-three drinking fountains and forty-two troughs were installed in the city. An ardent suffragist, she was the first Denver woman to wear a divided skirt while bicycling.[65]

Another Denver-area female physician was Dr. Rose Kidd Beere. Born in 1859 in Indiana, Rose began her medical training at Northwestern University Women's Medical College. In 1892 she moved to Durango, where the town's immigrant mining community welcomed her wholeheart-edly. Three years later Governor Alva Adams asked her to take over the State Home for Dependent and Neglected Children, which she did until the Spanish-American War broke out in 1898. Dr. Beere's father wrote her a letter stating that it was the first war in which no one in their family was fighting. To Beere, that was a call to action. With her father agreeing to take care of her sons, she went to San Francisco and convinced the commander in charge of the US forces in the Philippines to take her on as a nurse after he refused to allow her to be a doctor to the troops. Rose nursed American and Filipino soldiers for a year before returning to Colorado. She worked as the health officer for Denver Public Schools, establishing the city's first dental clinic for poor children. She was the doctor at the Poor Farm, ran Denver General Hospital, and later opened her own hospital for injured World War I soldiers.[66]

Female lawyers and scientists were few and far between. In 1896 Mary Florence Lathrop opened her law practice in the Equitable Building at Seventeenth and Stout Streets in downtown Denver. She was one of only six female attorneys in the state prior to 1900. In the natural sciences, Alice Eastwood began her professional life as a teacher at East High School in Denver. Her passion for botany drove her to Colorado's plains and moun-tains. Self-trained, Eastwood became a premier botanist, serving as curator at the California Academy of Science's herbarium. Like Martha Maxwell, the

Colorado naturalist, Eastwood is one of a few women to have been honored by the scientific community. The Colorado botanist has eight species named for her, including *Mertensia eastwoodiae* and *Eastwoodiae elegans.*[67] Of all the honors bestowed upon her, the one that pleased her the most was the renaming of the herbarium—her "child . . . dearer to me than life"—the Alice Eastwood Herbarium of the California Academy of Sciences.[68]

Although Lathrop and Eastwood enjoyed fruitful careers in male-dominated fields, for many men and women ensnared by promises of economic riches, the Centennial State proved a terrible disappointment. The Homestead Act's provision of 160 acres was often too little land for farming, as rain did not follow the plow as promised. Summers of drought were followed by devastating blizzards that wiped out not only agricultural crops but also the cattle herds of those who had hoped to supply the gold- and silver-mining mountain towns. As more families settled in cities and on homesteads, problems increased. Consumptives searching for a cure in the dry mountain air were often disappointed, but, having risked everything to migrate, they often lacked the money or the stamina to return to their home states. City dwellers faced increased amounts of garbage in the streets. The 1893 depression hit Coloradans particularly hard. Although many male civic leaders still extolled the promises of the Centennial State, it often fell upon the women in a community to ensure that economic progress did not leave the disenfranchised, sick, and uneducated in its dust. During the last quarter of the nineteenth century, Colorado women, like their eastern counterparts, organized and agitated for reform.

THE WOMEN OF WALKER RANCH

Phoebe Fidelia Skinner Walker gave birth to William, her only child, in 1877. She was thirty-five years old. From then on, she was never again as physically strong as she had been. Her mounting medical bills strained the family budget. To supplement the ranching operation, James Walker engaged in logging and lumbering. He took out loans and sold a piece of the ranch. Still struggling in 1902, he accepted an offer to sell the entire property. When the would-be purchaser could not make the annual payments, Walker regained his ranch by default.

As his wife grew older and more frail, Walker hired Veronica Kossler, the eldest daughter of a neighbor, to assist her. Like her patient, Kossler taught school. She also drove butter and eggs to Black Hawk to augment her income. Between school terms, she nursed Walker and did chores the older woman was no longer able to perform. Friends since childhood, William Walker and Kossler grew closer during this time. They married in 1902 and promptly moved in with his parents.

With her daughter-in-law's presence and help, Walker's health improved, and she was able to enjoy the births of her first two grandchildren, Leta and Ruth. Their grandmother and grandfather doted on both girls, and their grandfather shielded them when their mischievous antics drew a scowl and sometimes a small switch from their mother. Leta, the oldest, initiated their childhood adventures. As young children, they often defied their parents' wishes and played in the ranch's irrigation ditch, even though they were warned that the "Ditch Man" would get them. One day their aging grandmother decided to scare them into behaving. She donned an old hat and coat and hid in chokecherry bushes that lined the ditch. Leta, as was her style, sent Ruth, her "sidekick," into the ditch first. While both girls were merrily digging away, Grandmother Walker rose up from the bushes and startled the girls, who scurried up the embankment and ran back to the house. After their encounter with the "Ditch Man," Leta and Ruth never dug in the ditch again.[69] But this was not the end of their mischief. On another occasion, Leta convinced Ruth to pry open a beehive so they could watch the bees. The bees naturally became agitated, so Leta sprayed the hive with water. Thinking it was safe to examine the hive, the barefooted girls found that, rather than flying away, the bees had sought safety on the ground. When they stepped up to the hive, Leta and Ruth were stung by dozens of angry bees.[70]

Phoebe Walker's health continued to decline. In 1912 a winter storm dropped more than three feet of snow on Flagstaff Road, making it impossible for her doctor to reach her or for the family to drive the seriously ill woman into Boulder. The first woman of Walker Ranch succumbed to influenza on March 2, 1912. With the matriarch of the family buried in a little cemetery near the Kossler Ranch, it fell to Veronica Kossler Walker, the second woman of Walker Ranch, to help run the expanding ranching operation.

As Leta and Ruth got older, their chores increased, in part because they were capable of doing more but also because their mother had four more children. For Leta, her younger siblings "made a lot of extra work and we [Leta and Ruth] used to grumble a little bit once in awhile. And think, 'well, I just wish they weren't having another one' or 'I hope this is the last one' or something like that."[71] The two oldest daughters also took care of their siblings because their mother cooked for the ranch's hired men and visitors. In

FIGURE 4.5 *As the oldest child of William and Veronica Walker, Leta Walker's duties included taking care of her five younger siblings, working in the garden, and hunting coyotes that endangered the family's cattle. Courtesy, Stella Daniels Rodgers.*

addition, Leta helped her mother and grandfather plant the spring garden of radishes, lettuce, corn, onions, and cucumbers. She cared for the currants, rhubarb, and cherries planted next to the log cabin, which was alternately used as housing for hired help and friends and for rendering the lard of butchered animals. Walker children—like other farm and ranch children—carried wood into the house for fuel, peeled potatoes and apples, swept the floor, and set the table for meals.

The Walkers delayed Leta's first schooling until Ruth was also old enough to attend. They hired their first teacher, Patrice Whitten, at fifty dollars a month. The school room in their home was the start of District #30, Pine Grove.[72] Occasionally, the ranch's timbering families sent their children to classes in the Walker home when the men were working at the ranch. The Kosslers, Veronica's family, also hired a teacher for their children. Around 1928, Pine Grove School was built halfway between the Kossler and Walker Ranches for the children of the only two families living on the mountain. The teacher boarded with whichever family had the most children attending school at the time. During high school, Leta boarded with the Clynkes in Boulder and attended Mount St. Gertrude Academy. Meanwhile, Alice Clynke, the family's daughter, lived with Leta's family and taught the younger Walker children. The ranch's fourth teacher, Ruth Dunn, was twenty years old when she was hired. She walked from Eldorado Springs to the ranch every Sunday night and returned home on Friday evenings. The Walkers paid her ninety dollars a month. In return, she paid the Walkers twenty dollars a month for room and board. Accepted as part of the family, Dunn and the Walkers played cribbage in the evenings. She taught Jim his first lessons, Esther the second-grade curriculum, Helen the fourth, and Delia the sixth.[73]

After graduation, Leta attended dressmaker classes at the Opportunity School in Denver. She boarded with Dr. John Galen Locke. Leta's aunt Mary worked for the Lockes, and Leta did odd jobs. Although Dr. Locke gained notoriety as the Grand Dragon of Colorado's Ku Klux Klan, Leta insisted that he was "nothing like the man portrayed in the papers."[74] Locke wanted Leta "to have everything I never had—eating out, going to plays, and picture shows and everything . . . He was a godfather."[75] After three years of dressmaker school, Leta graduated. Needed at the ranch, she returned to Flagstaff Mountain. There she met Carl Daniels, who worked for her father in the timbering operation. They married in 1926 and moved to the south ranch until the Walker Ranch was sold in 1950 to Dr. Oliver Taylor. Daniels ran cattle and was caretaker of the ranch for Taylor before going to work for the Denver Water Department. Leta and Carl Daniels had one daughter, Stella, born in 1936.[76]

All of Leta Walker Daniels's siblings married, but only her family spent their lives on the Walker Ranch.[77] Her daughter, Stella, married Bill Rodgers. They had one daughter, Debra, born in 1955. First Stella and Bill Rodgers and later her parents bought parts of Walker Ranch from Taylor. Debra grew up on Flagstaff Mountain and followed her grandfather Carl onto the payroll of the Denver Water Department. Although she did not live on Walker Ranch property after high school, she has since returned to the mountain to live after building a home on the site where her grandparents, Carl and Leta Walker Daniels, once lived. Her parents continue to reside in her childhood home.[78]

The Walkers sold the ranch because development of Gross Reservoir increased traffic along Flagstaff Road, and Walker found it nearly impossible to contain his cattle as reservoir visitors regularly left gates open.[79] Nearly twenty years later, Boulder County began purchasing Walker Ranch land. It presently owns 3,818 acres. The open space property is listed on the National Register of Historic Places. Boulder County Parks and Open Space is recreating the original farmhouse of James and Phoebe Walker that burned in 1992. Further damage to the historic ranch occurred when the 2000 Eldorado fire burned over 1,000 acres. Each September, Boulder

County Parks and Open Space hosts a Walker Ranch Special Event at the homestead, during which costumed volunteers reenact the daily chores of a working ranch.

INSEPARABLE HOMESTEADERS: ANNIE AND KITTY HARBISON

In 1902, sisters Annie and Kitty Harbison proudly received Homestead Patents #5569 and #5570, signed by President Theodore Roosevelt, after five years of "proving up" their dairy farm.[80] Like most homesteaders, the Harbison girls faced many challenges in establishing their claims.

Annie and Kitty were born shortly after the Civil War to Andrew Harbison and Mary Quinlan, Andrew's second wife. Harbison had a daughter and a son from his pre–Civil War first marriage. When he met Quinlan, he and his son, Harry, told her that his first wife had died years earlier.[81] After their wedding, the Harbisons settled in eastern Nebraska where Harry was joined by Annie, Kitty, and Robert. Harry, as restless as other young men after the Civil War, headed west. The rest of the family followed, settling in Denver for a few years. Harry moved to the Grand Lake area, where he planned to raise commercial trout to sell to miners. When he realized that spring-fed Columbine Lake could not sustain trout, he spent two years digging a two-mile ditch from the river to the lake. During this time, Andrew Harbison filed for a homestead near Greeley, which he lost during the 1893 depression. This convinced him to join Harry in the Grand Lake area in 1896. Within months, the rest of the family joined him. Andrew could not file on another homestead because it had been less than five years since his Greeley claim. Instead, each of his daughters filed for a homestead in their own names (Robert was too young to file a claim). The sisters, born four years apart but virtually inseparable their entire lives, filed on adjoining land. Harry's ditch provided fresh water for Annie's land. Her cabin was used as the family's cooking space. The "Big Cabin," overlapping both sisters' land, was the family's living space. Because she preferred to be close to her older sister, Kitty seldom lived in her cabin, which was located away from Annie's and the Big Cabin.[82]

The Harbisons' only income in the early years of homesteading was Andrew's Civil War pension of four dollars a month, so his two daughters laundered, cooked, and waitressed at the Kauffman Hotel and other Grand Lake establishments.[83] Mary, Robert, and Andrew planted hay and a vegetable garden, cut trees, and plowed the land on the two homesteads. They also purchased cows to begin a dairy farm.

Henry Schnoor, a rancher, often visited the Harbisons during his supply trips from nearby Green Mountain to the town of Grand Lake. He proposed to Kitty, and she initially accepted until she realized that marriage would mean losing her homestead and leaving Annie to run the dairy ranch by herself when their parents died. So Kitty changed her mind and declined his offer. She and the rest of the family had worked too hard in the past year to lose ground now.

During the winter of 1898–1899, Mother Nature outdid herself and dumped forty-nine inches of snow in a region that typically received twenty inches of snow a year. Annie and Robert, who had livestock to feed and supply trips to make into town, tried to use horses to cut a path through the snow. But the horses sank through the crust hundreds of yards from the barn. The only solution was to get the horses turned around and back to safety before they all froze. Robert and Annie, clad in her usual long dress and winter coat—the sisters always wore dresses, never pants—cut a narrow channel through the snow and led the horses back to the barn. Despite these troubles, at the end of 1899 Andrew recorded in his journal that the family had a sewing machine, four horses, and several head of dairy cattle.[84] The family's hard work on the homesteads combined with the sisters' work in town allowed the family to finally gain a precarious foothold in the central mountains of Colorado.

Harry often left Columbine Lake for several weeks at a time. That meant that Mary took care of his place, Robert and Andrew worked the girls' homesteads, and Annie and Kitty worked either at the homestead or in town. At times, Mary made a day trip to check on Harry's homestead; other times she stayed overnight. Once when she was coming home the sleigh flipped, throwing her to the ground. Hurt but knowing that she could not wait for help because no one knew she was en route, she unhitched the horse and rode home. Her injured hip rendered her bedridden for many weeks. By 1901 Harry was weary of the Columbine Lake venture. His roving nature was more than geographic; he married for a second time—two years before divorcing his first wife.[85]

The long-awaited arrival of Annie's and Kitty's patents in 1902 proved that they were successful homesteaders. The dairy farm—the only one serving Grand Lake—prospered. The two homesteads had a pig pen, cow barn, horse barn, saddle barn, chicken coop, and four-hole outhouse. The sisters opened tourist cabins to accommodate city dwellers aching for fresh air and open vistas. But, after 1906, the family endured heartaches and surprises. First, Andrew died. The next year the family experienced a second jolt when Schnoor, Kitty's jilted suitor, arrived at their door with his two young daughters. After Kitty rejected his proposal, he had married another woman, with whom he had Beatrice and Mary. Tired of her isolated life on Green Mountain, his wife left him and their one- and three-year-old daughters. Schnoor, at a loss as to how to raise two girls, tried to leave them at a Denver orphanage but was turned away because the younger girl was sick. On his way home, he stopped and poured out his woes to the Harbisons. When he departed, he was alone. The three women kept the daughters to raise. Later, when Schnoor remarried, the older daughter rejoined her father but the younger, Mary (called Mame), refused, saying "the Harbisons are my moms."[86]

The third jolt arrived in a letter from the US government. After her husband's death, Mary Harbison applied for his Civil War pension. However, to her shock, the government's letter of reply reported that his first wife had already applied for the pension. Mary had no idea that the first wife was alive because Andrew and Harry had told her forty years earlier that she was dead. Mary was required to submit letters from neighbors saying that she and Andrew had been married and had lived as husband and wife for over thirty years. Eventually, the first wife backed off, stating that Mary obviously needed the money more than she did (she had also remarried). Mary was then awarded the pension.[87]

Mary Harbison died in 1923. Local papers extolled her as a great cook and valuable community member. Seven years later, officials from Rocky Mountain National Park (RMNP) offered to buy part of the sisters' ranch to build a road into the park. The sisters refused to sell. Negotiations went back and forth for eight years until a local judge and friend of the sisters intervened. After Kitty told RMNP officials where the road should go, the sisters sold the desired parcel.

In November 1938, nearly forty years after filing their initial homestead claims, both Annie and Kitty died of pneumonia. Kitty was sixty-six and Annie, who lingered for five days after Kitty's death, was seventy. Always together in life, the two sisters were buried together under one headstone at the Grand Lake Cemetery a few miles from their dairy farm.

Mame, Henry Schnoor's abandoned daughter, inherited the Harbison property. Years earlier she had married Clyde Gudgel, a Harbison ranch hand. The couple worked the ranch until they sold the remainder of the original homesteads to Rocky Mountain National Park in the mid-1950s. In the early 1960s a RMNP official proposed that the Harbison buildings be preserved for the educational benefit of future generations; the Park Service declined, citing a lack of funds. The structures remained on park property for visitors to see, but no effort was expended to preserve them as valuable historic buildings. In 1973 the new superintendent of Rocky Mountain National Park, interpreting the Park Service's original aim as meaning only the preservation of land, not manmade structures, ordered that the buildings be burned. This destroyed the physical evidence of the Harbison sisters' work and forced his removal as superintendent.[88]

"STRANGER WITHIN THE GATES": MARY C. MULLIGAN, DOMESTIC SERVANT

The twelfth US census (1900) enumerated 13,731 females engaged in domestic and personal service in Colorado. Of this number, 7,202 were employed as servants. In Denver, 5,597 females were engaged in domestic and personal service, of which 3,138 were servants and 277 were housekeepers.[89] Mary C. Mulligan, housekeeper and dressmaker for Margaret ("Molly") Brown, was representative of the women employed as live-in help at the turn of the century. Mulligan was a first-generation American, raised in Nebraska and Kansas by Irish-born parents. Sometime in her young adulthood she moved to Denver. By age thirty-six she was working for the Browns at 1340 Pennsylvania Street, the "House of Lions."

By the turn of the twentieth century there was a substantial domestic servant problem, caused by a number of factors. First was the social stigma attached to the work, which many people associated with black and immigrant women. Second, there was the feudal nature of the live-in arrangement. A servant lived with a master and depended upon him or her for food, shelter, and other necessities. Third, other jobs were becoming available for women that entailed fewer hours, less physical labor, and fewer intrusions into their leisure time. In Colorado, servant girls were scarce because most girls married before they were twenty.[90]

Prospective employers relied on recommendations from friends and relatives to find a servant. Depending on the size of the household, there could be one "maid of all jobs" or several female and male servants. It was important to distinguish between employees and employers. This was accomplished through dress, by the two groups not socializing, and by dividing the household into separate areas. Servants used back entrances and stairways. Servant areas were partitioned off, and there were often separate kitchens and dining rooms for servants. In this way, servants were in the household but not of it; in the language of a popular sympathetic description of their plight, they were "strangers within the gates."[91]

Servants' duties varied depending on the number of servants employed and the employer's needs or idiosyncrasies. A lady's maid was responsible for serving the mistress of the household. She had to be an accomplished hairdresser, seamstress, and dressmaker. She maintained her employer's clothing and jewelry and accompanied her on her travels. Parlor maids cleaned the main-floor hallways and parlors, libraries, dining rooms, and drawing rooms. Each morning they aired out the rooms and swept carpets. Until the advent of electric heat, parlor maids removed ashes and cinders from fireplaces, cleaned grates, prepared new fires, and filled coal shuttles. As Mrs. Brown's housekeeper and dressmaker, Mulligan would probably have assumed most of those responsibilities. For this, she earned enough to support herself. The average wage for domestic service was approximately twenty-five dollars a month. Living at the Brown house, Mulligan had the advantage of free room and board, although she worked long, difficult hours to please Maggie Brown's "feisty and demanding spirit."[92] Her room on the third floor was small and poorly ventilated. It likely had a bed, washstand, chair, and perhaps a chest of drawers. There was no place for Mulligan to relax at the end of the day except in the kitchen—where she had already spent a large portion of her work day—and her bedroom.

Mulligan worked six-and-a-half days per week. As a live-in domestic, she was always on call and sometimes worked up to sixteen hours a day. Most domestics were given half of Sunday and one evening a week off to rest. Mulligan possibly spent her free time sewing, mending, or writing letters. She probably had few close friends because domestic work was notorious for isolating women from their peers. Small wonder, then, that young women who had other jobs available to them refused to become domestic servants. Women with no other options who had to work as domestics preferred to live outside their employer's dwelling so they were not on call all hours of the day.

FIVE

ORGANIZING FOR CHANGE

(1878–1900)

Although not nearly as large or industrialized as cities in the East, Denver shared urban characteristics with them. Streets were filled with the pungent aroma of horse "road apples," rotting garbage, and roving bands of dogs. Soot from wood and coal fires darkened clothing, faces, and buildings. The poor lived in dimly lit, poorly heated, sparsely furnished, overcrowded dwellings.[1] The city's elite increasingly moved out to virgin property, untainted by city industries and the working poor. One characteristic Denver did not share with eastern cities was its reputation as a refuge for tuberculosis sufferers. Although leaders shunned the label and city newspapers would not print the word, many consumptives came to Colorado hoping the dry climate would cure them or at least lessen the severity of their illness.

In August 1892 Frances Wisebart Jacobs left her home in Denver and began her daily rounds. Walking the clay-packed, windy streets, she administered to those she found huddled in doorways and the dark recesses of alleys.

DOI: 10.5876/9781607322078.c05

Upon entering a shanty, she found sickness and abject poverty. Not all her patients were consumptives, but after seeing so many people sick with any one of a number of diseases, she could quickly recognize the ragged cough and gaunt face of impending death. Often there was little she could do. In her basket she carried soup, medicine, and soap. She left these items behind with a family before moving on to another home.[2]

Friends, concerned about her health, tried to dissuade Jacobs from making personal visits, but she ignored their pleas. She believed that if she stayed away, there was a good chance the sick would die. Her efforts, although gallant, could not help all the coughing and expectorating consumptives in Denver, so she founded a hospital for the poor. Unfortunately, in August 1892 it was only a foundation. There were not enough funds to begin building. After one visit, Jacobs collapsed. Overworked and worn down, she died three months later.[3] The entire city joined her sister clubwomen in mourning the loss of a generous soul.

WOMEN'S CLUBS

The women's club movement in the United States was initiated in 1868 by journalist Jane (Jennie June) Cunningham Croly, who founded the Sorosis (the botanical name for a fruit formed from the receptacles of many flowers merged together) Club in New York City, and reformer Caroline Severance, who founded Boston's New England Woman's Club. Between 1868 and 1900, white middle- and upper-class women banded together to form clubs across the nation. In 1890 Croly suggested a national organization. The General Federation of Women's Clubs (GFWC) was organized to "bring into communication with each other the various clubs throughout the world, in order that they may compare methods of work and become mutually helpful."[4] By the height of the Progressive Era in 1914, the GFWC's membership had grown to nearly 2 million American women active in reform legislation, public health, conservation, philanthropy, household economics, and child labor.

The first women's literary clubs were formed primarily for intellectual stimulation. Women studied classical literature, languages, history, and art. Clubs became, in Croly's words, "the middle-aged women's universities."[5] Meetings were held weekly or fortnightly for two hours in the evening or afternoon between the months of October and June when school was in session, which allowed women to meet, free of immediate motherly duties. To join, a candidate was sponsored by two or more members and approved by a

FIGURE 5.1 *Members of federated women's clubs were instrumental in establishing public libraries, national parks and monuments, and homes for orphaned and neglected children. Courtesy, Library of Congress Prints and Photographs Division, Washington, DC.*

large percentage of the executive committee or by the entire club. Most sponsors informally sounded out other members before a formal nomination was made, so a candidate was rarely rejected. In the early years of the club movement, criticisms were often directed toward the clubs for being pro–woman's suffrage. To avoid that label, many clubs chose innocuous names and forbade discussion of suffrage and religion.

A city library was usually the clubwomen's first project, many times in response to their own need for books for their club papers and discussions. In the 1870s and 1880s several clubs began to study the living and working conditions of the poor, public and private charities organized to help them, and laws concerning women. From this, clubwomen developed a permanent concern for the poor and the need for reform legislation. With the organization of the GFWC, the work of the women's literary clubs was standardized, with reform and philanthropy becoming a permanent part of club work. By

the 1890s, newer women's clubs in the United States were formed as "departmental clubs" that stressed philanthropy rather than beginning as literary
clubs as the first clubs had. Standardization was thus achieved: the GFWC
and state federations established permanent committees or departments,
each of which chose themes or particular projects. Individual clubs adapted
national and state projects to fit the specific needs of their communities.

The women's club pattern in Colorado was similar to that in the rest of
the nation. However, because of the state's youthfulness, the first women's
clubs were not organized until the early 1880s. In April 1881 eleven women
met at the home of Ella S. Denison to organize a women's literary club on the
model of the Fortnightly Club of Chicago, to which Denison's mother had
belonged. In addition to the hostess, other charter members of this newly
formed Denver Fortnightly Club (DFC) included Susan Riley Ashley,
Margaret Gray Evans, Ione Hanna, and Lavinia Spalding. The first minutes
described the purpose of the club as "a union of congenial minds for study
and discussion and for the furtherance of good in practical ways" and noted
the election of Margaret Evans as president.[6] Like the Denver Fortnightly
Club, the Pleasant Hours Club was organized in 1881 and renamed the
Monday Literary Club (MLC) in 1889.[7] A third club, the Round Table
Club (RTC), was founded in 1889 with twenty-five charter members. It
was founded, led, and dominated for thirty-two years by Alice Polk Hill.
Members of all three clubs presented papers on topics of general interest as
well as on contemporary issues.[8]

Unlike the three earlier organizations that had begun as literary clubs,
the Twenty-Second Avenue Study Club was originally founded as the Non-
Partisan Equal Suffrage League, an auxiliary of the Colorado Equal Suffrage
Association. After Colorado's electorate passed the suffrage amendment,
league women voted to study Shattuck's *Parliamentary Rules* and Fiske's
Civil Government of the United States and to report on relevant political
issues. During the summer and fall of 1894, members devoted their time
to activities relevant to the November election. Through their efforts, their
own Ione Hanna was elected to the school board.[9] Successful in winning suffrage and becoming educated voters, members voted to dissolve the league
and form in its place the Twenty-Second Avenue Study Club, with nineteen
charter members. In quick succession, other women's clubs were founded
in Colorado after 1881. By 1900, 100 women's clubs were meeting in forty
Colorado towns.[10]

In 1894 women in Colorado followed their eastern sisters' lead in
founding a departmental club. Denison led the drive along with twelve other

members of the DFC, MLC, and RTC. Two hundred women—including suffragists, reformers, and working women—met to organize the Woman's Club of Denver (WCD), divided into the Departments of Home, Reform, Education, Philanthropy, Art and Literature, and Science and Philosophy. The club's membership grew rapidly, reaching 1,000 within a decade.[11] When the four older clubs issued the call for a state federation of women's clubs, the WCD was included because it was the largest club in the Denver area (most literary clubs limited their membership; departmental clubs did not).

Members of the clubs were generally middle-class married women, the wives of businessmen, political leaders, physicians, and attorneys.[12] The exception was the Woman's Club of Denver, which had a proportionally higher number of single women and women who worked outside the home.[13] The WCD also had a larger number of reformers, suffragists, and public servants. Reformers included Elizabeth Byers, Margaret P. Campbell, Ella Denison, Margaret Evans, Eliza F. Routt, Elizabeth Iliff Warren, and Alice Hall Hill.[14] Suffragists who were charter members of the WCD—Ione Hanna, Katharine Patterson, Mary C.C. Bradford, Ellis Meredith, Minnie J. Reynolds, Ella Adams, and Helen Marsh Wixson—had been instrumental in the Colorado fight for suffrage. Bradford served as president of the National Women's Suffrage Association (1901). Reynolds was the first president of the Woman's Press Club. Denison and Evans had long histories of civic involvement.

Similar to eastern clubwomen, Colorado clubwomen, with their origins in literary study, very early on recognized the city's need for a public library. In 1885 the City Library Association's forming committee was composed of seven members. Three of the four women on the committee were DFC members. The WCD began the Traveling Library project in 1896 because it knew that many people did not have a library in their community. Boxes of books were sent all over the state without charge until the Colorado Federation of Women's Clubs (CFWC) took over the project. Under the auspices of the state federation, clubs donated boxes of books, usually in a past president's honor. Early directors were Minnie J. Reynolds and Julia V. Welles, who became nationally known for her work on this project. In 1903 the state legislature authorized the Free Traveling Libraries, a forerunner of bookmobiles, with a $1,000 appropriation. That year, sixty rural schools received chests of books.[15]

Clubwomen pushed vigorously for the establishment of institutions that would aid children, such as the State Home for Dependent and Neglected Children (1895) and the State Home and Industrial School for Girls (1899), both of which were initially located in Denver. Once founded, their boards of control were dominated by Denver clubwomen. The first president of the industrial school was Jane O. Cooper, a member of the DFC and the WCD. Dora Reynolds (DFC) was on the board of the state home from its inception until her death. Other clubs in the city and throughout the state supported these institutions with contributions of money, supplies, entertainment, and books and magazines. Clubwomen also dominated the offices of the State Superintendency of Public Instruction, the State Assistant Librarianship, and the State Board of Charities and Corrections.[16] These women, well placed for reform work, were key figures in the clubs' progressive work. Other institutions that drew the clubwomen's attention were the Newsboys' Union, the county hospital, the city jail, the Florence Crittenton Home, and the Old Ladies' Home. All of these institutions were regularly reported on in club meetings and supported through the years. In particular, the Old Ladies' Home was a favorite project of the clubs, many of which furnished rooms at the home and supplied magazine subscriptions.

Colorado clubwomen enthusiastically embraced the progressive cause of conservation. Prior to the founding of the Colorado Federation of Women's Clubs, the Monday Literary Club and the Denver Fortnightly Club signed a joint petition for designation of the cliff dwellings at Mesa Verde as a national park.[17] Over the next twelve years, individual clubs, the CFWC, and the GFWC vigorously lobbied national and state officials. Success finally came in 1906 when the federal government created Mesa Verde National Park. Later, additional efforts were exerted for the conservation and preservation of natural and historical lands.

In 1898 Colorado clubwomen were honored for their hard work when Denver was selected as the site for the national GFWC convention. Although the state federation was less than five years old, it boasted a membership of 108 clubs with approximately 4,700 members, representing 38 towns. Denver led the list with 12 clubs (including the National Colored Woman's League and the National Council of Jewish Women), followed by Colorado Springs, Fort Collins, and Trinidad with 4 clubs each.

The Denver convention of the General Federation of Women's Clubs was the impetus for another women's organization. Minnie J. Reynolds of the *Rocky Mountain News,* who was in charge of publicity for the convention, was asked by women across the nation if Denver had a club composed of newspaper women, writers, or pen women. Reynolds asked her friend and author Helen Wixson if she thought it would be a good idea to form one. Encouraged by Wixson, Reynolds sent invitations to Denver newspaperwomen and other writers. As Minnie Hall Krauser later recalled, "Four active newspaper girls rode our bicycles up to Mrs. Wixson's home on Clarkson Street, leaned our bikes up against the porch and organized a club."[18] As stated in the by-laws, "The object of this association shall be to advance and encourage women in literary work, to cultivate acquaintance and friendship among women of literary tastes, to secure the benefits arising from organized effort, and to drive dull care away."[19] The Denver Woman's Press Club began with nineteen charter members. It soon proved so resourceful and practical that it was able to buy its own clubhouse. The club remains active over 100 years later.

EQUAL SUFFRAGE CAMPAIGN

Clubwomen's accomplishments received favorable coverage in city newspapers. The same cannot be said about the vast majority of Colorado women, however. Although the lives and work of most women were invisible, original plans for the Colorado State Capitol building called for at least a representation of womanhood. Elijah Myers designed the building and work began in 1886; however, the Capitol Board of Managers dismissed Myers in 1889 to save money, explaining that because the state had his plans and had paid for them, the architect was no longer needed. Frank E. Edbrooke completed the structure in 1908, basically following Myers's design. One major change, though, was the disappearance of the female figure Myers had planned to place on top of the dome. Apparently, the legislature studied many models in various states of dress but could not agree on which one to use. Thus, the most invisible woman in Denver in the early twentieth century may well have been the missing woman of the Capitol dome.

This snub, though, did not deter suffrage proponents from continuing their campaign for equal rights in the Centennial State. During the Ninth General Assembly session in 1893, J. Warner Mills sponsored a bill to submit the issue of women's suffrage to voters in the next general election. When the bill passed both houses, suffragists had only a few months to rally their troops and convince the state's male electorate to support women's suffrage.

Without a sizable war chest, Colorado suffragists appealed to the National American Woman Suffrage Association (NAWSA) for help. But, remembering the defeat in 1877, national leaders held out little hope that western women would be successful just sixteen years later. Susan B. Anthony asked if they had "converted all those Mexicans out in the southern counties."[20] NAWSA did send Carrie Land Chapman (later Carrie

Chapman Catt, president of NAWSA) to the state. The Colorado Equal Suffrage Association also benefited from the work of its treasurer, Elizabeth Ensley. In addition to her role as treasurer, she was instrumental in winning over black male voters to the suffrage cause.[21]

Meetings were held and auxiliary leagues were formed throughout the state. Supporters distributed an enormous amount of suffrage literature. Because the vast majority of the state's newspapers supported equal suffrage, the cause was given favorable press coverage. Equally important was the work of female journalists. Minnie Reynolds, Ellis Meredith, and Caroline Churchill were indispensable to the cause.[22]

In previous campaigns, the liquor industry had been a major obstacle to woman's suffrage. Afraid that women would enact prohibition, those in the industry consistently opposed equal suffrage. Fortunately for the suffragists, Colorado's liquor interests did not take the 1893 campaign seriously until the late fall. When they did take note and tried to organize opposition to the measure, they made a significant mistake. A broadside that ridiculed suffragists and their supporters inadvertently identified the liquor industry as its sponsor, which strengthened the women's case.[23]

In November 1893, male voters in the Centennial State went to the polls as members of the Colorado Equal Suffrage Association looked on. Proving to be pioneers in every sense of the word, the men did not disappoint Colorado suffragists and pleasantly shocked eastern suffragists who, as mentioned, had held little hope that the measure would pass. The next morning the incomplete returns showed that, for the first time in the United States, male voters in a general election granted women equal suffrage. Later, complete returns tallied 35,698 in favor of the measure and 29,462 opposed.[24]

Following their successful campaign, suffragists focused their efforts on encouraging women to vote and electing women to public office. Three Republican women—Clara Cressingham, Frances Klock, and Carrie Clyde Holly—were elected state representatives in 1894. In the state assembly, Cressingham was elected secretary of the Republican House Caucus. Klock served as chair of the Indian and Veterans Affairs Committee and sponsored legislation to create a home for delinquent girls. She later served as the home's director. Holly, from Pueblo County, introduced a nineteenth-century version of the Equal Rights Amendment (ERA). In light of the fact that the twentieth-century national ERA was never ratified, Holly's bill was too radical an idea for the times. Her House Bill 59, defining the "age of consent" (the age at which a man can legally argue that a woman consented to sex), did pass. All three female state representatives worked for laws favorable

FIGURE 5.2 *Carrie Clyde Holly was one of the first three women elected to the Colorado General Assembly. During her term she sponsored an unsuccessful Equal Rights Amendment to the state constitution. Courtesy, History Colorado (Scan #10035441), Denver.*

to women and children. Between 1893 and 1898, other women were elected or appointed to state offices, many in the fields of education and reform. These offices included the Superintendent of Public Instruction, State Board of Charities and Corrections, State Home for Dependent and Neglected Children, and the Board of Control of the State Industrial School.

WOMAN'S CHRISTIAN TEMPERANCE UNION

The anti-suffragists' fears that women would vote to prohibit alcohol were not unfounded. The Woman's Christian Temperance Union (WCTU) grew out of the "Woman's Crusade" of 1873–1874 in which women held prayer vigils, led petition campaigns, demonstrated, and sang hymns to convince local saloonkeepers to destroy their liquor and close their doors. Within three months, women were successful in driving liquor out of 250 communities. Feeling empowered, they met in 1874 to form a national organization. The National Woman's Christian Temperance Union was organized to combat the influence of alcohol on families and society. Annie Wittenmyer was elected the organization's first president. Colorado's first local chapters were formed in 1878, and the state union was organized in 1880. By the time the Boulder Woman's Christian Temperance Union was organized in 1881, Frances E. Willard had been elected the WCTU's second president. A noted feminist whose personal motto was "do everything," Willard broadened the organization's scope. The concept of "home protection" and the WCTU's watchwords of "Agitate-Educate-Legislate" were enlarged to cover more than the prohibition of alcohol. In Boulder, the union was initially reluctant to engage in politics, and it developed programs directed at all age groups. During WCTU meetings, children from infants up to age six were presented for membership in the "Cradle Roll" as "white ribbon recruits." Older children were instructed on scientific temperance and encouraged to enter WCTU's anti-narcotic essay contests.

Local unions embraced the national agenda to varying degrees. Local WCTUs advocated the protection of women and children at home and at work, along with the establishment of shelters for abused women and children, the eight-hour workday, kindergartens, and stiffer penalties for sexual crimes against girls and women. One of the first projects in Boulder was the establishment of a reading room so young men would have an alternative to saloons.[25] To meet expenses, WCTU members collected small monthly subscriptions from townspeople. They held suppers, concerts, entertainments, and lectures to raise funds. Clara H. Savory, who later served as librarian for many years, founded this pioneer effort. At first, the reading room had 16 magazines, 4 daily papers, and 3 weeklies. In June a book reception was held at which 60 books were donated. By 1898 the library had 430 volumes, and average daily attendance was sixty. During the year the library moved into new quarters at the corner of Spruce and Twelfth Streets, and the city council voted an allowance of fifty dollars per month.

In 1883, only two years after George Crawford selected the town sites for Grand Junction and Delta, women in Grand Junction founded a local chapter of the WCTU. Six years later, Mesa County organized its first chapter. Impetus for forming local chapters came from labor unions and citizens. Unions were worried about liquor's effect on family life, as some husbands and fathers chose to drink away their wages. Members presented temperance lessons in churches, gave public lectures, and secured abstinence pledges. The

FIGURE 5.3 *The Woman's Christian Temperance Union brought prohibition to Colorado four years before the Eighteenth Amendment did the same for the rest of the nation. The organization established reading rooms as alternatives to saloons and founded mission homes for children. Courtesy, Denver Public Library Western History Collection, Joseph Collier, C-19.*

Western Slope chapters proved quite successful. In 1908 Mesa County voted to become a dry county. When the issue arose again in 1911, the drys reinforced their dominance and once again won by a 57 percent to 43 percent margin.[26]

GROUP HOMES AND HOSPITALS

In the 1880s an unmarried pregnant dance hall employee appealed to Catherine Beach, a WCTU member, for help. Beach tried to unite the young woman with her family, but they suggested that their daughter be sent to a reformatory. Despondent, the girl committed suicide in Beach's home.[27] The tragedy compelled Beach to seek the WCTU's help. Convinced that unwed mothers were degraded by unscrupulous men who promised marriage in exchange for sexual favors, the Colorado WCTU opened its first home in Colorado Springs before relocating to Denver. Its first matron was Sadie Likens, an experienced reformer. A former Civil War nurse, Likens had served as superintendent of the State Home and Industrial School for Girls, as matron of the county hospital, and as Denver's first police matron.[28]

The Colorado Cottage Home (CCH)—located for over thirty years at 427 Fairfax Street—provided a home for unmarried pregnant women, prenatal care, and placement of newborns with foster parents. Funding came from the WCTU, women's clubs, church auxiliaries, and residents. Although the state's local WCTU chapters donated two dollars a month, that amount was often insufficient to cover an increase in the CCH's population or emergencies. Only one-third to one-half of the women were able to pay the full cost of their stay.[29] Many of the women had lost one or both parents, and others had lost their jobs because of their pregnancy. The home purposely did not demand financial support from the fathers to protect the women's identities. Abandoned by the fathers-to-be, pregnant women were also often shunned by their families, who viewed them as humiliating stumbling blocks to their social climbing goals. When the CCH was shut down in 1903 for lack of funds, a contingent of WCTU women selected member Dinnie Hayes to solicit money. She earned a percentage of the funds she collected and by 1906 had amassed enough money to put a deposit on a new building. The mortgage was retired in 1911.[30]

Unwed mothers-to-be usually heard about the CCH through friends. It posted no advertisements, avoided publicizing the women's life stories, and did not allow visitors to meet residents. The number of admissions varied through the years, from a low of thirty-two in 1894 to a high of eighty-eight in 1923.[31] The 1915 report showed that thirty-two white women and one black woman were admitted that year. There were five teachers, five students, one telephone operator, and sixteen domestic servants.[32]

A president and supervisory board oversaw the operations of the CCH. Live-in staff members were responsible for day-to-day activities. The matron was almost always single or sometimes widowed.[33] To the extent that her health allowed, the mother-to-be was expected to practice cooking, laundering, and housekeeping in the hope that she would be hired as a domestic servant after the baby's birth. In an effort to persuade residents to convert to Protestant Christianity, the CCH conducted nondenominational church services.

In the eyes of CCH officials, it was best to place newborn children with foster parents. The matron and employees emphasized the future interests of the child, the financial burden of raising a child as a single mother, and the social stigma of illegitimacy. Some women, though, did keep their children, boarding them at the CCH while they worked for wages at a job outside the home. Women were grateful for the shelter and medical care they received. In 1892 one mother wrote that she believed poor girls would kill themselves if it were not for the CCH.[34]

By the 1920s the system was breaking down as morality changed, CCH officials saw that women were also to blame for their situation, and more opportunities existed for women—who in an earlier time might have been missionaries but now found jobs in business, government, social work, and academia. By the end of the 1920s rescue homes across the nation were regarded as repressive institutions, out of step with modern American culture. One by one their doors closed. For the Colorado Cottage Home, the end came in 1931. When some members of the governing board wanted to oust Adrianna Hungerford, who had been the home's president for twenty-five years, she initially withstood the challenge. The following year, however, she agreed to close the CCH.[35]

Fortunately, the closing of the Colorado Cottage Home did not leave "fallen women" and their newborns out on the streets. In November 1892 Denver hosted the National WCTU Convention. In attendance was Charles N. Crittenton, a wealthy merchant, who had opened the Florence Night Mission in 1883 in New York City in memory of his daughter, who had died at the age of four. The goal of the mission was to reform "fallen women" and preach salvation and hope while providing shelter for unmarried pregnant women and girls. At the convention, the work of the WCTU so impressed Crittenton that he pledged $5,000 to establish five Florence Crittenton Homes, including one in Denver, to be operated as part of the organization's purity campaign. In February 1893 fifty-eight women agreed to become members. A house was rented at 3138 Lawrence Street, although the home quickly moved from that site to one at 2312 Champa Street where it remained for the next six years. Dr. Minnie C.T. Love offered her services as house physician. The home's first two girls were typical of the residents.[36] In the early years, the home helped the occasional prostitute who wanted to make good, girls and women down on their luck, and females sent from police court or referred by a physician. As the first Florence Crittenton Home in the United States to actively cooperate with a juvenile court, its work was highly praised by Judge Benjamin Lindsey.[37]

In October 1899 the home purchased a twelve-room residence and six building lots at 4901 West Colfax Street. Within seven years, crowded conditions forced the construction of a three-story, steam-heated addition.

The bulk of the $17,000 bill was raised in a two-week campaign led by Ellis Meredith. The new building provided additional dining-room space, a kitchen and pantries, a laundry, large sunny nurseries, a venereal ward with separate bath and toilet, a delivery room, a six- to eight-bed maternity ward, a convalescent room, and isolation quarters. The girls' dormitory filled the entire third floor. Donations from grocers, butchers, and bakers enabled the home to run on a tight budget.[38]

As the years went by, more improvements were made. In 1913 lots donated by Charles Morey were fenced and planted with fruit trees that, along with berry and garden patches, provided fresh fruit and vegetables for residents. Anna Steele financed the Hattie Steele Memorial Schoolroom in honor of her daughter, who had been an active board member for many years.[39] The schoolroom included a large enclosed sun porch with a sleeping porch for babies below it. In 1916 the home endeavored to become even more self-sufficient when Morey bought lots to house chicken coops.

Without the support of the Charity Organization Society (which later became United Charities, in 1913 the Federated Charities, in 1932 the Denver Community Chest, and finally today's United Way), citizens, and the dedicated work of many professional women who freely gave of their time and expertise, the Crittenton Home would never have been successful. Mary Lathrop donated years of legal counsel, and physicians Mary A. Sperry, Mary Hawes, and Mary Bates provided free medical care to the residents.[40] During one particular year, Dr. Hawes made 439 visits to the home without charge. She served for six years on the Denver Board of Education, helped establish Denver's early medical dispensary, and was a staff member not only at the Crittenton Home but also at the Colorado Cottage Home and the Women's Hospital. Although denied a staff position at other Denver hospitals because of her sex, Dr. Bates, like many other professional women, carved out her niche in philanthropic work and within institutions that catered to women and children.

General hospitals also received help from Colorado women. In February 1881 the Reverend A. Gentile, S.J., petitioned the Sisters of Charity of Cincinnati to open a hospital in Pueblo. Sisters Maria Teresa O'Donnell and Cephas Bray visited Pueblo and asked their superiors for permission to do so. They were soon joined by six more sisters. On July 31, St. Mary's Hospital opened in a boardinghouse in the Grove neighborhood. Fifteen months later the frame building was replaced by a brick building on the corner of Grant and Quincy. At the dedication of an annex to the hospital, former governor Alva Adams praised the nuns, saying, "They do that for others, which we will not do . . . In them the ignorant find a teacher, the forsaken a friend, the orphan a mother, the sick a nurse, the sinful a refuge."[41] The Sisters of Charity also established St. Mary's Hospital at 11th and Colorado in Grand Junction. In response to an invitation from Father Carr, pastor of St. Joseph's Church in Grand Junction, Sisters Mary Balbina and Mary Lewis came from Fort Leavenworth, Kansas, in the summer of 1895. They were selected to run the new hospital, started by Dr. Herman Bull. The sisters chose the site, purchased three lots, and were given three additional lots by the town's mayor. Later, they bought the rest of the block for expansion of the hospital facility. Although the first building was made of wood, a brick structure was erected in 1912.

WOMEN'S WORK ON DISPLAY

In the summer of 1893, more than 27 million men, women, and children from all over the world visited the World's Columbian Exposition in Chicago, a "coming out" party for the United States. When the US Congress announced plans for the 400th anniversary celebration of Columbus's arrival in the Americas, a coalition of women's rights activists and working women demanded exhibit space and that women be assigned to all of the fair's governing boards. Public-spirited socialites and clubwomen also pressured Congress for space for a separate Woman's Building. The 117 members of the Board of Lady Managers, in charge of all business concerning women at the fair, included representatives from all the states and territories as well as a core group of nine women from the host city. Despite pressure from African American women's organizations, there were no black members. The Board of Lady Managers chose Sophia Hayden, a graduate of the architecture program at Massachusetts Institute of Technology, to design the Woman's Building. It was adorned with roof sculptures and murals created by other women. The board also raised funds for the Children's Building, which became a large child-care center for fair-going mothers. A dormitory housed women who were traveling alone or with children.

Women filled the completed building with exhibits sent by the states' committees. Colorado's contribution was a collection of forty-six publications. Caroline Romney's *Durango Daily Record* and *Durango Weekly Record,* Agnes Hill's "Hints on How to Talk," Alice Polk Hill's *Tales of the Colorado Pioneers*, Caroline Nichols Churchill's *Queen Bee* newspaper, and Ellis Meredith's *Scrapbook* were among those placed in the library of the Woman's Building. The Ramona Indian School, in the Children's Building, was named for Helen Hunt Jackson's novel *Ramona*. The school's method of teaching Native children was modeled in part on theories in Jackson's book. The official women's exposition handbook, *Art and Handicraft in the Woman's Building of the World's Columbian Exposition*, included two illustrations by Colorado's Mary Halleck Foote.[42] It was a fitting testament to the work accomplished by Colorado women in the years leading up to the twentieth century.

DENVER'S "MOTHER OF CHARITIES": FRANCES WISEBART JACOBS

In 1892, when Frances Wisebart Jacobs died of pneumonia at the young age of forty-nine, the entire city of Denver mourned the loss—and with good reason. Jacobs, Denver's "Mother of Charities," had dedicated her short life to aiding poor men and women, tuberculosis sufferers, the homeless, and children. Born in Harrodsburg, Kentucky, the second child of Bavarian Jewish immigrants, Wisebart became a schoolteacher before marrying a family friend and her brother's business partner, Abraham Jacobs. The two men, bitten by the gold bug, came to Colorado in 1859. They opened clothing stores in Central City and Denver before Jacobs returned to Ohio to wed the twenty-year-old Wisebart. Hard times befell the couple when fires in Denver and Central City wiped out their clothing stores. In 1864 the Jacobses moved to Denver, where she quickly saw the need for charity to aid the city's destitute and ill.

Colorado's climate enticed tuberculosis sufferers, much as its gold discovery lured miners. Thousands of "lungers" immigrated to the state on the heels of the gold seekers. In addition to TB sufferers, the city was home to Jewish refugees who had fled pogroms in Russia. In 1872 Jacobs spearheaded the formation of the Hebrew Ladies' Benevolent Society, designed to aid these refugees. She also served as the organization's first president. Two years later Jacobs joined with Elizabeth Byers and Margaret Evans, wife of territorial governor John Evans, to organize the Ladies' Relief Society. Continuing her philanthropic efforts, she joined with like-minded women to form the Jewish Relief Society. Through the Tabernacle Free Dispensary, it provided medication to "lungers." Jacobs, as always, took a particularly proactive role in the organization, personally delivering medicine, food, and soap to those who did not come to the dispensary. She was known to remark, "I never went anywhere that food was needed that soap wasn't needed more."[43]

As Denver became the destination for gold seekers and consumptives, city charities and churches were hard-pressed to meet the needs of those who were down on their luck. In 1887 Jacobs and Reverend Myron Reed, a Congregational minister, joined forces with Father William O'Ryan, a Catholic priest; Dean H. Martyn Hart, an Episcopalian minister; and Rabbi William S. Friedman of Temple Emanuel to form the Charity Organization Society (COS). Reed served as COS's first president. Jacobs volunteered to be secretary, a position she held until her death. Under the slogan "Not Alms, But a Friend," COS strove to ensure that the poor would be properly cared for while maintaining and reinforcing their self-respect. By 1900 COS was providing funds to fifteen charities, including the Ladies' Relief Society, Tabernacle Free Dispensary, Denver Flower Mission, Florence Crittenton Home, Working Boys' Home, and Denver Orphans' Home. Today's Mile Hi United Way evolved from COS. The national United Way still refers to Jacobs as one of its founders. It annually presents the Frances Wisebart Jacobs Award to recognize "the campaign leader who works in a most exemplary way during their workplace campaign."[44]

Although many causes tugged at Jacobs's heart strings—including homeless women, improved working conditions for women, and separate prison facilities for men and women—TB sufferers remained her strongest passion. In 1889 she helped organize the Jewish Hospital Association and raised $42,000 to build the Frances Jacobs Hospital. Because of the Panic of 1893, the hospital remained unfunded and shuttered until 1899, when it opened as the National Jewish Hospital for Consumptives after being adopted as B'nai B'rith's national project. Quickly overwhelmed by the number of tuberculosis cases, the hospital, whose motto was "none may enter who can pay; none can pay who enter," began admitting only those who had a good chance of recovery.[45] Because the hospital was non-kosher, Orthodox Jews sought treatment at the Jewish Charity Society for Consumptives (later renamed the Jewish Consumptives' Relief Society) on West Colfax Avenue in Lakewood.

Heedless of the health dangers she faced in administering aid to the sick and the poor, Jacobs continued her visits in all kinds of weather. One day in August 1892, after making her rounds through downtown Denver, she collapsed. On November 3, 1892, she succumbed to pneumonia. Her funeral service at Temple Emanuel was filled with 4,000 mourners of every faith, race, class, and economic status. A week later, a memorial service at First Congregational Church was similarly filled to capacity. The governor, mayor, and other community leaders lauded her philanthropic work and leadership.

FIGURE 5.4 *Frances Wisebart Jacobs is commemorated with this statue at National Jewish Health in Denver. A tireless campaigner for the sick, especially tuberculosis sufferers, Jacobs founded the first hospital dedicated to the care of "lungers." Courtesy, Beck Archives, Special Collections and Archives, Penrose Library, University of Denver.*

In 1900 Colorado's "Mother of Charities," taken from her adopted city much too soon, was the only woman among sixteen Colorado pioneers chosen to be commemorated with a stained-glass portrait in the rotunda of the State Capitol building. A century after her work to establish a hospital for needy consumptives, a bronze statue of her was placed in the lobby of National Jewish Health. Jacobs was inducted into the Colorado Women's Hall of Fame and is one of only a few Coloradans selected for the National Women's Hall of Fame in Seneca Falls, New York.

PRESSING ISSUES—WOMEN JOURNALISTS AND WOMEN'S RIGHTS: CAROLINE ROMNEY, CAROLINE NICHOLS CHURCHILL, AND MINNIE J. REYNOLDS

Newspaper work was one area in which women found they could make a difference, especially in the fight to win the right to vote in Colorado. During the last quarter of the nineteenth century, several women across the state were publishing newspapers or working as newspaper reporters. In the early 1880s Caroline Romney left Leadville and freighted her Gordon hand press by wagon because Durango, her destination, had no rail service. Once there, she set up her office in a tent and successfully raced to publish the town's first daily paper, the *Durango Record*. Forty years old and a widow, the New York–born woman gathered news, wrote editorials, managed the paper, and sold advertisements. In a town of only 3,500 people, Romney had to be sharp with her pen, quick with her wit, and strong in willpower and determination to compete successfully with the town's two other week-lies and four daily papers. As with other newspaperwomen in the state, the cause of women's rights was dear to Romney's heart. She encouraged women to move to Durango, criticized the Clipper Theatre and its "lewd girls," ran an exposé on opium dens, and worried about the proximity of the Southern Utes, asserting that their land could be better used by "hardworking white men"—an attitude not uncommon among western men and women at the time. In early 1882, Romney closed down the *Durango Record* and left town. She later worked for newspapers in Trinidad, Colorado, and El Paso, Texas.[46]

Like Romney, Caroline Nichols Churchill also published her own newspaper. Born in 1833 in Canada to American citizens, she began teaching in her native country at age fourteen. Sometime in the 1850s she married Mr. Churchill. He died sometime in the 1860s. She provided for her daughter by teaching and taking in sewing. She lived in Minnesota for two years until a war between the Dakota Indians and the US government made living

FIGURE 5.5 *Through the efforts of Colorado's female newspaper editors and writers, Colorado men voted to give the state's women the right to vote in 1893. Courtesy, History Colorado (Women-Suffrage-1907, Scan #10025803), Denver.*

there too dangerous. Churchill then moved to California and wrote a book about her experiences there. To publicize and sell her book, she embarked on a trip through the West, arriving in Denver in 1879. Finding the climate to her liking, she chose to stay. To support herself (her sister was caring for her daughter), Churchill combined her passions for writing and women's rights by starting a monthly newspaper, the *Colorado Antelope.* Her timing was auspicious, as Colorado had given women the right to vote in school elections but had denied them equal suffrage in the state constitution. Her newspaper, one of the few devoted to women's rights, steadily gained readers. In March 1881 she urged women to vote in the upcoming May school elections to help convince men that women were sincerely interested in political affairs and would exercise their political rights if granted equal suffrage.[47]

In 1882 Churchill renamed the paper the *Queen Bee* and made it a weekly. In its pages she regularly waged written battle against anti-suffrage editors and publishers. A staunch Populist, she also used her paper to advocate for labor unions, birth control, temperance, and the humane treatment of animals. When Colorado men voted in November 1893 to grant equal suffrage to the women of the state, the *Queen Bee's* headline proclaimed "Western Women Wild with Joy over Colorado's Election." The accompanying article relayed congratulations sent by suffrage associations in Kansas, Iowa, Nebraska, and Texas: "Such enthusiasm you never saw as among the women here. We are going to celebrate your victory next week. 1893 has been a memorable year. It has gained more for the suffrage cause than all the years preceding."[48] Unfortunately, American women would have to wait another quarter of a century for national suffrage to be won.

Winning enfranchisement was only one step toward political involvement and empowerment. Churchill appealed to her female readers to become politically active. After eighteen years of publication, in 1895 Churchill shut down the *Queen Bee*. In 1909 she published *Active Footsteps,* her autobiography. Churchill, a fighter for society's disenfranchised, died in Colorado Springs in 1926.

When Minnie J. Reynolds issued a call to other Denver women writers to found a club for newspaperwomen, she was a successful writer for the *Rocky Mountain News*. Born in New York, Reynolds began her career writing and selling articles to eastern newspapers. Her correspondence pieces for the *Rocky Mountain News* brought a job offer from the newspaper. Happily, she accepted the job and moved to Denver, only to find the editors surprised to be looking across the desk at M. J. Reynolds, a woman, rather than the male writer they were expecting.[49] Although they did not renege on their offer, they did reassign her to the society page. Unhappy but undaunted, Reynolds accepted the job and soon moved up to society page editor. Through this position she became friends with and a valuable contact for many influential women in Denver and around the state.

In the 1890s Reynolds's sister, Helen, became secretary of the Colorado Equal Suffrage Association while she served as press chairwoman. In this role, Reynolds was able to convince three-fourths of the state's newspapers to back the suffrage movement. Her work for woman's suffrage also put her in contact with members of the Populist Party. She ran for the state legislature on the Populist ticket in 1894. She was not elected.

Reynold's progressivism extended beyond woman's suffrage to racial injustice. She roundly criticized Denver Public Schools when it denied a black girl the academic honors she had earned. She also befriended those in Denver's Chinese community. Reynolds, in spite of working fourteen-hour days, founded the Woman's Club of Denver and started a statewide traveling library for the Colorado Federation of Women's Clubs. She was also a member of the Round Table Club, discussed earlier in the chapter. Her favorite club, though, was the one she founded in 1898: the Denver Woman's Press Club.[50]

"THAT DAMN[ED] WOMAN": MARY FLORENCE LATHROP

Although Mary Florence Lathrop became well-known and well-loved in Denver as the first woman attorney accepted for membership in the American Bar Association and for hosting thousands of American servicemen at wartime dinners, she was first known as a temperance worker and orator.

Lathrop was born on December 10, 1865, in Philadelphia to a Quaker couple, John and Anna Bell Campbell Lathrop. Her father died when she was only fourteen. Five years later she and her mother were left penniless when the bank holding her father's money failed. As many children and widows were forced to do under such circumstances, Lathrop went to work. She first reported for the *Philadelphia Press* and then worked for seven years as an industrial journalist for the McClure Syndicate. In addition, Lathrop lectured and wrote for the temperance movement. In 1884 she wrote about the evils of rum for a Philadelphia temperance publication: "The most remarkable thing about rum bottles is the amount they will hold. I saw one not long ago that looked as if it only held a quart, but a foolish man put his truth, honor, and good nature, all the money he earned, and a nicely furnished brick house in it."[51]

In 1885 she spoke on Practical Temperance Teaching at the Sixth Annual Institute of the Primary Teachers' Union in Philadelphia. The following year she gave the opening address at a conference of the Young Woman's Christian Temperance Union and spoke at the national WCTU meeting in Minnesota. As a result of her grueling schedule as a reporter and speaker, Lathrop was advised to go west with her mother to regain her health. They spent a year touring Wyoming. Upon her return to Pennsylvania, she resumed her work with McClure. Later, when she tried to resign, Sam McClure refused her letter of resignation, so she took a leave of absence. That leave extended more than fifty years; she never returned to reporting for the syndicate.

Stricken with tuberculosis, Lathrop again went west. Like many other consumptives, she hoped the Rocky Mountain climate would restore her health. In 1890 she and her mother moved to Denver permanently. For their first two years, the city directory listed her mother as an artistic needle worker and Mary as an "authoress," residing at 1420 Champa Street. Her January and February 1890 diary entries chronicle visits with friends, weekly

Sunday school teaching, and lectures given at area churches. Her reputa-tion as a forceful and effective temperance speaker followed her to Denver. Her workaholic habits continued, as she wrote for the National Union of Primary Sabbath School Teachers and traveled throughout the West advo-cating temperance. Between May and December 1890, Lathrop lectured in Wyoming, Utah, Nevada, and California. The many speeches given and miles traveled rendered her sick with a cold and laryngitis. In her final report to the Non-Partisan Woman's Christian Temperance Union, she recounted her work. She had traveled over 5,000 miles and attended 92 meetings. She had distributed nearly 120,000 pages of literature and written 1,000 let-ters, 57 news articles, and 200 newspaper notices. Her body rebelled against such a physically strenuous life. Although her mother urged her to go into medicine, Lathrop favored the legal profession. She graduated from the University of Denver's Law School in 1896. After passing the Colorado bar examination, she opened her law office in the Equitable Building, Denver's most prestigious office building and the address of the city's most prominent law firms. Mary remained at the Equitable Building, working eight hours a day six days a week, until her death in 1951 at age eighty-five.[52]

As a woman working in a field dominated by men, Lathrop encoun-tered her share of criticism. One Denver attorney referred to her as "that damn[ed] woman." From then on, whenever she overheard that phrase, she would answer "present." In 1898 she successfully argued the case *Clayton v. Hallett*, which prompted passage of a Colorado law on charitable bequests.[53] Although she no longer spoke on the temperance circuit, she continued her support for women and children who were sometimes at the mercy of the courts. During World War I, Lathrop served as the legal adviser for the Crittenton Home and the juvenile court. The first woman member of the American Bar Association (1917), she was active in organizing its Committee for Laws Concerning Women and Children. As a member of the Colorado Bar Association, she was instrumental in developing the Small Guardianship Law under which children could receive an inheritance of $300 or less before coming of age if the presiding judge approved. This eliminated the draining of small bequests by unnecessary fees.

But Lathrop, a single woman who worked outside the rigid limits of domesticity her entire life, did not advocate that a woman work outside the home unless she was the family's only wage earner. She argued that "a home means a mother. Not an absentee mother, but full-time, and a loving one. Poverty and luxury alike contribute to the rape of childhood." She pas-sionately believed "marriage is the right career for a woman" and insisted

FIGURE 5.6 *Mary Florence Lathrop was a successful temperance speaker and one of Colorado's first female attorneys. Courtesy, History Colorado (Scan #10038372), Denver.*

that "famous, rich women are paupers if they have no home, no husband, no children to love them."[54] In 1938 she responded to a reporter's inquiry as to whether young girls should go into law: "For a young woman it would still be pretty difficult. A boy can get along if he's just average. A girl has to know much more than that or she doesn't have a chance."[55] Since 1991, the Colorado Women's Bar Association has rewarded outstanding female attorneys with the Mary Lathrop Award. Lathrop's contributions to Denver citizens also earned her an honorary doctorate, the Founder's Day Award, and the Evans Award from the University of Denver.

During World War II, Lathrop entertained thousands of soldiers who were stationed in or passing through Denver. At first, she invited ten to twenty men to her home. Later, she moved the dinners to the Cosmopolitan Hotel, a twelve-story luxury hotel at Eighteenth and Broadway. Between 1941 and 1951, Lathrop hosted dinners for over 12,000 soldiers and sailors. Even after her death, Denver servicemen and servicewomen were treated to dinner as a provision in her will. The final dinner was held in December 1954, as the last of the $1,000 she bequeathed for the dinners was spent. The majority of her estate was left to the University of Denver to establish a student aid fund. She also left many antiques and historical possessions to the Denver Art Museum.

───── S I X ─────
BREAKING WITH TRADITION
───── (1901–1919) ─────

In comparison to states on the Pacific Coast, relatively few Chinese or Japanese were living in Colorado in the late nineteenth and early twentieth centuries. The 1880 census recorded only 593 Chinese and 19 Japanese in the state. For men looking for a wife, the prospects were bleak. Female Chinese and Japanese comprised less than 4 percent of the total number of both populations. The 1910 US census revealed no better news for single Japanese men. Japanese women still made up less than 5 percent of the 2,300 Japanese recorded as living in Colorado. There were more than 2,000 Japanese men for every 100 Japanese women, in contrast to the situation for whites and blacks, where there were 116 males for every 100 females.[1] Picture brides became the solution. The 1907–1908 "Gentlemen's Agreement" prohibited further emigration of Japanese laborers but allowed wives and families to join Japanese men already in the United States. Based on the *omaiai-kekkon*, or arranged marriage custom, women in Japan exchanged photographs with

DOI: 10.5876/9781607322078.c06

prospective husbands in the United States, had their names entered into their spouse's family registers, and then applied for passports to join husbands they had never met.

Twenty thousand Japanese women immigrated to the United States prior to 1920, when the Japanese government prohibited further female emigration because of growing US anti-Japanese sentiment. As a result of the picture bride system (*shashin kekkon,* or "photo-marriage"), the percentage of Japanese American women in Colorado skyrocketed, from less than 5 percent in 1910 to 35 percent in 1920.[2] One picture bride was Some Kosuge. In 1912 the teacher disembarked from a ship in Seattle, Washington. In the waiting crowd was her intended husband, Shichirobei Nakane. Like Some, Shichirobei was a college graduate from a successful family. In Japan, his family members were prosperous farmers and manufacturers of shoy (soy sauce).[3] Nakane and Kosuge were married on June 11, 1912, with Shichirobei taking Kosuge's last name, as she was the oldest daughter in a family with no sons. This practice was known as *yoshi.* Nakane had older brothers to carry on his family name; the Kosuge family had none.[4]

From Seattle, the Kosuges took the train east. They stopped along the South Platte River at Merino, eleven miles southwest of Sterling, where he began a farming venture with two other men. Merino, located on the high plains of Colorado, was once home to buffalo and antelope, hunted by Native Americans before their removal to reservations in the 1870s and 1880s. Both Kosuges worked in the fields during planting and harvesting seasons. Kosuge labored even when she was pregnant. The couple had ten children, all born at home. Dr. W. B. Lutes, the Merino physician, helped deliver some of the infants. The Kosuges farmed their land in Merino until 1938. They then spent five years in the Iliff area and three years at Kersey. Tiring of drought and dust, they sold their farm and moved to Denver.[5]

IMMIGRANTS

Between 1901 and 1920, immigration to the United States peaked, with nearly 1 million newcomers in 1907 alone. Midwestern and western states lured countless immigrants with advertisements in the eastern states and in Europe. In Colorado, Italian men arrived to work on the railroads, in the mines, and at the smelters. Russian Germans settled in eastern Colorado, while Japanese men, immigrating without wives or families, moved to both the southeastern and northeastern plains. Some Japanese men, no longer needed by the railroads, were recruited to work in the steel mills in Pueblo.

During spring and summer layoffs, they worked in sugar beet fields in south-eastern Colorado or worked their homesteads along the Arkansas River, growing melons and other crops for city markets.

Mexicans also migrated north to southern Colorado to work in the beet fields. They lived in tents during the work season and moved back to Mexico in the off season. Sometime around 1910, sugar beet companies built camps in which the workers and their families lived year-round. The camps were rows of adobe-walled rooms with common walls. At first, the sugar companies guaranteed bills for workers' purchases during the winter at the town's grocery stores, but they later opened a commissary in one of the factory's storerooms. After 1910 the revolution in Mexico made it easier for labor contractors to persuade Mexicans to move north to work in Colorado fields. In 1900 the US census recorded only 274 persons born in Mexico or born to parents who were native-born Mexicans. By the time of the 1930 US census, over 13,000 Coloradans listed Mexico as their country of birth; nearly 58,000 Coloradans reported themselves as Mexicans.[6] Entire families worked in the fields under extremely harsh conditions. Mothers left their babies at the end of a row as they weeded and harvested the sugar beet plants. In the winter, families bought 100-pound sacks of pinto beans and buck-ets of lard at the company store. There was little money for meat. Families shared a garden plot to grow chili peppers. In the spring, asparagus, dande-lion, and purslane were gathered along riverbanks.

MINING WOES

The promised riches of the twentieth century stood in stark contrast to the reality experienced by coal miners and their families. By its very nature, coal mining is an extremely dangerous job. In Colorado it was especially deadly. Between 1884 and 1912, nearly 43,000 coal miners were killed in mining accidents in the United States. That number included more than 1,700 Colorado workers, twice the national average. Colorado coal miners were predominantly Italian, Slavic, and Greek immigrants. To push for improved labor conditions, miners, like other industrial workers, joined unions and held strikes.[7]

In 1903 and 1904, strikes by miners broke out statewide. Confrontations in the Cripple Creek District quickly turned violent. In February 1903 the Western Federation of Miners (WFM) tried to secure an eight-hour workday for smelter workers in Colorado City by leading a sympathy strike against mine owners in Cripple Creek. Colorado governor James H. Peabody, responding to pleas by local businessmen, ordered National Guard units to Teller County and Colorado City. Late on the night of September 29, 1903, a unit of the National Guard led by Major Thomas McClelland invaded the offices of the *Victor Daily Record*—the WFM's local official organ—and arrested manager George E. Kyner, foreman H. J. Reynolds, circulator W. L. Sweet, and two linotype operators, brothers F. W. and Charles G. Langdon. Before being marched off to the makeshift jail, Kyner called his wife, who hurried to the house of Emma Langdon, Charles Langdon's wife. Rousing her from bed, Mrs. Kyner told her that the *Record* force had been arrested. Knowing it was crucial to publish the paper, Langdon "broke all records in dressing" while Mrs. Kyner ran off to round up two other employees, Miller and Conrad.[8] As she dashed through dark alleys to the *Record* office, Langdon kept a keen eye out for soldiers. Arriving at the same time as the two men, she helped them lock, bolt, and bar the doors just before the soldiers returned demanding entrance. Rebuffed, the militia left, and the three set about printing the paper. Langdon manned one of the linotype machines and set type.

By 3:00 a.m. the issue was ready. Langdon grabbed a fresh paper and shoved it under Mrs. Kyner's door so she would know they had been successful in printing it. Returning to the office, she found that the carriers had left after seeing the doors locked, so she "immediately hurried out and ran down the alley, finding two of them several blocks away."[9] She told them to get the other delivery boys together and meet her at the office. Clad only in a dressing gown and unlaced shoes, she went home to change as dawn approached. Once again reporting to the office, she took the papers and rushed to the makeshift jail. Overhearing an officer gloating that the miners' *Victor Daily Record* would not be published that day, she boldly handed him one of her copies, eliciting a stream of profanity from the man. Assured by her husband that the five arrested men were fine, Langdon rushed back to the office and started composing the next issue. She worked continuously until Kyner, Sweet, Richmond, and the Langdon brothers were released and ready to take their places at the machines. Galvanized by the event, Emma Langdon went on to serve as vice president of the Victor Trades Assembly, a member of the Typographical Union in Victor, and later of Union No. 49 in Denver after being expelled from Victor.[10]

Although Langdon was successful in issuing the *Victor Daily Record*, the strike ultimately failed. Mine management also won other Colorado strikes. Over the next several months, Governor Peabody sent the militia into San Miguel and Las Animas Counties to support mine owners. Labor troubles were not confined to those areas, however. In 1903 and 1904 miners in the northern coalfields shut down several companies in Clear Creek County, and smelter workers struck the American Smelting and Refining Company. Both efforts were to no avail as corporate owners, in alliance with Colorado's governor and state militia, crushed the strikes. By 1906 Colorado workers' unions in the coalfields had been beaten.

But troubles continued. In 1910, disasters at the Primero, Starkville, and Delagua mines killed more than 200 men. In the aftermath of these tragedies, miners and their families demanded mining reforms. In Lafayette, Elizabeth Beranek, a wife and mother of miners, took it upon herself to lead a group of picketers. During the Long Strike of 1910–1914, she left her kitchen to rally men, women, and children to picket and sing labor songs. The Czechoslovakian-born Beranek, who was only five feet two inches tall, led numerous picket lines carrying a large American flag. Her spunk and courage earned her the title "the Amazon" among miners and their families.[11]

Small changes did occur as a result of the pickets and strikes. In 1913 a Colorado mine safety bill passed that required better ventilation, increased inspections, and control of coal dust in mines. However, the miners and union leaders knew that enforcement of the bill's provisions was not guaranteed. Further, the bill did not rectify other labor issues, such as implementing the eight-hour workday or assuring payment in US currency instead of company scrip. Unresolved, these demands became the focus of future strikes.

WOMEN AT WORK

In the first two decades of the twentieth century, many businesswomen owned boardinghouses, laundries, or dressmaking shops. In DeBeque, young Jennie L. Jackson worked for her room and board while she attended school. At age nineteen she married J. Elvin Harris, the owner and operator of the town's general store. For the next several years, the couple moved from town to town until they settled in a one-room cabin on Plateau Creek near Mesa. The Harris Ranch became a halfway station for freighters and farmers. Harris and her two daughters usually fed eight to ten people every day. For twenty-five cents, weary travelers, the local schoolteacher, and hired help received a meal of biscuits, fried ham, oatmeal, coffee and cream, and homemade jellies.[12]

While their husbands concentrated on ranching operations, some wives took advantage of a town's growing population to run their own successful businesses, selling the products of their farm effort. Maude May Griffith

FIGURE 6.1 *To supplement the family income or as their sole income, women ran boardinghouses, providing meals for men who greatly outnumbered women in the early years of Anglo settlement. Courtesy, Carnegie Branch Library for Local History, Boulder Historical Society Collection, Boulder, CO.*

Russell sold her poultry and eggs to Montrose hotels and restaurants while her husband tended their peach and pear orchards.[13] The Italian-born Marietta Martucci Mancuso left her five-year-old son with family in Italy to join her husband, who worked for the Denver and Rio Grande Railroad. The couple had fourteen children, including three sets of twins born within a three-year period. To support their large family, the Mancusos farmed in the Riverside area of Grand Junction. Marietta was often seen carrying baskets of fruit on each hip as she walked to market. She also raised her own pigs, bottled much of her own produce, and prepared her own tomato paste. Although she rarely spoke English, she was an astute businesswoman who bought five homes during her lifetime.[14]

Other women worked side by side with their husbands in the family business. In 1915 Mabelle Delight Gardner Clymer and her husband, Fred, bought a herd of milk cows and opened the Rose Glen Dairy. They later bought the Arctic Dairy. She drove the truck and picked up cans of milk from other farms. When full, the cans weighed over 100 pounds each. If farmers' wives tried to help, she refused, saying, "I can lift the milk but I can't lift you too."[15] As Clymer aged, she left the trucking to others while she managed the dairy's bookkeeping department.

Although the new century presented more opportunities for women, most continued to work in traditionally female jobs. In rare cases, isolated rural areas and small towns afforded the most intrepid women an opportunity to engage in a highly unusual occupation. On the Western Slope, Hattie Pearson became Grand Junction's first female undertaker. After the death of her first husband, Pearson moved with her two daughters and son to the town at the confluence of the Colorado and Gunnison Rivers. In 1907 she and her daughter Ruth were working as clerks at J. E. Wheatly's notions store. Two years later the Grand Junction/Mesa County directory listed her as "undertaker and licensed embalmer." Working out of her office at 115 North Fifth Street, Pearson employed a "gentleman assistant" to prepare male corpses. Even after she married her second husband, William Murr, a Grand Junction businessman, Hattie continued to work as an undertaker. Attired in "tails" and a top hat, she drove a horse-drawn buggy around town.[16]

Also living and working on the Western Slope was Ola Anfenson, pioneer photographer. Born in the Dakotas in 1874 to Swedish immigrants, Anfenson was introduced to the art of negative retouching as a young girl. After learning the technique, she moved to Des Moines, Iowa, where she plied her craft at the Edinger Gallery.[17] Beginning in the late 1890s Anfenson bounced back and forth from California to Grand Junction, Colorado, to the Midwest to Nevada, working alternately as a photographer and a hotel parlor maid. While visiting her sister in Grand Junction, she worked for photographer Frank Dean. Seemingly nomadic by nature, Anfenson joined her parents in Grand Junction after they moved there for her father's health. Dean rehired her to work in his photography studio. After her father's death, Anfenson and her mother moved to DeBeque, where her sister and her sister's husband ranched. DeBeque was in a boom cycle precipitated by oil discoveries. Anfenson bought a town lot and, with her brother-in-law's help, built a photograph gallery. With a large supply of pretty clothes, throws, lace capes, and shawls for her subjects, her business was a success. In 1914 the oil boom in DeBeque "busted" and her business declined. Fortuitously, at this time Fred Garrison visited her gallery. He convinced Anfenson to move to Rifle to manage his gallery while he tended his ranch on Hunter Mesa. Although reluctant to leave her gallery in DeBeque, business was so slow that Anfenson accepted his offer. Within a year, she also accepted his marriage proposal. She was forty years old. She gave birth to a daughter, Grace, but the infant survived only a few weeks.[18] For the next twenty-five years, the Garrisons ran their gallery in Rifle.

Sisters-in-law Josie and Ellen Hupp parlayed their entrepreneurial skills into successful real estate ventures. The Hupps bought and sold a number of hotels in the mountain resort town of Estes Park. On the southwest corner of what later became Elkhorn and Moraine Avenues, they built the Hupp Hotel. For two dollars or more a night, a visitor enjoyed one of the hotel's twenty-three rooms, steam heat, and hot and cold running water. Next, they purchased the property on the northeast corner of the intersection and renamed it the Hupp Annex. In 1913 Josie purchased Boyd Market, which her husband, a butcher, operated. Ellen's death in 1917 did not dampen Josie's entrepreneurial spirit. She joined with other Estes Park business owners to charter the first bank in town. Ever the shrewd businesswoman, Hupp built the bank between her two hotels. She also served as the town's postmistress for several years. As was often the case in fledging towns, a post office operated out of someone's home or business. Hupp ran the Estes Park post office from her hotels, bringing additional foot traffic to her establishments. At one time, she owned or operated three hotels and two restaurants.[19]

THE "HELLO GIRLS"

In 1871 Alexander Graham Bell of Scotland immigrated to Boston, Massachusetts, to instruct the hearing-impaired. After experimenting with an electric current to transmit sounds, he achieved a "talking telegraph" in 1876, the year of Colorado statehood. Bell set up his own telephone company and sold rights to other entrepreneurs to establish local telephone companies. In 1879 Frederick O. Vaille established the Colorado Telephone Company, with 161 subscribers. The central office moved in 1880 to the top floor of the newly completed Tabor Block at Sixteenth and Larimer Streets. Within three years of its founding, the company had nearly 600 subscribers, having overcome early resistance by lawyers, doctors, and businessmen who feared being disturbed at home by clients or patients. Over the years, lines were completed to Colorado Springs, Pueblo, New York City, and San Francisco. By 1915 Denver subscribers constituted 45 percent of Colorado's 92,561 total subscribers.[20]

The Colorado Telephone Company originally only hired men as operators but soon discovered that they were less solicitous than female operators and often escalated problems with customers by being undiplomatic and even rude.[21] Another important consideration for the company was the fact that it could pay women less than men. Within a short time, male operators were replaced by women, all of whom were white and nearly 70

FIGURE 6.2 *At the telephone operator's school, a job applicant has her arm reach measured to ascertain that she can stretch far enough physically to connect calls. Colorado Telephone Company (renamed Mountain States Telegraph and Telephone Company in 1911) first hired male operators but quickly switched to females when men proved rude and unsolicitous to customers. Courtesy, History Colorado (Mountain States Telephone Collection, Scan #200007498), Denver.*

percent native-born. Originally, an operator shouted out connections to young boys in the next room who dashed around, behind, and often into each other to make the correct connections for the phone calls. The office was so chaotic and noisy that passers-by on the street were known to run into the building thinking a fight was in progress. New technology and feminine grace eventually ended this bedlam. After six months of training, "hello girls" clad in black uniforms, broad white collars, and black ties were ready for work. In 1901 the main Denver exchange employed 120 women, and another 80 worked at the York and South branch offices. Sixty women worked the phones during the busy hours, 9:00 a.m. to 5:00 p.m.; only 7 or 8 were on duty at night. Thirty operators ran the toll line department. Supervisors, each watching over 9 operators, walked back and forth during the entire shift. Information clerks sat at desks in the middle of the workplace to answer questions from the public. In addition to the work areas, the company provided an employees' dining room and a sitting room furnished with couches, easy chairs, magazines, and books. A matron and her assistant were in charge of company-provided lockers.[22]

Smaller communities did not acquire telephone exchanges until years after Denver got its exchange. In Lamar, service began in 1901, with fifty phones. As was the case in the larger cities, young single white women made up the ranks of "hello girls." Amy Mourning managed the Lamar office from 7:00 a.m. to 9:00 p.m. Succeeding her was Rose Foster, until the switchboard was moved to a modest room off the lobby of the Union Hotel at the corner of Main and Olive. At that location the King sisters, Birdie and Grace, were acclaimed as exceptionally efficient, capable, and helpful.[23]

Another occupation filled predominantly by white women was sales clerking. Of the 2,183 Colorado saleswomen in 1910, all but 6 were white. Young women were increasingly hired by the Denver Dry Goods Store, which, like the telephone exchange, offered its employees amenities such as a tidy lunchroom. The biggest draw, though, was the higher prestige accorded salesclerks and operators over that of women employed as domestic servants, dressmakers, or laundresses.[24]

The vast majority of women wage earners, however, still worked in the traditional field of domestic service. In 1910 more than 53,600 Colorado females were employed outside the home. Of this number, 51,443 were native or foreign-born whites, 2,132 were "Negroes," and 66 were "Indian, Chinese, Japanese, and all other." Nearly half of the "Negroes" worked as domestic servants, as did a third of the latter category, while less than 15.5 percent of the whites fell into the category.[25]

SCHOOLTEACHERS

Teaching continued to be an occupation in which an educated white woman could work outside the home. Nearly 10 percent (12 percent when musicians and music teachers were included) of white women in Colorado were teachers.[26] If a woman remained single, she could work for decades as a teacher, even perhaps working her way up the educational ladder to become an elementary school principal. Dora Moore, who began teaching in Denver, became the principal at Corona Elementary School in 1893, a position she held until ill health forced her into early retirement in 1929. To honor this well-loved and respected principal, Corona was renamed Dora Moore Elementary School in 1929.[27]

Other teachers solidified their financial standing by homesteading or running a business when school was not in session. In Larimer County, Josephine Lamb taught in the county schools during the winter and at mountain communities in the summer. At age twenty-one, she homesteaded in the Livermore area and became the owner of the Livermore Hotel. She bought a total of 1,300 acres of farm and ranchland on which she ran cattle in the summer. In exchange for her help in their hay fields, neighbors took care of her herd while she taught school.[28] Another female teacher who homesteaded was Alice C. Newberry, who began her teaching career in Kit Carson County when she was only fourteen. She "proved up" on her homestead in 1909, at which time she moved to Denver to teach in its public schools. With her teaching salary and income from her farm, she was able to build a house at 1421 South Grant Street, where she lived for the rest of her life.[29]

Rural schoolteachers faced a variety of challenges. Josephine Dyekman's first school was Waverly, which was poor. Although she had to walk a mile and a half to a primitive wooden schoolhouse, she did not complain because "the school boards always gave me a good axe" with which to split kindling for the classroom. Like other teachers, Dyekman boarded and ate with her students' families. When she lived with one particularly poor family, her dinner bucket contained only three pancakes.[30] Her chores included sweeping the floor, carrying out ashes, and building fires in the schoolroom's stove. After one year at Waverly, Dyekman "got raised" (transferred to a "better" school). As she was en route, the stage driver told her that every former teacher had "carried off" one of their young men. Dyekman kept the tradition alive, marrying Stewart McNey, the town's sole remaining bachelor, the following year.[31] Although some teachers quit after they married, McNey only took several years off while her son was young and then returned to teaching. Because her husband was a rancher, her steady teaching income was important—especially the year the family's house caught fire, followed the next day by a flood that swept away what the fire had not destroyed.

For at least two women, teaching in the West was an escape from unfulfilled lives back East. In 1916, Rosamond Underwood and Dorothy Woodruff stepped off the train at the Hayden depot. Although not trained teachers, the two twenty-nine-year-olds had decided that teaching in Elkhead would be an adventure and a way to leave Auburn, New York, the hometown to which they had returned after graduating from Smith College. Farrington (Ferry) Carpenter, a cattle rancher who was responsible for the new school and hiring its teachers, had more than education on his mind. He viewed a new school as the solution to the area's biggest problem—the lack of single, eligible women. One of his friends was Bob (also known as Robert or Robin) Perry, a mine supervisor in Oak Creek. Perry's two sisters, Marjorie and Charlotte, knew Underwood and Woodruff from college. When Carpenter heard that the Perry sisters considered the two applicants "the prettiest and liveliest girls in their class," he quickly hired them. They boarded with Uriah and Mary Harrison, who had recently moved from Lower Elkhead to Upper Elkhead. When Underwood and Woodruff arrived, the house had no dividing walls, only partitions made of bedclothes and rugs that rendered the abode "especially sociable" whenever the wind blew. As primitive as their housing was, their new stone schoolhouse was considered lavish. Amazingly, the school had electricity and a projector with educational slides donated by the Ford Motor Company.[32]

Perry and Carpenter set their hearts on marrying the two teachers. Carpenter's scheme to marry one of them did not pan out, at least not for several decades. In 1917 Underwood married Perry. Woodruff, who had been secretly engaged, married a Grand Rapids banker three days after her colleague's wedding. Although Carpenter initially missed out on marrying either of these teachers, he persuaded Eunice Pleasant, another teacher he had recruited, to be his wife. Bob Perry died in 1934 and Eunice in 1954. One year after Eunice's death—four decades after he had hired her—Carpenter married Rosamond Underwood Perry. The Elkhead School, the catalyst for their initial friendship, closed in 1938, a victim of declining enrollment as families found making a living in the northern Rockies too difficult to sustain.

LIBRARIANS

The 1910 US census did not have a category for librarians, but by 1920, 155 female librarians were employed in Colorado, vastly outnumbering the state's 14 male librarians.[33] Often, as was the case in the early years of libraries in Brush, Del Norte, Fowler, Hugo, Ordway, Salida, and Sedgwick, members of women's clubs or civic organizations voluntarily staffed the library on a rotating basis. Libraries in larger cities were often fortunate enough to have paid trained librarians.

The first libraries were subscription libraries. Town residents generally paid one dollar to check out books, most of which were donated by private citizens. Subscription libraries soon gave way to public libraries. At the forefront of the public library movement were clubwomen. Between 1886 and 1929, over thirty Colorado town libraries were either founded or heavily supported by women's clubs. A partial list includes libraries in Aurora, Buena Vista, Delta, Flagler, Huerfano County (Walsenburg), Las Animas, Littleton, Meeker, Monte Vista, Windsor, and Yuma. Members of the Woman's Christian Temperance Society established libraries and reading rooms in Boulder and Eaton as alternatives to saloons. The idea for a library in Loveland originated when members of the Women's Improvement Society discovered they had nothing left to improve after residents voted to abolish the town's saloons.[34]

With the support of clubs and city governments, library collections started finding permanent homes in converted buildings and in Carnegie Foundation–funded stone edifices. That stability also encouraged the libraries to hire librarians, even though they were usually untrained. In the early years, a librarian's pay ranged from Florence Bonds's weekly salary of $1.50 in Estes Park to 10 cents an hour for Mrs. John Wadell at the Fleming Community Library.[35] To raise funds, women held bake sales, dances, teas, theater performances, and raffles. In time, most libraries came under the auspices of town governments, although fundraising remained a critical part of many libraries' mission.

The need for trained librarians increased as more libraries were established. By the late nineteenth century, library training schools had been founded in eastern and midwestern states.[36] But for many western women who wanted to be librarians, enrolling in a library school in the Midwest or the East was financially impractical. For them, training classes held at a local library filled the bill. Charlotte Baker began her library career at the Denver Public Library's training school after her teaching career was cut short by a physical breakdown and tuberculosis. Ordered to move to a drier climate, she and her sister Anna came to Colorado. Baker enrolled in Colorado College to become a math teacher but suffered another breakdown. After deciding that she could not make a living in an occupation that required the constant

FIGURE 6.3 *Unable to withstand the physical rigors of teaching, Charlotte Baker graduated from the Denver Public Library's training school. As the librarian at Colorado State Agricultural College (now Colorado State University), she mentored librarians throughout the state. Courtesy, Fort Collins Museum and Discovery Science Center, #H00144, Fort Collins, CO.*

use of her voice, she took the entrance examination for the Denver Public Library's (DPL) training class. After she graduated in 1894, she joined the DPL staff, but her health woes continued.[37] Dependent on crutches, she served mostly in the Catalog Room and taught literature to students in the library training classes.[38] She and her sister became restless and moved to Las Cruces, New Mexico, where Baker accepted a job as librarian at New Mexico College of Agriculture and Mechanic Arts (now New Mexico State University). Administrators "exhibited" her to visitors as a trained librarian. She was less than thrilled at being treated as a rare and exotic animal: "If I only could have had a string tied to my belt and a hand organ to dance to the illusion would have been complete."[39] Circus commodity or not, Baker enjoyed good health in New Mexico's climate, as she regularly danced and rode horseback.

By 1906 she longed for "civilization" and returned to Colorado. First hired as assistant librarian at Colorado State Agricultural College (now Colorado State University) in Fort Collins, Baker later replaced head librarian Josh Daniels when he left for California in 1910. She quickly became a valuable mentor to other librarians, as she spent her spare time and vacations visiting libraries throughout the state, witnessing firsthand the rugged working and living conditions untrained library workers faced. Most librarians lodged in hotels, boardinghouses, private homes, and dormitories. Their room and board, which ranged from twenty to forty dollars a month, generally consumed at least half of their monthly income. Dirt, pests, fire, odors, and flies were common problems in the libraries. Without assistants or secretarial help, librarians were overwhelmed with menial tasks. In 1912 Camille Wallace (Mesa County Public Library) wrote to Baker that her daily work consisted of "an infinite amount of detail work," such as cataloging, mending, and cleaning. Wallace's only assistants were a schoolgirl who gave a few hours daily in exchange for training and a young boy who considered his work done after he "built a fire in the furnace and swept the middle of the floor."[40] Baker was not immune from such work conditions. One winter day she was forced to put a paper torch in a stovepipe elbow and trot up and down the frozen pipes for an hour and a half to thaw them out.[41]

Some town librarians seriously embraced their role as literary missionaries, combining it with a strong sense of morality. Josephine Silver, head of the Lamar Library from 1915 to 1953, fiercely guarded her young readers' morals by refusing to allow them to read books she thought were inappropriate.[42] Another "straight-laced spinster" who took it upon herself to protect young patrons from "unsuitable books" was Camille Wallace. One patron referred to the restricted shelf as "Miss Wallace's Inferno," although he doubted the sequestered volumes were torrid enough to justify being called an inferno.[43] At the DPL, books considered controversial—such as *Huckleberry Finn, Zola,* and *The Arabian Nights*—were marked with an "S" for Special Collection. With closed shelves, a patron first looked at the library's catalog of holdings to find a book and then asked a librarian to get the book from the caged shelves. In this way, librarians limited access to the collection. The process, however, did not stop male librarians from spending many of their working hours perusing the catalog to find "off-limit" books.[44]

NURSES AND PHYSICIANS

Nursing was also a traditional job for women. After the Civil War, training for nurses provided employment for the increasing number of native-born women migrating to American cities for work. As one nursing reformer stated, "The domestic order created by a good wife, the altruistic caring expressed by a good mother, and the self-discipline of a good soldier were to be combined in the training of a good nurse."[45] Influenced by Florence Nightingale, who believed adamantly in women's duties and responsibilities, nurses' training emphasized character building and strict discipline.

It soon became advantageous for a hospital to open its own nursing school. Hospital trainees were paid an "allowance" of eight to twelve dollars a month for personal expenses plus room and board. They worked thirteen-hour days, six days a week, fifty weeks a year. The majority of nurse trainees' work consisted of cleaning bathrooms, floors, towels, and sheets. Trainees attended lectures by the hospital's doctors after a full day's work. Often, the doctors were ineffectual teachers. At the Colorado State Insane Asylum, the Board of Lunacy hired two chief nurses, one for the men's department and one for the women's department. One of their responsibilities was to instruct nurses for an hour one evening a week for ten months of the year, which equaled less than fifty hours of instruction a year. Nurses at the asylum assisted patients with dressing, washing, and getting to the dining room in time for breakfast. They bathed patients and changed their clothes and bed linens at least once a week.[46]

A woman who chose nursing as a profession had limited options. She could become a hospital nurse, a private nurse, a superintendent of nursing, enter hospital administration, or work in smaller charitable and church-affiliated institutions. Gertrude Potts graduated from Dr. Sutherland's Hospital

FIGURE 6.4 *Beth-El student nurses in Colorado Springs were often glorified maids and servants. The majority of their education consisted of cleaning bathrooms, floors, towels, and sheets. Courtesy, Special Collections, Pikes Peak Library District, 001-2171, Colorado Springs.*

school in 1907. After six months of graduate study at California Hospital in Los Angeles, she worked as the operating supervisor in the Wallace (Idaho) Hospital before returning to Colorado in 1909. From that time until Dr. Sutherland's death in 1917 forced the hospital to close, Potts was the supervisor of Loveland General Hospital. Widowed after three years of marriage to David Ragan, she steadily progressed through the nursing ranks, from nurse to operating supervisor to superintendent at Greeley Hospital.[47] Another Colorado woman, nurse Anna Fender, operated St. Luke's Hospital in Montrose County from 1916 to 1948, delivering more than 4,000 babies at an average cost of twenty-five dollars. When she retired she gave furnishings and equipment to the new hospital, Montrose Memorial, spurring it to name the new maternity ward after her.[48]

Oca Cushman entered St. Luke's Hospital Training School for Nurses in Denver in 1900. After graduating, she became a nursing supervisor at St. Luke's until Children's Hospital opened. The idea for a children's hospital in Denver began with summer tent hospitals for babies, inspired by Dr. Minnie

C.T. Love. Aided by Colorado's fresh air and sunshine, six medical staff and volunteer nurses treated up to fifty children under age five. Early on, the staff saw the need for a permanent hospital that would care for sick, injured, and crippled children and be supported mainly by volunteer contributions. In 1910 Children's Hospital began admitting patients in a former residence at 2221 Downing Street. As the demand for child health care services increased throughout the region, the hospital quickly outgrew its original location and raised more than $200,000 to build a new facility at Nineteenth Avenue and Downing Street in downtown Denver. Cushman was its superintendent from 1910 until her retirement in 1955 at age eighty-five. Hailed as the "first, formidable, and forever" superintendent of Children's Hospital, she was instrumental in the hospital's day-to-day affairs, procuring financial contributions, and founding its nursing school.[49]

Just as traditional male occupations established professional organizations and licensure or certification requirements to gain legitimacy and respect, so did the traditionally female occupation of nursing. In 1904 Louise Croft Boyd wrote the bill introduced into the Colorado General Assembly to create legal licensure for nurses. Boyd, an 1899 graduate of the Colorado Training School for Nurses and a founder of the Colorado State Trained Nurses Association (later the Colorado State Nurses Association and now the Colorado Nurses Association), applied for and became Colorado's first licensed nurse after the bill passed.

After the Civil War, a few progressive medical schools opened their doors to female students. By 1890 the University of Michigan, Woman's Medical College of the New York Infirmary, and the Women's College of Philadelphia had graduated nearly 800 women doctors.[50] Many female doctors established their own practices because hospitals refused to hire them. Female doctors who found cities on the Front Range intolerant of professionally trained women settled in communities in the mountains, on the Western Slope, or on the eastern plains. Dr. Susan Anderson, "Doc Susie," was a mainstay in the mountain town of Fraser.[51] In Fort Collins, Dr. Mary D. Reckly was the city's first female physician to open an office after graduating from both a regular school of medicine and a school of osteopathy. Several years later Nora Rice Miller opened her practice in Fort Collins after her husband's death left her with two young children to support. Rather than teach, as she had done before her marriage, she studied medicine, graduating from the University of Colorado Medical School. As a physician, she often traveled long distances by horse-drawn buggy to reach her rural patients, many of whom were pregnant.[52]

Another female doctor in rural Colorado was Harriette Collins Lingham. Trained at Boston University Hospital, Lingham first worked in "Beantown's" tenement districts before coming to Colorado. Arriving in 1897 with her older sister, she spent four years as a doctor in the Cripple Creek District. In 1901 she became a physician at Hartman Sanitarium six miles outside of Montrose. Because of the scattered population, she traveled to her patients by horse-drawn buggy. On the way to see a patient her horses trotted at a fast clip, sensing the urgency. On the return journey, they jogged along at a comfortable pace as Dr. Lingham slept. Although a worried friend gave her a loaded revolver, she complied with the request to always carry it with her only after she removed the shells and locked them in her desk.[53] Another Colorado woman doctor who came to the practice of medicine later in life was Mary Isabella Hudson Lang, originally a homesteader in Bent County. She moved to Eads after a broken hip made performing ranch chores too difficult. In town, she owned the drugstore and practiced medicine after receiving a Colorado license in 1914. Traveling by horse and buggy, by train, and on foot, Lang saw patients up to the day she died in 1929.[54]

AFRICAN AMERICAN WOMEN

Between 1860 and 1920, Colorado's black population increased steadily, with the largest growth occurring between 1860 and 1880. Females constituted less than 8 percent of the black population in 1860; by 1880, they represented nearly 30 percent. That percentage increased to 48 percent by 1890. The majority of Colorado's black population resided in Arapahoe, El Paso, and Pueblo Counties, home of three of the state's largest cities: Denver, Colorado Springs, and Pueblo.[55]

When Ruth Flowers moved to Boulder in 1917, there were only sixty black families in town. That group included only twenty males because there were few jobs for black men in Boulder. Instead, the men worked in Denver or worked on the railroad as dining and sleeping car porters. When they had time off, they returned to their families, but in the meantime women kept Boulder's black community together. As Flowers recalled, they were "the backbone of the church, the backbone of the family, they were the backbone of the social life."[56] Black communities were segregated and restricted to the poorest part of town; Methodist and Baptist churches were the centers of their social lives. Barred from movie theaters, Flowers and her sister visited friends who owned a piano. Another favorite activity was hiking.[57] Although black men had to leave Boulder to find work, the existence of the university combined with Boulder's affluence meant traditional jobs were available for black women as cooks, maids, and laundresses.

The experiences of black women in Denver were similar to those of their black sisters in Boulder. In 1909 two-year-old Sarah Sims came to Denver with her parents. Her father, a foundry worker, felt the western city had more opportunities for advancement than his hometown of Atchison, Kansas. Although there were more jobs for black men in Denver than there were in Boulder, segregation and discrimination were just as prevalent. One difference, though, was the existence of the YWCA. Although basically a white philanthropic organization, one branch in Denver was all black. The YWCA and YMCA sponsored picnics, summer camps in the mountains, and sports days. The YWCA also encouraged young black women to join the network of women's clubs. Sims and others formed the Yakawana Club, which gave food baskets and coal to needy families. They held bake sales, teas, and dances to pay for the items they gave away.[58]

Although most black women were mired in domestic service, a few were able to combine business acumen with a sense of their culture to become highly successful. One case in point was Madame C. J. Walker. Born Sarah Breedlove, she was orphaned at age seven, married at age fourteen, and a mother at age seventeen. Her husband died after three years of marriage. In 1905 she joined her sister-in-law, Lucy Breedlove Crockett, who was living in Denver with her four daughters. Breedlove found a job as a cook in a boardinghouse, earning thirty dollars a month. She sold Annie Pope-Turnbo hair products on the side and created her own formula for hair care products for black women. She peddled her products door-to-door and placed ads in the *Statesmen* newspaper.

After she married C. J. Walker in 1906, she took the moniker Madame C. J. Walker and began marketing Madame Walker's Wonderful Hair Grower products.[59] Traveling south from Denver to Colorado Springs, Pueblo, and Trinidad, she touted her unique formula and trained African American women in hair care. Walker's daughter, A'Lelia McWilliams, came to Denver to take care of the Colorado business while Madame and C. J. Walker left to market their mail-order business. In 1907 Madame Walker closed the Denver store to concentrate on the more lucrative southern and northern US cities. As she parlayed her formula into a fortune, Madame Walker contributed substantially to homes for the aged in St. Louis and Indianapolis, the National Association for the Advancement of Colored People, and scholarships for female students at Tuskegee Institute. One of the wealthiest self-made businesswomen in the United States, she had homes built in

New York City and at Irvington-on-the-Hudson. Troubled by hyperten-
sion, Walker died in 1919. Her philanthropic gifts continued after her death
through a trust fund that provided for the establishment of an industrial
and mission school in Africa and bequests to black orphans' and old folks'
homes, branches of the Young Women's Christian Association, and private
secondary and collegiate institutions.[60]

Of course, one did not need to be as wealthy as Madame C. J. Walker to
be charitable. At the other end of the economic spectrum was Julia Greeley.
She was born into slavery, freed during the Civil War, and brought west from
St. Louis by Sarah Pratte Dickerson Gilpin (wife of Territorial Governor
William Gilpin). A devout Catholic, Sarah Gilpin was the catalyst for the
former slave's conversion to Catholicism. Greeley attended the old Catholic
Cathedral on Stout Street for a few years but switched to Sacred Heart after
its establishment in 1879. She became the church's most enthusiastic, pious,
and dedicated layperson. Each month she delivered copies of the Catholic
periodical *The Messenger of the Sacred Heart* to every Denver firehouse and
gave the firemen, both Catholics and non-Catholics, other Catholic literature. As regularly as clockwork every year, she garnered fifty subscriptions to
the *Messenger* and sold almost 200 Catholic almanacs.[61]

Even though she herself was poor, having lost her life savings when a
Denver bank failed, Greeley constantly visited the poor and gave them assistance. She aided poor white people as well as blacks, although she was sensitive to the fact that whites might be hesitant to receive aid from a "Negress"
and especially reluctant for their neighbors to know about it. Therefore, she
delivered the goods she begged for on their behalf to their homes at night.
Policemen reported seeing her with mattresses, a baby carriage, coal, and groceries as she made her rounds in the parish.

Greeley, single and childless, loved children and was always available to
look after the children of parish mothers. She earned ten to twelve dollars
a month sweeping and dusting Sacred Heart Church every week as well as
doing other odd jobs. Loved by many, especially the Catholic sisters to whom
she gave so much, the aged Negress was considered beautiful by those she
helped. When Mother Mary Pancratia Bonfils, founder of Loretto Heights
College, died, Greeley went to the Sacred Heart rectory and arranged to
have a High Mass sung for her soul. "She was good to me," she said. "She told
me that I would be White in Heaven."[62]

Greeley died on July 7, 1918, the day of the Feast of the Sacred Heart.
Unlike the deaths of most blacks in the capital city, hers was well-noted,
written about in the *Denver Catholic Register* and mourned by hundreds

of Denverites. She was given the highest honor possible for a deceased lay-person when her body lay in state in a Catholic church, a first in Denver's history. The city's rich arrived in limousines and touring cars to pay their respects. The poor whom she had helped with her generosity flocked to the chapel in throngs. At Mount Olivet Cemetery, Greeley was buried in the Franciscan habit as a member of the Third Order of St. Francis at St. Elizabeth's Church.[63]

AFRICAN AMERICAN AGRICULTURAL COMMUNITIES

Like Greeley, most African Americans in Colorado lived in large cities, but blacks also established two notable agricultural communities. On the eastern plains of Colorado, one group of settlers tried to scratch out an agrarian life in Weld County thirty miles east of Greeley. The Dearfield Colony was founded by Oliver Toussaint Jackson in 1910. The name Dearfield was suggested by Dr. J.H.P. Westbrook, an early colonist. It was adopted because the land would become very dear to the homesteaders. Many of the settlers had little agricultural experience, but by using dry-land farming techniques and raising livestock and poultry, they established a tenuous hold on the prairie land. In 1921, the *Weld County News* reported that 700 people inhabited Dearfield. The improved lands were worth $750,000, with livestock and poultry worth another $200,000. Annual agricultural production was valued at $125,000.[64]

At least eight single women homesteaded at Dearfield. Olietta Moore's widowed mother and her aunt were two of those women. Her mother, who worked in Denver, homesteaded 160 acres so her grandfather would have a garden in which to putter and grow corn. Her aunt, a teacher, homesteaded because no one was hiring black teachers in Colorado. In the 1930s the community was reduced to nearly nothing by drought, dust storms, and the Great Depression. By 1950 Dearfield's lone inhabitant was Jennie Jackson, Oliver's niece, who had stayed in hopes that others would return. No one did, and when she died, tumbling weeds and blowing sand buried the story of Dearfield for decades.[65]

A lesser-known black colony was founded eight miles south of Manzanola by sisters Kitty (Lanore) and Jose (Josephine) Rucker. Established in 1912, the colony—like many in arid southeastern Colorado—struggled the first few years but by 1915 was prospering. Families built their own dugout homes, six feet deep with a fireplace and scant furniture. Settlers planted crops and raised cattle. Some men joined the local cattlemen's association.

George Swink, a successful white rancher, let them haul water from his wells and loaned them his tools. At its height the colony numbered approximately thirty families, or 100 residents. Its Prairie Valley School housed grades one through eight. Some students continued their education at high schools in Manzanola, Pueblo, and Colorado Springs. The year Prairie Valley School opened, Lulu Craig, the daughter of former slaves, moved to Manzanola with her husband and children. Craig had been a Kansas teacher since she was eighteen. She taught at Prairie Valley and other area schools until her retirement in 1939 at age seventy-one. Like other agricultural communities, the black colony at Manzanola suffered immensely during the Great Depression and eventually succumbed to the harsh realities of dry-land farming. In 1933, with only six remaining resident families, the school closed. Lulu Craig was one of the few still living on the original land at the time of her death in 1972 at age 104. By the mid-1970s all the residents had moved away, leaving few traces of the colony's existence as a black community.[66]

"PICTURE BRIDES"

Some Kosuge was one of many Japanese "picture brides" who came to the United States primarily between 1907 and 1921 to marry Japanese men who had immigrated years earlier to work in the mines, on the railroads, or in the fields. Also arriving from Japan in 1912 was Tomi Ogawa. She came to the United States reluctantly to marry Minosuke Noguchi, a man fifteen years her senior. Ogawa had been attending the Women's University of Japan for two years and wanted to complete her education. As the daughter of a prosperous family in Japan, she had been enjoying a comfortable life—playing tennis, arranging flowers, and mastering musical instruments. However, when the family fortune was wiped out, she was sent to Colorado to pave the way for her younger brothers to follow and rebuild the family fortune. A dutiful daughter, Ogawa followed her parents' dictates. In the United States she discovered that her husband had once attended college and, rather than approaching farming as a way to simply survive, he viewed it as a creative endeavor, often experimenting with new crops. Although strangers to one another prior to their marriage, the couple soon discovered that they were united in their pursuit of beauty and grew to love each other.[67]

In 1905 Matsu Kobayashi left Japan for Rock Springs, Wyoming, to join her husband, Seiichi (Harry), who was working for the railroad. They moved

FIGURE 6.5 *Japanese men greatly outnumbered Japanese women in Colorado, so their only hope for marriage was a picture bride. Courtesy, Denver Public Library Western History Collection, Cyril F. Norred, X-21645.*

to Sterling, Colorado, when the sugar factory was built there. As one of the earliest Japanese women in the area, it fell upon Kobayashi to cook for the growing number of single Japanese males moving to the region to work in the sugar beet industry.

Because she knew having more women nearby would lighten her load, she began arranging marriages.[68] One marriage she arranged was between Tsuchi Tanabe and Kansuke Kinoshita. Nineteen-year old Tanabe had immigrated to Colorado to be reunited with her husband, who had left Japan the previous year shortly after their wedding. But after they were reunited her husband died, so Kobayashi arranged for Tanabe to marry Kinoshita, a man twenty-three years older than she. They were married for fifty-three years before he died at age ninety-five. The couple had fourteen children. When Tanabe died in 1980 at age eighty-one, she left behind twenty-eight grandchildren and nineteen great-grandchildren.[69]

Another picture bride, Ai Wada, left Hiroshima to marry Hirosaku Tomita, who in 1899 was one of the first Japanese men to settle in the South

Platte area of northeastern Colorado. Like many other picture brides, Wada was many years younger than her husband. They worked side by side as wage laborers in the sugar beet fields near Proctor until they were able to buy their own land near Merino.[70]

The first Japanese men Charles Koike recruited to the Pueblo steel mills were single. They were soon joined by their own picture brides. When Hanaye Todoo Kameoka joined her husband, he was able to move out of the Robinson Hotel where single Japanese men lived. Mary Yagami's father worked in the Pueblo steel mill before being hired by the railroad in La Junta and later the Swink sugar factory. After his marriage, the family farmed and opened a produce stand west of Swink.[71]

COAL MINERS' WIVES: DOMESTICITY AND MILITANCY

Japanese agricultural workers were not the only men to send for picture brides. In southern Colorado, eastern and southern European immigrant miners went to great lengths to secure brides. Some of these men were already engaged to women from their hometowns. Other immigrant women came after being persuaded by stories of hundreds of eligible miners seeking wives. Maria Batuello came at the urging of her aunt, who was engaged to a Colorado miner. She sent a picture of herself to her future uncle, who showed it to his best friend. Eight months after she and her aunt arrived in Walsenburg, Batuello married her uncle's friend. Another woman, arriving at the boardinghouse of her husband-to-be, decided she did not like the looks of him, so she chose another boarder to marry. The jilted man had paid her passage to Colorado, so her new husband had to repay him.[72]

Mining accidents, maternal deaths, and disease left widows and widowers with attendant children. Remarriage was common. Bill Massarotti recounted the beginning of his second marriage. A friend arranged for him to meet a widow with two small children. She greeted him with "you're doing pretty good." He proposed, and they were married one month later.[73]

Although the men earned wages, their wives were responsible for everything else. A healthy, well-fed miner worked hard and received the highest pay. His working day began when he entered the mine and ended when he walked out. In contrast, his wife's workday began when she rose before him and ended when she collapsed into bed eighteen or twenty hours later. A miner's wife prepared three meals a day from scratch for her family and, in some cases, for boarders also. Mining was a physically taxing job that required consuming large amounts of food. In the morning, a wife prepared two meals. Breakfast consisted of eggs, meat, bread, and coffee. Lunch was assembled in a bucket—water and fruit in the bottom half and dairy products, meat, and bread in the top half. Josephine Bazanelle packed her husband's bucket with sliced bread, cheese, salami, boiled eggs, and fried leg of cottontail. Caroline Tomsic included sandwiches, pork chops, and bread for her husband's lunch.[74]

Although camp residents shopped at the camp store for flour, sugar, and coffee, they grew most of their produce and hunted and fished for much of their meat. Almost every yard had a garden that often yielded enough fruit, vegetables, and herbs to last through the winter. Rabbit hutches and chicken coops were common. The gardens and animals were women's purview. Men fished and hunted wild game such as squirrels, jackrabbits, and birds.

Although maintaining a mining household was grueling, miners' wives—like their ranching or farming counterparts—also worked to supplement the family income. Such work was especially critical during mine shutdowns or strikes. Taking in boarders was the most common job. Wives also took in laundry and cleaned houses. In southern Colorado, Angela Tonso always had boarders in her home. She charged three dollars a week to feed them and do their laundry. Beatrice Nogare took care of her father, brothers, and six additional boarding miners.[75] Other miners' wives worked as servants for the wives of company managers. Those jobs did more than bring in wages. A pit boss assigned workplaces ("rooms") at the face of the coal mine. Because miners were paid by the ton, a good room could mean the difference between a living wage and starvation, so some men bribed the pit boss with their wives' unpaid labor to secure a good room. Labor organizer Mary Harris "Mother" Jones was all too aware of this practice. Speaking to a group of miners' wives in Starkville, she was greeted with applause when she said, "Did Jack ever tell you, 'Say Mary, you go down and scrub the floor for the superintendent's wife, or the boss's wife, and then I will get a good room.'"[76] Single daughters also contributed income to the family. Twelve-year-old Emma Zanetell did laundry for coal-camp residents in Las Animas County.[77]

In addition to their daily back-breaking work, women suffered from a lack of labor-free recreational outlets. Weddings, family celebrations, and religious feasts—all of which required women's preparation, cooking, cleaning, and child care—only added to their chores. While middle-class women formed literary clubs, attended movie theaters, and enjoyed automobile rides to parks, miners' wives remained isolated by day and exhausted at night. To survive required "a certain toughness, strength, and resiliency."[78]

Most of the time, such individual resilience and collective unity remained inconspicuous, if not invisible. Women went about their daily work, spiritually and materially supporting their husbands and families and helping other women in the community who were ill or incapacitated. But during periods of labor unrest, women's underlying strength came to the surface. Women participated heavily—and often militantly—in strike activities. During the 1903 strike a crowd of women attacked a man supervising the demolition of company housing from which striking miners had been evicted. The bitter strike in 1913–1914 elevated women's militancy to a new level. A group of Segundo women attacked a pro-company priest, forcing him to flee to safety. At the Walsen camp, female picketers assaulted a track layer who had refused to join the union. They rolled him in the mud, kicked him, hit him with a heavy bucket, and broke his nose.[79]

Colorado's Southern Coal Field is situated on the east side of the Rockies in Las Animas and Huerfano Counties. In the early twentieth century, John D. Rockefeller's Colorado Fuel and Iron Company (CF&I) was the region's largest operator. Most miners lived in canyons where erosion exposed the coal seams. They and their families lived in company towns and bought food at company stores. Supporting townspeople—the doctor, priests, schoolteacher, and law enforcement officials—were usually company employees. In September 1913 members of the United Mine Workers (UMW) announced a strike after mine operators refused their demands. Approximately 90 percent (10,000–12,000 miners and their families) of the workforce struck. Forced out of company housing, workers moved their families to union tent colonies on the plains. Ludlow, the largest colony with 200 tents, housed 1,200 miners and their families. In the winter months that followed, mining families struggled to survive.

Mother Jones spent time in the Colorado coalfields. In January 1914 she was "deported," only to return to Trinidad where she was arrested. Two hundred women marched in protest. They were met by 100 soldiers on horseback. Ordered to halt, the women instead inched forward. General John Chase ordered the troops to charge after the women laughed when he was thrown by his spooked horse. Swinging rifles and sabers, the soldiers scattered the protesters who, in their flight to safety, found sticks and bottles to use against the men. At the end of the day, women from Trinidad's tent colonies met and formed the Women's Voting Association of Southern Colorado to protest the militia's presence.

As the months dragged on, the pattern of labor strife established only a decade earlier repeated itself. Governor Elias M. Ammons dispatched the

FIGURE 6.6 *When striking miners and their families were expelled from company housing during the Ludlow strike, the Western Federation of Miners set up a tent colony in Las Animas County. On April 20, 1914, National Guardsmen set fire to the tents. Women and children, who had taken refuge in pits dug under the tents, suffocated. Courtesy, Denver Public Library Western History Collection, Z-217.*

National Guard, which detained UMW leaders without charges and periodically raided strikers' camps. As CF&I replaced National Guard troops with company guards, tensions intensified. The six-month stalemate ended on April 20, 1914, when a detachment attacked Ludlow. The militia sprayed machine gun fire into the colony and set fire to the tents. Mary Petrucci awoke the next morning surrounded by the dead bodies of her three children, two women, and eight other children, all of whom had sought safety in a pit under one of the tents. Suffocated in this "death pit" were six children under age five, four under age nine, and one eleven-year-old. Gunfire killed union leader Louis Tikas, along with James Fyler and John Bartotti.[80]

When members of other tent colonies heard of the massacre, they attacked and destroyed mines. During the ten-day guerrilla-style war that followed, Angela Tonso and other women smuggled guns past militia checkpoints. More than a thousand miners fought along a forty-mile front between Trinidad and Walsenburg. An equal number of women held a sit-in outside Governor Ammons's office in Denver to demand that he request federal aid from President Wilson. State senator Helen Ring Robinson and Representative Alma Lafferty led the Women's Peace Association in a day-long vigil. A besieged Ammons capitulated. Although the strike dragged on for another seven months, US Army soldiers eventually brought order to the Southern Coal Fields.[81]

Although it ended in defeat for the UMW, the strike focused national attention on the Colorado coal camps. Mary Petrucci, hoping to secure "a better place for all babies," joined Mary Thomas, Margaret Dominski, and Pearl Jolly in speaking across the United States about conditions in the Colorado mines.[82] Midway through the tour, however, Petrucci—who had lost all her children in the Ludlow disaster—was unable to continue. Before returning to Colorado, she told a reporter: "I used to sing around my work and playing with my babies. Well, I don't sing anymore. And my husband doesn't laugh as he used to. I'm twenty-four years old and I suppose I'll live a long time, but I don't see how I can ever be happy again. But I try to be cheerful on account of my husband. It is so hard for him when he comes home from work to find only me in the house, and none of the children."[83]

The public's horrified reaction prompted the US Commission on Industrial Relations to investigate Colorado mining conditions. Recognizing that public opinion was against the mine owners, Rockefeller announced that employees would be given a grievance procedure and be allowed to elect representatives to joint worker-management committees to address working conditions, sanitation, and safety. In 1915 the state legislature created the Colorado Industrial Commission, which had the power to investigate all disputes over wages, hours, and working conditions. Although it was a step forward, the commission was only marginally successful. Strikes throughout the next decade proved that there was still a long way to go to secure the "better place for all babies" of which Mary Petrucci dreamed.

A DEARFIELD COLONIST: ERMA DOWNEY INGRAM

In 1918 Henry William Downey, his wife, Nellie Weyms-Downey, and their three children—nine-year-old-Ralph, five-year-old Erma, and two-year-old Frankie—settled in the African American colony of Dearfield, Colorado. Henry's sister, Ada, and her husband, Walter, owned property in the community and needed someone to live on it and farm the land. For the next seven years, the Downeys struggled to make a living. They grew corn, potatoes, and pinto beans and raised milk cows, hogs, turkeys, and chickens. Henry Downey worked as a foreman for the Union Pacific Railroad while his wife and children tended the farm crops and animals. As Ingram later recalled, the family did whatever was necessary to eke out a living: "My mother and my brother took care of what little crop that come in. And then also, the people on the other side of the ditch where they have irrigation, when potato crop come in, we—my sister and I—would go before them, after they had plowed the potatoes up, and shook the potatoes off the vine. And my mother and father and my brother would pick. They paid them by the peck . . . And so that's another way they had money."[84] Another resident, Sarah Fountain, explained, "There was too much for women to do in their homes and fields to hire out—those dry fields took all their effort. Money came from crops and men working outside . . . Every household expected the woman in the home to do the work. A woman works everywhere, she worked in the home, would put her cooking on before she went to the field, and then came back and tended to it, serve it, and if necessary go back out to the fields, or milk the cows."[85]

The Downeys worked land owned by the Pritchards and the Danforths. Her parents wanted to buy ten acres of land of their own for $300, but even with Henry's railroad salary, they were never able to afford it. However, they always had plenty to eat because, in addition to raising chickens and turkeys, they also milked the cows and sold the cream. The noonday meal was the biggest meal of the day, which also meant it generated the most dishes. Nellie Weyms-Downey served fried chicken, potatoes, green beans or pinto beans, and corn. Greens were gathered by the riverbanks. During the winter there were few vegetables on the table, which held plenty of milk, tea, coffee, and sugar. Weyms-Downey always made bread pudding and donuts, her daughters' favorite. Turkeys were dressed for holiday meals. Leftovers from

FIGURE 6.7 *Dearfield Colony was founded by Oliver Toussaint Jackson, an African American, in 1910. In 1921 it boasted a school, a church, and improved lands worth $750,000. Courtesy, City of Greeley Museums, Permanent Collection, Greeley, CO.*

the noon meal provided the evening meal. Henry made a wooden trough and put spaces in it; as the water ran through, Nellie put the leftovers in a pot in the trough where the cold water kept it cold until the next meal. That meal "was fun 'cause we didn't have so many dishes to wash as the last. But that midday was dishes, pots and pans and you name it. And of course my sister and I caught the dishwashing [chores]."[86]

With her father working for the railroad, Ingram's mother acquired skills she may not have needed in an urban setting. Nellie carried a shotgun with her out in the yard or garden. Ingram recalled her mother shooting a rattlesnake and having the gun's "kickback" knock her to the ground.[87]

As was common and even necessary for survival, everyone pulled together in Dearfield. The children attended a one-room schoolhouse. They either walked to school or, in inclement weather, drove a one-horse buggy. Children were watched over by whatever adults were around and banded together to butcher hogs and divide the meat. Community socials were occasions to relax, catch up on news, and play.

But working and relaxing together did not constitute a panacea for the harsh reality of eking out a living from the arid land. Years of drought were followed by dust storms that ravaged the arid land. Ingram vividly remembered "the dust—you could see it coming. And when it got there you couldn't keep it out of any crack or anything. If you had to go out it was just like you was grinding it between your teeth. Sometime[s] it would clear up and then the next thing you'd look and see it coming—a great big, black dark—and the closer it got to you it just looked like dust . . . It was terrible because it'd get in your food, it'd get in your bed, . . . and you'd have to shake your bed out before you [could] get in it."[88]

By 1925, having had enough, the Downeys left Dearfield. They moved to Denver, where William was hired by the Denver and Rio Grande Railroad. Ingram, who had completed sixth grade in Dearfield, began attending the newly constructed Cole Junior High. Her brother, Ralph, finished ninth grade but quit school when their father was stricken with arthritis and could no longer work. By the time William was well enough to return to his job, Ralph had married and was out of the family home. For many years, Nellie Downey did not work outside the home. Later, she joined other members of her extended family in working for a wealthy Denver family. She sewed their silk pajamas and knitted woolen socks.[89]

Erma Downey married King W. Ingram in Denver in 1937. The couple moved to Terre Haute, Indiana, where they lived for twelve years before returning to Denver to help her parents. The Ingrams had ten children, seven sons (one died in infancy from influenza) and three daughters.[90] King Ingram first worked for the Shirley Savoy before being hired by the US Post Office. Erma Downey Ingram, possibly the last surviving Dearfield resident, died in 2007.

HISPANIC VILLAGE WOMEN OF SOUTHERN COLORADO

Living in isolated villages in the mountains of northern New Mexico and the arid lands of southern Colorado, Hispanics relied on the entire family to survive. While stereotypes of Hispanic women portray them as powerless and submissive, the truth is much different. As historian Sarah Deutsch notes, Hispanic women "not only shared in the community, they were instrumental in creating it, socially and physically, and in sustaining it."[91]

Women were important in creating the physical community. Although men made adobe and built the basic structure of the houses, women plastered them each fall inside and out with a compound made by mixing burned and ground rock with water. Women built fireplaces and outdoor ovens and were also essential in maintaining the physical bodies that inhabited the village. The "most fundamental work of women . . . centered around food in all its stages: production, processing, provision, and exchange."[92] They tended the garden plots, joined with other women to bake bread for special occasions, fed their families and visitors, and exchanged food for services and other food items.

Although their "most fundamental work" centered around food, Hispanic village women were also important in maintaining kinship ties and acting as community healers and midwives.[93] Women reinforced community ties through their actions as mothers, hosts, *comadres*, healers, producers, and consumers. Extended families of parents, aunts, uncles, and grandparents participated in raising the children. New parents usually selected the wife's parents to be co-parents (*comadre* and *copadre*) for the firstborn and the husband's parents for their second child. Co-parents participated in naming the child, acted as chaperones, and weighed in on child-rearing techniques. They were consulted on the choice of the child's mate.[94] In the plaza setting, women were instrumental in maintaining social networks, regularly visiting one another's homes and traveling to other villages to visit kin.

Curanderas (healers) and *parteras* (midwives) were respected members of the village. *Curanderas* used a holistic approach and a variety of medicinal plants (*remedios*) to heal physical and spiritual illnesses. *Remedios* were passed orally from one woman to another. *Parteras* were equally important in the villages. A mother-to-be chose a female neighbor known for her kindness, strength of character, and intelligence to be her midwife. It was generally not a self-chosen occupation. Because the *partera* needed to be available at a moment's notice, the person selected was often an older woman who could leave her family for what might be several days as the mother gave birth and settled in with her newborn. Once selected, a new *partera* apprenticed herself to an experienced midwife to learn as much as she could. Like *curanderas*, midwives charged nothing, accepting as payment (usually in-kind) anything the family would give them. The amount varied between fifty cents and ten dollars.[95]

From the time of their settlement, the villages of southern Colorado and northern New Mexico were isolated from, first, the Spanish and, later, Mexican institutions of government and religion. Just as Anglos had circuit-riding Protestant ministers who visited outlying settlements on a monthly or bi-monthly schedule, Hispanic villages were often visited by a Catholic priest only once a month. In the interim, village women led services. As members of Penitente auxiliaries, they also made Lenten meals, cleaned chapels, and cared for sick members. In addition, Holy Week preparations were the purview of women, who prepared feasts and participated in church services.[96]

Hispanic women's roles faced a challenge in the late nineteenth century. After 1880, encroaching Anglo businesses (railroads and mining companies) and settlers disrupted the lives of Hispanic villagers in southern Colorado. By 1900 another threat was throwing a shadow over the plaza. Protestant missionaries targeted the villages as bastions of Catholicism, while reform-minded Anglo women focused their personal missionary zeal on Hispanic women. Between 1900 and 1914 more than 200 female missionaries moved to the villages of northern New Mexico and southern Colorado.[97] In addition to their Catholicism, the communal nature of Hispanic homes appalled Protestant women. Families slept on the floor and ate from a common dish. As had their counterparts on Indian reservations in southwestern Colorado, female missionaries assumed that a different, more communal society from their own middle-class Anglo upbringing was less moral and more degrading to women. Therefore, they tried to change Hispanic women's homes. They were no more successful than those working with the Indians had been. Although missionaries rejoiced at what they considered victories—Hispanic women adopting Anglo stoves, dishes, and cooking utensils—their impact was less monumental. Similar to Anglo efforts on the reservations, female missionaries were most successful in bringing Anglo medicine and health care to the villages.[98]

Mission schools were also used to convert young Hispanics to Anglo ways. Earlier schools had been staffed by, at best, inexperienced teachers and at worst incompetent ones. In addition, the existence of boarding schools required that Hispanic children be separated from their families. Like the Native Americans, it was no surprise that Hispanic families did not embrace these schools for their children. Prior to 1900, efforts to fill day schools also met with resistance from villagers who did not see the importance of educating girls. After 1900, though, villagers agreed with missionaries who argued that education for both sexes was necessary in the changing world. Ironically, however, missionaries still emphasized domestic skills for Hispanic girls.[99]

Female Protestant missionaries also threatened Hispanic women's status within religion. In their condemnation of what they considered the worship of the Virgin Mary, they attacked a featured role for Hispanic women in the villages. Missionaries provided free services for religious rites, such as baptism and marriage, at a time when priests often required cash payments for the same. This, coupled with the missionaries' everyday presence in contrast to the virtual absence of the Catholic priest, undermined the latter's role in the community. A Hispanic woman who converted to Protestantism lived an existence in limbo, caught between Anglos who did not fully accept her and sister Hispanics who rejected her.[100]

SEVEN
THE PROGRESSIVE ERA
(1901–1919)

In a crowded room at the Astor Hotel in New York City in November 1913, Helen Ring Robinson was introduced as the first woman state senator in the state of Colorado. In a nation in which only eleven states had granted women full voting rights, Robinson was an exotic creature to those awaiting her speech on woman's suffrage.[1] Some were there to be inspired; others were waiting for an opening in which to heckle her. On a lecture tour of five northeastern states, Robinson was forced to rely on skills developed in her earlier career to handle the "antis" in her audiences. She had been an educator at Wolfe Hall and at the Wolcott School, as well as an editor for the *Rocky Mountain News*, so she knew how to draw upon her personal charm, unwavering confidence, and a strong command of the facts to refute her opponents' arguments.

To dispel the physical stereotype of female politicians as women who had "faces like vinegar jugs," the state senator dressed in a dark skirt and white

DOI: 10.5876/9781607322078.c07

Helen Ring Robinson

FIGURE 7.1 *Helen Ring Robinson, Colorado's first female state senator, drew crowds to her suffrage speeches in New York in 1913. Courtesy, History Colorado (Scan #10030252), Denver.*

high-necked blouse adorned with a silver brooch. She customarily wore her long hair piled high on her head in a fashionable bun. Detractors criticized her for trying to fulfill a man's role and for neglecting her family. In response, she reminded them of something she had told a Denver news reporter soon after she was sworn into office: "I am going to be the housewife of the senate. There will be so many men there that I shall let them look after themselves and I shall take it upon myself to look after the women and children . . . I believe a woman who has qualified as a capable mother and housewife can qualify as a capable legislator. I hold my new responsibilities to the people of the state as sacred as I hold my responsibilities to my husband and my daughter."[2]

At the Astor Hotel, Robinson expanded on that theme, telling New Yorkers that every city needed motherliness: "Some of the women want to leave all these things to the men, who have always been proverbially careless housekeepers. Business interests get along very well in the hands of men, but women are more interested in persons. Laws will not get by a woman without her seeing how they will affect the individual."[3] Like other activists for women's rights before her, she used commonly held beliefs regarding women's natural nurturing capabilities to argue that qualities that held her in good stead as a mother would be equally valuable for a female politician.[4]

Two years later, Robinson returned to support New York suffragists. Encountering recurrent criticism of Colorado from easterners, she jumped to her state's defense, emphasizing that it provided an eight-hour day for its cannery workers while the same workers in New Jersey labored "as long as flesh and blood" could stand it.[5]

Back home, Robinson discussed her experience as a novelty from a state seen as backward and uncivilized. Unfazed by her reception from easterners, she explained that she was glad to be heckled because it gave her the opportunity to set the record straight regarding woman's suffrage. Her aim was "to allay that haunting, panicky fear among the men that when the women get the ballot they would take the American home out in the back yard and shoot it full of holes." She knew that some audience members came to see what "sort of creature a woman senator was."[6] After her speeches, they left disappointed because her petticoats and unshorn hair belied their image of a female politician. But the Wellesley College graduate did not disappoint the women voters in her home state. During her two terms as state senator, she pushed for a variety of progressive legislation.

A HEROIC AND PROGRESSIVE WOMAN

The arrival of a new century generated enthusiasm and hope that many of the old problems could be solved in the coming years. In the United States, the period from 1890 to 1920 is commonly referred to as the Progressive Era, a time in which men and women worked vigorously for change. They wanted honest government in the hands of the people rather than in the clutches of Big Business. They favored social reforms that would make life better for people in the cities; they supported improved labor conditions for workers, especially women and children. Muckrakers graphically portrayed abuses by Big Business and municipal governments. Ida Tarbell's *History of the Standard Oil Company,* Lincoln Steffen's *The Shame of the Cities,* and Upton Sinclair's *The Jungle* exposed pervasive abuses in the United States. Awakened by these books, by numerous magazine and newspaper articles, and by their own work with the city's poor, progressives worked for change at all levels of government. Their champion at the national level was President Theodore Roosevelt (1901–1909). His years in office brought to fruition a number of reforms, including the conservation of natural resources and legislation providing for meat inspection and pure food and drugs.

The progressive movement joined professionals in the fields of education, medicine, law, and business with members of municipal agencies, civic organizations, and women's clubs. At the state level, John Shafroth and Edward Costigan were well-known for their reform work. In Denver, notable male progressives Robert Speer and Judge Benjamin Lindsey were complemented by educator Emily Griffith, police matron Josephine Roche, and the intrepid Margaret Tobin Brown. Brown, one of six children of Irish immigrants, is best known as the "Unsinkable Molly Brown" of the 1912 *Titanic* disaster. However, Maggie (she was never known as Molly during her lifetime) was also a philanthropist, political activist, and suffragist. Born in Hannibal, Missouri, in 1867, she moved to Leadville in 1886 and shortly thereafter married James Joseph (J.J.) Brown. In the mining town she helped establish the Colorado chapter of the National American Woman Suffrage Association and worked in soup kitchens that aided miners and their families. Two children, Lawrence Palmer Brown and Catherine Ellen (nicknamed Helen), were born to the Browns. After striking it rich in 1893, the Browns moved to Denver, settling initially at 1152 York Street. Later, they bought a Queen Anne home at 1340 Pennsylvania Street for $30,000.

Brown became a charter member of the Woman's Club of Denver, raised funds for Denver's Cathedral of the Immaculate Conception and St. Joseph's

Hospital, supported woman's suffrage, and worked with Judge Ben Lindsey, whose juvenile court became a prototype in penal reform.

Brown was in Europe with her daughter in 1912 when she found out that her grandson Lawrence was ill. She immediately booked passage on the first available ship, the RMS *Titanic*. On its maiden voyage across the Atlantic Ocean, the *Titanic*'s passenger list read like a Who's Who of the rich and famous. Among the first-class passengers were industrialist Benjamin Guggenheim, millionaire John Jacob Astor IV and his pregnant wife, Isidor Straus (owner of Macy's Department Store) and his wife, and Dorothy Gibson, an American silent film actress. Steerage was occupied by hundreds of immigrants making their way to the United States. On April 15, 1912, after striking an iceberg, the ship floundered and sank. Brown, who had helped other women and children into lifeboats, was finally put in one herself. For six hours the passengers rowed and waited for rescue. Brown, ever mindful of women's capabilities, demanded that the women be allowed to row along with the men. Quartermaster Robert Hichens, in charge of lifeboat no. 6, alternated between panic and resignation. Finally, the survivors were rescued by the *Carpathia*. Safely aboard the ship, Brown comforted other survivors, helped prepare survivor lists, interpreted for other survivors, and organized a relief drive. She also headed the *Titanic* Survivors' Committee, a group of wealthy passengers who raised funds to aid less fortunate passengers and crew members. By the time the *Carpathia* reached New York City, Brown had collected $10,000 from the ship's passengers and *Titanic* survivors. Later, she raised funds to reward Captain Arthur Henry Rostron and his *Carpathia* crew, presenting a loving cup to Rostron on behalf of *Titanic* survivors. Brown was interviewed several times by the national media, which hailed her as a heroine. Although she reportedly replied to a reporter's question as to how she survived the disaster that had claimed about 1,500 passengers by asserting "it was typical Brown luck; we're unsinkable," no real evidence substantiates the quote.[7]

THE PROGRESSIVE WORK OF THE COLORADO FEDERATION OF WOMEN'S CLUBS

In Colorado, Brown continued to support various causes and participate in the Woman's Club of Denver. By 1919 the club was able to cite an impressive list of accomplishments in four areas: libraries and education, health and welfare, youth, and conservation. Because Colorado's Traveling Library project was unique among the nation's federated clubs, the Colorado Federation of Women's Clubs (CFWC) was asked to submit one box of books to the

1902 St. Louis Exposition. When the Library Commission was established in 1903, three of the five members were from federated clubs.

In the area of education, the CFWC sponsored a college scholarship for a needy Colorado girl and urged the passage of bills designed to enhance educational opportunities. Consolidated schools, manual training programs, art and music education, and domestic science classes were advocated. The clubs endorsed bills to increase teachers' salaries, inspect school buildings, and provide for a teachers' pension program. Realizing that their voices would be more readily heard if they were members of the educational community, clubwomen ran for school boards and pushed for the appointment of clubwomen to state educational agencies and university boards. A small sampling of these women includes Ione Hanna (school board member), Anne Shuler (first dean of women at the University of Denver), and Anna Wolcott Vaile, founder of the prestigious Miss Wolcott's School and first woman regent at the University of Colorado. Katherine Craig served three two-year terms as the state superintendent of public instruction.

To benefit the state's youth, women's clubs supported the State Home and Industrial School for Girls, the State Industrial School for Boys, and the State Home for Dependent and Neglected Children. Individual women served as members on these organizations' Boards of Control. Judge Lindsey insisted that "had it not been for the votes of women and their unceasing donations of time and money, few if any of our great welfare measures would have been enacted into law."[8]

An even more extensive list of achievements is found in the area of health and welfare. The Old Ladies' Home, a free employment bureau, free dispensary, and Day Nursery were initiated by clubwomen. The Day Nursery for children of working women, initiated by the Woman's Club of Denver, is now the Marjory Reed Mayo Nursery, named after its later benefactor. Legislation sponsored or supported by the clubs included the State Employment Bureau, the State Board of Charities and Corrections, the Mothers Compensation Act, and the Child Labor Act, both passed in 1912. Through the years, many club members served on the State Board of Charities and Corrections, including the first president, Sarah Platt Decker. After the death of her second husband, Sarah turned her attention, considerable energy, and leadership skills to charity work and the successful 1893 Colorado woman's suffrage campaign. In 1894 she was chosen president of the newly formed Woman's Club of Denver.

Conservation was a favorite area for progressives, especially President Theodore Roosevelt. A passionate champion of conservation, Decker was the only woman delegate Roosevelt appointed to the national convention on the conservation of natural resources in 1908.[9] She was especially proud of the federation's role in the establishment of Mesa Verde and Rocky Mountain National Parks.

Decker's vigor, sense of humor, and easy platform manner impressed clubwomen at all levels, including General Federation of Women's Clubs (GFWC) delegates at their biennial convention in Denver in 1896.[10] Two years later she was elected vice president of the GFWC shortly before her marriage to Westbrook S. Decker, a well-known member of the Colorado bar. She had refused the GFWC presidential nomination in 1902 but accepted it in 1904 after the death of her husband. She served two terms as GFWC president. Her addresses to the federation reveal "a keen sense of the practical, the ability to cut to the core of a problem and devise workable solutions." The president of a New York music club once wrote to her complaining that her club members were bored with singing to themselves. Decker's terse reply—"Try to sing to others. My busy day. Excuse brevity"—was indicative of her practical nature.[11] A year later, after the club had sung in hospitals, orphanages, and schools, Decker received a warm letter of thanks.

Decker employed her many talents in state and city affairs as well. As chairwoman and longtime member of the State Board of Charities and Correction (1898–1912), she was credited with instigating needed reforms in the state penal system. She served as a member of the State Civil Service Commission, as president of the Denver Civic Federation, and as president of the Woman's Public Service League, a Denver civic organization she had founded. In 1912 Decker was being considered for the US Senate until she died unexpectedly that July in San Francisco. In her honor, Denver City and County offices were closed at noon the day of her funeral, and flags were flown at half-mast. A year later, the Denver Public Library opened a branch library, the Sarah Platt Decker Library, at 1501 South Logan Street in her honor.

In addition to the work of strong leaders such as Decker, women's clubs were successful for a number of other reasons. Club members themselves—white, middle or upper class, most of them married—were perceived as responsible mothers, wives, and citizens. It would have been difficult to paint these women as rabble-rousers or rabid destroyers of the status quo. Clubwomen thoroughly studied social conditions, existing laws, and possible solutions to problems. They asked prominent men such as governors, mayors, and judges to address club meetings. Male guest speakers were won over by the women's sincerity, knowledge, and well-placed praise. They were so impressed with Susan Riley Ashley's political expertise that state legislators convened a special evening session to hear her speak on the need for a state home for dependent children, after which the assembly voted in favor of establishing such an institution. Notable progressive men—such as John Shafroth, Judge Benjamin Lindsey, Thomas Patterson, and George Creel—were just a few of the women's supporters and co-reformers.[12] Newspapers regularly published a women's section filled with articles on club activities. In Denver, this section often ran several pages. A final reason for the clubwomen's success was their choice of causes—the rights of children, the aged, the poor, and women.

AFRICAN AMERICAN WOMEN'S CLUBS

Rural women, black and white, were generally too isolated and laden with family and farm chores to form women's clubs for literary study or philanthropic endeavors. But in Colorado Springs and Denver, the situation was different. Although few individual women, black or white, could emulate the fortune and philanthropic contributions of Madame C. J. Walker, African American women—like their white counterparts—established benevolent, social welfare, and social reform organizations. Led by Fannie Barrier Williams and Josephine St. Pierre Muffin, thirty-six women's clubs in twelve states formed the National Federation of Afro-American Women in 1895. That same year Mary Church Terrell organized black women's clubs into the National League of Colored Women. The following year the two groups united and became the National Association of Colored Women (NACW). The NACW soon became the most powerful African American women's organization in the country.[13] As more blacks moved to Colorado cities, black women from other states who had experience with women's clubs began forming them in Colorado. In addition to her work as a suffragist, Elizabeth Ensley was an active clubwoman. In 1904 Ensley founded the Colorado Association of Colored Women's Clubs.[14] Member clubs of the state association—which included the Colored Ladies Legal Rights Association, Colored Women's Republican Club (founded by Ensley and Ida DePriest in 1894), and the Woman's League of Denver—focused on political issues.

By the turn of the twentieth century, as the long-hoped-for civil rights and economic gains were dashed in the repressive post–Reconstruction Era, black leaders turned from full participation in society to preparation for full participation. Although economic advancement and full assimilation continued to be long-term goals, they were superseded by the accepted belief that blacks must first accumulate wealth and develop the virtues of cleanliness, thrift, and high moral character. The argument was that once these goals were achieved, blacks would gain the respect of whites and be "worthy" of full citizenship. African American organizations throughout the country focused on self-help and racial solidarity. Undermining the efforts of black women were the usual scoundrels: southern de jure segregation, northern de facto segregation, the apathy of national white leaders, and racist stereotyping.

A primary goal of African American women's organizations was to combat the prevailing racial stereotype of black women as immoral. To that end, the clubs established in the early years of the twentieth century emphasized self-improvement through the study of art, literature, music, and needlework. The names of Denver clubs show this shift in emphasis: Pond Lily Art Club, Book Lovers Club, Carnation Art Club, and Taka Art and Literary Club. This did not mean they ignored broader issues, such as helping the needy. In fact, members used their skills in needlework, art, and music to raise money for the less fortunate. Between 1900 and 1925, over thirty Colorado clubs were organized, joined the National Association of Colored Women, and positively affected their communities in Denver, Pueblo, and other Front Range cities. Needy families in black communities received coal, clothing, food, and money. In Denver the clubs' crowning achievement was the Negro Woman's Club Home; in Pueblo it was the Colored Orphanage and Old Folks Home, preserved to this day as a National Register historic site. The idea for the home, which is located at 306 East First Avenue and was incorporated in 1907, came from the City Federation of Colored Women's Clubs. Lucille Hargrove served as the home's manager, and Laura Johnson was its matron. Almost ten years later the home moved from First Avenue to 2713–2715 North Grand Avenue. It was later renamed the Lincoln Home in honor of Abraham Lincoln. Operating until 1963, the home was supported by Pueblo's black community and all sixteen Federated Women's Clubs in Colorado.[15]

JEWISH WOMEN

As was the case with African American communities, Colorado's immigrant Jewish population benefited from the philanthropic efforts of its women. Carrie Shevelson Benjamin, born in Russian Poland, immigrated to the United States as a young child. At age fifteen she enrolled in Syracuse

FIGURE 7.2 *Seraphine Eppstein Pisko organized the Denver Jewish Settlement House and raised funds for National Jewish Hospital. Courtesy, Denver Public Library Western History Collection, Z-8004.*

University, where she became the school's first Jewish woman to earn a BA before completing a master's degree. After teaching high school foreign language classes, she married Maurice Benjamin, a manager or clerk in several Denver businesses. A strong believer in women's innate aptitude for charitable work, she joined the Woman's Club of Denver and became chair of its Department of Philanthropy. She was appointed to the State Board of Charities and Corrections and authored several published articles. Eastern European Jewish women rarely held leadership positions in the early days of the National Council of Jewish Women (NCJW). Denver's relatively small Jewish population, however, had a more flexible social structure, providing Benjamin with the opportunity to become the first president of the Denver chapter of the NCJW, a state vice president, and the chairwoman of philanthropy for the national organization.[16]

Another president of the local NCJW chapter was Seraphine Eppstein Pisko, who, like her mother, was also president of the Hebrew Ladies' Benevolent Society. Pisko helped organize the Denver Jewish Settlement House and free kindergarten for Eastern European immigrants on Denver's west side. She served as vice president of the National Conference of Jewish Charities and was a member of the national board of the NCJW. When National Jewish Hospital opened, she accepted a paid position as a traveling fundraiser.[17]

Also working among the Jews on the west side of Denver was Fannie Eller Lorber. Born in Russia, she moved to Colorado in 1896 and married Jacob Lorber, a Hungarian immigrant who owned a successful shoe business. In 1907, with her close friend Bessie Willens and a small group of women in the West Colfax area, Lorber founded the Denver Sheltering Home for Jewish Children. It opened the next year in a rented house, with eight children and a matron. One of the home's primary goals was to provide a Jewish environment for Jewish children and remove them from the proselytizing influence of Catholic and Protestant institutions. The home accepted the most neglected children, those whose parents were unable to care for them because one or both parents had tuberculosis. The home served only kosher food and operated along Orthodox lines in regard to Jewish holidays and religious observance. Lorber served as the home's unpaid president for fifty years until her death. Initially, she raised funds locally, but in 1920 the board decided that the institution needed to go national, as the children came from all over the United States. Lorber was sent to New York, where she opened a local office, hired fundraisers, and began to establish ladies auxiliaries in major cities. Soon, there were 100,000 members nationwide, a true testament to Lorber's hard work and passionate nature. As one person stated, "Whatever Fannie wanted, Fannie got ... She was a very dynamic person."[18] The Denver Sheltering Home eventually evolved into the renowned Children's Asthma Research Institute and Hospital before merging with National Jewish Hospital.

Fundraiser Anna Hillkowitz, a Russian-born immigrant, first worked as a librarian for the Denver Public Library. She and her parents, Rabbi Elias and Rebecca Hillkowitz, had moved to Denver in hopes of improving her father's asthma. An active member of the Young Women's Jewish Alliance, Hillkowitz was soon lecturing for the NCJW. In 1904 the Jewish Consumptives' Relief Society (JCRS) was founded by a group of Eastern European immigrants, many of whom were themselves victims of tuberculosis. Leaders included Anna's brother, Dr. Philip Hillkowitz, and Dr. Charles Spivak. Even before the society opened, she collected furnishings for the early patient tent-cottages. In 1906 she took a leave of absence from her librarian position to become a traveling "field secretary." Earning $200 a month, Hillkowitz solicited contributions in over forty cities during the first six months alone. She spoke to women's groups, federations, and synagogues. On the advice of Dr. Spivak, she concentrated on acquiring numerous small donations rather than seeking large donations from wealthy individuals, as Seraphine Pisko did for National Jewish Hospital.[19]

While Benjamin, Pisko, Lorber, and Hillkowitz concentrated the majority of their efforts on Jewish residents, Ray Morris David was involved in a number of causes. In 1885 she married David David, a pioneer Aspen businessman. When he died, she was left a young widow with five children. In 1914 she was elected president of the Denver section of the NCJW. She was also a quasi–social worker for National Jewish Hospital, assisting former patients in securing jobs, housing, and financial assistance if necessary. This position earned her the moniker "Little Mother of the Poor."[20] In 1915, when the Denver Jewish Aid Society was reorganized, David was hired as superintendent of relief activities. By this time her expertise was also recognized by city and state leaders. She was appointed to the Denver Board of Charities and Corrections, the State Board of Pardons, and the Child Center Committee.

COLORADO WOMEN AND WORLD WAR I

Although the philanthropic projects of individual women and women's clubs and organizations continued during the first two decades of the twentieth century, World War I brought new challenges. The assassination of Archduke Franz Ferdinand of Austria-Hungary in the Serbian town of Sarajevo soon exploded into a war that engulfed the entire European continent and the British Isles. In the United States, President Woodrow Wilson exhorted the American people to be neutral "in thought as well as in deed." However, other forces were stronger than the president's plea. Allied propaganda, strong ties to ancestral homes, and German submarine warfare against all seafaring vessels combined to bring the nation into the worldwide conflict on April 6, 1917. With the declaration of war, munitions, medical supplies and services, money, and soldiers were needed in large quantities. Coloradans quickly exceeded the goals of two Red Cross membership drives.[21] Liberty Bond drives, the YWCA, the Salvation Army, and the American Library Association ("For a million dollars for a million books for a million men") were also well-supported by Colorado citizens. Articles of clothing, medical supplies, entertainment, and food were provided to the Red Cross, servicemen's centers, and hospitals.

Governor Julius Gunter appointed men's and women's councils of defense, both of which consisted of prominent Coloradans.[22] Having proven themselves capable of mobilizing large numbers of women in support of progressive reforms, clubwomen were often appointed chairs of committees. The state chair of the women's Liberty Loan Committee was former state senator Helen Ring Robinson. As a member of the Woman's Club of Denver, Robinson had ties to the statewide network of clubwomen who fervently bought and sold bonds. At an October 1917 meeting of the Denver Fortnightly Club, Mary F. Fisher reported that $6,300 in bonds had been sold in the club's name. In addition, in 1918 the club joined other women's clubs in providing entertainment at Central Presbyterian Church, which raised $1,000 for the war funds.[23]

In addition to the Liberty Loan drives, councilwomen traveled throughout the city appealing to citizens' patriotism and calling for their support. Mass meetings of Denver clubwomen were held at the clubhouse of the Woman's Club of Denver, where in 1918 Beatrice Forbes-Robinson Hale, a representative of Herbert Hoover's Food Administration Board, spoke to 500 women about the necessity of food conservation. When queried by a news reporter, the "rich women of Denver" promised to do their part in this effort: "It is the only fair thing for those who can afford things, to adjust their living to set an example for all. Buying flour will make a proportionately greater hardship on those with small income[s] than with those who can afford luxury. Those who can should certainly ration themselves."[24] To that end, Colorado women observed wheat-less and meatless days, as did women throughout the country.

It was perhaps through their Red Cross work that Colorado women made their greatest impact. Individual women, like Mate Smith Hottel of Longmont, traveled from district to district teaching girls and women to knit and spending hours manning Red Cross offices.[25] Other Coloradans regularly donated money to the Red Cross, beginning with the Belgian Flour Fund and the Belgian War Relief Fund. By 1916 the Red Cross "army" had enlisted hundreds of volunteers for relief work. Because clothes, surgical dressings, and other medical supplies were priorities, women sewed, knitted, and rolled bandages during social gatherings and club meetings. "We dispensed with papers," said one, "and instead . . . worked at our knitting [while] one of our members read American history."[26]

The Red Cross provided canteens and entertainment for military personnel arriving at, stationed at, and departing from cities along the Front Range. Pueblo's Canteen Department was responsible for meeting every troop train that arrived in the southern city. The largest canteen was located at Denver's Union Station. The room was open twenty-four hours a day. "Sammies" received free cigarettes, candy, and stationery. Pueblo's Red Cross chapter had a similar setup. Men marched to a little brown hut one block from the depot for sandwiches, coffee, cookies, fruit, and cigarettes. Jennie Baker, a member of the Council of Defense, "exhausted herself in her work, giving up nearly everything, even her own home. Returning one day, quite worn out, she stopped on her way to bed to write in the dust of her piano, 'I am a patriot.' "[27] Perhaps one of the biggest sacrifices made on the home front was that of Elizabeth Keely, appointed chief of commissariat of the Fifth National Service School at Loretto Heights Academy. She was also in charge of the Union Station canteen and faithfully visited soldiers at Fitzsimons Army Hospital. Ultimately, Keely worked herself to exhaustion and died.[28]

Although the Red Cross Motor Corps was generally made up of young women, some of its officers were older. The *Rocky Mountain News* reported in 1918, "The motor branch reads like a social register of Denver but these society women, volunteering primarily because they are experienced at driving their own cars, mean business."[29] The women took special courses in motor mechanics and auto repair under Tom Botterill, at the YMCA motor school, or in one of the two courses in the Opportunity School garage. They were given communication duties after completing their training.

The first military service center in Denver was the Soldiers' and Sailors' Club at 1436 Glenarm Place, site of the Woman's Club of Denver. In the meantime, the women met at Calvary Baptist Church. Clubs also contributed money to recuperation centers for American soldiers in France. The smaller clubs gave between $10 and $50, while the 356-member Woman's Club of Denver gave $400.[30]

In July 1917, as World War I raged in Europe, the Sisters of Loretto offered their Loretto Heights campus as the location of the Fifth National Service School. The purpose of the school, which was held for three weeks in July, was "to give efficient training to women in caring for the wounded, feeding the hungry, and keeping things going while the men were actively engaged at the front."[31] The school was never intended to train women to be soldiers, though they were lightheartedly referred to as "soldierettes." Compulsory courses for 200 women included Red Cross courses, wigwag (using flags to send messages), military drills, and calisthenics. Living conditions for the women were spartan. For the 105 boarding students (another 20 women commuted, and 70 sisters remained in their own housing), US Army tents were pitched on the western campus between the clubhouse and Pancratia Hall. Officers' quarters were south of the tents, near the tennis courts. For commuters, bus service was installed from the Englewood car line to the academy (the school gained college status in 1918). Women were given plain food, a tin basin of cold water for their ablutions, and an army cot. Boarding students were instructed to bring a handbag and a suitcase containing the bare necessities. Cigarettes were strictly forbidden. Women wore khaki uniforms and stout drill shoes.[32]

According to Mrs. Alexander Sharp, who was in charge of the service school, the coordination of effort and concentration of energy were the chief accomplishments. Girls learned to perform the same task every day regardless of whether they were in the mood, to adapt to working with different people, and to develop a sense of responsibility. The women had a daily routine: up at 6:30 a.m., fifteen minutes for dressing, followed by military calisthenics promptly at 6:45. At 7:30 the women reported to the mess and at 8:00 to police call. Inspection was held at 8:30. Military drill began at 9:00 and continued for thirty minutes. For the next three hours the women attended Red Cross classes. Following mess, there were classes in wireless and plain telegraphy, typewriting, stenography, wigwagging, and knitting. Soldierettes attended lectures, studied, and drilled before evening mess. After dinner, there was another hour for studying and voluntary drill. Taps was played at 9:30 p.m. At the end of the camp, the women took examinations.[33]

In addition to the Fifth National Service School held on its campus, Loretto Heights sisters, students, and alumnae organized under the name

FIGURE 7.3 *Loretto Heights Academy (later College) founded a service camp during World War I. Sisters of the Order and laywomen rolled bandages for the Red Cross. Day and boarding students trained as "soldierettes." Courtesy, Denver Public Library Western History Collection, George L. Beam, GB-7545.*

Loretto Heights Auxiliary for the Red Cross, knit 350 items, and made 50 hospital wraps and 600 surgical dressings by April 1918. For the War Saving Stamp and Liberty Loan drives, several members of the Loretto Heights Alumnae Association served as leaders, while students at the academy invested in War Savings Stamps and held monthly Thrift Stamp days. The families of students invested nearly $7,000 in Third Liberty Loan Bonds. The school also supplied nearby Fort Logan with books and magazines.[34]

As the war drew to a close, women who had been active in the efforts on the home front envisioned women's continuing involvement in state affairs. Carrie O. Kistler, chair of the Women's State Council of Defense, suggested establishing local bureaus for placement of released army personnel, a listing of jobs so women who no longer had war work could find employment, and the continuation of thrift and economy—habits developed during the war years. Realizing that demobilization would increase the need for local charities, she advocated drafting experienced women into permanent social work. Unfortunately, Kistler was generations ahead of her time, and nothing came of her suggestions.[35]

INFLUENZA EPIDEMIC

The ink on the Versailles Treaty was scarcely dry before another calamity struck the world. From 1918 to 1919, the Spanish influenza epidemic (so named because at the time it was erroneously believed to have originated in Spain) spread worldwide, killing between 20 million and 40 million people. The pandemic affected everyone, although it was particularly deadly for those between ages twenty and forty. Throughout the United States, those lucky enough to avoid infection had to deal with public health restrictions imposed to contain the spread of the disease. Businesses, churches, and schools were forced to shut their doors, and stricken citizens were quarantined in their homes, while brave residents went about their business wearing gauze masks provided by public health departments. As the pandemic spread, as many as 675,000 Americans died. In Pueblo, the first flu case was reported to the City Health Office on October 5, 1918. Soon, St. Mary's Hospital, established in 1891 by the Sisters of Charity of Cincinnati, was so overcrowded with influenza-stricken patients that the sisters gave up their beds to the ill. Although public places were ordered closed, by the spring Pueblo County had more than 5,000 influenza cases. A shortage of nurses compounded the problem, so schoolteachers were called into emergency service to dispatch nursing care to over 2,400 people in the community. Some homes also received clothing, drugs, and food. At the request of the local Red Cross chapter, Pueblo opened an emergency hospital. A community kitchen was also established under the joint direction of the Red Cross, the Women's Council of Defense, and the City of Pueblo. The Women's Motor Corps of the Service League delivered meals provided by the Domestic Science Department of Central High School. In a single day, the garment department made over 500 pneumonia jackets and 4,000 gauze masks.[36] By February 1919, the worst of the epidemic was over.

NATIONAL EQUAL SUFFRAGE

Although the first two decades of the twentieth century were filled with tragedy, violence, heartbreak, and toil, by 1920 the nation's women finally had something to celebrate. Congress ratified the Nineteenth Amendment, giving women throughout the United States the right to vote. After more than 150 years of struggle by thousands of women and a variety of local, state, and national organizations, the so-called Susan B. Anthony Amendment finally gave women of other states the same voting rights enjoyed by their sisters in Colorado and other western states. Unfortunately, the high hopes that the progressive reforms of the first two decades of the twentieth century would continue into the 1920s were quickly dashed. As the doughboys of World War I returned home, the United States quickly withdrew into a cocoon of isolationism and nativism. For Colorado women, the next ten years offered a dichotomy of freedom and repression, of opportunity and challenge.

FROM TEACHER TO SENATOR: HELEN RING ROBINSON

Helen Ring was born in Eastport, Maine, the daughter of Thomas and Mary (Prescott) Ring. After graduating from Wellesley College, she came to Denver, where the "Yankee schoolmarm" first taught a subscription school in a room on Larimer Street.[37] She later taught at Wolfe Hall and the Wolcott School for Girls. In 1902 she married Ewing Robinson, a Denver attorney. Moving from teaching to writing, she joined the staff at the *Rocky Mountain News* as an editorial writer and the staff of the *Denver Times* as a book critic.[38]

Robinson was a prominent member of the Women's Independent Party, but it was under the Democratic Party flag that she won a state senate seat in 1912, serving from 1913 to 1917. As an anomaly in the male-dominated world of politics and a strong supporter of woman's suffrage, Robinson was in high demand as a public speaker. At the conclusion of her speeches, Robinson answered questions from audience members. Sometimes the lack of reasoning implicit in someone's question left her no choice but to make an equally illogical reply. In Hartford, Connecticut, for example, a man argued that women should not be in the legislature because they had never been there before. He reasoned that the fact that there was only one woman to thirty-four men in the Colorado Senate proved that no woman should be there. Robinson replied: "I asked him what inference he would draw as to the general fitness of women from the fact that in another Colorado institution the men predominate much more largely than in the Senate. In the State Penitentiary there are 803 men and only 37 women."[39] Such quick thinking and wit earned her many accolades.

In the Colorado Assembly, Robinson introduced legislation in keeping with her self-proclaimed title "Housewife of the Senate." Bills included financial support for the State Home for Neglected and Dependent Children, the establishment of county boards of education, and minimum salaries for teachers. She successfully called for the formation of a joint house and senate committee to investigate conditions at the Insane Asylum in Pueblo. A true progressive, she introduced legislation promoting safety of food and drugs as well as a minimum wage for women and minors. It passed in 1913.[40] That same year, she investigated the site of the Ludlow Massacre.

Following her term in the state senate, Robinson became enmeshed in the nation's World War I efforts. In addition to acting as chair and director of the women's Liberty Loan Committee, she lectured for the National Food Administration and served on the Federal Commission on Training Camp Activities. During the war, she argued in her book *Preparing Women for Citizenship* that although the war was a terrible thing, it forced women to look beyond their homes and develop a sense of nation.[41] She observed that the war was more effective in teaching women about citizenship and giving them a national outlook "than ten thousand writers could" ever be. She "watched women's minds, so sealed it seemed only can-openers could unclose them, opening everywhere under that War's impact."[42] Unfortunately, Robinson's war work was a tremendous burden. The many demands on her time and energy damaged her health so greatly that she suffered a breakdown after the armistice. She moved to California in hopes of improving her health but returned to Colorado in 1922. She died of heart failure in July 1923. In a deathbed message to newspaper friends, she blamed the overwork during the war years for causing her death.[43] In recognition of her contributions to the people of the state of Colorado, Robinson became only the second woman in history to lie in state in Colorado's Capitol rotunda.

WOMEN OF THE KIVA: VIRGINIA DONAGHE McCLURG AND LUCY PEABODY

In 1900 the Colorado Cliff Dwellings Association (CCDA) was incorporated for the sole purpose of preserving the ancient Indian ruins in the far southwestern corner of the state. It was the culmination of over a decade of work by a number of people, principally Virginia Donaghe McClurg, a transplanted New York writer. But forming the CCDA was only one step toward her ultimate goal.

In 1877 Donaghe moved to Colorado seeking better health. A woman of impeccable heritage (she was descended from colonial and state governors as well as the founders of Yale and Harvard Universities), she was a well-known writer in the East. In Colorado Springs Donaghe opened a select school for young women at the corner of Platte and Nevada Avenues. A New York newspaper asked her to write a story about "buried cities and lost homes." She accepted the assignment, took a train to Durango, and, because of local problems between Indians and whites, was escorted by federal troops to see the Sandal House, a cliff dwelling on the Mancos River. She was the first white woman to visit this Mesa Verde area. Entranced, Donaghe returned in 1886 with her own expedition, which included a guide and a photographer. She published sketches of sites from this trip and gave public lectures on the cliff dwellings. She became more interested in sharing stories about Mesa Verde dwellings than in teaching young girls, so Donaghe closed her school and went on the lecture circuit. In 1893 she spoke at the Columbian Exposition in Chicago; the next year she taught a short course, "The Prehistoric West," at St. John's Cathedral in Denver. After the final lecture, Mary Bancroft, wife of a prominent Denver physician who founded the Colorado Medical Society and the Colorado Historical Society, circulated a petition asking that Mesa Verde be set aside as a national park. The petition was presented to the US Congress, where it was left to wither.[44]

For Virginia Donaghe McClurg (she married Gilbert McClurg in 1889), the fight was just beginning. She persuaded the Colorado Federation of Women's Clubs to appoint a standing committee to investigate and promote the cause of the cliff dwellings. She rightly knew that the federation of 5,000 women would be an invaluable ally. The committee held lectures and paid for the first mapping of the area and the first wagon road to the ruins. In 1900 the committee was incorporated as the Colorado Cliff Dwellings Association. In addition to McClurg, there were nineteen charter members from all parts of the state. She was elected regent (although she often referred to herself as the "regent general"), and Lucy Peabody was elected vice-regent.[45]

The first problem to overcome was the fact that the lands of the Mesa Verde ruins were within the reservation boundaries of the Weeminuche Utes. Thus, it was necessary to procure a lease of this land from the Utes until permanent protection could be provided for the ruins. This task proved rather trying, as the women found it difficult to ascertain which Ute chiefs and sub-chiefs had the authority to negotiate a lease with the association. The lease was necessary to protect the ruins and its artifacts from people such as the Swedish anthropologist Gustaf Nordenskjold, who had visited the ruins in 1891 and taken 600 relics back to Sweden. His book describing his actions infuriated Americans.[46] Another obvious problem in negotiating with the Utes was the language barrier. This was compounded by bureaucratic insistence on the use of certain language for the documents.

McClurg traveled the 450 miles from her home in Colorado Springs to the Ute reservation twice before returning with a signed lease. The first time, the required signators were not on the reservation during her visit. When she made the journey a second time by train and wagon to meet with Chiefs Ignacio and Acawitz, she found the former was ill. She offered him two mustard plasters, followed up with a cherry bounce—an alcoholic drink made with fresh cherries, spices, and corn whiskey.[47] Feeling better, Ignacio signed the treaty that gave the Colorado Cliff Dwellings Association water rights and permission to build and improve roads, collect tolls for the roads, and put up a rest house. The rest house ran for ten years at a cost of $300 a year. Some of the cost was raised by soliciting 25 cents from each member of the Colorado Federation of Women's Clubs.

The year 1901 continued to shine on the women and the association. Gilbert McClurg invited Vice President Theodore Roosevelt to be an honored guest at Colorado's Quarto-Centennial Jubilee of statehood, where members of the association presented him with a prehistoric Indian bowl. Courting Roosevelt appeared even more providential when President William McKinley was assassinated in 1901. As president of the United States, Roosevelt became a staunch supporter of the association's drive to protect the ruins of southwestern Colorado.

McClurg spoke throughout the country on behalf of the cliff dwellings and the association's work. Peabody led a committee that submitted an official report to the CCDA on the restoration and preservation of the Indian ruins. Peabody was well-versed in prehistoric Indian ruins. Schooled in Washington, DC, she had been a secretarial assistant in the Bureau of Ethnology, where she met and married William Sloane Peabody, an executive officer of the US Geological Survey. After his retirement, they moved to Denver. She quickly immersed herself in state politics and women's clubs.

The CCDA made headway in its quest for preservation of the ruins, but by 1904 the members had become disenchanted with the association's board, feeling that the leaders were too independent of the entire group. McClurg tried to placate them by explaining that such independence was necessary to avoid misunderstandings and inaccurate press releases, but the grumbling continued. In late 1905, the situation blew up.[48] McClurg, whose goal had always been to make Mesa Verde a national park, changed course and proposed that it become a state park managed by her CCDA, much as the Mount Vernon Ladies' Association operates George Washington's home. McClurg feared that the US Department of the Interior would permit museums and universities to conduct excavations at Mesa Verde. Peabody was equally adamant that Mesa Verde would do best under federal protection and control. When the two women could not agree, Peabody left the association, taking members with her. While McClurg stayed in Colorado trying to gain support for a Mesa Verde State Park, Peabody headed to Washington to campaign for the Hogg Bill to establish the ruins as a federal park. She emerged victorious when President Roosevelt signed the bill into law in June 1906.[49]

Curiously, McClurg later built her own Indian ruins in Manitou Springs. These ruins replicate part of the Spruce Tree House, Cliff Palace, and Balcony House. A prospectus for the ruins stated: "The Cliff Canyon, near Manitou [Springs] is an exact counterpart of many of the canons in Southern Colorado where the cliff dwellings were made, and the work of carefully removing the whole of Cliff Canyon undertaken. More than a million pounds of rock have been brought to the new location and the houses erected in exact dimensions and appearance, stone by stone."[50] Even today, tourists are confused as to whether these are authentic ruins, rebuilt ruins, or merely a convenient tourist stop.

A HOME AWAY FROM HOME: THE NEGRO WOMAN'S CLUB HOME

By the 1890s Denver was home to nearly three-quarters of the African Americans living in Colorado. Unlike the Chinese and Japanese contingents, in which males greatly outnumbered females, the number of black women nearly equaled that of black men.[51] Families established homes and businesses in the northeast part of the city. For middle-class African American women, the lure of women's clubs was as strong as it was for their Anglo counterparts. Between 1900 and 1925, over twenty clubs were founded in Denver.[52] Like Anglo women's clubs, many were formed with the goal of self-improvement and evolved into clubs in which the major focus was on bettering the community and society at large. Clubwomen formed city and state federations and joined the National Association of Colored Women. One recipient of the clubs' philanthropy was the Colored Orphanage and Old Folks Home in Pueblo. Club activities focused on efforts to develop members' skills as well as their musical, literary, and intellectual abilities; helping the poor and needy; battling discrimination; working with children to encourage higher educational standards; and sponsoring mothers' meetings, girls' clubs, and fundraising activities. Of these efforts, assisting the needy and supporting the Negro Woman's Club Home were the highest priorities.[53]

Georgia Contee of the Self-Improvement Club first suggested the idea of a club home where young black women might stay. Because this was too ambitious an undertaking for one group, she invited other club presidents to consider joining the effort. The seven clubs that responded to the challenge—Taka Art, Pond Lily, Carnation Art, Self-Improvement, Progressive Art, Sojourner Truth, and Twentieth Century—became known collectively as the Negro Woman's Club Home Association.[54]

Between late 1915 and early 1916, the association met regularly. Each club submitted an idea for the ideal club home. Most ideas emphasized a concern for charity, a nursery, employment, education, and the rights of arrested black children. The Taka Club suggested a fundraising campaign, which began with a mass meeting held in July 1916 at Shorter Chapel. On December 16, 1916, the clubs moved into a modern two-story, eight-room brick home at 2357 Clarkson Street.[55] The main floor held the dormitory, and the lower floor housed the nursery. Clubs were responsible for soliciting sustaining members—either individuals or groups who would pay a sustaining fee of twelve dollars—and associate members, who paid six dollars per year toward the home's maintenance. In addition to raising money for the home, clubs contributed whatever was needed, such as dishes, window screens, and lawn rakes for the home and milk, bread, and clothing for the residents. Perhaps most important was volunteering at the home. Members changed diapers, cooked meals, and found inventive ways to save money, such as Lillian Bondurant's suggestion to buy meat wholesale and to contact Oliver Toussaint Jackson, head of Dearfield Colony, to solicit fresh vegetables for the home.[56]

The home's most important staff member was the matron. She was responsible for an infinite number of tasks, especially those that involved the dormitory. Young working women could rent a dormitory room for $1.25 a week, including kitchen privileges (the price rose to $1.50 in 1920 and to $2.00 in 1924). As head of the dormitory and substitute mother to the "inmates," as the residents were called, the matron enforced strict rules that clearly indicated the clubwomen's desire to instill proper training and morality in the girls. The matron opened and closed the building, prepared menus, handled emergencies, itemized weekly reports of transactions, and collected fees for entertainments. In compensation for these duties, the matron received a salary of $40 per month in 1920.[57]

Both the nursery and the dormitory proved successful. In 1921 the association reported to the State Board of Charities and Corrections that the home had four paid officers—one man and three women— including a second matron. Thirty children were cared for in the nursery. The dormitory housed nine girls. The home allowed community organizations to rent its facilities for a $3 fee. Women's clubs were charged 50 cents to hold weekly meetings there. In addition, activities such as Harvest Home (a yearly bazaar), raffles, and a charity ball were held to secure funds. By the early 1920s, concerned about raising funds for the home, the association solicited help from the Denver Federation of Charities. In 1922 it joined the Community Chest.

Other changes occurred at the home during the early 1920s. The need for its dormitory declined after the YWCA sponsored one for black women. This fact, coupled with an increasing need for its nursery, led the association to shut its dormitory and expand the nursery. In 1946 the name was changed to the George Washington Carver Day Nursery. Currently the Mile High Montessori Early Learning Centers–George Washington Carver Day Nursery, the center continues to provide quality child care and education to children from struggling families.[58]

EIGHT

CONFORMITY AND CHANGE

(1920–1929)

In 1914 Charlotte Perry and Portia Mansfield founded a summer dance camp near Nederland. Although the inaugural camp was successful over-all, there were problems. The camp was located too close to Denver, which meant proximity to the peering eyes of men anxious to see "scantily clad nymphs" dancing on the hillsides. At 9,000 feet above sea level, the rarified mountain air exhausted the dancers. Lightning storms frightened campers as well as their leaders, who were not known for their timidness. After all, how many women founded their own dance camp on a shoestring budget, even in the intoxicating Roaring Twenties? Only Perry and Mansfield, defying their parents and conventional wisdom, proved adventurous enough.[1] Unwilling to abandon their dream, Perry and Mansfield crossed the Continental Divide and settled in Steamboat Springs, where they continued to shock and intrigue local citizens who alternately complained about their existence and eagerly sought out news and views of the camp and its denizens.

DOI: 10.5876/9781607322078.c08

FIGURE 8.1 *Dancers, clad in flowing garments, at the Perry-Mansfield Camp captivated the attention of Steamboat Springs delivery personnel and set townspeople's tongues wagging. The innovative camp still operates from its home in Strawberry Park. Courtesy, Tread of Pioneers Museum, Steamboat Springs, CO.*

Although their cows provided milk and their garden provided vegetables for the dining room, Perry and Mansfield purchased meat from neighboring ranches. Delivery boys were treated to a multitude of sights and sounds. Girls and young women not involved in practices rode horses, splashed in the stream, and swam in the lake. Others hiked along narrow paths woven between strands of pine and aspen trees. If practice was in session, delivery boys caught glimpses of dancers clad in skin-fitting tights, sinewy wraps, and flowing chiffon robes.[2] At mealtime, the dining room was a beehive of noise, as laughter and chatter emanated from every corner of the room made of rough-hewn wood. These sights and sounds were duly relayed to friends, who further spread the news. Many townspeople were shocked, but their disapproval did not affect the popularity of the Perry-Mansfield Camp among dancers, as the 1920s proved to be a time of artistic innovation and creativity. That, however, was not the case for everyone.

A DECADE OF CONTRASTS

For American citizens, the password of the 1920s was conformity. The Great Crusade of World War I had only disillusioned progressive reformers and internationalists. The peace treaty process at Versailles and President

Woodrow Wilson's unsuccessful struggle for its ratification had reinforced the views of cynics and isolationists. War-induced nativism not only endured but actually worsened during the 1919–1920 Red Scare, when the Bolshevists became the scapegoat for the country's labor-capital troubles. The public and politicians, seeing Red everywhere and encouraged by the yellow journalism of Randolph Hearst and others, made mass accusations and clamored for the arrest and deportation of suspected troublemakers. The *Denver Post*'s pro-management articles incited such animosity from labor that its offices fell victim to rioting during the Denver Tramway Strike in August 1920. But with little substantial proof of any real Red danger, the scare petered out in the early 1920s. However, this was not the case for nativism or its silent partner, Americanism.

As was true in other states, the influx of large numbers of immigrants influenced state and local politics, demographics, and progressive reforms in Colorado. Starting in the 1880s, as boat after boat disgorged thousands of immigrants from southern and eastern Europe, nativists gained political strength by wailing over the new immigrants' racial inferiority, drinking culture, and non-Protestant religion. One way to counteract the foreigners' different-ness was through Americanization, or assimilation into American society. The federated women's clubs made Americanization their project for 1918–1920. In their efforts to Americanize foreigners, clubwomen realized that they needed to study American government and citizenship. The North Side Woman's Club of Denver invited Emily Griffith of the Opportunity School to discuss the topic, while other club meetings discussed "immigration and naturalization" and "American ideals." The House of Neighborly Service Association in Greeley was founded in 1926 to help Spanish Colony residents adjust to the local culture. It sponsored classes in health, education, arts and crafts, and recreation. Miss Wilson, a trained social worker from West Virginia, established an Americanization school for adult residents.[3]

WOMEN OF THE KU KLUX KLAN

Other Coloradans' response to unassimilated persons was less charitable and more judgmental. Anything or anyone who did not conform was labeled un-American. Traditional "outsiders" in American history—including Jews, blacks, and Catholics—found themselves the targets of the Ku Klux Klan. The KKK, originally established in the South as a social club for former Confederates but which quickly degenerated into a white supremacist group, reemerged in the 1920s. This time, however, it was not simply a southern phenomenon. Colorado, Indiana, Illinois, Kansas, Oregon, and Oklahoma were a few of the non-southern states that experienced the rise of the second Klan. The Colorado KKK appealed to a large number of people who feared more immigration, increased crime, labor unrest, and political corruption. In 1921 Dr. John Galen Locke founded the Colorado Klan. With no substantial counterattack in Denver, the Klan established a stronghold in the capital city. Klan kaverns were also founded in Grand Junction, Trinidad, and Cañon City.

Perhaps it was political expediency, fear of the growing immigrant population and its failure to assimilate, or the desire to recapture the power and notoriety of her earlier years as a reformer that compelled a Denver federated clubwoman to join with other women to incorporate the Women of the Ku Klux Klan. In December 1924 Meta L. Gremmels, Dr. Ester B. Hunt, and Laurena H. Senter filed incorporation papers with the secretary of state for the Women of the Ku Klux Klan. The organization's objectives were given as "the procuring and enforcement of just and equitable laws, upholding the constitution of the United States and the state of Colorado, teaching of respect for laws and law-enforcing authorities, furtherance of American principles, ideals, and institutions, and relief work to alleviate suffering and distress."[4] Only white women over age eighteen were eligible for membership. Two members of the Woman's Club of Denver became top leaders in the Denver Klan. Laurena Senter became imperial commander of Denver Klan No. 1; Dr. Minnie C.T. Love held the office of excellent commander.

Dr. Love—chief medical officer for the Florence Crittenton Home, suffragist, and a member of the Woman's Club of Denver and the Woman's Christian Temperance Union—would at first glance seem an unlikely Klanswoman. However, her passion for children's health and well-being drove her to what many considered extremes. Throughout her medical career, she focused on diseases of women and children. In 1897 she was the foremost figure in helping organize the Babies Summer Hospital (later Children's Hospital). In 1920, stumping for moral reform and Americanism, she won a seat in the state house of representatives. During her time in office she sponsored bills to regulate families and oversee prenatal care. She pushed for health examinations for those wanting to marry to ensure that neither prospective spouse had a venereal disease. Love pushed for laws requiring unwed mothers to breastfeed their babies. Although not reelected in 1922, she was reelected in 1924 with the help of the Klan.

As one of only a few Klanswomen in the state assembly, Love passionately pushed reform proposals. She advocated sterilizing epileptics and the insane because she strongly believed "heredity plays a very important part in the transmission of crime, idiocy, and imbecility."[5] To counteract the influence of the Catholic Church, she led the charge for compulsory public education attendance and introduced a measure that required all orphans to attend public schools. Most measures introduced by Klansmen and Klanswomen in the state house were unsuccessful (largely because the Klan did not have control of the state senate).

Thirty-five chapters of the Women of the KKK were formed in Colorado. In Limon, the Chapter 11 auxiliary was chartered on September 24, 1925, with members from the town and outlying Lincoln County. As outlined in the booklet "Invisible Empire, Women of the KKK," the organization was open only to "true and loyal citizens of the United States of America, being white, female, Gentile person of temperate habits, sound in mind and believes in tenets of the Christian religion, the maintenance of White Supremacy, and the principles of 'pure Americanism.'"[6] The first meeting was held in the Masonic Temple following a Klansmen meeting. The charter was read and accepted, and officers were elected. Women took an oath that was three pages long. Members swore to follow the Klan's constitution, maintain the secrecy of the KKK, pay dues, protect KKK property, and defend the "home, reputation, and physical and business interest of a *swoman and that of a *swoman's family."[7] The membership application card required the woman's name, address, maiden name, and place of birth, as well as her husband's name and business. The applicant also recorded her religious affiliation and that of her mother, father, and husband. Other questions included the length of her residency in the city or community, the number of children she had, and the school(s) they attended. The application card had space for the names, addresses, and phone numbers of three or four references.

In November, fourteen women attended the Limon Klan chapter meeting and voted to pay national dues. Mrs. Wright gave a short talk about her visit to an Iowa Klanswomen meeting. Two new members, Dora Lee Shockley and Maude Preston McConnell, both of Limon, were accepted. At the last meeting of the year, attendance was up to twenty-five women. They voted to make a fifteen dollar donation to Christian Church Orphanage in Denver, the only Protestant orphanage in Colorado.

Attendance was often an issue, though. In January 1926 the chapter agreed that an officer who missed three consecutive meetings without reporting a reasonable excuse to the excellent commander would forfeit her office. In February, only fifteen Klanswomen marched in force to the Baptist Church to hear Reverend Ellyson speak.[8] The white robes they wore had been ordered from the national Klanswomen organization. The order form showed how to measure for length, width, and sleeve length. It also required a woman's signature agreeing that she would return the robe should she sever relations with the Klan.[9]

The Limon auxiliary did not last long. Interest dwindled rapidly through the fall of 1926, perhaps because records show that very little was accomplished at meetings attended by as few as six members. The dissension over leadership and activities that shattered the men's organization also fatally infected the women's Klan in Denver. State representatives and Klanswomen Josie J. Jackson and Metta Gremmels joined with Lutie N. Bosley to form the Minute Women opposite Locke's Minute Men organization. Dr. Love and hundreds of other Klanswomen exchanged their robes for Betsy Ross outfits. Senter and the Denver Klanswomen initially took a neutral stand on the rift between Locke and the Colorado KKK before deciding to support Locke. Although the idea was to have Senter and Love work together, the two rivals were unable to do so. Senter returned to the Denver Klanswomen, taking about fifty members with her. In 1929 the US District Court ruled that the Denver group could no longer call itself Klanswomen unless it obeyed the national organization. Senter, grand dragon of the Colorado Klanswomen, subsequently converted the Denver chapter to the Colorado Cycle Club. The group met in her home and lasted until 1945, although it met only sporadically over the years.[10]

AGE OF THE FLAPPER

While Klanswomen in Limon and Denver fretted about the state of affairs in the United States, other women found the 1920s an exciting time. New technology, the advent of affordable automobiles, economic opportunities in burgeoning white-collar fields, and educational opportunities offered by colleges and universities combined to create a lifestyle befitting the "New Woman." World War I had destroyed the idealism of the early twentieth century and ushered in a desire for fun and frivolity. Fueled by modern products, tempting advertisements, and easy credit, Americans embraced the newness of the decade. For American women who had gained equal suffrage with the passage of the Nineteenth Amendment and helped win the war with their work at home, it was a heady time.

The image of the "flapper" became an enduring icon of the 1920s. Young women bobbed their hair, exchanged hourglass-fitting clothes for boyish knee-length sheaths, and painted their faces. They went on dates unchaperoned, drank illegal alcohol from flasks, and rode in and even drove automobiles. For a young single woman—not yet occupied with a husband, children, and a household to manage—movie houses, speakeasies, amusement parks, and ethnic gathering places were enticing. The emergence of this so-called New Woman of the 1920s sparked heated debates. Mainstream magazines such as *Ladies' Home Journal* and *Saturday Evening Post* offered radical challenges to Victorian notions of female propriety. The *Post* published stories about young, college-educated women who drank gin cocktails and smoked cigarettes. Magazines, books, radio, and the movies created a national culture. Novelist F. Scott Fitzgerald and his wife, Zelda Fitzgerald, were illustrative of this new national culture, as they drank and partied excessively. His collection of stories, *Flappers and Philosophers,* and his novel, *The Great Gatsby,* aptly described the era.

Young working women appropriated movie stars as role models. Modern theaters were as glamorous and appealing as the male and female stars who graced the scenes. Denver was home to more than forty-five movie houses, many of them crowded along Curtis Street between Sixteenth and Eighteenth Avenues. The Colonial, Princess, and Empress Theaters enticed the public with thousands of electric marquee lights. Other cities and towns converted opera houses into movie theaters to draw potential viewers to movies starring Clara Bow, Rudolph Valentino, Mary Pickford, Douglas Fairbanks, and Charlie Chaplin. In addition to theaters, Denver's Lakeside Amusement Park and Elitch Gardens were favorite places to meet beaus, ride the Ferris wheel, and dance away the night.

Although the image of the flapper personified the youthful rebellion of the 1920s, most women were married and more concerned with household matters than with bobbed hair and speakeasies. Electric washing machines, refrigerators, and vacuum cleaners became the rage. Actually adding to housewives' work, the advent of these gleaming new devices created new standards of cleanliness. Advertisements chided a woman who continued to wash clothes using a scrub board and wringer when an electric washing machine would allow her to spend her day in leisure listening to "soap operas" on the radio. Sales of electrical appliances increased as buyers were lured in by promises of cleaner homes and more leisure time. As the number of middle-class households rose, the number of American homes with electricity increased from 14 percent in 1910 to 70 percent in 1930. However, for most households, electricity's promises were not realized during the 1920s. For many families in urban areas, electricity was unaffordable; in rural areas, electricity was not available until the late 1930s.[11]

LIFE IN THE *COLONIAS*

One group of Colorado women who continued to live without electricity were those in *colonias*. Some of those women were American-born, while others and their families were recruited from Mexico by Colorado sugar companies. Company housing in a *colonia* consisted of connected adobe homes or apartments, ten to a row. In Grand Junction an apartment had two rooms with wood floors, two windows, a front door, and one back door. A wood stove provided heat. A single outside water faucet served all the families in the row. Outhouses were located in backyards. As many as fifteen persons from an extended family lived in these apartments. If working, residents were charged little or no rent. Holly Sugar also provided company stores at which workers bought food and clothing at inflated prices. In preparation for the winter months when they would not be working in the beet fields, Hispanic families stockpiled large quantities of food to survive the next several months. They bought flour and sugar in 200-pound cans and coffee in 25-pound cans, as well as large quantities of canned milk. They purchased potatoes, beans, and other vegetables from local farmers and meat from local sheepherders. Men hunted deer in the surrounding hills for winter meals of venison. They hoped this food cache would be sufficient to feed the family through the winter months before the sugar beet cycle of planting, hoeing, thinning, and harvesting began again in the spring.[12]

Sugar beet farming also dominated the South Platte Valley in northeastern Colorado. The Great Western Sugar Company (GWSC) contracted with farmers, taught them the latest techniques, and lent growers new equipment. GWSC first brought in German Russian families from Nebraska who had farming experience. In the early twentieth century, the company recruited Japanese men. By 1916, though, neither group was working as laborers, as they had become landowners and tenant farmers. GWSC began advertising for workers in southern Colorado, New Mexico, and Texas. At first, most Mexican laborers worked the fields and then returned to Mexico, but by the 1920s that situation had changed.

The Mexican Revolution and availability of work in the American Southwest encouraged more workers to stay year-round. Sugar company recruiters enticed Hispanic families to the northeastern beet fields with promises of family garden plots and decent housing. In 1922 a company agent visited the family home of Magdalena Arellano. Although she had a job caring for the children of a wealthy family in Antonito, the rest of her family was unemployed so she, her mother, father, uncle, and aunt moved to Fort Collins. The sugar company paid for their rail fare and an overnight stay

FIGURE 8.2 *Jovita Ortega (left), who married Marciano Aguayo in 1929, and Severa Varela worked in the beet fields near Sedgwick. Ortega and her family moved north when she was a young girl. Every morning she arose at 3:00 a.m. to prepare breakfast and lunch before joining her brothers in the fields. Courtesy, José Aguayo.*

at the Linden Hotel. The next morning they were contracted out to a farmer and moved to a shack on his ranch.[13]

Jovita Ortega and her family also came to northeastern Colorado to work in the beet fields. For Ortega, the days were long and the nights short. Her uncle lit a stove for her every morning at 3:00 a.m. so she could make a hearty breakfast for her many brothers, who had jobs thinning and topping beets. Making breakfast was only the first of her jobs: "After breakfast, at about 4 a.m., I would also go out to the fields to work, but not before making a large stack of tortillas and putting beans to cook. I would return at noon to help my *tia* prepare the noon meal. While the boys rested in the shade, I would wash dishes and then return to the fields with them until it got dark. After dinner, I ironed clothes, finally going to bed at 11 p.m. Oh, those were tough times, so many boys in the family, so many clothes to wash and iron."[14] In all, Ortega worked eighteen to twenty hours a day among working in the fields, cooking meals, cleaning dishes, and washing and ironing clothes.

Pay for beet work varied from year to year and from district to district. Magdalena Arellano earned $18 an acre in 1923. She also worked as a domestic servant, using her wages to buy a house on Howe Street in Fort Collins for $500. Without her husband's knowledge, she arranged a loan and made several payments before he realized they were becoming home-owners.[15] Other beet workers in the northeast lived in housing provided by the farmer to whom they were under contract. Although recruiters promised that farmers would provide decent housing, most was inadequate. Often it consisted of an 8'-by-8' farm shack with a single door and a tiny window.

Better housing was sometimes available in *colonias* built by the Great Western Sugar Company. In 1922 the company branch in Fort Morgan built its first adobe colony, which soon led to the construction of others in Weld County. One of these was the Spanish Colony five miles northwest of Greeley. Families highly recommended by sugar beet foremen for their work ethic were invited to live in the colony. The sugar company contracted with beet laborers to build their own houses of two rooms or more. After a five-year lease, the company required that the residents purchase the home. A benefit provided by both the contract farmer and the sugar company's *colonias* was a patch of land on which beet workers could grow vegetables to can for winter meals. Jovita Ortega, who had married Marciano Aguayo in 1929, eventually had a half block to garden in Sedgwick. Their first home was a one-room shack they shared with three other people. Later, the Aguayos moved to a two-room brick home, but the young mother still had to put her infant daughters in a washtub balanced on two chairs to keep them safe from the rats that patrolled the dwelling. Despite such primitive conditions, Aguayo required all her children to attend school. Those who were old enough to work in the fields were allowed to do so only when school was not in session. Her emphasis on education reaped many benefits for her children. Among them, they earned five masters degrees and one doctorate.[16]

AFRICAN AMERICAN WOMEN

African American families also valued education as a means of upward mobility. There were 284,441 African American women in Colorado in 1930, an increase of 28,371 over the 1920 census. Although they represented less than 3 percent of all women in Colorado, they constituted nearly 14 percent of those employed as domestic servants in 1930. However, they represented less than one-quarter of a percent of women employed in clerical occupations and less than half of 1 percent of women in professional service.[17]

Part of the reason for their paucity in professional occupations was the fact that many professional jobs required a college education, something generally unavailable to women of color. An exception was Ruth Cave Flowers, an African American graduate of the University of Colorado (CU). After her mother's death when she was eleven, Ruth and her sister, Dorothy, were taken care of by their grandmother, Minnesota Waters. In 1917 the three moved from Cripple Creek to Boulder, where the girls attended school. The high school principal vowed that no black student would ever graduate from his high school, so he erased one of Ruth's credits so she did not have enough to graduate. However, Flowers did have enough credits to enroll at the university. She washed and ironed other students' clothing and washed dishes in a restaurant to pay her tuition and help with household expenses. During her last year at the university the wife of CU's president created a job just for her. She became Mrs. George Norlin's upstairs girl. When she graduated, discrimination prevented her from finding a teaching job in the West. Of the 2,875 schoolteachers in Colorado, only 11 were black females, as recorded in the 1930 census.[18] Ruth obtained a job teaching Latin and French at Claflin College in South Carolina before returning to Boulder to take care of her grandmother and earn an MA from CU in French and education.[19]

COLORADO WOMEN BY THE NUMBERS

Although few opportunities existed for Hispanic and black women, the economic sphere widened for Anglo women in the 1920s. Between 1900 and 1930 their main occupations underwent a subtle but important change, reflecting similar changes for women across the United States and indicative of the technological and market changes in the American workplace. Between the 1900 and 1930 censuses, the number of white women gainfully employed in the United States increased gradually by over 10 percent. In Colorado the number rose from 15.6 percent in 1900 to 23.6 percent in 1930.[20] The proliferation of offices, department stores, and telephone exchanges provided jobs for middle-class white women. As women came to dominate these positions, they became dead-end jobs for females rather than an upward path for male workers. Previously, capable clerks had been promoted to managerial positions, much as factory workers were promoted to foremen. But as companies grew in size, managers came from the ranks of college-educated men, leaving the multiplying clerk jobs for women trained in stenography and typing. In time, these entry-level positions were coined "pink-collar" jobs.[21]

Figures for the entire nation reveal that the percentage of women working in domestic service and kindred occupations decreased steadily from 1870 (61 percent) to 1890 (40 percent) to 1920 (less than 20 percent).[22] Likewise, the proportion of Colorado women employed in domestic and personal service decreased from 1870 (70 percent) to 1890 (54 percent) to 1920 (31 percent). However, reflecting the rise of consumerism and the growth in the number of department stores during the 1920s, the number of female store clerks increased from 3,855 at the beginning of the decade to 6,611 in 1930.[23] Saleswomen in department stores enjoyed the social status of white-collar work but earned lower wages than those in clerical fields. Expected to cater to their customers' whims and personalities, some parts of saleswomen's jobs mirrored those of domestic servants, but the freedom to live in their own homes and to interact with coworkers and the public helped compensate for low wages. The vast majority of saleswomen were white and native-born. The same held true for female bookkeepers, cashiers, stenographers, and typists. In 1930 all but 3 percent of women holding clerical jobs were white.

In both the 1920 and 1930 censuses, domestic and professional service categories were numbers one and two, respectively, for female jobs.[24] In 1930, 20 percent of the female labor force in the United States was made up of office workers. Within a decade that number rose to nearly 33 percent. In 1930, over 40 percent of those in the clerical field were stenographers and typists. In Colorado, "clerical, sales, and kindred workers" leapfrogged over "domestic and personal service" and "professional service" to become the new leading category of employment by the 1940 census.[25] Just over 69 percent of stenographers and typists were single women, a percentage that nearly matched that of single teachers (70 percent), single nurses (72 percent), and single telephone operators (69.5 percent).[26]

In addition to dominating clerical and sales jobs, white women also nearly exclusively filled the ranks of telephone operators. By 1930, all but 3 of the state's 1,925 telephone operators were native- or foreign-born white women.[27] Between 1879 and 1929 a female telephone operator "was the voice of reassurance, compassion, and solace; the purveyor of the town's gossip; and, on momentous occasions, the savior of lives."[28] On June 3, 1921, for example, thirteen telephone operators heroically warned Pueblo residents about an Arkansas River flood as twelve feet of water threatened the Exchange Building.[29] However, by 1930 technological advances had altered the role of the telephone operator. The new dial phones largely replaced the amiable female operator on the other end of the line. A caller now listened for a dial tone before personally calling a number by spinning the dial with his or her finger. No longer would an operator routinely place calls. Henceforth, she served only special functions and seldom communicated with the average caller.

Similar to the domestic and personal service field, the percentages of women employed in professional services remained constant from 1900 to 1930, hovering at around 20 percent. White women accounted for 95 percent of those employed in the sector. The vast majority of professional women were teachers—nearly 10,000 of the 16,846 women listed as employed in professional service in the 1930 census.[30] Few of them, however, had the monumental impact Emily Griffith had. Her Opportunity School led the way in educating, training, and helping immigrants and working-class men and women become successful. Although women filled the ranks of schoolteachers, they were underrepresented in the college teaching ranks at a time when more and more women were attending institutions of higher learning. Only 223 Colorado women were listed as professors or college presidents in 1930.[31]

ARTISTIC AND LITERARY WOMEN

Although fewer than 200 Colorado women were enumerated as dancers and actresses by US census workers in the 1920s and 1930s, the Perry-Mansfield School of Dance gained worldwide renown under the tutelage of Charlotte Perry and Portia Mansfield. Other Colorado artists thrived in different artistic fields. In Colorado Springs, Laura Gilpin photographed and designed brochures for the newly opened Broadmoor Art Academy. Her photographs of Native peoples and Southwest ruins made her an artistic icon in that region. A Colorado Springs native, Gilpin first took photographs with a Brownie camera. She studied in New York City and abroad before returning to Colorado. In 1924 she made her first trip to Mesa Verde with Betsy Forster, a Colorado Springs nurse. The trip launched a lifetime connection to the region's American Indians. In the early 1930s, when Forster became a visiting nurse to the Navaho community in Red Rocks, Arizona, Gilpin joined her. Her photographs were published in a number of works, including *The Pueblos: A Camera Chronicle* and *The Rio Grande: River of Destiny*.[32]

Other women became successful writers. Slightly over 200 female authors, editors, and reporters were recorded in the 1930 census. Almost half of those were residents of Denver, where the Denver Woman's Press Club (DWPC) continued to prosper. The DWPC bought the home of George and Elizabeth Burr in 1924 after hosting a new social event, the Denver Woman's Press Club Ball, to raise funds for its purchase. Attended by society leaders Louise (Mrs. Crawford) Hill of Denver and Julie (Mrs. Spencer) Penrose of Colorado Springs, the ball was a grand affair. Netting enough money to put a down-payment on the house, the ball was such a success that the club held one each fall for the next several years until the mortgage was retired. Through the years, club members cranked out articles and books. In 1936 six of the women were writing children's books, five were writing poetry, three were writing adult fiction, and three had produced textbooks. In deference to the conditions of the Great Depression, the club extended its philanthropic work to include donations to its own members in need.[33]

Two successful writers who did not live in Denver were Helen Rich and Belle Turnbull. The younger of the two by twelve years, Rich was born in 1894 in Minnesota, the daughter of a prominent dentist. Although trained to be a teacher, she had no interest in teaching and quickly became a newspaper reporter. Belle Turnbull and her family moved to Colorado in 1890. The two women met in Colorado Springs when Turnbull was chair of the high school English department and Rich a reporter and former society editor for the *Colorado Springs Gazette-Telegraph*. As was common, Rich was initially assigned the more "feminine" beat on the society page; once she realized that she hated parties, she became a top feature writer reporting on the courthouse beat and focusing on crime stories that emanated from the sheriff's office. For years the two women took extended summer vacations in Frisco, renting a cabin during their stay. They supported themselves by teaching and reporting. By the 1930s they were both eager to write poetry and novels rather than grade papers and meet deadlines. In 1938 they moved permanently into a primitive cabin in Breckenridge. Although it had no indoor plumbing, electricity, or telephone, the cabin did have stunning views from all its windows.

For the next thirty years, Rich and Turnbull focused their energies on writing. Keen observers of the people and physical environment surrounding them, they each drew upon their setting for their works. Rich published *The Spring Begins* (1947) and *The Willow-Bender* (1950). Turnbull's books of poetry include *Goldboat* (1940), *The Far Side of the Hill* (1953), and *The Tenmile Range* (1957). Rich also worked as chief assistant to Susan Badger in the Summit County Welfare Office. Badger became a close friend of the two writers, often joining them for poker parties in their parlor. Because of their no-nonsense approach to life at 10,000 feet above sea level, Rich and Turnbull were accepted by Summit County residents. They dressed casually and appropriately for tromping around town in all kinds of weather. Turnbull, handsome and petite, always wore blue jeans. Rich donned men's shirts and slacks topped off by a French beret. Hiking through mining areas with a former miner, she carried a *Saturday Evening Post* delivery bag stuffed with books, manuscripts, and groceries.

Turnbull and Rich embraced their new lifestyle in the cabin on French Street, although it was unlike the one they had left behind in Colorado Springs. Turnbull acknowledged that her Vassar education had not taught her "to deal with frozen water pipes, or how to break a trail through 14-inch fall of snow with the webs [snowshoes], or how to get rid of packrats, or how long to hang a haunch of venison, or how to cut up a jag of firewood for a Franklin stove."[34] They learned through trial and error and by observing their neighbors. Both women found the physical labor required to sustain their home invigorating. Rich once explained, "The beauty of the thing about living where I do is I've got a woodpile when I come home from a day's work with the nerves all frayed out. I go to work on the woodpile, saw wood, then split it into kindling if necessary; then I'm ready to go to work on the typewriter."[35] In 1970 Turnbull died at age eighty-eight. The following year Rich, her companion and friend for the last forty years, also died.

PROFESSIONAL WOMEN

Although some women made inroads into traditional male jobs, men continued to dominate the medical and legal professions. In Colorado in 1920 there were 1,642 male physicians and surgeons compared with 130 females; 1,517 male lawyers, judges, and justices to a mere 22 females.[36] One female doctor was Helen McCarty Fickel. Born in Berthoud in 1907, McCarty enrolled in the University of Colorado's medical school, intending to become a nurse. However, her father, a physician, did not want her to become a nurse because in his day they had been "janitors and scrubbed and did the laundry."[37] He told her that if she insisted on being a nurse after graduation she could do so, but he asked her to remain open to other options. After her first year at CU, she agreed with her father. She graduated in 1932, interned for a year at Colorado General Hospital, and returned to Berthoud. Although she wanted to become a psychiatrist, her father persuaded her to succeed him in his medical practice, sweetening his proposal with an offer to buy her a car and to let her use his office equipment. She opened her office in a back room of his house, where her father's patients readily accepted her as their new doctor.[38]

Social work was one occupation that showed a steady increase in the number of female workers through the first three decades of the twentieth century. In 1898 the New York School of Social Work at Columbia University began offering classes; by 1910 it had established a two-year program. The US Census Bureau recognized the rise of this occupation with a new classification: religious, charity, and welfare workers. By the early 1920s the American Association of Social Workers, American Association of Medical Social Workers, and American Association of Professional Social Work had been established. That same year 60 percent of Colorado's social workers were female, compared with 66 percent nationwide.[39] Women who had started their careers in settlement houses moved into positions with private agencies in the 1920s. Gertrude Vaile, a Colorado native, earned a sociology degree from Vassar College. In 1910 she graduated from the Chicago School of Civic Philanthropy and began to work with Chicago United Charities. After two years she returned to Denver to work with the City Board of Charities and was director of civilian relief for the American Red Cross Mountain Division. Later, she served as president of the National Conference of Social Work.[40] Florence Hutsinpillar served as executive secretary and case supervisor for the Denver Bureau of Charities. During Vaile's presidency, Hutsinpillar served on the board of the National Conference of Social Work.[41]

WOMEN IN POLITICS

Following their successful campaign for equal suffrage in 1893, some Colorado women ran for political office. They knew they were setting precedents not only for themselves and future Coloradans but also for women in other states who, along with their male counterparts, were keeping informed about western women's political work. Colorado suffrage leaders and male politicians agreed that the state superintendent of public instruction would be "the woman's office." By guaranteeing that women would appear as candidates in every election, Republican and Democratic men were hoping to draw women into their respective parties. Suffragists, satisfied with the arrangement, feared that pushing for more would harm suffrage movements in other states. As it turned out, the agreement had numerous ramifications. On the positive side, women occupied the office of state superintendent for more than fifty years. On the negative side, the existence of a "female" office ended up limiting women's access to other political positions. Because it was off-limits to men, the office lost its prestige. In the words of educator Aaron Gove, it became the "least attractive" of all state offices—for men.[42]

For women, however, it was a plum position. Helen Loring Grenfell was the first woman elected, winning the office in 1898, 1900, and 1902. When she ran for a fourth term in 1904, however, she faced a Republican Party intent on removing her from office. Although both the party and the press had worn kid gloves during earlier elections, they took them off in 1904. The *Denver Republican* charged that Grenfell had won the 1902 election fraudulently and criticized her political flexibility because she had first run as a candidate for the Fusion Party (a coalition of Republicans, Democrats, and Populists who supported silver currency), then as a Democrat, and finally as a Republican on the Democratic slate in 1904. Pitted against Katherine Craig, a schoolteacher, Grenfell retaliated with criticism of the Republican administration. In a close election, Craig beat Grenfell and was reelected in 1906. In 1910 the office was again hotly contested. Two years later she lost her seat to Katherine Cook, bringing the position back into the Democratic fold. The incumbent Cook defeated Helen Ring Robinson to become the Democratic candidate, much to the disgust of Alice Rohe, a *Rocky Mountain News* reporter who maintained that the political "machine" had pushed aside the best candidate.[43] On the Republican side, Helen Wixson defeated Grace Shoe. In the general election, the tireless Wixson was the only Republican elected to a state office.

A handful of other women ran for state representative, state treasurer, state auditor, and University of Colorado regent. At first, some succeeded; but as time went on, fewer and fewer women were elected to public office at the state level. Between 1894 and 1900, seven women were sent to the state legislature. Only one won in 1902, however, and no women won in 1904 and 1906. While Helen Wixson, president of the Woman's Republican League, accused the male-dominated state committee of undermining women's participation, women themselves were sometimes to blame for their omission from the political arena. Those who held the position of state superintendent of public instruction did not attempt to run for other offices.[44] Holding tight to their monopoly on that office—Helen Grenfell, Katherine Craig, and Mary Bradford controlled the position for all but four years between

1898 and 1920—they failed to mentor or encourage other women to run for leadership positions. Some women were elected to local offices, many of which were education-based positions. Nettie S. Freed taught in Fruita before teaching German and social studies at Pueblo's Centennial High School. She was elected the Pueblo County superintendent of schools in 1931, 1932, 1934, and 1936. In 1947 and 1949 she was elected state superintendent of instruction; later, she became the first commissioner of education in Colorado.[45]

A rare instance of women dominating political positions occurred in Grover. In this small community fifty miles northeast of Greeley, women seized control of city offices after becoming frustrated by the idleness of male elected officials. In 1929 thirteen women ran for a variety of city and county offices; all were elected. Elizabeth Lower was the town's new mayor. The "petticoat government," as the men routinely referred to it, did so well that the slate of women was elected to two additional terms.[46]

THE EARLY BIRTH CONTROL MOVEMENT IN COLORADO

In 1925 state representative Dr. Minnie C.T. Love introduced a bill into the Colorado General Assembly advocating the distribution of birth control information and the manufacture and distribution of contraceptives. The founder of the birth control movement in the United States, Margaret Sanger, opened the first birth control clinic in Brooklyn in 1916. The daughter of a radical Irish father and a mother who died at age fifty after bearing eleven children, Sanger had personally witnessed the burden and dangers women faced in bearing and raising a large number of children in urban areas rife with unsanitary conditions. After World War I, as Sanger turned to medical doctors for support, the birth control movement became much less radical.

Sanger visited Denver three times over a fifteen-year period. In 1916 she spoke to a gathering in support of the National Woman's Party. The ideas that married couples engaged in sexual activity for reasons other than procreation and that they would try to limit their family size were radical. Although some couples asked their family doctor for help, the poor had no resources available. Sanger returned a second time in 1923 and was entertained with a buffet dinner hosted by Imogene Daly. The guest list included the founder of Denver's juvenile court, Judge Benjamin Lindsey, and his wife. Ruth Vincent, a social worker in the juvenile court, was the first director of its Girls Division. She married Dr. T. Donald Cunningham, a Denver doctor. Seeing "an obvious corollary between overpopulation in individual families—unplanned, unwanted children—harassed, hopeless parents— and the Juvenile Court," she decided to found an organization dedicated to sponsoring birth control for the needy.[47] Other early supporters were Grace Kassler, Marie Dines, and Sarah Arneill. The women's first fundraising effort brought in $100. They opened the first birth control clinic in 1926 in the basement of the Seventeenth Avenue Community Church. Volunteers raised money, provided transportation to and from the clinic, and sometimes cared for patients' children while the mothers were examined and fitted with diaphragms. Interns, residents, and medical students provided care in the clinic on a rotating basis. The first year, 150 women used the clinic's facilities. In 1928 it moved to the obstetrical and gynecological outpatient clinic at Colorado General Hospital. In 1930, after Sanger spoke at the Capitol Life Auditorium, she attracted Mary (Mrs. Verner Z.) Reed as a supporter. Reed donated $100 that year and $1,000 the next year and later served as treasurer of the Denver Birth Control League.[48]

Birth control clinics were established in other Colorado towns as well. Marka Webb Bennett Stewart was one of the founders of the first clinic in Colorado Springs. Boulder and Pueblo also had clinics. Dr. Ella A. Mead opened a clinic in Greeley in the 1920s. Mead graduated from the University of Colorado Medical School and completed internships in Denver before opening her own practice in Greeley. She initially biked to patients' homes but soon acquired a 1906 Maxwell automobile. She kept it running for 150,000 miles by using hairpins to mend the fan belt, adhesive tape to patch a leaky radiator hose, and a hot flatiron against the manifold to help start the car in the dead of winter. After more than fifty years as a private physician and public health officer, Mead retired. Her leadership in promoting children's clinics, a public health department, and Weld County General Hospital garnered her awards from the American Medical Women's Association and the Colorado State Medical Society.[49] Weld County General Hospital named its nurses' building in her honor.

BLAZING NEW TRAILS

Although some women took risks in their professional careers by promoting controversial causes, other Colorado women pursued more physical challenges. The oldest female professional athletic organization did not form until 1948, but professional women athletes were wowing audiences in the nineteenth century. Cowgirls were members of Wild West shows in

FIGURE 8.3 *To make house calls, Dr. Ella A. Mead of Greeley drove her 1906 Maxwell automobile. A Weld County physician for over fifty years, Mead was instrumental in persuading county commissioners to establish the nation's first birth control clinic supported by a county. Courtesy, City of Greeley Museums, Hazel E. Johnson Collection, Greeley, CO.*

the 1880s and 1890s. In the early twentieth century, Bertha Kaepernick, the daughter of German immigrants, first participated in a bronco riding exhibition at Cheyenne (Wyoming) Frontier Days. At the 1912 Calgary Stampede she won the relay race, took second in trick riding, and was awarded third in both bronco and trick riding. Her winnings totaled $1,150. Although she retired from competitive rodeo in 1919, she continued to make guest appearances at rodeos and worked as a rodeo "pickup"—riding out to capture runaway horses—through the 1930s.[50] Sisters Vaughn and Gene Krieg grew up on a Colorado ranch, learning to ride before they were five years old. On the ranch, they helped their brothers break wild horses and pursue stray cattle. At age sixteen, Gene became the youngest female to win the bronco riding contest at Cheyenne Frontier Days. Hired as a relay rider for Verne Elliott's rodeo company, she also competed in bronco and trick riding. She married bulldogger Shorty Creed in 1931. Competing all over the country and in international rodeos, the couple won numerous titles. Vaughn joined the rodeo circuit in 1927 and was soon known for her riding as well as her original costumes. She married and divorced a number of times before happily settling down with cowboy Lynn Huskey in 1933. She later told a

FIGURE 8.4 *Fearless Mary Geneva "Gene" Krieg Creed rides bronco Spider in a rodeo at Rocky Ford. She and her sister, Vaughn, learned to ride at a young age, broke wild horses, and pursued stray cattle before joining the rodeo circuit. Courtesy, Fort Collins Museum and Discovery Science Center, #H09921, Fort Collins, CO.*

reporter that she married him because she could always be sure she could be a cowgirl with him.[51]

In the rugged San Juan Mountains near Durango, Olga Schaaf Little spent almost forty years as a mule skinner. With her train of thirty burros, she brought supplies in to mines and brought ore back. She charged five dollars a ton for transporting coal on burros. Each burro carried the ore in three seventy-pound sacks. She also freighted with a wagon and teams and a big bobsled. One winter, when one burro kicked, another reared in response and disengaged itself from the bobsled. Practically buried in four feet of snow, the burro could not be dislodged until the spring snowmelt. Little brought the trapped animal hay to eat every week until it could be freed.[52]

While some women chose to take risks riding wild broncos or leading mule trains along treacherous mountain paths, other women scaled Colorado's "fourteeners" in defiance of conventional wisdom. The Colorado Mountain Club (CMC), formed in 1912, was not primarily a climbing organization, but would-be members qualified by climbing a fourteener. Nine women were among the twenty-five charter members. They were soon joined by other women, including Harriet Vaille and her younger sister, Agnes. Harriet was appointed to chair the CMC's Nomenclature

Committee, whose task was to research appropriate names for features in what would become Rocky Mountain National Park. With fellow CMC member Edna Hendrie, Vaille found elderly Arapaho men from Wyoming's Wind River Reservation to lead the party. As a result of the trip, Big Meadow, Lumpy Creek, and Never Summer Range were added to the map. Vaille became so interested in Indian culture that she decided to attend the University of Chicago, but she returned home when her mother suffered a stroke.[53]

Agnes Vaille was one of Colorado's first female technical climbers. A graduate of Smith College, she volunteered with the Red Cross during World War I. After the war she attended the National School for Commercial and Trade Executives at Northwestern University in Chicago. In 1924 Vaille was hired as secretary of the Denver Chamber of Commerce, performing the job so ably that businessmen said she had "the brains of a man."[54] A fearless climber, she made the first known solo ascent of James Peak in winter, designed her own lightweight sleeping bag, and made an ascent of the Bishop, a 120-foot rock formation in Platte Canyon. In the early 1920s, through the CMC, she met Walter Kiener, a Swiss immigrant. They decided to climb the east face of Longs Peak, a technical climb of 1,600 feet. After aborting two attempts, they tried again in January 1925 against the advice of Vaille's friends and relatives, who regarded the winter attempt an "obsession."[55] Accounts differ regarding the decision to climb on January 10, but no one can dispute what occurred. The ascent was frighteningly slow amid waist-deep snow and treacherous ice. On the descent, the exhausted Vaille fell and skidded. Kiener, also exhausted, helped her to some rocks for protection from the wind and started across Boulder Field for help. With three others, he started back up the mountain. Two of the men turned back; Herbert Sortland lost his way and died near Longs Peak Inn. When Kiener returned to the spot at which he had left her, Vaille was dead and frozen. The tragedy jolted the climbing community. In 1927 a stone shelter was erected near the Keyhole commemorating Vaille and Sortland.[56]

Agnes Vaille was by no means the only renegade in the Colorado Mountain Club. Many would argue that any woman who joined a climbing club in the early twentieth century was a rebel in her own right. Marjorie Perry preferred the term *social outlaw* to describe herself.[57] Born in Chicago on November 15, 1882, she was the oldest daughter of Sam and Ella Perry. A brother, Robert (Bob), joined her within two years, but in the meantime she was "the son of the family," happily accompanying her father on hunting and camping trips in the Colorado Rockies. Her schooling at Manual High School in Denver suited her perfectly, as she was able to take classes in the manual arts. The skills she learned there stood her in good stead when she later owned her own ranch. But first she went to Smith College, where her secret aim "was to play basket ball [*sic*] and to learn to skate well." When she graduated, she saw no need to find a worthwhile occupation: "There's no use trying to make a lady or a scholar out of a hoodlum and I had in mind my future life."[58] Instead, she enjoyed long horseback rides with her father and participated in skiing and climbing expeditions with friends. On one trip she met Carl Howelsen, a champion Swedish skier. She convinced him to check out the snow in Steamboat Springs. He was immediately captivated, bought land, and established a ski jump. Howelsen Hill and the Winter Ski Carnival he established still exist nearly 100 years later.

When her sister, Charlotte, and Portia Mansfield founded the Perry-Mansfield Camp in Steamboat Springs, Perry became their first riding instructor. To have her own horse at the camp in the days before horse trailers, she rode her horse 200 miles to Steamboat in the spring and back to Denver in the fall.[59] Perry met Eleanor Bliss, a new camper at Perry-Mansfield. An able horsewoman, Bliss returned to camp the following year as Perry's assistant. Thus began a lifelong friendship and partnership. From 1925 to 1947, the two wrote letters and visited one another. Perry, who had bought 10 acres of land in Littleton after her parents' death in 1936, continually increased her holdings until she had acquired 200 acres. Bliss, who lived in New York, cared for her deceased sister's son and daughter and then her aging parents. After her parents died, Bliss quit her job and moved to Colorado to be with Perry. They initially lived in Perry's ranch house off the Highline Canal and at her place in Steamboat Springs. Bliss knew she needed her own home because Perry, her senior by seventeen years, would likely die before she did. For the next twenty years, the two women lived the winter months in Littleton at Perry's home and the other months in Steamboat, each with her own home but together every day. In a paper she presented to the Denver Fortnightly Club, Perry recalled her life with Eleanor Bliss: "For the last 17 years, I've been blessed with the companionship of a most congenial partner, who loves the horses, dogs and all the animals as much as I do. I'm sure the wild country and my free life are the reason for her joining me and keeping me young. Once in a while she quietly heads me in the right direction if I get too far off the beaten track, but not enuf [*sic*] to spoil the fairy tale and keep it from ending 'They lived happily ever after.'"[60] After Perry's death in 1969, Bliss spoke of Perry's impact on her life: "Have you ever been in a certain place at a certain time and met someone who made all the difference in your life? Steamboat Springs was my place and Marjorie Perry was that person and the year was 1924."[61]

The Marjorie Perry Nature Reserve, a fifty-five-acre site in Greenwood Village, Colorado, serves as a primary wildlife preserve. The "social outlaw" would be happy to know that the land on which she lovingly raised sheep, horses, cows, and chickens is still home to the wild geese, waterfowl, and coyotes that inhabited the land when she owned it.

Nona Lovell Brooks, described as a prophet of modern mystical Christianity, was a different kind of renegade than Agnes Vaille or Marjorie Perry. Born in 1861 in Louisville, Kentucky, she was the youngest daughter of Chauncey and Lavinia Brooks. When her father's salt-mining business collapsed, the family moved to Pueblo. Her sister Althea (also spelled Alethea and Alethe) Brooks Small became acquainted with the teaching of Kate Bingham, a follower of the New Thought philosophy that developed in the United States in the late nineteenth century. Composed of three major denominations—Unity Church, Religious Science, and Church of Divine Science—the philosophy emphasizes metaphysical beliefs. The three Brooks daughters, Nona and her two married sisters, Alethea Brooks Small and Fannie Brooks James, began attending Bingham's classes. On the third day of class, Brooks was suddenly cured of a severe throat ailment. A witness to other cures, she became a firm believer. James began teaching classes in her home and corresponding with Malinda Cramer, a California woman who had labeled her teachings *Divine Science*. Realizing that their teachings were very similar, Brooks asked Cramer for permission to share the term. Having secured permission, she founded the Divine Science Church of Denver in 1898. A Divine Science College to educate teachers and practitioners, organize churches, and ordain ministers was also established.[62]

A DANCE FOR LIFE: PERRY-MANSFIELD DANCE COMPANY

When Charlotte Perry and Portia Mansfield opened their Rocky Mountain Dancing Club in Nederland in 1913, they were fulfilling a dream hatched three years earlier. Charlotte Perry, the youngest of the three Perry children, was born in Denver in 1889 and lived a privileged life that included earning a degree from Smith College in Northampton, Massachusetts. There she built upon her love of drama, acting in a number of productions. In 1910 she met fellow student Portia Mansfield Swett (she later dropped the Swett). Mansfield, born in 1887, had a much different childhood than Perry's. Her father, a struggling hotel keeper, constantly moved his family. He died shortly after she enrolled at Smith. Needing to support herself, she crocheted Irish collars and sold them to classmates for two dollars apiece. She also tutored philosophy students and taught tennis. While a student, she visited the state mental hospital and began Saturday evening "dance therapy" for its patients. After graduating from college the year she met Perry, Mansfield studied dance in Europe and the United States before running a dance studio in Omaha, Nebraska. In 1912 she visited Perry, who had returned to Denver after graduation. Perry's father, a railroad and mining man, took the young women bear hunting in the mountains. Captivated by the natural beauty, the two decided to live together in the mountains and pursue their dual passions of dance and theater. For the next two years they saved money for their dream camp. Mansfield taught dance at Miss Morgan's Dramatic School and secured a secretarial job there for Perry. They both also taught private ballroom dance lessons.[63]

When Perry and Mansfield decided to find a new location for their dance camp, they enlisted the help of Perry's brother, Bob, who had a coal-mining operation at Oak Creek, south of Steamboat Springs.[64] For $200, the women bought a log cabin and several acres in Strawberry Park, two miles north of Steamboat Springs. Then they returned to Chicago to work and take classes at the Lewis Institute for Coffin Makers so they could build camp furniture. Laden with those items, they returned to Colorado and enlisted the help of Bob Perry and several of his carpenters to build a main lodge and six cabins with canvas roofs in time for the camp's summer opening. Years later, Mansfield recalled the six hectic weeks during which they prepared the camp for its first students: "One day the foreman told us all the men were quitting—they couldn't stand our cooking. Weeping, Miss Perry went to her brother and asked what was wrong. He told us to soak the potatoes in grease, overcook the meat, boil the coffee and serve them soggy pie. We tried this formula on them and they loved every bite."[65] The women also cleared trails, made curtains, and stained the floors and walls of the main house. For the first ten years, candles provided the only light. Water was drawn from a spring at the bottom of a 100-foot cliff. The road to the main house was a quarter of a mile long, over which hand baggage had to be carried. A team of horses transported campers' trunks. For a trip into town, the women hitched a cart to Tango, a mule who had proven too nasty for mine work and was given to them.

Although they had moved away from the leering countenances of men on the Eastern Slope, the camp founders and dancers still had to contend with suspicious and wary Yampa Valley residents who were afraid that Perry, Mansfield, and the unorthodox dances would corrupt their young daughters. Husbands refused to let their wives deliver eggs and other products to the camp, so the items were left under a culvert on the main road. Soon, a few brave parents allowed their daughters to attend the camp; when they suffered no ill effects, townspeople relaxed their vigilance. Camp enrollment steadily grew. In 1917 a drama department, headed by Perry, accommodated fifty students.[66]

In the summer of 1921, Mansfield established her first dance company, the Portia Mansfield Dancers (later the Perry-Mansfield Dancers). After the troupe auditioned at Denver's Orpheum Theatre, it was hired to perform on the vaudeville circuit that autumn. By 1927 as many as four Perry-Mansfield companies were touring simultaneously. Mansfield, inspired by the work of Isadora Duncan and Ruth St. Denis, created the choreography. Perry, general designer and technical director, became one of the company's leading dancers. Just as the founders and dancers had drawn criticism from Steamboat Springs residents, they faced similar problems on the road. Responding to a minister who suggested that a better way to bring the arts to his town would be through a lecture, dance company member Harold Ames defended Mansfield's scholarship and artistic skills. Other towns welcomed the dancers, however. One reporter raved that the finale was "particularly interesting as the dancers wave long streamers of silk over their heads in multicolors corresponding with those of [the] costumes."[67] The group disbanded in 1930, a casualty of vaudeville's declining quality and the precarious economic conditions.[68] Perry-Mansfield performers continued to tour Colorado and Wyoming, giving small-town residents their first experience with professional dancers.

The camp consumed its founders during the summer months. For the next quarter of a century, Perry and Mansfield spent the other months of the year in the New York City area, teaching and pursuing formal studies in the arts. Mansfield earned an MA in physical education and a PhD in anthropology. Perry studied acting and directing. She earned a master's degree in drama from New York University and in the late 1940s became a member of the Hunter College drama staff, where she helped develop the children's theater program.

The 1930s were a time of rapid expansion of the Perry-Mansfield dance curriculum. Highly influential dancers, choreographers, and dance composers came to the camp over the next thirty years. Faculty members included Doris Humphrey, Agnes de Mille, Jose Limon, and Louis Horst. Promising acting students Julie Harris, Lee Remick, and Dustin Hoffman attended the camp.

Through the years, the Perry-Mansfield School of Theatre and Dance, as it was later named, sponsored a wide variety of activities. Building on the early days of horseback riding, the camp became the home of the first National Rating Center for Riding in 1953. Mountaineering camps for young boys and girls operated on and off beginning in the 1930s. From 1952 to 1954, Mansfield and Perry organized and hosted a Symposium of the Arts. Designed to investigate the ways teachers, artists, and laypeople could promote cultural development, the symposium was instrumental in the creation of the Colorado Council of the Arts (Colorado Creative Industries today).

By the 1960s Perry and Mansfield were in their early seventies. They sold the camp to Stephens College and moved to California.[69] Mansfield's death in 1979 ended their life and work together. Perry died in 1983. The camp, however, continues. In 1994 Julie Harris, best known for her starring role in *East of Eden,* wrote a letter to the State Historical Fund supporting the nomination of the Perry-Mansfield Performing Arts School and Camp to the National Register of Historic Places.[70] Work began the following year, with a preservation master plan. The Main Lodge, which still serves as a kitchen and dining room, has been restored. As Tricia Henry asserted, "Perry-Mansfield was an oasis for creativity at a time when few venues were available to either professional performing artists or students."[71]

"AN ATMOSPHERE OF PLEASANT COMFORT": PHYLLIS WHEATLEY BRANCH, YWCA

In 1916 the YWCA for Colored Women was organized at Shorter A.M.E. Church by Isabel Champand and Mrs. A. M. War to serve Denver's black community. Its first headquarters were at 3318 25th Street. It was the forerunner of the Phyllis Wheatley Branch (named after the first African American female poet of stature) of the YWCA, established in 1920. Located at 2460 Welton Street, the three-story home offered residence and meeting rooms and recreational facilities. Gertie N. Ross was the first chairwoman of the Committee of Management. To fill the position of executive secretary, the branch used the YWCA national board to search for worthy applicants, ultimately selecting Josephine Davis, a graduate of Fisk University, at a salary of $1,200 a year. Davis, who exercised general supervision over the home,

FIGURE 8.5 *The Phyllis Wheatley Branch of the YWCA was popular among young African American women living in or visiting Denver. Courtesy, Denver Public Library Western History Collection, Charles S. Price, X-22345.*

was given rent-free quarters. Although Davis did an outstanding job, she did not last long as executive secretary. By 1922 she had married and resigned her position. This would become a common occurrence for the branch. Mrs. Fairfax Butler Richey arrived from Iowa to replace Davis. Highly regarded, she commanded a salary of $1,500 a year before she, too, remarried and resigned. Next, Helen Taylor, known for her leadership in acquiring Camp Nizhoni, became the new secretary until she followed Davis and Richey down the matrimonial aisle and out the YWCA door.[72] That move necessitated another search by the national board. Grace Sheppard, secretary of the Personnel Bureau of the national board in New York City, strongly recommended Anna M. Arnold and forwarded her credentials and qualifications to the Denver office. Her references stated that she possessed the necessary qualities: a Christian girl with a winning personality, poise, intelligence, and a pleasing appearance.[73] However, Arnold was not hired. Instead, the board hired Dorothy Guinn, a Radcliff College graduate, who must have had sterling qualifications to be hired over Arnold. Guinn stayed for six years before landing a plum national staff position in 1932. Her successor, EsCobedo Sarreals, served three years until she, too, was stricken by Cupid's arrow.

The Phyllis Wheatley Branch proved very popular with Denver's black residents. In her 1920 report, Josephine Davis recorded 208 paid members, two grade school clubs, one business girls' club, and 12 residents. In 1925 the executive secretary reported 326 residents; 301 of 339 applicants had been placed in jobs. Word-of-mouth testimonials and printed advertisements informed African Americans traveling through, visiting, or moving to Denver of the services offered by the Phyllis Wheatley Branch. One 1930s advertisement was printed on eye-catching orange paper, enticing young women to the residence with its "attractive and bright" rooms, cooking and laundry privileges without charge, and a "spacious living room" in which to "entertain the boy friend" rather than doing so on a local street corner.[74] Summer rates were seventy-five cents a night or two dollars per week.

Through the 1920s and 1930s, more departments were formed to serve the black community. Initially, the Branch Employment Department found women jobs in laundries, as maids and cooks, and in secretarial positions. The Business and Employed Girls Clubs later split into Business (secretarial, retail, and accounting) and Industrial (domestic science, factory, and laundry) Clubs. The Industrial Club was the most active and largest of the clubs. It held weekly club suppers, hosted carnivals, sponsored dances, published its own newsletter, and had its own lending library. Schoolgirls from elementary grades through high school joined the Girl Reserves Club.[75]

Branch leaders quickly recognized the need for a summer camp. Because Camp Lookout, the YWCA camp, was closed to non-whites and city baths were segregated, very few facilities were available for African American youth. In 1926 the branch established Camp Nizhoni near Lincoln Hills on Pine Creek in Gilpin County. Onsite was a large old house in need of windows. The owners agreed to deed the property to the branch in three years if the YWCA installed new windows. For the next two decades, girls stayed overnight at the camp while others attended as day visitors. In 1928 the camp hosted 22 girls overnight for two weeks, 42 weekend guests, and nearly 1,100 day visitors.[76]

Black leaders at the Wheatley Branch who worked closely with Denver's Central Branch and the national board were often praised for their abilities and results. Gertie Ross was admired by whites and blacks for her "amazing organizational ability and perseverance."[77] As proof, she became the first African American to serve on Denver's YWCA Central board. Lillian Bondurant, also a chairwoman at Wheatley (1930–1935), became the first black woman to serve on Central's Finance Committee. Records and reports of the Wheatley Branch show several references to interracial friendships.

Many branch leaders were also involved in other interracial organizations. Gertie Ross and Beatrice Thompson helped organize the Denver branch of the National Association for the Advancement of Colored People, headed by George Gross, Dr. Clarence Holmes, and George Ross. Other leaders among Denver's white and black YWCA branches formed the Interracial Committee in the late 1920s to campaign against racial prejudice in Denver's press, police department, real estate practices, and recreational facilities. Especially visible in the 1930s, the group initiated Interracial Sunday, a series of ecumenical gatherings held each year on the Sunday closest to Lincoln's birthday. Denverites of all races and religions prayed and listened to national and local leaders speak. As more and more of Denver's diverse population took part in Interracial Sunday, it expanded to become Race Relations Week.[78] In the 1930s the Interracial Committee also fought for more blacks to be hired for Works Progress Administration jobs, suggested boycotting and picketing segregated movie theaters, and promoted black history, literature, and art. Through their efforts, members of the committee were able to have the signs "Negro Day," "Mexican Day," and "Mixed Day" removed from the Municipal Bath House. They challenged the all-white hiring practices of Denver Public Schools and were happy to report in October 1934 that Miss Burdine had been hired as the first black teacher at Whittier School.[79]

During the 1940s and 1950s the Phyllis Wheatley Branch continued serving Denver's blacks, but as the racial makeup of the neighborhood changed, so did its name. In 1950 it was renamed the Welton Branch to reflect its multiracial constituency. In 1964 the branch was discontinued.[80]

OPPORTUNITY FOR ALL: EMILY GRIFFITH AND THE OPPORTUNITY SCHOOL

Born in Cincinnati, Ohio, in 1868 (although she always gave her birth year as 1880), Emily Griffith began teaching in Nebraska. Her family—mother, father, brother, and two sisters—moved to Denver in 1895. Emily had no high school education or teaching certificate, so the Denver School Board hired her as a substitute teacher before giving her a job teaching sixth graders at Central School in the Auraria neighborhood. Her students, children of the poor working class, often skipped school to supplement the family income with jobs as newsboys, maids, and telegram deliverers. More than once, Griffith dipped into her meager earnings to buy groceries, clothing, and medicine for the families. When Denver Public Schools transferred her to the Twenty-Fourth Street School in the Five Points neighborhood, Griffith found herself teaching children with diverse backgrounds. The neighborhood housed African American, Chinese, Hispanic, Japanese, Italian, Jewish, and Native American families. The student body represented thirty-seven nationalities. As Griffith worked with her students, visited their homes, and spoke with their parents, she realized that their struggles in school were seldom a result of simplemindedness or laziness. For many, English was not their native language. Like the children at Central School, they often missed school to help the family. Many parents were illiterate in the English language and possessed few marketable job skills beyond physical strength. Griffith believed education was the ticket to self-sufficiency for her students and their parents. She began teaching classes in arithmetic, reading, and English for adults and working children in the evenings and during lunch periods.

Her successes and herculean efforts were noted by the Denver School Board and others. In 1904 she was appointed deputy state superintendent under Superintendent Katherine L. Craig. She missed the children, though, and returned to the classroom two years later. In 1909 she received a complimentary state teaching diploma for her excellent service. She returned to the office of public instruction the next year as deputy superintendent under Superintendent Helen Marsh Wixson. But once again, feeling that she made the biggest difference with her teaching, she returned to the Twenty-Fourth Street School in 1913.

Emily's two stints in the state office introduced her to numerous officials and workers in the legislature and at schools, charitable institutions, and social agencies. By 1915 she was ready to lobby for her vision of a school, one which students of all ages could attend for free, become literate in English, take classes they wanted to take (instead of those someone thought they should take), and learn marketable job skills. Griffith attended women's club meetings in the evenings and on weekends to solicit club members' support. She talked to ministers and social workers, attended board meetings at the YMCA and the YWCA, and badgered Denver School Board members until her idea was approved in 1916. At a salary of $1,800 a year, she was named principal of the new Opportunity School at Longfellow, a condemned school at Fourteenth and Welton Streets. Open from 8:30 a.m. to 10:00 p.m., the school offered classes in reading, writing, and speaking English and in marketable job skills. A sign above the door read "Public Opportunity School—For All Who Wish to Learn."[81] Not knowing how many students

FIGURE 8.6 *The educator who may have had the most profound impact on Denver students was Emily Griffith. As founder of the Opportunity School, her influence has been felt by generations from the early 1900s to the present. Courtesy, History Colorado (Scan #10026598), Denver.*

the school would draw on opening day, Griffith and her small staff were ecstatic when ten times the expected number attended. Always alert to the needs of the students and the workplace, the school offered classes in radio communication, gasoline engine maintenance, ambulance driving, nursing, and first aid during World War I. By 1926 the school had outgrown the

Longfellow School building, and a new building was erected. Two years later the school opened an Employment Bureau.

In the meantime, its founder was appointed or elected to a number of positions. In 1920 Griffith was appointed to the State Child Welfare Board. Two years later she was elected president of the Colorado Education Association; in 1924 she was appointed to the Board of Control of the State Industrial School for Boys. By 1933 her workload was too heavy. Surprising everyone who believed she was only in her early fifties (she was actually twelve years older), Emily retired from the Opportunity School. Although she protested, the Denver School Board renamed the Opportunity School the Emily Griffith Opportunity School the following year. Griffith and her sister Florence, whom she had taken care of all her life, moved to Pinecliffe, Colorado. Fred W. Lundy, a carpenter and teacher at the Opportunity School, built them a primitive four-room cabin. He lived in a cabin nearby and did odd jobs for the two sisters.

In June 1947 Emily and Florence Griffith were found dead in the cabin, shot in the back of the head. When police went looking for Fred Lundy, he was nowhere to be found. Two months later a young fisherman discovered his body in a creek. Although some surmised that Lundy shot both sisters as a mercy killing, others have pointed the finger at Evan Gurtner, the husband of Evelyn, the third Griffith sister. She was the sole heiress to Griffith's estate, which included a sizable amount of cash from the sale of Emily's Denver home the previous year. The case remains unsolved.[82]

The Emily Griffith Opportunity School continues to honor its founder's vision. A part of the Colorado Community College System, it is largely supported through the Emily Griffith Foundation. Students can become bricklayers, certified chefs, or electricians; be trained in cosmetology, event management, or the culinary arts; pursue a career as a legal secretary, automobile technician, medical assistant, dental aide, or nurses' assistant. Classes are taught in welding and real estate. The Corporate Training Division offers workforce development classes, while the Extended Learning Center offers classes in parenting and GED preparation. The Language Learning Center provides English, Arabic, and Spanish lessons. Emily Griffith High School offers career and technical courses and houses the Emily Griffith Adult High School.

NINE

THE GREAT DEPRESSION

(1930-1939)

As the nation reeled during the Great Depression, Franklin D. Roosevelt was elected the thirty-second president of the United States. The voters' displeasure with Herbert Hoover was as much a factor in Roosevelt's election as were his campaign promises to do whatever was necessary to move the nation forward. Once in office, Roosevelt and the US Congress passed a litany of bills and created dozens of agencies aimed at "relief, recovery, and reform." Not everyone was pleased with the results, in theory or in practice. One disgruntled woman was Gertrude Rader of Loma, Colorado.[1]

Although a variety of programs were created to aid American farmers and ranchers, the Raders found the government "helpers" a "nuisance." A young male helper would arrive at any time of day, first wasting Gertrude's time by trying to make a believer out of her by giving her a summary of his college education. Then he wanted to see the livestock, the irrigation canal, or the fields. Whatever it was, it kept her from her chores for much too long.

DOI: 10.5876/9781607322078.c09

The practice of a helper coming unannounced, disrupting chores or meals, wasting time building up his ego, and wanting to see various areas of the ranch was repeated each time a new government "character" showed up at the doorstep. Making matters even worse were the decisions the young men made regarding the Raders' livestock and crops. Two officials decided that the Raders had too many "bovine critters" and pigs, so they selected and killed a yearling heifer and two runt pigs and told the Raders to bury them. The Raders, with no electricity or icebox, refused to let meat go to waste, so they bought chemicals and Morton's pork cure salt in Fruita. They cut the beef into small pieces to fit into fruit canning jars, covered the pieces with corned beef solution, and sealed the jars. They rubbed the forty-pound pigs with pork cure and rolled them in flour sacks. Only after these steps had been taken did the Raders follow the government helpers' instructions—they buried all the meat under the vegetables in their root storage cellar. The next government official who visited the ranch decided they had too many acres of wheat and ordered the Raders to plow them under. Once again, the couple followed the order but only after they ran the wheat through their cattle's digestive systems.[2]

The land of western Colorado has its own beauty. There are red canyon walls, shrubby mesas, and winding rivers and streams. It is a land—like much of Colorado—dependent upon irrigation. For over thirty years, Rader served as secretary-treasurer of the Loma Ditch and Lateral Company and its spur ditches. One government helper managed to rile Rader as both the water expert and a woman in one ill-advised tirade. When he wanted to see the irrigation ditch, she led him to a headgate and demonstrated how it worked. This stole two precious hours from her day. Back at the house, she tried to explain how to figure irrigation water for each of the farms. He refused to listen and declared that he was "angry, frustrated, and embarrassed at having a WOMAN show him how to figure water needs." Infuriated by his contemptuous tone of voice, she threw her figures into the fire and left him standing there.[3]

The Raders were not the only ones in the Loma area to experience the ignorance of government helpers. Their neighboring ranchers and farmers could have regaled each other with stories about the helpers. One evening a visitor to the Raders thought he heard sheep bleating, which surprised them because they didn't own any sheep. It was simply a croaking frog. Another official couldn't distinguish yellow clover seeds from oat seeds, which prompted the owner of Knowles' Feed and Seed to declare, "Even a jackass knows the difference between oats and clover seeds." Rader could have told them about the young man who did not know how to step off property and accurately figure square footage. One of her neighbors could have mentioned the official who said he was sent about some unproductive ewes but pronounced it "e-was." He further illustrated his ignorance when the report he had the farmer sign said he had slaughtered five "yous."[4]

Rader did praise two New Deal programs, however. The Resettlement Program provided construction work for the area, and the Civilian Conservation Corps (CCC) hired many of the area's young men. But the latter program was a mixed blessing for the Raders, as local CCC campers poisoned several of their milk cows when they put out bait to kill prairie dogs.[5] In all, it is easy to see why the Raders—like many other Americans—yearned for the previous decade.

THE GREAT DEPRESSION

During the 1920s, dancing the Charleston, sipping illegal liquor, and buying modern appliances on credit blinded many Americans to the problems lurking in the nation's economy, but it was impossible to stave off the Great Depression of the 1930s. In October 1929 the financial house of cards, the pseudo-prosperity of the 1920s, came crashing down with the collapse of the stock market. By 1932 nearly one in four Americans was without a job. Thousands of people wandered around the country looking for work. The suffering of the farmers, who had not experienced the good times of the 1920s, worsened when serious drought and wind turned the southern Great Plains into the Dust Bowl. Fewer industries existed in Colorado than in the eastern and midwestern states, and those that were present were largely agriculture-based and subsequently experienced hard times along with the farmers. Although substantial suffering existed, Governor Edwin C. Johnson and Colorado legislators were so opposed to federal involvement in the state's affairs that they tried to cripple New Deal programs. In January 1934 federal emergency relief officials stopped payments to the state because the general assembly refused to appropriate matching funds. Only the threat of violence by citizens spurred the legislature into action.

Unfortunately for Spanish-speaking workers, the economic crisis only exacerbated nativist sentiments against Mexicans. Under President Hoover's administration the federal government began to expatriate and deport aliens, most of whom were Mexican, arguing that their jobs could be filled by US citizens. Many legal residents and citizens were ensnared in the roundups. In

1932 the Godina family from Longmont was among the 20,000 Colorado residents repatriated to Mexico, even though Mrs. Godina and the six children were citizens and Mr. Godina was a legal resident. Later, the family was allowed to return to Longmont.[6]

In 1936 Governor Johnson proclaimed martial law in a mile-wide strip along the state's southern border, declaring that individuals in Colorado were "acting in conjunction with large numbers of persons outside of said state who are aliens and indigent persons to effect an invasion of said state."[7] The National Guard was authorized to search persons on trains, in vehicles, and on foot. Those who were undocumented or deemed unable to support themselves were deported or turned away. As Adjutant General Neil Kimball patrolled from the air, his troops halted travelers at the state's southern border. More than 300 people were turned away. But the blockade proved less than airtight as "smugglers" entered Colorado through Nebraska and Kansas. When some guardsmen ventured into New Mexico to conduct "intelligence missions," the state's governor warned them to stay in Colorado, protesting that Johnson had no right to treat New Mexicans as aliens because their ancestors had settled in the area when Colorado was part of Mexico. The Roman Catholic Church, the Communist Party, and others called for an end to the blockade. Employers also protested, saying they needed workers. Although the state labor bureau reported that 1,300 jobs were now available as a result of the blockade, few Anglo Coloradans applied for beet field work that paid only $1.10 a day. In the end, even though he continued to defend the blockade, Johnson finally lifted it, stating that the problem of cheap alien labor required a national solution.[8]

While Johnson was driving Hispanics from the state, the 355 residents of the Spanish Colony tried to survive with the help of the House of Neighborly Service Association (HNSA). Although useful, its efforts were insufficient, as economic conditions worsened in the 1930s. By 1935 the demand for beet labor had decreased by 45 percent, leaving many residents jobless. To alleviate the worst of the suffering, the Greeley Woman's Club donated milk, clothing, gifts, and money. In response to appeals for help from the HNSA social worker, the club raised money, hosted Christmas parties for colony children, and provided dress material for older children.[9] But neither group could provide jobs for the families. Faced with few jobs, increased discrimination, and possible deportation, farmworkers left the barren beet fields for Denver and other cities. There, they shared what they received in relief and took advantage of the lack of work to enroll their children in public schools.[10]

African Americans also experienced increased discrimination and hardship during the Depression. The Phyllis Wheatley Branch of the YWCA noted significant differences in attendance and participation from the 1920s to 1940. Its January 1931 report noted that it had deferred girls' rent payments and that the Industrial Club was down from eighty-five to forty members because young women could not afford the supper. Fewer members attended the Girl Reserves Club because they did not have money for carfare. As Dorothy C. Guinn reported, hardships for African Americans were the same as those for any other group of workers who belonged to the YWCA, but they had an added burden "when, as is so often the case, the racial element is injected into the employment situation."[11]

The following year, representatives from black women's groups released findings on employment conditions for black women. The first section of the report suggested actions the black community could take. Hiring blacks to do laundry or lawn chores, appealing to white friends, soliciting commodities (eggs and milk), patronizing black establishments, and boycotting were mentioned. The organizations discovered that blacks were losing ground in jobs they had traditionally filled, primarily domestic service and as employees of the Denver Dry Goods Store. Housework that had paid fifteen dollars a week the previous year was down to ten and in some cases only five dollars a week. The report stressed the importance of doing one's job conscientiously. Leaders pointed out that the situation was exacerbated by the few women who did not fulfill their duties responsibly. Employer criticism of black employees increased, with comments such as "does good work but invariable [sic] walks off with food from larder" and "a fine cook, but keeps a filthy kitchen."[12] Branch records also revealed a disturbing trend. In 1923, more than 71 percent of applicants were placed in jobs. By 1930 the percentage had dropped to 56; in 1931, only 43 percent of applicants were placed in jobs.[13] Compounding the problem was the fact that New Deal programs seldom helped women or minorities.

CHANGES FOR THE UTE INDIANS

Native Americans were equally ignored. By 1900 Colorado and federal authorities had succeeded in relegating what remained of Ute tribal members to two reservations in the southwestern corner of the state. The goal of reservations was to drive the "Indian" out of the Native American. They were to abandon their nomadic ways, live in permanent homes, and adopt the Anglos' patriarchal culture. Their children would attend boarding

FIGURE 9.1 *Boarding schools for Native Americans tried to teach Anglo ways of life, such as Anglo child care and dress. The schools were also notorious for their unhealthy conditions. Children contracted trachoma and other diseases. Courtesy, Denver Public Library Western History Collection, X-30675.*

schools, preferably off-reservation, where they would leave behind their culture and become indoctrinated in Anglo ways. Both Ute men and women were subject to these assimilationist policies, but the women were most affected by the campaign to turn their culture of gender equality into one of patriarchy. In this matter, as with other reservation plans, Ute women sought their own path. Before their removal to reservations in southwestern Colorado, Ute women "participated in councils, were active in warfare, and provided leadership and power in spiritual matters."[14] After relocation, Ute women continued to insist on equal participation. Although agents implemented the policies of the Office of Indian Affairs through Ute men, Ute women resisted attempts to render them passive in political, economic, or social matters. They participated in councils and public debates. They petitioned Washington, DC, for the annuities, supplies, and rations that had been promised them. They attended public forums on reservation policy, attended tribal councils, and adamantly opposed boarding schools for their children.

While men received training and incentives to be producers, Ute women were expected to adopt the Anglo middle-class homemaker lifestyle. Instead, they defiantly engaged in wage work, made and sold craft items, leased and sold their land, ran farms, raised livestock, and gathered and processed wild foods. All of these tasks were necessary for the survival of the tribe's members, who were trying to scratch out a living on land that was barely arable.

Although field matrons hired by the Office of Indian Affairs introduced "Euro-American standards of cleanliness, subsistence tasks, and aesthetics," Ute women were selective in adopting these standards.[15] They continued to complete household chores communally and to live in temporary homes through the 1920s. Native women did go to field matrons for medicine and prenatal care. In short, confined to the reservation and subject to assimilationist policies, Ute women did not acquiesce. Rather, they deliberately adopted parts of Anglo culture (such as labor-saving technology) but maintained a distinctly Ute identity on the reservation. As active members of their tribes, Ute women—and men—were further challenged in the 1930s by a significant change in American Indian policy.

In 1934, in the midst of the Great Depression, Congress passed the Indian Reorganization Act (IRA). After a century of assimilation attempts, the act ushered in a new era. The IRA required the political reorganization of tribes through the creation of elected tribal councils to manage tribal affairs in accordance with new tribal constitutions. Economic reorganization would be accomplished through the granting of corporate charters. The establishment of a $10 million revolving credit fund would promote economic development on reservations. One of the most significant facets of the IRA was a package of reforms designed to protect and increase Indian landholdings. The allotment policy was abolished. The IRA also permitted the voluntary exchange of allotments and heirship land, restored remaining surplus land to tribal ownership, and authorized annual appropriation of federal funds for the purchase of new tribal lands. For those living on the Southern Ute and Ute Mountain Ute Reservations, the IRA required a paradigm shift in attitude toward, and tribal relations with, the federal government. Following a pattern established in the late 1800s when the two reservations were formed, the two Ute groups reacted differently to the IRA. In 1935 the Southern Utes accepted the IRA with a referendum vote and ratified a tribal constitution in 1936. The Ute Mountain Utes, traditionally more isolated and wary of the federal government, did not create a constitution until 1940.[16]

For Ute women, the new tribal governments provided opportunities for increased involvement. Two women, Aileen Hatch and Emma South Beecher, served on the Ute Mountain Ute's first council. Although the Southern Utes did not elect a woman (Euterpe Taylor) until 1948, from that point forward they almost always had a female representative, often more than one. Taylor, who served four times, was soon followed by Sunshine Smith, who served a total of ten years between 1952 and 1966. In 1960 the election of two new female members gave the six-person Southern Ute Tribal Council four women members.

As reservation Utes dealt with the ramifications of the Indian Reorganization Act, they faced issues surrounding the education of their children. From the earliest attempts at assimilation, Utes fought sending their children to boarding schools, which were notoriously unhealthy. A day school was established near the agency, but attendance was so low after it was converted to a boarding school that by 1890 it had closed. In its place, Fort Lewis was converted from a military post to a boarding school, but enrollment there was no better. In 1894 a Southern Ute agent reported that half of the students attending boarding school in Albuquerque had died and a quarter of the students at Fort Lewis had contracted trachoma, which led to blindness. During the next two decades, the Southern Ute Boarding School and Allen Day School (established 1909) educated Ute students. By 1920 the boarding school was closed, and Utes were enrolled in public schools.

Although more Ute children attended public schools through the 1930s, that alone did not guarantee them an equal and integrated education. Like Hispanics, American Indian students were usually segregated from white students because of their lack of English-language skills. For Ute Mountain Utes, the situation was bleak. In 1934 most students attended Ute Mountain Boarding School, a few attended the boarding school at Ignacio, four were enrolled in an off-reservation boarding school, and one attended public school. Ute Mountain Utes' educational problems were compounded by geographic isolation, suspicion of outsiders, and seasonal migration habits as stock-raising families.[17]

WOMEN AND NEW DEAL PROGRAMS

The federal government created a smorgasbord of New Deal programs designed to help American workers in urban areas. Few proved of much assistance to women workers. Title I of the National Industrial Recovery Act, passed in 1933, included wage differentials based on sex. The National Woman's Party and the League of Women Voters protested, and officers of the National Federation of Business and Professional Women's Clubs sent telegrams to the president. Although First Lady Eleanor Roosevelt and Secretary of Labor Frances Perkins assured women's groups that the codes were only temporary, when the bill was signed it contained eight codes with gender-based wage differentials.[18]

Other New Deal programs also ignored women workers. The Public Works Administration created work on schools, bridges, hospitals, and government buildings—projects that required hundreds of workers in construction, engineering, and design, fields in which female workers were virtually absent. The popular Civilian Conservation Corps hired young men for national, state, and local park projects. Only later, at the urging of the First Lady, did the government open eighty-six CCC camps for young women. Even then, the CCC's comparatively few females (6,400 versus 3.5 million males) received only fifty cents to the men's dollar-a-day wage.[19] Another work relief program, the Civilian Works Administration, slightly improved the lot of unemployed women by hiring 100,000 female workers nationwide, but it also paid them a lower wage than men received.

Significant change occurred with the creation of the Works Progress Administration (WPA). Nationally, the proportions of women on WPA work relief varied between 12 percent and 19 percent of females.[20] Male laborers built bridges, repaired roads, laid riprap along creek banks for erosion control, and constructed public buildings. As with other New Deal programs, minorities were not hired in the same proportion as whites. In Colorado, Hispanics hired by the WPA were removed from the payroll before harvest season so they would be available for stoop labor in the beet fields.[21]

Although the WPA had the largest positive impact of all New Deal programs on the plight of unemployed women, the program's criteria for eligibility hampered females. No more than one member of a family could be hired, and an individual had to prove that he or she was the head of the household. In some states, previous lack of work experience outside the home disqualified women. Under the largest WPA project for Colorado women—the sewing project—more than 7 million garments, quilts, and clothing accessories were completed between 1935 and 1942. The items were given to needy persons in the state. The WPA hired Spanish-speaking women in southern Colorado to weave rugs. Its food-canning project used meat, vegetables, and fruits from the federal government's agricultural purchase programs. Cans of food were distributed to the needy and to the hot lunch program. The latter was usually sponsored by local boards of education and aided by civic organizations and parent-teacher associations. Prior to participating in the hot lunch program, children in some parts of Colorado ate only a piece of cornbread or a cold pancake for lunch. Meat, if included, was salt pork. Initially,

FIGURE 9.2 *The Works Progress Administration established a weaving project in southern Colorado in which women were hired to spin and weave wool. Courtesy, Denver Public Library Western History Collection, Z-3036.*

an effort was made to have children bring a piece of bread from home to supplement the hot lunch provided through the WPA program. However, that practice was discontinued because the bread the children brought was dirty, dry, and moldy. For some schoolchildren, the hot lunch program, which included milk, was their only hot meal of the day.[22] The program also gave

Colorado women a work relief job and work experience. Colorado women on the WPA payroll served over 21 million school lunches.[23]

Under other WPA programs, unemployed nurses were hired to help in relief homes where sickness prevented mothers from caring for their children. WPA employees also worked in twenty-eight Colorado nursery schools. In Denver, Colorado Springs, Pueblo, and Greeley, the WPA rented houses to provide a two-month course-in-residence to train young women in domestic service to be aides in motherless homes. Although initially opposed by clubwomen as unworthy work for women, the program became popular. Nearly half a million visits were made to motherless homes.[24]

Just as unemployed white-collar men were given jobs in the WPA as historians and accountants, professional women were also put to work using their skills and training. Over 5,000 Denver women prepared a card file of all Colorado war records. Other women conducted surveys on schools, the parole system, mineral and water resources, roads, game refuges, spending habits, and records of communicable diseases.[25]

The Public Works Administration Project commissioned artists to create sculptural pieces for public buildings. Gladys Caldwell Fisher was paid thirty-five dollars a week to carve a relief, *American Indian Orpheus and the Animals,* which was placed in the Denver City and County Building. Two years later she carved two massive bighorn sheep for the entrance of the US Post Office (now the Byron R. White Federal Courthouse) in Denver. With the ninety-eight dollars a month she was paid, she was able to hire two more artists and a stone carver from relief rolls. The project took over a year to complete and brought Fisher favorable publicity. Her last public commission was carving two bear cubs for the Mammoth Hot Springs Post Office in Yellowstone National Park.[26]

Louise W. Brand, a WPA employee, worked for the Denver Public Schools as a crafts teacher. Struggling to survive on her salary, she took adult education classes at a local YWCA in leather and metal work. Jonas Fur and Taxidermy hired her to make glass eyes for its "stuffed" animals. When her stepfather, who worked for the WPA Federal Art Project, hurt his back and could not work, she asked to take over his job. Because of her work at Jonas Fur, she was put on the staff at the Natural History Museum. Her first assignment was working with other women making flowers for exhibits of Colorado fauna. She traveled throughout the state and brought back samples of Colorado flora. She also perused reference books, which, although old, contained valuable information. Because of their dilapidated state, she learned book binding and salvaged many of the books for the museum's library. Brand earned ninety-five dollars every two weeks. She worked with twenty other women and was the last to go when the WPA program ended. Creating displays of Colorado fauna was an enriching experience for Brand. Forty years later, when interviewed for the WPA Oral History Project sponsored by the Friends of the Denver Public Library, she stated, "Nothing has given me as much pleasure."[27]

Ethel and Jenne Magafan, twin sisters born in 1916 in Chicago, Illinois, to Peter J. and Julia P. Magafan, also received WPA commissions. After graduating from high school in Denver, the sisters studied with regionalist painters Frank Mechau and Boardman Robinson at the Colorado Springs Fine Arts Center (formerly the Broadmoor Art School). Mechau later hired them as mural assistants and encouraged them to enter competitions sponsored by the US Treasury Department's Section of Fine Arts. In this program, a master artist was awarded a commission and used relief artists as assistants. The sisters painted murals in midwestern and western states, some as the sole artist and others as Mechau's assistants. Although Ethel was awarded a commission for the Lawrence, Kansas, post office, local authorities rejected her idea of depicting the 1863 massacre. Also known as Quantrell's Raid, the massacre was a rebel guerilla attack led by William Clarke Quantrell on the pro-Union town of Lawrence. Quantrell's men set fire to the town and killed most of its male residents. Ethel's mural *Threshing,* a contemporary agricultural scene, for the Auburn, Nebraska, post office, was accepted, however. In 1941 she painted *Horse Corral,* which still survives in the South Denver Post Office. In all, she won five commissions. She and her sister also painted *Mountains in the Snow* for the Social Security Building in Washington, DC.[28]

Jenne assisted Mechau on several pieces. For the Glenwood Springs Post Office, the two artists and another assistant, Eduardo Chavez (who was married to Jenne), painted *Wild Horse Race* in 1937. That same year Jenne and Eduardo painted *Decorative Map,* also for the post office. This mural depicts Glenwood Springs's economic and recreational activities set against a background of mountains, trees, and canyons. The three artists also collaborated on *Indian Fight* and *The Corral* for the Colorado Springs Post Office (these two panels are presently in Building 41 of the Denver Federal Center). In addition, Jenne painted murals for post offices in Anson (Texas), Albion (Nebraska), and Helper (Utah).[29]

Like the Magafans, Louise Emerson Ronnebeck was not a Colorado native. She came to Colorado when her husband was appointed the art director at the Denver Art Museum. Ronnebeck was commissioned to paint

FIGURE 9.3 *Ila McAfee Turner, a native of Sargents, south of Gunnison, painted Wealth of the West for the Gunnison Post Office. Murals by Turner, Louise Ronnebeck, and Jenne and Ethel Magafan were commissioned by the Works Progress Administration. Courtesy, Denver Public Library Western History Collection, X-9357.*

murals for the Worland (Wyoming) and Grand Junction Post Offices. In 1973 *The Harvest,* which showed a man and woman harvesting peaches, was sent to Washington, DC, for restoration. It was forgotten about for nearly twenty years before it was found and returned to Grand Junction, where it now resides in the city's Wayne Aspinall Federal Building.

Two native-born Coloradans received their artistic inspiration from their home state. Ila McAfee Turner completed murals for post offices in Clifton (Texas), Edmond (Oklahoma), and Gunnison and the public library in Greeley. She was born in 1897 and raised on her family's ranch in Sargents, south of Gunnison. After graduating from Western State College, she studied art in Chicago and New York before marrying Elmer Page Turner, another artist. They moved to Taos, New Mexico, in 1928. Although a neurological disease ended her husband's work as a painter, Ila thrived in the artist colony. Her 1934 oil painting *Mountain Lions,* depicting two large cats overlooking the Black Canyon of the Gunnison, is owned by the Smithsonian Institution. Turner moved back to her home state in 1993 (her husband died in 1966) and died in Pueblo two years later.

Nadine Kent Drummond, born in Trinidad, worked for the Federal Art Project. Her lithograph *Mountain Town* showed a gathering of buildings hemmed in by towering hills of pine trees and mining structures. Drummond frequently depicted the windswept desolation of Colorado's farming regions. *Farm Auction in Trinidad* portrayed a common event during the Great Depression: the bidding for a farm that neither the resident nor his neighbors could afford to buy and on which they could not earn a living.

THE DUST BOWL

During the 1930s, Colorado's southeastern plains communities were on the verge of blowing away. The area experienced extreme hardship when years of severe drought compounded the problems of agricultural overproduction in the 1920s. Winds blew away the topsoil of fallow fields. Great clouds of dust hid the sun, turning day into night. Towns were forced to put on their streetlights at midday to aid visibility. Dust invaded buildings and homes, obliterated roads, and interrupted airplane, railroad, and automobile traffic. One particularly huge dust cloud swirled out of Colorado and across the Texas Panhandle before settling on ships in the Gulf of Mexico. Another storm dropped its dust on the nation's East Coast. In 1934 and 1935, the wind carried away precious topsoil nearly every day.

In early June 1934, after a state labor convention in Pueblo, an old cowpuncher drove two social workers through 200 miles of drought area, where they were caught in one of the infamous dust storms. One of the social workers reported: "In an hour you couldn't see two feet ahead of the car. All of my clothes will have to be cleaned. Even my hat. When I got home at 9:30 last night I had to wash my hair it was so filthy. Even with all of the windows of the car closed there was a thick layer of dust on the seat and in our laps—everywhere. In all those miles of driving we didn't see one drop of water or one crop which had come up. Just a little cactus and a bit of sagebrush."[30] Acre by acre, Colorado disappeared into thick, dusty air. Perhaps the only positive immediate effect of these "black blizzards" was that they uncovered a number of archaeological artifacts, providing scientists with evidence about the migrations of early Indians.

Dust storms created serious health issues for Coloradans. Hundreds of people fell sick, particularly children and the aged who were especially sensitive to "dust pneumonia." In the spring of 1935 the disease reached epidemic proportions in southeastern Colorado, not only among humans but among animals as well. R. M. McMillin, president of the Bent-Prowers Cattle and Horse Growers Association, reported that 50,000 cattle needed to be removed from Bent, Prowers, and Baca Counties and relocated to South Park and the San Luis Valley because sand covered their ranges to a depth of several inches.[31]

The storms also disturbed urban Coloradans. When it rained on April 9, 1935, beads of mud showered down on Denver. Less than a week later a storm that struck Denver at 2:00 p.m. "blotted out the sun, blew up sand drifts that stopped trains and automobiles, and grounded airplanes. The gale-like winds tore down wires . . . and filled homes and stores with a thick film of powdery dust."[32] Near Durango, one storm created dust drifts nine feet high.[33] Residents in eastern Colorado appealed to the federal government for aid. The Federal Emergency Relief Administration provided food rations and livestock feed, as well as special work projects. The Farm Credit Administration extended special drought loans, and the Resettlement Administration initiated its program of relocating farmers. The Civilian Conservation Corps started an intense program of soil conservation. Although some farmers on the eastern plains welcomed help from the Agricultural Adjustment and Resettlement Administrations, others were less enamored with the federal programs.[34]

In May 1935, when rain momentarily ended the Dust Bowl drought, thousands of farmers transferred off of relief and once again began farming. Unfortunately, the rain continued to be so heavy that the dry earth could not absorb it quickly enough, causing terrible spring floods, particularly in Kiowa and Elbert Counties. To compound farmers' problems, the change in weather did not last long. Clear and sunny skies returned to blister the farms of southeastern Colorado. Unlike 1934, when farmers fed tumbleweed and Russian thistle to their livestock, not even those plants were growing in 1935. Desperate ranchers in southern Colorado burned thorns off cactus plants to feed to their animals, which were ready to eat any available vegetation.

For thousands of farmers in southeastern Colorado, this was the last straw. Four years of drought and crop failures had depleted their savings and their hope. Packing up what few possessions remained, Colorado farmers joined the mass exodus from the plains. Not knowing what the future held for them in the cities and towns to which they emigrated, the busted and broken agricultural souls moved on, leaving behind dust-filled homes and infertile soil.[35] Almost a quarter of Kit Carson County's residents moved away, while Baca County's population declined by 41 percent.[36]

MEETING THE CHALLENGES

Some middle-class urban families on the Western Slope found the going a bit easier, not having to contend with either the "black blizzards" of the eastern plains or the government helpers who plagued Gertrude Rader and her ranching neighbors. Grand Junction was still a relatively small city on the eve of the Great Depression, with few industries. Subsequently, it was able to avoid the massive layoffs and significant social disruptions that plagued Pueblo and Denver in the 1930s. Unlike their rural eastern plains counterparts, agricultural production for farmers in the Grand Valley was relatively unharmed. Thus, the women of Grand Junction, although needing to conserve and be resourceful, faced fewer challenges than others in the state. When necessity called, they were able to draw upon their skills of "canning, cooking, sewing, and those other things that made it possible to keep their households nearly self-sufficient."[37] Women stretched paychecks until they nearly snapped back. They raised vegetables in their own gardens and bought fresh fruit from Grand Valley orchards to eat in the summer and fall and to can for winter and spring consumption. Edna Copley Sutherland kept a "canning book" in which she wrote recipes and recorded the number of quart jars she canned. In 1937 she put up an incredible 510 quarts of fruits, vegetables, meat, soup, and juices.[38]

Most families owned a grinder with which to make their own sausage, using the Morton Salt Company's prepared spice mixture and stuffing the meat in homemade cheesecloth sacks that were then stored in a cool place, such as a root cellar or a basement. Dairy and meat products that were not canned required either electrical refrigeration—not an option for many families before or during the Depression—or an icebox. Women baked their own bread, biscuits, and rolls.

Keeping the family well-clothed during the Great Depression presented another challenge. Women made clothes using thread purchased for five cents a spool and patterns for fifteen cents apiece. Cotton cloth sold for fifteen cents per yard, and cotton sacks in which flour was purchased were another source of material. Most flour sacks were white but were stamped with the brand name of the flour. Removing these markings took a great deal of "elbow grease," soap, bleach, and ingenuity. The sacks were fashioned into dishcloths, handkerchiefs, tea towels, and petticoats. "Hand-me-down" clothing was also important. Clothing was sometimes worn "as is" by someone else; other times, a man's cast-out overalls contained enough material to make a young boy's jeans. Most women owned a treadle sewing machine. Friends borrowed and altered clothing patterns as needed. Readymade clothing from a department store was often worn only for special occasions, such as church. Many Depression-era children went barefoot because shoes were too expensive to buy as often as necessary for a growing boy or girl.

Regardless of whether clothing was made or purchased, it had to be cleaned. Washing clothes was a woman's most odious chore, as evidenced by the fact that the moment she could hire it out or purchase a labor-saving electrical washer and dryer, she did so. Doing laundry was an all-day chore. Water was carried in, boiled, used for washing and rinsing the clothes, and hauled outside again. Clothes were wet, soaped, and rubbed on the corrugated metal sheets of a washboard. Repeated washings and rinsings were followed by hand-wringing before the item was hung on the line to dry. In cold weather, clothing was often brought in frozen stiff to dry inside before being ironed with heavy metal irons heated on the stove. For families with electricity and the money to allow them the luxury, electrical irons replaced metal ones.

In addition to making do with what they had, women found work outside the home, if possible. In Grand Junction, women found seasonal work with seed companies and canning factories. Other women quit their jobs following marriage because they believed a family did not have the right to collect two paychecks. Eva Larson, a fifth grade teacher at Hawthorne School, resigned from her job when she married N. Franklin Cheek, who worked for the Public Service Company. Likewise, Mary Aspinall quit her teaching job when she married Leonard White, a railroader.[39] A reader of the *Denver Post,* after learning that over 400 married women taught in the Denver schools, suggested that women who "would look better in their homes living on their husband's salaries" should be replaced with jobless men.[40] The reader failed to realize that many women continued to teach because it provided either the family's only paycheck or a necessary supplement to ward off the wolf at the door. Velma Burdick Deaver taught school in northeastern Colorado. Ironically, because she had a teaching job, her husband was denied work. For eighty-five dollars a month, Leona Rector Hinricks taught in a one-room school in Morappos while her husband—a ranch hand—and son lived in Rangely. Education also provided Norinne Holland's mother with a job. The family lost their ranch after Norinne's father died in 1933: "The bank came out and settled everything that there was. My brother was only 15 and still attending school. There was no way we could keep the ranch." Mrs. Holland later ran for county superintendent of schools and won.[41]

When the nation's fortunes and individuals' pipe dreams of "easy money" disappeared in the stock market crash, Colorado women rose to the challenge. Clubwomen stocked pantry shelves and held food drives for the needy, farmwomen on the eastern plains coped with mountains of dust in their homes, and married women contended with policies against hiring them. Women helped their fellow citizens and transients in many ways. Men looking for any kind of work came through communities along major roads and railroads. Although struggling to provide for their own families, housewives allowed these men to spend a few hours weeding a garden, chopping wood, or repairing items around the farm or house in exchange for a home-cooked meal. New Deal programs helped women indirectly by providing work relief for male members of their families, but only a few were instrumental in directly benefiting unemployed women looking for work. In addition, all New Deal programs gave preference to Anglo workers over needy minorities.

Most New Deal programs were terminated either before the United States entered World War II or shortly thereafter. One important piece of New Deal legislation, though, endured the transition from Depression relief to war work. In 1935 Congress passed the Social Security Act, a revolutionary concept for the United States, which lagged behind other developed nations in providing old-age insurance plans for citizens. Domestic servants and large proportions of farm laborers, as well as charitable, educational, and hospital personnel, were exempted. Women filled a majority of those job categories. Revisions to the act in 1939 added widows' benefits and provided wives of insured workers with old-age payments equal to 50 percent of their husbands' payments when they both reached retirement age. The method of computing benefits and the eligibility requirements changed in such a manner that a working wife paid the same taxes as her husband for less insurance. Inequities in the Social Security program existed for decades, rendering it less beneficial to many employee groups, particularly women.[42]

DEATH OF AN ICON

The same year Congress passed the Social Security Act, a Colorado icon was found frozen to death in a cabin in Leadville. Elizabeth Bonduel McCourt "Baby" Doe Tabor had not survived the winter in the old mining camp. A widow for thirty-six years, Tabor had outlived most of her detractors. As she endured years of abject poverty at the Matchless Mine, her reputation evolved from "wanton divorcée" to madwoman.[43] Numerous books, movies, and an opera have fed the public's fascination with the love triangle and scandal involving Horace Tabor, his first wife, Augusta, and Baby Doe.

They recount the adultery, the messy divorce, Denver snubbing the new couple, and Tabor's alleged deathbed instructions to Baby Doe to hold on to the Matchless Mine, believing it would one day prove valuable again. Many accounts praised Augusta as the hardworking, long-suffering wife. Supporters of Baby Doe, however, criticized Augusta as cold and prudish. Tabor—sometimes only on the periphery of the scandal—is portrayed as a man so smitten by a beautiful woman nearly half his age that he threw away a political career and squandered his fortune to keep her clothed in furs and lavishly entertained.

When Baby Doe's body was discovered, the public was inundated with lurid details of her death, as decades earlier they had been scandalized by her life. In death, however, she was treated less harshly. Leadville residents contrasted her appearance in the town—"dressed in baggy, gender-crossing clothing from which dangled a large crucifix, her feet wrapped in rags"—with earlier photographs of her as a young, vibrant woman. Newspapers printed pictures of her cabin, crammed with papers and decidedly slovenly. Her attire and appearance in Leadville had earned her the title of madwoman. One historian, though, begs to differ. Over the course of twenty years, Judy Nolte Temple read, organized, and tried to decipher thousands of Baby Doe's "Dreams and Visions" found after her death. In *Baby Doe Tabor: The Madwoman in the Cabin*, Temple concludes that Tabor's writings suggest that "she was not mad but, instead, a most unconventional autobiographer, a pioneer of marvelous realism, or even a religious mystic-in-the-rough." She termed the widow's madwoman costume a case of "strategic madness" that "demanded community attention to her plight," much as Emily Dickinson's reclusiveness had.[44] Adulteress, seductress, heroic widow, or madwoman? In the middle of the Great Depression, Coloradans found a respite from their worries in the death of an icon from an earlier era.

DISPENSING RELIEF: ELIZABETH KLETZSCH AND THE BUREAU OF PUBLIC WELFARE

In the early 1930s, because of its moderate climate and relatively few industries, Denver was weathering the Depression better than many other communities. However, these advantages did not outweigh the disadvantage of having a mayor and a governor who were virulently opposed to federal interference. In 1933 the general assembly reaffirmed that county and municipal authorities were responsible for public relief. When Colorado refused to match funds dispensed by the Federal Emergency Relief Administration, Director Harry Hopkins threatened to withhold funds. The legislature raised the monies. Into this war of wills, Benjamin Glassberg, the administration's regional director, appointed Elizabeth Schroeder Kletzsch the new Denver director, ignoring the city's recommendation of Eunice Robinson. Kletzsch spent March to July 1934 in the center of a firestorm over federal monies and matching state funds. Later, there were turf battles within her own bureau and between Kletzsch and the city council.

Kletzsch, like earlier social workers, had a female network of supporters and mentors. Her first mentor was Glassberg who knew her from Milwaukee when he had been superintendent of the city's relief department. When she arrived at Denver's Union Station, Kletzsch was met by Glassberg; Esther K. Sudler, chairwoman of the board of directors of the Bureau of City Charities; and Robinson, former head of the bureau (until Kletzsch's arrival). Over the next several days, she observed Glassberg's management style until he left town. Even after his departure, she relied on his guidance. In April 1934 she despairingly wrote to her parents that her authority was being challenged by Robinson—who had been demoted to general case supervisor when Kletzsch was appointed—and Sudler, president of the board.[45] When Glassberg learned about the situation, he threatened to withdraw federal funds unless Robinson resigned. Only after a long meeting with Sudler did he relent and allow Robinson—and the federal funds—to remain.

Kletzsch also relied on Alice van Diest, the state director of relief. A native Coloradan, van Diest taught for several years after graduating from Colorado College before deciding that social service was more valuable to society than foreign language teaching was. She became a social worker in New York City. Because of her foreign language skills, she was assigned to the homes of poor Mexican, Puerto Rican, and Spanish residents on the Lower East Side. When she was called back to Colorado because of parental illnesses, she taught at her alma mater and served as director of the El Paso County Welfare Department. Kletzsch spent many weekends with van Diest. Before her first weekend in Colorado Springs, she wrote "it will be heaven to be in a private home with no reporters or politicians within seventy-five miles."[46] Later, she reported that she could now face "a very strenuous week."[47] Van Diest's fourteen-room home included five master bedrooms and a guest room that overlooked Pikes Peak. Van Diest's companionship and tour guide efforts rejuvenated Kletzsch. Van Diest, too, must have enjoyed the visits. She often sent Kletzsch a begonia when she returned to Denver.

Kletzsch also valued the expertise of Josephine Roche, president and general manager of the Rocky Mountain Fuel Company. The two women met at the Blue Parrot Restaurant in Denver when Kletzsch and Robinson were having lunch. Roche invited them both to dinner. Kletzsch was impressed with the fuel company owner, praising her as "a charming, good-looking brilliant woman."[48] In May, the two women crossed paths again for lunch one day, followed by dinner the next. Kletzsch reported: "I'm very proud of the fact that she seems to like me for she is one of the really great women in the US today and one who doesn't bother [with] just being polite to people. She is tremendously busy with very important people and therefore I'm especially pleased to have her bother with me."[49]

Frances ("Pinky") Wayne of the *Denver Post*, originally one of Kletzsch's nemeses, soon became one of her supporters. How many of Wayne's initial criticisms were her own and how many were made as a reporter for the *Post*—a vehement opponent of federal authority in Colorado relief matters—is unknown, but early on Wayne noted that Kletzsch's personal charm was accentuated by "two playful, delightful dimples."[50] Eventually, Kletzsch's executive skills won over both the reporter and her newspaper.[51]

Just as a cluster of reform-minded men and women had electrified the atmosphere at Hull House and the University of Chicago at the turn of the century, Denver in the early 1930s was glowing. Judge Benjamin Lindsey (juvenile court), Elizabeth Byers (Ladies Union Aid Society), Sarah Platt Decker (Woman's Club of Denver), and Gertrude Vaile (City Charities) had built a strong foundation of relief and reform work. Although the magnitude of the problems posed by the Great Depression taxed local relief organizations, relief workers were undaunted. When the federal government took control of monies and the disbursement of funds, most local social relief workers simply changed employers. But for Robinson and Sudler, Kletzsch's appointment was intolerable. Both had served many years with the organization and did not welcome an "outsider." Robinson, a Coloradan with a degree from the University of Denver, was initially a teacher. Soon tiring of that, she volunteered at the public welfare office, then she took a paid position, and in 1926 she became Denver's director of public welfare until Kletzsch's arrival. She never accepted her reduced role with the bureau. More than once, she threatened to resign, although it appears she never took her complaints directly to Kletzsch.

Sudler was also a thorn in Kletzsch's side. She accused her of being ineffective, despite the fact that Kletzsch hired over 4,000 men for public works projects, created a sewing circle for unemployed women, doled out relief funds, and established the bureau as a model relief agency. She increased the number of field workers and raised their salaries to be competitive with other city workers' wages (Robinson's salary increased by more than 30 percent). Kletzsch acknowledged that Sudler was a capable woman who should have had a paid position that would have deterred her from meddling.[52]

Other problems also arose. In April, she wrote that she was sick about Glassberg leaving the area because she needed his backing. She appealed to her parents not to repeat what she told them: "Since I've been here I've learned that gossip can do a great deal of harm. Just now the Ku Klux Klan is circulating a story about my being Jewish and trying to arouse opposition."[53] The Jewish issue arose again two days later. An article in the Colorado Engineers Society magazine alleged that Glassberg had appointed Kletzsch because she was "a personal friend of his" and "of his own faith." The society's president quickly assured her that they would print an apology in the next edition.[54] The remark about Kletzsch being Glassberg's "personal friend" troubled her. Asking her parents not to talk about her and Glassberg, she reminded them that "whenever a married man is kind to a divorcee there's bound to be talk and in consequence the wife might be upset which would be ridiculous as you know."[55]

Directing the bureau was a feather in Kletzsch's cap. The "Denver situation" was the talk of the 1934 National Conference of Social Work. Her professionalism brought praise from other social workers, especially when earlier critics now voiced ardent support. It also earned her a state supervisor job in Wisconsin, which she accepted because it allowed her to move closer to her family. After she left Denver, the travails of the Bureau of Public Welfare continued. The selection of Carrie Lee Moellendick of Boulder as the bureau's new director prompted Robinson to resign. At the end of 1935, the bureau was dismantled. Care of Denver's needy was transferred to the poor department under the Department of Health and Charity.[56]

A MINER'S BEST FRIEND: JOSEPHINE ROCHE

Although many women have been the wives, mothers, and daughters of mine workers and several were miners themselves, very few women ever controlled a mine company and used her position to further the rights of miners rather than increase the value of company stock. Josephine Aspinwall Roche, the only child of John J. and Ella Aspinwall Roche, was the exception. Born on

FIGURE 9.4 *Josephine Roche became the majority owner of Rocky Mountain Fuel Company shortly after the death of her father. She invited the United Mine Workers to unionize her employees, an act that prompted her competitors to undercut prices in an effort to drive her out of business. Courtesy, History Colorado (Scan #10025012), Denver.*

December 2, 1886, in Nebraska, she graduated from a private school before enrolling at Vassar College in 1904. She plunged into college life, joining the basketball and track clubs and visiting slum settlements in Poughkeepsie. During the summers, she volunteered at the New York juvenile court. In 1908 she graduated with a double major in economics and the classics. She continued her studies at Columbia University, earning a master's degree in 1910. Her thesis, "Economic Conditions in Relation to the Delinquency of Girls," foretold her future work.[57] For two years she investigated working conditions of children and immigrants for the Russell Sage Foundation and Columbia University. In the evenings she directed classes at Greenwich House, a pioneering social service agency.

Her father, involved with the Rocky Mountain Fuel Company (RMFC), and her mother moved to Denver in 1908. She soon joined them in the West when George Creel, a Denver city commissioner, offered her the job of police matron. As "inspector of amusements," it was Roche's job to oversee the town's many dance halls and protect children from prostitution rings and abuse. When that job ended, she became a probation officer for Judge Ben Lindsey's juvenile court.[58]

Roche's earlier concern for the working conditions of immigrant laborers came into play in 1914 following the Ludlow Massacre. She recruited wives of Colorado Fuel and Iron miners to testify about the massacre before the US Industrial Relations Commission.

The outbreak of World War I provided another avenue for Roche's activism. Appointed a special agent for the Belgian Relief Committee, she went to England and later organized a relief drive in the northeastern US states. As US isolation ended, she created the Foreign Language Information Service to translate US news for foreign press agencies. In the middle of this venture, she married Edward Hale Bierstadt. They divorced after two years of marriage. From 1923 to 1925, Roche was director of the Editorial and Special Studies Department of the Children's Bureau in Washington, DC.

When her father fell ill, Roche returned to Denver. After he died in January 1927, she became a minority owner of the RMFC. Less than twelve months later the company and its workers were immersed in a bitter strike over higher wages and better working conditions. In November, six miners were killed by company guards at the Columbine mine in Serene, Colorado. A lifelong advocate for laborers and children, Roche was galvanized by the tragedy.[59] She borrowed money from friends and quietly began buying interests in the RMFC until she gained majority power. Shocking both the company and the coal-mining industry, Roche promptly invited the

United Mine Workers (UMW) to unionize the workers, paid them the unheard-of wage of $7.00 a day, rehired strikers, eliminated company scrip, and instituted workmen's compensation. Although these measures endeared her to miners and their families, they spurred a conspiracy by the state's other coal companies to break her company. Her most virulent and powerful enemy was John D. Rockefeller's Colorado Fuel and Iron Company, which cut prices below cost. RMFC miners rallied around Roche and the RMFC, loaning her $80,000 to stay afloat. Other coal companies joined Rockefeller's ploy.[60] The RMFC barely hung on during the Great Depression and was forced into trusteeship in the 1940s.

In 1934, convinced that the state and its people needed a leader who would work with New Dealers, Roche challenged Governor Ed Johnson in the Democratic primary. After a bitter fight, Roche lost. Although she failed in her bid to be elected governor, she remained in the political arena. Within days of the election President Franklin Roosevelt appointed her to serve as assistant secretary of the treasury. In this position she was in charge of health service and welfare work, specifically overseeing the US Public Health Service. In 1935 Roche added chairwoman of the Executive Committee of the National Youth Administration to her duties. Roche resigned her treasury position in 1937 but continued to chair the Interdepartmental Health Committee. She served as president of the National Consumers League from 1938 to 1944. In 1947 she was named assistant to John L. Lewis, head of the UMW. From 1947 to 1971, she directed the UMW's Welfare and Retirement Fund.[61]

Roche, a tireless activist for the rights of workers and children, was honored many times. She received honorary degrees from Smith College, Oglethorpe College, Mount Holyoke College, and the University of Colorado. The General Federation of Women's Clubs named her an outstanding American woman, and US Steel awarded her its National Achievement gold medal in 1935. Another noteworthy American woman who devoted her life's work to women, children, laborers, and others on the "margins of society"—none other than Eleanor Roosevelt—called Roche one of the country's greatest women. Roche died in Bethesda, Maryland, on July 29, 1976, at age eighty-one.

LEGISLATIVE ACTIVIST: EUDOCHIA BELL SMITH

Although Colorado women were granted the right to vote in 1893, they did not have the right to sit on juries until various women's groups took up the cause and a noted member of the Colorado General Assembly, Eudochia Bell Smith, sponsored the bill.

A native of San Antonio, Texas, Smith did not start out as a legislative activist. Her first career was as a journalist. In 1920 she and her husband, Joseph Emerson Smith, moved to Denver, where he continued his career in journalism while she did freelance writing before joining the *Rocky Mountain News* as editor of its women's department. One day she was sent to listen to a report about the State Industrial School for Boys in Golden. Horrified at what she heard, Eudochia believed the state legislature should enact reforms.[62] She decided to run for the Colorado House of Representatives on the Democratic ticket. Stumping through her Denver district in her high heels and trademark hat, Smith spread her message. In January 1937 she was sworn in and immediately set to work investigating the state school. She brought in Father Edward Flanagan of Boys Town, Nebraska. Basing her bill on his findings, she offered a three-point remedy: improve the parole system, create cottages to provide a homier atmosphere, and have service clubs appoint a Big Brother for each boy. This law, when passed, convinced her that the welfare of women and children needed the "feel of a woman's handclasp, her guidance and protection."[63] During her four terms as a state legislator, Smith sponsored bills calling for food service regulation and removing the word "illegitimate" from birth certificates. She unsuccessfully introduced a bill to raise the driving age to eighteen after a sixteen-year-old driver hit and killed a fourteen-year-old bicyclist.

Although Smith's driver's license bill failed, she did not receive threatening calls about that bill as she did in 1936 when, as a representative, she sponsored a resolution calling for a state investigation of un-American activities. Although she dismissed the callers as "crackpots," Mayor Benjamin Stapleton took the threats seriously and offered police protection to committee members, who were also urged to report all threats to their lives and safety to police headquarters. Smith's proposed legislation was similar to that of the congressional Dies committee. Members of the Colorado committee were informed that an allegedly Communist organization had discussed their investigation at a special meeting several days earlier and vigorously condemned it. The members received scores of messages from individuals and organizations offering assistance to the committee, asking if information could be submitted to it, and praising its aim. Numerous veterans' groups promised full support, and some offered to raise funds to finance the committee's work. Vernon A. Cheever, a Colorado Springs representative, declared that it was unlikely that the committee's investigation would result in criminal prosecution: "So far as I know, there is no prohibitive law applicable to most of the subversive activities we will seek to expose. I believe, however, that the exposure itself will accomplish our purposes and that public opinion will unite to stamp out the activities which threaten our democracy once those activities are disclosed in their true colors."[64]

In 1940, on the strength of her tenure in the house, Smith was elected to the state senate. She joined with women's organizations to amend the state constitution to allow females to serve on juries. Although the League of Women Voters, the Business and Professional Women's Club, and the Colorado Federation of Women's Clubs had written and lobbied for the bill, it had never been enacted. Supporters were adamant that it would not be defeated again. On the day of the debate in the senate, women filled the seats on the senate floor and in the balcony. The calm opening turned chaotic. One male senator shouted that women were too emotional to sit on juries, not realizing the irony of the statement delivered with the full force of his voice. Another argued that women like Smith were responsible for juvenile delinquency. Some used the argument that building restrooms for female jurors was a waste of precious supplies and manpower during wartime. Amid all the chaos, Smith reminded male senators of their campaign promises to support the bill and asked whether they were ready to alienate the most powerful women's bloc in the state. She also pointed out that it would be the voters who would ultimately decide whether women would be allowed to be jurors. The legislature was only voting to decide if the bill would be placed before the electorate. Smith's calmness and leadership amid the hysteria won out. By a narrow margin, the general assembly passed the bill. In the next general election, Colorado voters passed the amendment to the original Women's Suffrage Clause by a landslide. Fifty-one years to the day after winning the right to vote in the Centennial State, Colorado women gained the right to serve on juries. That same election saw passage of the Smith-Hornbaker Old Age Pension Bill, which provided a forty-five-dollar monthly pension to eligible elderly Coloradans.

After one term as senator Smith tried to retire, but the Democratic Party would not hear of it. She ran for a second term, was elected, but resigned to become registrar of the US District Land Office. In this position she was responsible for collecting oil, grazing, and homestead fees. She left this job in 1961. The former journalist and stateswoman died at age ninety.

——— T E N ———
STEPPING UP
——— (1940–1945) ———

With World War II raging in Europe and the United States precipitously close to joining the Allied forces, Oleta Lawanda Crain, a black teacher, quit her job in a segregated school in Oklahoma and moved to Colorado to look for a better-paying job. By late 1942 she had found a job cleaning toilets and mopping floors at the Remington Arms Plant just west of Denver.[1]

Although the company claimed publicly that it did not discriminate, Remington Arms initially hired African American women in only one of three areas—the restrooms, the cafeteria, or the lead shop. The first two positions paid much less than the lead shop. Working in the lead shop, though, had a disadvantage. Although men and women in the other areas of the plant were not given physical exams, workers in the lead shop were tested every three weeks for lead poisoning. If the level of lead in their blood was too high, they were removed from the shop and temporarily assigned to cafeteria

DOI: 10.5876/9781607322078.c10

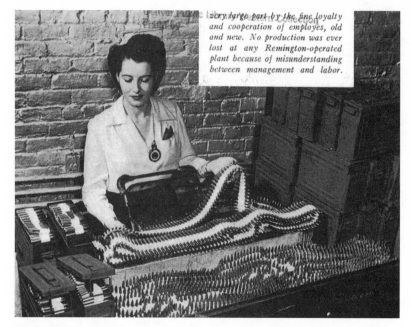

very large part by the fine loyalty and cooperation of employees, old and new. No production was ever lost at any Remington-operated plant because of misunderstanding between management and labor.

FIGURE 10.1 *During World War II, women made up nearly half of the workforce at the Denver Ordnance Plant. Run by the Remington Arms Company, the plant produced as many as 6 million .30 caliber bullets a day. Women worked on the production line, clerked in the administration office, and served meals in the cafeterias. Courtesy, Denver Public Library Western History Collection, Z-123.*

or restroom work.[2] Although this was done for the workers' protection, it also meant a decrease in pay.

In contrast, Anglos who worked at the Denver Ordnance Plant (DOP) had the luxury of several different available jobs. Those with secretarial skills typed, took dictation, and filed paperwork in the administration building. Others—clad in denim overalls or one-piece navy jumpsuits, their hair corralled in brightly colored bandanas or snoods—made or inspected .30 caliber bullets. Although female employees ranged in age from their late teens to their sixties, male workers were generally older, especially as men volunteered or were called to military service after the attack on Pearl Harbor.

All plant workers presented identification badges to guards at the gate off Sixth Avenue and Alameda before going off in different directions. Those in overalls or jumpsuits fanned out to one of four manufacturing buildings or to the shops.[3] Women dressed in skirts and crisp white blouses walked to the administration building, while most men headed to the storage buildings or the railroad depot. Crain's time at the plant was short. She had already seen an advertisement for her dream job.[4]

WOMEN WAR WORKERS

Although the United States did not officially enter World War II until December 8, 1941, it had been supplying Allied countries with war materials through the Lend-Lease Program for nearly a year. In 1940, when the federal government announced plans to build an ordnance factory, Denver officials lobbied earnestly for the plant. Through the efforts of US representative Lawrence Lewis and Denver manager of parks and improvements George Cramner, Denver was chosen as the site for a munitions plant. Nearly 2,000 acres just west of town were purchased from a widow, St. Claire Oakie Hayden, and two other ranchers. Rail lines were extended out to the site, and construction began on what would be 200 buildings. The buildings included manufacturing buildings, a health clinic, numerous guard towers, office space, and other necessary structures.[5]

Pledging to avoid discrimination, Remington Arms hired 10,000 workers to manufacture .30 caliber bullets. Of the original number, 40 percent were women, many hired to be secretaries, clerks, and inspectors. Women also made bullets. The first female applicants in the fall of 1941 were looking for jobs that paid better than their current ones. Denver-area teachers mimicked Crain in quitting poor-paying teaching jobs. Other women stopped attending college at the University of Denver, University of Colorado, and Colorado Woman's College to work at the plant. Women—earning an average of less than twenty-five dollars a week in laundries, department stores, restaurants, and hotels—left their jobs for war manufacturing jobs that paid more than forty dollars a week.[6] After the attack on Pearl Harbor, women also applied for jobs at the Remington plant out of a sense of patriotic duty.

Work areas, rest areas, and cafeterias were initially segregated.[7] With the help of the Phyllis Wheatley Branch of the YWCA, African American women were later hired as inspectors and bullet makers. Although her real goal was to join the Women's Auxiliary Army Corps (WAAC), Crain replaced a white female high school dropout in the lead shop. Crain was one of thirteen black women who worked outside the restrooms and kitchens. Another was Marguerite Grant Baker. Baker's mother worked for the William Gray Evans family, but, like many other domestic servants, she wanted a better life for her daughter. Born in 1919, Baker attended the

Opportunity School in Denver to become a dietitian. When she was unable to find a job as one, sadly, she became a domestic servant, following in her mother's footsteps. She worked first in the cafeteria at the Remington Arms Plant before moving on to the production line.[8]

One of Baker's coworkers in the cafeteria was Jennie Walker Rucker, whose family had been driven out of Texas by a boll weevil infestation. Originally settling in Pueblo to work in the steel mill, her father later moved the family to Denver where he could earn more money cleaning coaches for the Union Pacific Railroad. Rucker's mother lived with and cooked for a white family, so Jennie only saw her mother on Thursdays and Sundays. Because her mother wanted her to earn a college education, Rucker tried to sign up for shorthand and typing classes in high school. The school counselor, however, said she would never find a job as a secretary and refused to approve the classes. Instead, she registered Rucker for a cooking class. When she told her mother what had transpired, her mother replied, "You tell the teacher to teach you shorthand and typing. I'll teach you how to cook and sew!"[9] In the summer of 1941, after her freshman year at the University of Colorado, Rucker took a job in the Remington cafeteria but did not work there long. Her score of 97 on a civil service shorthand and typing examination earned her a call to Washington, DC. She was one of 600 blacks who passed the test. However, because of blatant racial discrimination, none of the 600 was assigned a job, so they sat idle in Washington from December until the end of May drawing the equivalent of a $1,440-a-year-salary. Rucker was finally assigned to work with the Corps of Engineers. She spent seven years in the nation's capital before being called to the corps' Omaha office to fill a stenography vacancy. When she reported, she was told that no charwoman's work was available. Announcing that she was there for the stenographer's job, she was told that they "didn't hire coloreds for office jobs."[10]

Although Crain resigned from the plant to join the WAAC in hopes of playing in the band, women who remained at the DOP through the duration of the war faced other problems in addition to discrimination. One was the lack of a day-care center. There were only 3,000 day-care centers in the entire country.[11] Although young mothers were initially discouraged from applying for war defense jobs, as the demand for workers grew, women with young children began working in the factories. Neither the Denver Council of Defense nor the Council of Social Agencies had planned for child care for working mothers. Finally, to aid its female employees, the DOP published a list of low-cost child-care centers and licensed private homes in August 1943.[12]

Mothers with children in school tried to balance motherhood with a full-time job. The *DOP Bulletin* periodically showcased women who were trying to be "supermoms" long before the "soccer moms" of the late twentieth century. Cora Hope operated a machine in Building 2-A. She worked the swing shift, wrote letters to her three sons in the army, kept house, and cared for four daughters and one son who were still in school. She did not mind having little time for recreation or the many other things she had enjoyed before the war because she knew she was helping her boys.[13] Hope and other older married women without pre-school-age children at home made up the fastest-growing group in the paid labor force. During the war, 25 percent of married women were employed, up from 15 percent during the Depression. By the end of the war, 18 million American women were working outside the home, an increase of 50 percent since 1939.[14]

In addition to child care, women faced the hassles of shift changes. One woman recounted that her commute by streetcar took two hours each way. When plant managers changed her schedule from a day shift to a night or graveyard shift, she was able to sleep only a few hours before returning to work.[15]

Women across the nation were also hired to work in machine shops, steel mills, oil refineries, railroad roundhouses, and lumber mills. At the national level, women made up half of the workforce. Women were hired by the Colorado Fuel and Iron Company (CF&I). Originally hired for the machine shop, women eventually worked in all departments at CF&I as vacancies increased when male employees entered the armed forces. Insisting that women would not be barred from any job simply because of their sex, CF&I hired women for jobs ranging from operating cranes to handling molds.[16]

Northeast of Denver, employees at the Rocky Mountain Arsenal manufactured incendiary bombs and poisonous gases. Workers at Gates Rubber Company made fanbelts. Bluhill Foods canned 454,320 peanuts for American servicemen, and Groswold Ski Company produced 33,000 snowshoes.[17] Women workers numbered among the thousands in these manufacturing plants. War work was a break from the usual occupations for women; it also represented a cataclysmic change for the manufacturing industry. The July 1943 issue of *Transportation* published guidelines for male supervisors:

> Pick young married women. They usually have more of a sense of responsibility than their unmarried sisters, they're less likely to be flirtatious, they need the work or they wouldn't be doing it. Give the female employee[s] a definite daylong schedule of duties so that they'll remain

FIGURE 10.2 *As American men hustled off to World War II battlefields, the country's women were actively recruited to fill jobs traditionally held by men. Courtesy, Library of Congress Prints and Photographs Division, Washington, DC.*

busy without bothering management for instructions every few minutes. Give every girl an adequate number of rest periods during the day. A girl has more confidence and is more efficient if she can keep her hair tidy, apply fresh lipstick and wash her hands several times a day. Be tactful when issuing instructions and in making criticisms. Women are often sensitive; they can't shrug off harsh words the way men do. Get enough size variety in operator's uniforms so that each girl can have a proper fit. This point can't be stressed too much in keeping women happy.[18]

There were many benefits to working at the DOP. The pay was good, and the work supported the war effort. In addition, the plant provided recreational opportunities. There were softball, basketball, and bowling leagues for women; penny days at Lakeside Amusement Park; and picnics for workers. All of that ended, however, when the Japanese surrendered on August 15, 1945. Production ceased immediately, and layoffs began. In October the plant was declared surplus property.[19]

THE HOME FRONT

For all Americans on the home front, the war meant ration stamps, recycling programs, and restrictions. Thousands of women grew their own vegetables in Victory Gardens, canned produce, and kept a wary eye on kitchen pantry supplies. The war presented a difficult dilemma for Colorado farmers, ranchers, and city dwellers. Agriculturists increased their output to feed American soldiers and allies abroad at the same time they faced a labor shortage because nearly one-eighth of Colorado's population had entered military service. In addition, farms in Texas, Southern California, and Arizona no longer shipped harvests to Colorado because of gas rationing and rail cutbacks.

To counter these difficulties, federal and state governments formulated a three-part plan. They authorized prisoners of war (POWs) to work in Colorado's fields. Ultimately, 3,000 Italian and German POWs harvested sugar beets, onions, cabbage, and potatoes in Larimer, Morgan, and Weld Counties. Unemployed students were recruited for after-school hoeing and shoveling. A massive Victory Garden program was established that taught citizens how to convert empty lots and backyards into gardens. Larger plots belonging to factories, businesses, and schools were dedicated as community gardens. Erstwhile gardeners were inundated with promotional posters and how-to pamphlets. Slogans such as "Eat what you can, can what you can't" and "Grow your living. It may not be available for you to buy" encouraged citizens to start plants in window boxes and transplant them in gardens, use table scraps for fertilizer, share gardening tools, and can leftovers in Mason jars sealed with molten paraffin and lids. With men fighting in the war, laboring in the fields, or working jobs in town, it was women's responsibility to plant, reap, and later cook or can the produce.

Outstanding Victory Gardeners were proclaimed Green Thumb Contest winners. Lula R. Moore harvested thirty-two varieties of vegetables in her 1,400-square-foot plot, earning her the title of the state's best adult Victory Gardener. Barbara Ann Bocovich of Colorado Springs, the elementary school winner, planted 2,100 square feet in her grandmother's vacant lot. She harvested 27 dozen ears of corn, 350 pounds of cabbage, 1½ bushels of tomatoes, 4 bushels of beans, 7 bushels of root crops, 47 squash, 6 pumpkins, and "an abundance of leafy crops." Eighty-eight pints of the vegetables were canned for winter use.[20] Foods were stored in a cool basement or dugout cellar. Elbert County women set the record for Victory Gardens. All but 34 of the county's 989 rural families harvested gardens, and 275 of the 315 town families did the same. Gardening efforts in tiny Laird, near the Nebraska border, were also impressive. Twelve members of the Liberty Club tended thirteen gardens (one woman boasted of having one garden in town and one in the country).[21]

The federal government instituted rationing almost immediately after the United States entered the war. Metal, rubber, and gasoline were at the top of the list, but rationed foodstuffs concerned Americans the most. Red ration stamps were issued for purchasing meats and dairy products, and blue stamps were used for canned foods. Grocery ads in newspapers included ration stamp numbers and amounts for the various goods. Bread was available only between 9:00 and 10:00 a.m. and 4:00 and 5:00 p.m., no loaves could be reserved, and only one loaf was allowed per customer. For women who worked full-time, these restrictions required strategic planning. Women's magazines regularly published recipes that substituted applesauce for sugar and stretched quantities of rationed items. "Making do without" became an art form. At the end of a visit to her mother in Iowa, May Wilkins packed her car with bushels of walnuts, apples, cabbage, carrots, and turnips. In a letter to her husband, Don, who had remained behind at his job as a Fort Collins newspaper editor, she worried that she would not have enough sugar for canning the produce.[22]

Gasoline was also rationed. Because Wilkins drove to her mother's farm each spring, she constantly fretted about her allotment. In 1943 she decided to bring her mother to Colorado for the winter because she was becoming frail. She contacted her mother's physician, who wrote a letter on her behalf for additional gas rations.[23] Don reassured her that she would have enough coupons for her trip home because each one represented two gallons of gas, approximately thirty miles.[24]

Rationed metal and rubber led to recycling efforts. Homemakers were urged to recycle kitchen fats and grease, which could be taken back to the butcher. They were then converted to nitroglycerin for use in making explosives. Schoolchildren collected used lipstick containers, pots, pans, and other metal objects. Citizens melted down cannons from the town square, turned in old barber chairs, and replaced steel car bumpers with wooden planks. Most of America's rubber had come from Africa and the Dutch East Indies, areas now under Axis domination. To compensate, Americans donated old tires, garden hoses, and women's bathing caps for a national rubber scrap drive. Women had to give up silk and nylon stockings because they were vital for parachutes, medical supplies, and gunpowder bags. Some women artificially "colored" their legs with face cream and drew stocking "seams" on the backs of their legs with eyebrow pencils. Others rejoiced when they did come across a rare commodity. In late 1942, Wilkins gleefully reported that she had found three pairs of silk hose.[25] Other women simply did without and chalked up the new stocking-less style to the demands of war.

Across the nation, American women bought war bonds—many as members of "10 percent clubs" (workers who spent 10 percent of their income to buy war bonds)—and supported Red Cross work. Women regularly donated blood, took classes in nutrition and first aid, and sewed and knitted items for convalescing soldiers. They also donated money to local Red Cross chapters. Women's organizations opened their clubhouses to Red Cross recruiting drives.

WOMEN ON THE DIAMOND

Through the war years, American women took up the slack as men went off to fight the Axis Powers, even taking over men's positions in the athletic arena. In 1943 Philip K. Wrigley, owner of the Chicago Cubs, formed the All-American Girls Professional Baseball League, later renamed the All-American Girls Professional Ball League (AAGPBL). Scouts held tryouts in dozens of major cities. Nearly 300 women were invited to the final auditions in Chicago, where 60 were chosen to become the first US women to play professional baseball. Racine and Kenosha, Wisconsin, Rockford, Illinois, and South Bend, Indiana, were selected to field the first teams, which consisted of 15 players, a manager (coach), a business manager, and a female chaperone. One of the Kenosha Comets was Coloradan Lucille "Lou" Appugliese Colacito.[26] After her husband was sent overseas, she played two seasons for the Comets as a catcher. Her baseball card—similar to the cards of professional male baseball players—listed her as a right-hand thrower and batter.

Spring training began in May 1943 at Chicago's Wrigley Field. Those whose baseball skills survived the scrutiny were signed to professional contracts. Salaries ranged from forty-five dollars to eighty-five dollars a week, a rate that exceeded the pay of many skilled workers. Players had to comply with the league's high moral standards and rules of conduct. Femininity was a high priority. After daily practices, Wrigley required players to attend evening charm school classes at Helen Rubenstein's Beauty Salon. Proper etiquette, personal hygiene, mannerisms, and dress code were stressed. Each player was given a beauty kit and instructions on its use. Players visited military hospitals and played exhibition games to support the Red Cross.

IN THE MILITARY

After the United States officially entered World War II, nearly 400,000 women joined female military auxiliaries. They served as nurses, stenographers, dietitians, translators, pilots, mechanics, physical therapists, physicians, technicians, and cooks. Across the nation, 140,000 women enlisted in the Women's Auxiliary Army Corps (WAAC) or the Women's Army Corps (WAC). The WAAC existed from early 1942 until July 1943, when it was replaced by the WAC. The WAAC was only an auxiliary to the regular US Army. WAACs were given the option of continuing on in the WAC or leaving the service; 25 percent chose to leave. Another 100,000 enlisted in the navy's Women Accepted for Voluntary Emergency Service (WAVES), and 1,000 civilian pilots joined the Women's Airforce Service Pilots (WASP).[27]

The first two Denverites selected for WAAC training were Sophia Whiting and Sally Davis. Whiting held a master's degree and had worked as the registrar at Nebraska State Teachers College (Chadron). Before resigning to join the army, she was secretary to the dean of the College of Arts and Sciences at the University of Denver. Colonel T. N. Gimperling stated that Whiting's experience in secretarial and personnel work was a good foundation for officer's training. He was also pleased with Davis's qualifications. A Denver native, she had been captain of the Red Cross motor corps for the past eighteen months. Both women reported to Fort Des Moines (Iowa) to train for their commissions.[28] They were soon joined by other Colorado women, including Catherine McCleary of Ordway who was joining the army band to play piccolo. In November another thirty-one recruits were sworn in. Twenty-three were from Denver, with one each from Durango, Colorado Springs, Sterling, Fort Collins, Boulder, and Springfield. Two were from Wyoming. The new recruits had previously been switchboard operators, teachers, housewives, insurance workers, milliners, stenographers, waitresses, laboratory technicians, and cryptographers.[29] By the end of 1942, another fifty-five women from Colorado and Wyoming had enlisted. One, Iris Watanabe, was the first Nisei woman to join after the federal government permitted them to do so in July 1943.[30] For all recruits, military life was far from glamorous. May Wilkins visited Fort Des Moines and reported to her husband that "the sleeping quarters are pretty gloomy—old dark walls—no mirrors no dressers just a small army trunk at the head of the cot—that holds all belongings."[31]

Other Coloradans enlisted in the different women's branches. Pueblo native Kay Keating joined the WAVES after graduating from Central High School and Pueblo Junior College. She was shipped to Hawaii where she became a radio operator, a job that sometimes entailed working in an underground station in a pineapple field. Because the area was infested with flies, she brought in a frog and trained it to eat flies.[32] Another Colorado native, Virginia Moore, quit her job as a social worker and joined the WAVES in 1943. Moore was seldom hesitant about following her own path. During the 1930s she worked for the State Emergency Relief Association in California as a social worker before resigning to travel to the Orient. Upon her return, she stopped in Hawaii where she took a job placing children in foster homes. She resigned to attend the University of Washington to earn a master's degree in social work, during which time the Japanese bombed Pearl Harbor. With her mother's blessing, she joined the navy. At age thirty-two, she was older than most enlistees. She received basic training at Smith and Mount Holyoke Colleges for communications training. Although she preferred to stay in the East because she had spent a number of years in the West, Seaman Moore was assigned to San Diego. She and the other WAVE officers shared rooms in a barrack on Coronado Island. Each morning they were taken by boat to the base. One of their duties was to attend pistol practice. To deliver top-secret messages to ship captains, she rode in a motorcycle sidecar with her "little pistol" at her waist.[33]

Nationally, female marines totaled 19,000. Bea Leist, a Denver native who had always "wanted to be a little boy" so she could be a marine, enlisted as soon as she could in 1943, graduating in the third class of women. She was assigned to an aviation supply house in California, the last stop for planes on their way to the Pacific. While most women's decisions to join one of the military branches were supported, others were confronted with skepticism. When Velma Brooke enlisted, her boss said, "Now, why would a nice girl like you want to go off and join the Marines?"[34]

In 1938 Lowry Army Air Base in Aurora began training soldiers in aerial photography; five years later the first group of WACs arrived in line with the War Department's policy of replacing soldiers with WACs or civilian employees. After graduation they became lab operators and technicians. One officer was Second Lieutenant Dorothy L. Starbuck, a Brighton native and graduate of Loretto Heights College.[35] Of the original fifty women, forty-three graduated. Major Joe M. Cates, the base's director, said the first class completed courses in a manner "as satisfactory as [that] of the enlisted men."[36]

ARMY NURSES

Lowry was also home to army nurses. To qualify, a woman had to have good character, be a US citizen between ages twenty-one and forty-five, hold a high school diploma, and be a graduate of an accredited nursing school and a member of the American Nurses Association. She also had to pass a strict physical examination. Her starting salary was ninety dollars a month plus medical, dental, and maintenance expenses. The uniform consisted of a dark blue covert cloth overcoat, a dark blue covert garrison cap with maroon trim, dark blue covert cloth skirt, black tie, and black laced oxfords. First Lieutenant Kathleen L. McNulty, Lowry's chief nurse, performed administrative and supervisory work and assigned duties to staff nurses who supervised the ward, made rounds with the ward surgeon, and were responsible for the cleanliness of the ward and the safety of the patients.[37]

Other women also worked at or visited Lowry. Mrs. Elliot Todhunter Dewey—the first senior social hostess—secured over 7,000 volumes for the post and service club libraries, furnished the WACs' dayroom, and procured pianos and radios for squadron dayrooms. She invited female students (from the University of Denver, Colorado Woman's College, and Denver high schools) and female employees (from the Daniels and Fisher Company, May Company, Denver Dry Goods Company, Public Service, and the telephone company) to Lowry dances.[38] Years later, Rosalyn Mastrioianni Hersch fondly recalled the dances: "The guys were always polite in those days. Although I was a history major at the University of Denver, I was really studying boys."[39]

To accommodate army nurses, civilian workers, WACs, and wives of officers and enlisted men, the base commander sponsored the Lowry Women's Club, believed to have been the first of its kind in the nation. It served as a semi-official social center and meeting place for Lowry women. The first floor housed a nursery, playroom, lounge, kitchen, and two Red Cross sewing rooms. On the second floor were two rooms with additional kitchen equipment, a room for fabricating surgical dressings and bandages, and restrooms.[40]

Men and women were also stationed at other Colorado military establishments: Fitzsimons, Fort Logan, Buckley Air Field, Camp Carson, and Pueblo Air Base. At Camp Hale between Minturn and Leadville, 16,000 men trained for mountain combat. A regiment of 200 WACs, including Mary Kelles, served at the camp in finance, supply, communications, and the motor pool.[41]

The need for skilled nurses and nurses' aids was acute. In June 1942, Mary C. Walker, chairwoman of the State Committee on Supply and Distribution, sent letters to district presidents of the Colorado State Nurses Association (after 1947 the Colorado Nurses Association) asking for help in meeting federal quotas. Colorado was required to enroll 500 nurses in the Red Cross Nursing Service and certify their readiness to respond to military service. Through national recruitment efforts, over 55,000 registered nurses served during the war. Coloradan Althea Williams was one of them. She was appointed as second lieutenant and assigned to Fitzsimons Army Hospital in Aurora. As she and other nurses were sent to American bases and overseas combat stations, the nursing void was filled by registered nurses returning to hospital work and by nurses' aids, such as May Wilkins, who helped free up trained nurses for other work. Wilkins debated between becoming a nurses' aid and helping the war effort or accepting a paying job that would bring in money. She decided to join the Red Cross nurses' aid program, which made her husband so proud that "his vest about [broke] open."[42]

Another Red Cross worker was Marjorie Carol Jarrett, a graduate of North High School and the University of Denver (DU). Jarrett was among "the first contingent of American Negroes to go to England to run the first American Red Cross club for colored troops."[43] After graduating from DU, she studied at the Bishop Tuttle Training School for Social Services (North Carolina) before working for twelve years in social services in St. Louis. Her degree and experience qualified her to become one of the first five women sent to Britain. In a letter to her aunt, Jarrett explained that "in an unnamed town in war-torn England" she worked from 10:00 a.m. to 10:00 p.m. taking care of injured soldiers in an Episcopal church.[44]

AMACHE RELOCATION CAMP

For some Americans, World War II was not a time of opportunity but rather a period of increased discrimination. After the attack on Pearl Harbor, citizens on the Pacific Coast, home to the largest number of mainland residents of Japanese descent, demanded the removal of Japanese Americans. Colorado governor Ralph Carr was one of the few statesmen of the hour. Risking political suicide, he welcomed Japanese Americans, informing the *Rocky Mountain News* that they were just as loyal to American institutions as any other American citizen. Virginia Moore, the WAVE from Fort Collins, agreed with her governor: "I had lots of Japanese friends that were all in camps . . . [It was wrong] because they were Americans. I didn't really feel they were going to be against us."[45] A small percentage of Japanese Americans voluntarily left their homes in California and resettled in other states with communities of Nisei and Sansei inhabitants. This did not quell fears of Japanese sabotage and attacks on the mainland, so President Roosevelt issued Executive Order 9066 authorizing the secretary of war to establish military zones and remove "any or all persons" from those zones.

The War Relocation Authority subsequently moved 110,000 Japanese Americans—citizens and non-citizens alike—to ten internment camps in remote areas across the country. Southeastern Colorado was chosen as one of those sites. The camp, officially known as the Granada Relocation Camp, was situated on 10,500 acres of desolate prairie. This instant city soon became the tenth largest in Colorado, with a population of nearly 8,000 people in 1942.[46] To distinguish the camp from the town of Granada, it was called Amache in honor of Amache Ochinee Prowers. Most of the Japanese Americans at Amache came from California after being processed at the Merced and Santa Anita centers. The camp was laid out in twenty-nine blocks. Each block consisted of twelve barracks, with each barrack divided into twelve one-room units. A typical unit—housing a family of seven or fewer—included a closet, coal stove, folding cots, mattresses, and quilts. When the camp opened in August 1942, it was only partially completed. Hot and cold water was available in only a few of the blocks, and many evacuees had to walk several blocks to find a bathhouse with water. The evacuees themselves assisted in completing the camp by the end of 1942. Camp residents were supplied with food, fuel, and a small monthly allowance for clothing.

Monthly wages for workers inside the camp were twelve dollars for unskilled labor, sixteen dollars for skilled labor, and nineteen dollars for professional work. Chiyoko Sakamoto, a Los Angeles attorney and the first Japanese American woman to practice law in the United States, lived

FIGURE 10.3 *Colorado's internment center housed almost 8,000 Japanese Americans. Internees worked in the fields, school, and hospital at Camp Amache. Courtesy, History Colorado (Amache Collection, Scan #10027415), Denver.*

at Amache. She, two other Japanese Americans, and one Caucasian offered legal advice to camp residents.[47] Doctors and nurses also earned a professional wage in the camp's 150-bed hospital. Matilda Honda, a graduate of the University of California School of Nursing and a former public health nurse with the Los Angeles County Health Department, worked as a staff nurse. Her father, mother, and sister lived in Broomfield, while another sister was interned at the Central Utah Center. Although Honda was a voluntary evacuee, most of the other members of the nursing staff were Anglo residents of surrounding counties. Mildred L. Finley served as head nurse and Wanda Oliver was the chief nurse.[48]

The nursery and schools at Amache provided jobs for evacuees and townspeople alike. Many teachers commuted from Lamar. One of the commuters, Gladys Seevers, taught social studies and English. Sumi Kashiwage, an evacuee, was one of the nursery teachers.[49]

Other women found employment at Amache as stenographers, clerks, and telephone operators. Hatsuye Sato, a twenty-seven-year-old American-born evacuee, was working as a stenographer in the public relations office when Ross Thompson, city editor for the *Lamar Daily News,* interviewed her during his visit to the camp. She said the Japanese evacuees would have liked to have stayed home, but "if their move would further the war effort on behalf of America, then that was what they wanted." Sato explained that evacuees intended to prove that they were loyal Americans "by working for, and cooperating with America's war effort."[50] One place in which camp residents showed their cooperation was the silk-screening department. Taye Namura created colorful propaganda posters imploring American citizens to enlist, recycle metal, buy war bonds, and plant Victory Gardens. Two Japanese American stenographers were True Shibata and Ruth Noda.[51] The 1943 Amache Directory listed twelve clerks or clerk-stenographers, including Shibata and Noda; three telephone operators; and one social case worker.[52]

Most internees, though, worked in the fields. In addition to growing food for their own needs, Japanese Americans harvested enough vegetables to ship sixteen railroad carloads to other relocation camps. The War Relocation Authority released Japanese American men and women who volunteered to do farm work in the local area outside the camp. In 1943 farmers in Prowers County faced the loss of 60,000 tons of sugar beets if more laborers weren't found. Their first volunteers were twenty high school students and twenty women from Amache who helped save their crops.[53]

A LIFETIME OF SERVICE: OLETA CRAIN

Oleta Crain started at the Denver Ordnance Plant cleaning toilets before being promoted to the lead shop. During her short stint at the plant, she became one of its most respected workers. She was also one of its most vocal critics. At first, there were only two jobs "open to Negro girls—being a service operator, which is a maid's job, or working in the lead shop." Although originally told there was no chance for advancement, she was later offered a job in the lead shop because she had a college education and had been working on her master's degree—an indication that she could be trusted because managers believed "colored girls who have gone to college are honest."[54] The white girl she replaced had just graduated from Gove Junior High School.

For the first year or so of operations, the DOP ran a segregated plant. Blacks had to walk two blocks to the cafeteria and a restroom. They had no couch, chair, or table; if they got tired they had to walk two blocks to another building to rest. On two or three occasions the forewoman found girls lying on the floor to rest, so, after a restroom in another building was closed, the black workers were given one of its couches.[55]

When Crain read a 1942 recruiting poster stating "Women can play in the Army band and help win the war," she enlisted in the WAAC (later the WAC). However, when she reported for duty she was told that the poster did not mean "colored women." Part Cherokee, Crain was the first woman of color in the Rocky Mountain region to join the army. She completed basic training and then went on for officer training. One of only 3 blacks among the 300 women to enter officer training, Crain and the other 2 women were housed in private rooms rather than with the white officer candidates in the barracks. "I was so happy to be black, and not have to put up with barracks life," Crain said. "We got up earlier in the morning than the others and hurried over to take our showers, segregation, you know; at least we weren't bothered by crowded shoulders. I didn't have a chip on my shoulder, and seldom made an issue of things like that. If you can't do anything about something, you just as well make the best of it."[56]

Crain rose through the ranks, retiring as an air force major in 1963. Ironically, although she never played in a military women's band as she had originally hoped, Crain later served in a regimental office that had control over those bands.

In 1964 Crain joined the Department of Labor in Washington as a contract expert. After earning a master's degree in public administration at Northeastern University and serving as assistant regional administrator with the Office of Job Service for the New England states, she transferred to Denver in 1984. For the next fourteen years, Crain was the regional administrator of the US Department of Labor's Women's Bureau. In this capacity she worked with six states, networking with women and women's groups to improve wages, working conditions, and career opportunities. In December 1998 Crain retired after fifty-six years of public service. Her many honors include induction into the Colorado Women's Hall of Fame, the Dr. Mary McLeod Bethune Legacy Award from the National Council of Negro Women (Denver Section), and a US Department of Labor Award for Distinguished Career Service.[57]

SEWING FOR THE RED CROSS AND BUYING BOMBERS: DENVER CLUBWOMEN

During World War I, clubwomen sat on the Council of Defense, led war bond drives, and headed Red Cross campaigns. They ably mobilized and directed large numbers of club and non-club women for the war effort. By 1940 those 1917 leaders were deceased or no longer taking an active role in community and state affairs. The new club leaders were less well-known to "outsiders" than their 1917 predecessors had been. Thus, when Governor Carr named nearly 200 citizens to a State Defense Council, no clubwoman was included.[58] This is not to imply, however, that clubwomen were any less active in service to their country during World War II than they had been during World War I.

Because women were preoccupied with war service work, Denver clubs maintained their usual contributions and did not attempt any new undertakings. The State Home and Industrial School for Girls, the State Industrial School for Boys, the Old Ladies' Home, and the YWCA Rest and Recreation Rooms received their usual contributions. The Twenty-Second Avenue Study Club continued its luncheons at the Adult Workshop for the Blind during the war, although rationing caused problems. Zimmie Rupp's sister sent her red stamps so Rupp could buy meat for her Sunday dinners for soldiers, but there were not enough stamps for the workshop luncheons. When Rupp wrote Senator Edwin C. Johnson asking for more meat coupons, the senator sent her a cookbook instead. The clubwomen carried on in spite of the senator's misplaced help, using red stamps sent by Rupp's farm relatives.[59]

In 1943 the club also received an appeal for an endorsement, this time for the Equal Rights Amendment to the US Constitution. Although the endorsement was approved, Lucile Kling, the lone dissenter and club historian, questioned, "Why on earth do club women, whose lives have very seldom given them any actual contact with working conditions, insist on supporting this monstrosity, anathema to every working woman?" Kling later referred to the secretary's job of notifying senators and representatives that the club would support the amendment as a "task."[60] She was no more enthusiastic when club members rejoiced after winning the privilege of jury duty.[61]

Clubwomen participated in nearly every drive and campaign during the war years. They sent money for "Bundles for Britain," collected food and clothing, and donated books to the Victory Book Campaign. They also worked tirelessly for the Red Cross. By 1945, the Denver chapter had 74 paid staff members and over 13,000 volunteers. When the organization outgrew its first house at 300 East Eighth Avenue, it relocated to the Claude Boettcher Mansion at 800 Logan Street. The Red Cross also used the basement of the Grant-Humphreys Mansion, community centers, and the clubhouse of the Woman's Club of Denver. Club members regularly donated blood and gave money to local Red Cross chapters from club treasuries. During meetings, North Side Woman's Club (Denver) members made five afghans, fifty garments, fourteen lap robes for recuperating soldiers, thirty pairs of slippers, and twenty-three turtleneck sweaters for the Red Cross between 1942 and 1944.[62]

Members of the Twenty-Second Avenue Study Club met twice a month to sew for the Red Cross. They arrived between 10:00 a.m. and noon, sewed until breaking for a lunch of sandwiches, had a meeting at 2:00 p.m., and adjourned by 4:00 p.m.—otherwise the trolley cars would be full of war workers.[63] The luncheon chatter generally centered on the women's canning—what, how much, and how. In fourteen informal meetings between the spring of 1943 and October 1943, they made buddy bags, slumber robes, nightshirts, and diapers—putting in 784 hours of labor. In November 1943 women filled little pillows to support an injured soldier's arm or leg. The annual report for 1943–1944 shows the club members' productivity and dedication: 620½ articles made; 120 yards of tape dyed, pressed, and rolled; 24 sewing meetings; and 1,759½ hours spent on sewing work for the Red Cross. Regarding the last figure, one woman alone donated 234 hours.[64]

The Twenty-Second Avenue Study Club members were particularly interested in the salvage operations of the American Women's Voluntary Services, of which their own Jennie Steidley was chairwoman. In 1943 Denver women turned in 500,000 pounds of old stockings and 540 tons of tin cans to the Salvage Bureau at 139 Fifteenth Street. Steidley later received a US treasury citation for her salvage efforts.[65] In addition to nylon and tin cans, members of the Twenty-Second Avenue Study Club salvaged over 100 pounds of fat during the 1945–1946 club year.[66]

Women distributed gifts to the Fort Logan Convalescent Ward, gave books and playing cards to the United Service Organization (USO), and entertained recuperating soldiers at Fitzsimons Army Hospital. The Denver Woman's Club passed a resolution stating that each member should entertain at least two soldiers a month.[67] Many did that and more. For the USO "March of Cookies," the Twenty-Second Avenue Study Club baked more than 110 dozen cookies over the course of two years.[68] The Parachute Home Culture Club on the Western Slope baked cookies for the Glenwood Springs Red Cross and the USO in addition to supporting other Red Cross initiatives.

As they had during World War I, Colorado clubwomen actively participated in bond drives. The Colorado Federation of Women's Clubs reported that its members purchased $97,000 and sold over $200,000 worth of bonds and stamps during the war.[69] The North Side Woman's Club reported that its members alone had bought $7,000 in bonds in 1942.[70]

In 1943 the Colorado Federation of Women's Clubs participated in a novel project, the "Buy a Bomber" campaign. Federated clubs in the state raised enough money for the purchase of one heavy bomber named for the Colorado federation, nine pursuit planes—one for each district—one complete mobile laundry unit, and two motor scooters with side cars.[71]

WARTIME NURSING: OMI JENSEN AND ALTHEA WILLIAMS

Answering their nation's call, thousands of nurses reported to duty. Some were sent overseas to tend to the battlefield wounded, while others remained state-bound. Omi Jensen was one of only 122 women who earned Flight Nurse Wings during World War II. She was part of a pioneering group of navy nurses who flew into Pacific battle zones on evacuation aircraft and cared for badly wounded marines as they were flown to safety thousands of miles away. Jensen and her colleagues were officially designated VRE-1 but were nicknamed "Hell's Angels" by the servicemen they aided. On each evacuation trip, one nurse and one corpsman treated up to thirty-five wounded soldiers. Medical planes flew eight hours from Guam, spent twenty minutes on a war-scarred airstrip on Okinawa, then roared back into the air for the return trip. Over a three-month period, nearly 10,000 wounded soldiers were evacuated from Okinawa, where the casualties were more than double those of Iwo Jima and Guadalcanal combined. The twenty-four-year-old Jensen knelt on the airplane's floor to help the soldiers in the lowest berths before pulling herself up to help the men in the top berths. "I talked to them, wanted to know where they were from, if they were married," she said. "I would go around to the amputees because I wanted to offer to make phone calls to their families because (the loss of a limb) would be a sudden shock to their loved ones."[72] Although they suffered from head injuries, burns, and amputations, Jensen insisted that the men never complained; they were simply interested in getting home. Of more help than the medicine, she said, was the food. The sheer logistics of battle, where men had little time to do anything but fight, left the wounded famished and constantly talking about food.[73]

Another Colorado nurse was Althea Williams. Born in Platteville in 1920, Williams graduated from Bethel Nursing School in Colorado Springs and began working at Poudre Valley Hospital in Fort Collins. She was working there when Pearl Harbor was bombed. At first, she and her fellow hospital employees did not believe what they were hearing, assuming it "was an Orson Welles activity" (like the radio broadcast of *The War of the Worlds* in 1938).[74] Williams was immediately placed on active duty, appointed as second lieutenant, and assigned to Fitzsimons Army Hospital. Next she was sent to Kearns, Utah, before being transferred to a surgical hospital in the California desert. The 400-bed semi-mobile evacuation hospital was ordered to the Pacific by way of San Francisco. Without an armed escort, the ship had to change its route every seven seconds to avoid enemy attack. For a year and a half the unit was stationed on a tiny Pacific island. Most of the soldiers suffered from malaria, dengue fever, and scrub typhus. Day after day, Williams nursed soldiers and sailors.

When she separated from the service in 1945, she had over three months' leave coming to her because "it was a full-time, hour after hour, day after day [job], so we had no R and R." But she also had no complaints: "They asked us to serve, we served, and I was serving because of the fact that all of my friends, boyfriends, brothers, and all were serving. They had a right to have the best equipment and good nursing and medical care." When asked how she felt about the atomic bombs the United States had dropped on the two Japanese cities of Hiroshima and Nagasaki, Williams replied, "Oh, we were thrilled to death, because we knew we were getting ready to go into Japan. If the atomic bomb had not been dropped, we knew we would be having thousands and thousands of casualties on both sides. I get very upset when the people are trying to revise history and trying to change what actually took place in those days. My brother was a B29 pilot and he was on the island of Saipan. He had to go in and bomb Japan."[75]

By November 1945 Williams was stateside and back at the university taking classes toward a degree in home economics and occupational therapy. Like male veterans, Williams used her GI Bill for tuition and to support herself and her mother. But she never separated from the navy. She joined the reserves and was recalled when the Korean War broke out. For the next ten years she was stationed in Japan, Germany, and the United States. Her next wartime stint was in Vietnam as the US Army Vietnam chief nurse, having risen to full colonel in 1967. Medical care in Vietnam developed from the experiences in Korea. Helicopters, MASH (mobile army surgical hospital) units, and the treatment of trauma victims helped medical staffs. MUST (medical unit self-contained transportables), a 60-bed unit with a utility pack, provided correct atmospheric pressure in its operating room.

Williams experienced some discrimination in the military but not much because "I was raised with three brothers and so if I had any difficulties I just went to the individuals and took care of it. I never really had overt type of discrimination ever. Mainly because I wouldn't put up with it."[76]

A RABBIT'S TALE: MARY COYLE CHASE

In 1944, amid the destruction of World War II, *Harvey*, the tale of a six-foot-tall invisible white rabbit and Elwood P. Dowd, the only person who could see him, opened on Broadway. Written by Mary McDonough Coyle Chase, the play became a long-running success. Born in 1906 in Denver, the author was enchanted with the Irish folk tales her Irish-born mother, father, and uncles told to entertain her. Banshees, leprechauns, and pookas inhabited her daydreams and later reappeared in her plays. Starting at the *Rocky Mountain News* as a part-time summer reporter, Coyle blossomed into a gallant investigative reporter, often dashing to crime scenes in a Model T driven by *News* photographer Harry Rhoads. In 1928 she married *News* city editor Robert Chase and had three children.[77]

In 1931 Chase resigned from the *Rocky Mountain News* to raise her children and concentrate on her own writing. The Federal Theater Project in Denver staged her first play, *Me Third,* in 1936. Purchased by a New York producer, the play was rewritten and renamed *Now You've Done It*. Although directed by Denver native Antoinette Perry, it flopped in its Broadway debut.

Drawing upon the Irish stories of her childhood, Chase wrote *Harvey,* originally called *The Pooka* after the Irish folklore creature. It opened in Denver as *The White Rabbit* but was renamed *Harvey* for its Broadway debut. The story of the alcoholic Elwood Dowd and his imaginary rabbit won rave reviews and enriched the Chases, who moved into "the house that Harvey built," as she called it, in Denver's posh Country Club district. In 1945 *Harvey* earned Chase the Pulitzer Prize for Drama.[78]

Over the next thirty years Chase wrote many plays, including *Mrs. McThing,* a comedy about a witch who created duplicates of people from sticks, and two children's books, *Loretta Mason Potts* (1958) and *The Wicked, Wicked Ladies in the Haunted House* (1968).[79]

Mary McDonough Coyle Chase, taking her sense of humor to the grave, picked a plot in Crown Hill Cemetery next to a tombstone inscribed "Harvey." She was buried there after suffering a fatal heart attack on October 20, 1981. She was seventy-five.[80]

ELEVEN

CONFORMITY AND CHANGE, TAKE TWO

(1946-1960)

"1958 Miss America Runner Up: Miss Georgia, Jody Elizabeth Shattuck."
With that pronouncement, Marilyn Van Derbur became the second Miss
Colorado in three years to be named the nation's ranking beauty queen.
Crowned by the 1957 winner, Van Derbur walked calmly down the 120-
foot runway in Atlantic City's Convention Hall before a wildly applauding
audience. Although she had not won top places in the preliminary judging,
Van Derbur's victory was not a surprise. Two of her three older sisters and
her mother, Gwendolyn "Boots," were former beauty queens at the University
of Colorado (CU). Van Derbur started her climb to Miss America as the Phi
Beta Kappa candidate for Miss CU. Winning that crown placed her in the
Miss Colorado contest, where she was chosen to represent the state in the 1958
Miss America competition. Although part of her piano recital was blacked out
to television viewers by a local advertisement, every member of the Van Derbur
family was in the audience to cheer her and to join her onstage.[1]

DOI: 10.5876/9781607322078.c11

The new Miss America, a beautiful and articulate young woman, was a daughter and granddaughter of one of Colorado's leading families.[2] No one attending the contest or watching the televised event realized, however, that in other ways the new Miss America was straddling a chasm. Her title conveyed America's splendor and hope and portrayed the image of the ideal American woman. Yet Van Derbur carried a terrible secret. Very few knew that evening that Van Derbur's smiling face hid the trauma of sexual abuse at the hands of one who was supposed to have been her protector—her father, Francis Van Derbur. When Van Derbur disclosed this secret in 1991, the lie she had been living was finally exposed.[3] The postwar ideal of daddy protecting his little daughter, of safety within the white picket fences of suburban lawns was belied by her announcement.

BACK HOME

Van Derbur's situation was not the only one in which things were not as they first appeared. Employee numbers for women after World War II also obscured the truth. While the numbers and percentages of working women remained stable, the jobs at which they worked changed after 1945. With the Allied victory over the Axis Powers, defense plants quickly shut down or were converted to commercial factories for consumer goods. "Rosie the Riveter" was quickly dismissed and sent home to await her man. The Denver Ordnance Plant (DOP) shut its doors before being reopened as the Denver Federal Center, a western "capital" of federal departments and agencies. Colorado's emergence as a desirable location for military bases, military research and development companies, and federal agencies created jobs for women. Most of the jobs were clerical in nature, however. Although most female military personnel were mustered out, some, like Oleta Crain, remained in the armed forces. Well-entrenched as an officer in the Women's Army Corps (WAC), she was more fortunate than her former DOP coworkers, who were ushered out the factory door and through the Sixth Avenue gate.

As previously noted, the demands of World War II dramatically increased the numbers of women working, women working in industrial jobs, and married and older women working. The end of the war reversed that trend, as women were laid off from wartime jobs and replaced by returning veterans. By the 1950 census, a quarter of white working women were employed in professional and related services and another quarter in wholesale and retail trade. Over a third of black women remained in personal ser-

FIGURE 11.1 *Released from war factory jobs after 1945, women reverted to the traditional jobs they had held before the war. At Shepard's Citation in Colorado Springs, women were concentrated in the typing pool under the supervision of male managers. Photograph by Stewarts Commercial Photographers, © Pikes Peak Library District, 013-1012, Colorado Springs, CO.*

vice (72 percent working in private households) and over a quarter in professional and related services (most in medical and other health services). Ten years later, in the 1960 census, the top two categories for white and black women remained the same.[4]

JUSTINA L. FORD, MD

One African American woman who was successful in a professional field was Dr. Justina L. Ford. By the time of her death at age eighty-one, Ford had delivered approximately 7,000 babies, treated thousands of children, and visited and cared for countless numbers of adults. She was the doctor of choice for African American families in Denver.[5] As late as 1950, she was the only African American woman doctor in the capital city. Dr. Ford could not join the American Medical Association because she was not a member of the

Colorado Medical Society (CMS), and she could not join the CMS because of her race. That left her just two routes by which to provide medical care. One was in her office on the first floor of her home at 2335 Arapahoe Street in Denver. The second was to go to her patients' homes. At first she took a horse and buggy or walked to their homes. Later she rode streetcars and trolleys or traveled in an automobile with her husband at the wheel. When she arrived to deliver a baby, Dr. Ford removed her dress so she would not contaminate the newborn or the mother. Immigrant Greek, Hispanic, Korean, Japanese, and other ethnic peoples, as well as African Americans and poor whites—fearing that Anglo doctors would not touch them and would charge high fees—called on Dr. Ford. She made home visits in which she delivered the baby first and then asked about payment, which sometimes consisted of produce, poultry, or handmade blankets. If she was paid in cash, it came after family members pulled coins stashed in tin cans or under floorboards. Ford was aware that the families did not have the fifteen or twenty dollars she charged for prenatal care and delivery, and it was not unusual for her to provide free health care and also bring the struggling family some coal.[6]

After many years, Dr. Ford was finally allowed to practice medicine at Denver General and a few other hospitals. Almost forty years after her death the CMS, which had barred her from membership while she was alive, called her an outstanding Colorado figure in the development and furtherance of health care. Other honors were also extended. The Ford-Warren Branch Library of the Denver Public Library system is named in her honor. Her home, slated for demolition, was saved and moved to 3091 California Street, where it houses the Black American West Museum and Heritage Center.[7] Dr. Ford, who brought so many people into the world, said goodbye to this one in 1952.

COLORADO WOMEN BY THE NUMBERS

Oleta Crain never married or had children, in stark contrast to the ideals and practices of the majority of women in the postwar years. In 1940, 62 percent of women in Colorado were married. By 1950, that number had risen to 67 percent. Correspondingly, the proportion of single Colorado women decreased from 24 percent (1940) to 18 percent (1950 and 1960). In 1960, nearly 66 percent of white women and 62.5 percent of nonwhite females were married.[8]

Newspaper and magazine articles extolled the virtues of marriage and stay-at-home motherhood. Although that may have been the ideal for many, the reality was much different. By the late 1990s, 60 percent of American mothers whose children were not yet of school age worked outside the home.[9] The desire to buy houses, move to the suburbs, and purchase newly available consumer goods drove the need for more family income. Other women worked not to acquire material goods but to help provide the necessities of life for their families.

Percentage-wise, professional women lost ground after World War II, continuing a trend that started in the 1930s. Although single white women were twice as likely to enter college as their mothers had been, they were less likely (only 37 percent) to complete a degree.[10] The push to marry and set up households with which to support their husbands' schooling and, later, his career led white women to marry the person *they* wanted to be. As one woman explained, "If we wanted to be a lawyer or a doctor we married one."[11] Ironically, black women were often free of the constraints white women experienced in regard to working outside the home and obtaining college degrees. Although middle-class white society frowned on women who worked outside the home, the black press praised black married working women as connected to the struggle for racial equality. This attitude extended into higher education. In contrast to white women, who found completing a college degree detrimental to their marriage prospects, 90 percent of black women who enrolled in college completed their degrees.[12]

AN AUTHOR, A CONDUCTOR, AND A WEAVER

Women in the arts were more immune to the economic trends of the 1940s and 1950s. In the middle of World War II, Lenora Mattingly Weber wrote her first Beany Malone book, *Meet the Malones*. Beany starred in fourteen Malone books and also appeared as a minor character in Weber's Katie Rose Belford and Stacy Belford series. Weber's writing career was already established by the time she created Beany Malone. Born in Missouri, she spent her childhood on a homestead in Deer Trail, Colorado. She boarded in Denver to attend Manual High School, where she was captain of the girls' basketball team and school reporter for the *Denver Post*. The year after she graduated she married Albert Herman Weber, her high school coach. Her first book, *Wind on the Prairie*, was published in 1929. For the next thirty years, Weber wrote short stories for the *Saturday Evening Post, McCalls,* and *Good Housekeeping,* drawing upon her love of horses (she won the ladies' relay race at a Cheyenne, Wyoming, rodeo at age seventeen) and life in Denver. Weber ultimately wrote more than eighty short stories and thirty-four books, the last one published posthumously in 1972.[13]

Another Colorado woman who was successful in the arts was Antonio Brico. Although a trained and talented orchestra conductor, she found that, as a woman, symphony orchestra posts were unavailable to her. Unable to secure a conducting position with an established orchestra, she founded her own, the Women's Symphony Orchestra (later the Brico Symphony Orchestra), in New York. In the 1940s Brico moved to Denver, where she taught and served as a guest conductor. One of her students was Judy Collins, who became a famous folksinger. In 1947 Brico became director of the Denver Businessmen's Symphony (later renamed the Brico Symphony), a position she held until 1985. She also directed the Denver Opera Association, the Boulder Philharmonic, and the Women's String Orchestra.[14]

An artist in the traditional craft of weaving, Eppie Archuleta moved to the San Luis Valley with her husband, Frank, and their eight children. They worked in potato and lettuce fields and raised sheep. As a child in New Mexico, Archuleta had learned weaving from her mother and worked alongside her parents and siblings making blankets and rugs to sell. She was also taught how to collect and use various plants for dyes. In Colorado, Archuleta processed her own wool by carding, spinning, and dyeing it. Because she worked in the fields and cooked for her family during the day, she did her spinning and weaving at night after everyone else was asleep. Within a decade, she was passing her craft on to others as an instructor for the Los Artes del Valle crafts cooperative and the Virginia Neal Blue Women's Resource Center. She also taught younger weavers. Her weaving reflects traditional Hispanic designs, Navajo patterns, and representational forms such as landscapes, animals, and portraits of people. In the 1990s Archuleta moved to tiny Capulin, where she built a wool mill and continues to design and weave. She was named a National Heritage Fellow by the National Endowment for the Arts in recognition of her artistic contribution to the nation's traditional arts heritage.[15]

FAMILY LIFE

While urbanization isolated Americans from their natural landscapes, it also created improved technology for the home. Between 1940 and 1950, electricity, private toilets, showers and bathtubs, electric or gas stoves, and electric vacuum cleaners became commonplace household amenities. Unfortunately, these advances did not mean more leisure time for housewives. Even with these amenities, women were still spending an average of fifty-five hours a week on household chores. Rising expectations were to blame. Another reason was the greater number of children, which generally translated into a larger house and more clothing to clean.[16] From the late 1940s to the mid-1960s, American men and women married at younger ages, had more children, and divorced less often than had been the case in previous generations. Four children was considered the ideal number, double that of twenty years earlier. Reversing a national trend of declining birthrates since 1820, the nation's birthrate soared in the twenty years following the end of World War II. In 1930 the nation's birthrate was 19 births for every 1,000 women; by the 1950s it had risen to 24 per 1,000 women. Between 1945 and 1965, the "baby-boom" years, 4.3 million births were recorded in the United States, with the peak in 1957.[17]

Family life was altered by more than baby-boomer children, however. Families also moved more often. Discharged veterans and their brides moved away from the towns in which they had been born and raised. If they were white and middle class, the move was often to one of the new suburbs, perhaps across the country. Cut off from extended family, newlyweds relied more on each other. This "nuclear family" meant a renewed commitment to a family in which the husband was the primary wage earner and the wife the caretaker of the home and children. To reinforce a woman's role, numerous authors of books and magazine articles as well as so-called experts touted her as essential to the proper running of the household and rearing of children. To be a good wife, one high school home economics textbook advised, "Take fifteen minutes to rest so that you will be refreshed when he arrives. Touch up your makeup, put a ribbon in your hair and be fresh looking. Try to encourage the children to be quiet." Some "don'ts" included: "Don't greet him with problems or complaints. Don't complain if he's late for dinner. Count this as minor compared with what he might have gone through that day."[18] The home was a man's sanctuary. Ironically, it was the woman's place of work, one she could not escape. For the stay-at-home wife and mother, the standard chores of shopping, cleaning, cooking, washing, ironing, and child care required herculean efforts to meet society's expectations. For women who worked outside the home, household chores awaited her return. Small wonder, then, that for many mothers the 1950s and 1960s were a blur of diapers and children's birthday parties.[19]

New advances in birth control allowed husbands and wives to regulate family size and the spacing of children's births. In 1942 the Birth Control Federation of America became Planned Parenthood Federation of America. Condoms, diaphragms, jellies, and foams were widely available. Inter-uterine devices and oral contraceptives were developed in the late 1950s and early

1960s. The US Food and Drug Administration approved "the pill" in 1960. The following year, the National Council of Churches of Christ approved the use of birth control for church members.

Although birth control measures aided in family planning, a legal abortion was harder to obtain. Women's experiences with out-of-wedlock births depended on their economic status and, even more, their race. Young white pregnant women either married the baby's father before giving birth or were sent away to have the child and give it up for adoption. Young black women were more likely to keep their babies.[20] By the late 1960s, though, as the availability of birth control devices grew, Americans adopted more liberal views toward premarital sex. In 1967 Democratic state representative Richard Lamm sponsored a bill to liberalize Colorado's anti-abortion law. Although he became the face of the bill, he credited Ruth Nunn Steel as the driving force. Campaigning in "impeccable white gloves and a stylish hat," Steel met with legislators and discussed abortion at a time when doing so was unusual in mixed company.[21] Governor John Love signed Lamm's bill six years before the US Supreme Court affirmed a woman's right to an abortion in *Roe v. Wade*. It was a sign of changing attitudes toward morality and premarital sex. Between 1969 and 1974, the number of women who felt premarital sex was wrong dropped from 75 percent to 53 percent.[22]

FLORENCE CRITTENTON HOME

Changes in policy at the Florence Crittenton Home reflected these changes in attitudes. Whereas young pregnant women were once encouraged to give up their babies for adoption, in the late 1940s the home began offering mothers-to-be training on how to care for their newborns. In the early 1960s the home launched a $300,000 fundraising drive to build a new hospital wing and an educational activities building and to improve the nursery facilities and living quarters because of a significant increase in the number of pregnant thirteen- to seventeen-year-old girls. During the previous decade, the number of girls at the home had soared from 167 to 516. Director Frances Whitefield insisted that the decision to keep a baby or to place it for adoption belonged solely to the mother. To that end, the home employed a full-time nursing staff, case workers, medical teams from the University of Colorado Medical School, and a consulting psychiatrist.[23] Within a year, the home also began working with Denver Public Schools so the girls could earn high school diplomas.[24] By 1968 Whitefield, the director for twenty-one years, boasted that the home included a complete maternity ward at its Mary

FIGURE 11.2 *The Florence Crittenton Home was established in 1893 as a home for unwed mothers-to-be. The facility and mission have expanded over the years to include additional services for women and men. Courtesy, History Colorado (Denver Post Historical Collection, Scan #10041259), Denver.*

Donaldson Hospital. She reported that the average resident—nineteen years old, white, beginning college, and due in four months—typically gave her baby up for adoption.[25]

CIVIL RIGHTS MOVEMENTS

Other significant changes occurred in people's attitudes and behavior after the war. The transformations were shaped by individuals such as Rosa Parks and Betty Friedan and were part of larger national movements. Assaults on racism and sexism launched by blacks and feminists, respectively, changed the landscape of American life. Some of the two movements' goals were similar in nature—to end discrimination and gain access to previously closed or limited educational and economic avenues. Other demands, such as desegregation of public facilities and abortion rights, were more relevant to a particular group.

Increasingly, blacks demanded an end to segregated public facilities. As the movement spread from southern states to the rest of the nation, African Americans in Colorado joined the cause. Blacks, who made up only 2 percent of the state's population, faced discrimination in housing as well as segregation in schools and public facilities. Concentrated in Denver, Colorado Springs, and Pueblo, blacks enjoyed vibrant communities of black-owned businesses, churches, and private homes but were separated from the rest of the city. In response to the growing number of African Americans in Denver, in 1947 Mayor Quigg Newton assembled a task force to study the city's minority population. Data revealed that many hospitals did not treat blacks, realtors did not sell to blacks, and restaurants did not serve blacks. There were only two African Americans and one Hispanic on the police force. Black firefighters were assigned only to the station in Five Points, the historic Denver neighborhood for African Americans.[26] When George Brown, the *Denver Post*'s first black reporter, tried to register at various motels and trailer camps in an attempt to study Denver's racial atmosphere, most of the establishments refused to admit him. The manager of the Crestview Trailer Camp on Federal Boulevard told him bluntly, "We don't have restrictions on pets, but we have to draw the line on Negroes."[27] Although a southern reporter thought Denver was doing a splendid job in making progress toward racial integration, his opinion must be viewed as coming from a southerner accustomed to much harsher conditions. Blacks were segregated in Five Points, although some African American families had begun moving further east beginning in the 1930s. The stumbling blocks, or gates, to blacks moving

FIGURE 11.3 *Fannie Mae Duncan opened the Cotton Club in Colorado Springs in the mid-1950s. Headline entertainers such as Duke Ellington and Fats Domino packed in crowds of African and Anglo Americans. Courtesy, Special Collections, Pikes Peak Library District, 099-10735, Colorado Springs, CO.*

into historically white neighborhoods were restrictive covenants in property deeds. After the US Supreme Court made such clauses legally unenforceable, it was racism, banks' reluctance to lend to blacks, and real estate agents' unwillingness to show blacks homes in white areas that continued to keep African Americans from white enclaves. It became harder to do so after 1965, however, when the state strengthened its fair-housing statutes to align with the national Civil Rights Movement.

Colorado Springs witnessed political action and protests by African Americans. During World War II, Gretchen D. McRae became the first black woman to run for the Colorado Springs City Council. She lost by only seven votes. In 1944 Juanita Cassius Hairston was ejected from the Ute Theater for refusing to move to the segregated balcony section. Three years later she was awarded $600 in damages in a civil suit against the theater. After students staged sit-ins in Colorado Springs restaurants, the local National Association for the Advancement of Colored People filed lawsuits against the businesses. In 1954 Nina Stroud Pellerin became the first African American teacher in Colorado Springs District 11. Fannie Mae Duncan opened her Cotton Club on Colorado Avenue in the mid-1950s. As black music became more popular, white members of the Colorado Springs community asked if they could attend the club. Duncan posted a huge sign reading "Everybody Welcome" and opened the doors to all. Headline entertainers—Lionel Hampton, Fats Domino, and Duke Ellington—packed in the crowds.[28]

In the 1940s a small, racially mixed group formed the Denver chapter of the Congress on Racial Equality (CORE). CORE targeted the discriminatory hiring practices of Denver businesses. They picketed theaters and sat in restaurants that refused to serve African Americans. Skip Reynolds Crownhart, a sophomore at the University of Denver (DU), walked the picket lines. Later, she saw her efforts come to fruition when she was hired in the accounting department of Mountain Bell after graduating from DU.[29] The National Urban League's Denver chapter's push for better jobs was rewarded when the May Company hired a black cashier and Safeway a black checker.[30]

Traditionally, the largest concentration of Hispanics had been in the southern and northeastern parts of Colorado, but Denver's Hispanic population grew during and after the war years. Newton's task force on human relations, which showed widespread discrimination against blacks, found a similar situation for Hispanics. Of the nearly 200 businesses surveyed, less than 60 percent employed Spanish Americans. Three years later the Denver Area Welfare Council reported that the average Spanish American family made less than black families and only 61 percent of the average white family's income. The council estimated that 60 percent of Hispanics lived in substandard housing and 90 percent did not complete high school.[31] Spanish-speaking citizens established the GI Forum, the League of Latin American Citizens, and the Colorado Latin American Conference to address these issues.[32]

CHANGES ON THE UTE RESERVATIONS

Native Americans were clustered on two reservations in the southwestern corner of Colorado. Beginning in the 1940s, Ute women were elected to the Southern Ute and Ute Mountain Ute Tribal Councils. The education of their children was a top priority. In 1955 the Southern Utes began negotiations with the Ignacio Public School District to obtain the transfer of all Ute students from the Ute Vocational School to public schools. The following year, the public school and the Ute school consolidated into one school system. At Towaoc, Ute Mountain School reopened for grades one through six in

1953 after an eleven-year hiatus. As students moved through the grades, they enrolled in Cortez's public high school until 1961, when all Ute Mountain Ute students were attending public schools. However, public education was a "perpetual source of frustration."[33] There were no Ute teachers, and no Ute Mountain tribal member was ever elected to the Montezuma-Cortez school board. Cynthia Kent, educational coordinator for the Southern Utes, claimed the school board was prejudiced. The first female chairperson of the Ute Mountain Ute tribe, Judy Pinnecoose, complained that Cortez school officials wouldn't work with Ute parents. One school counselor argued that Ute students' low performance resulted from unstable homes and a lack of interest in education. To spark interest, special programs were offered on the Ute language, culture, and history in the Ignacio schools, but they were unsuccessful and were discontinued in 1981. Another bone of contention between Ute leaders and education leaders was the use of Johnson-O'Malley federal funds, monies given to school districts with large Indian populations. Ute Indians complained when the district used the monies for programs or expenditures that did not directly affect Ute students.[34]

Native Americans also had to adapt to changes wrought by passage of the Indian Reorganization Act (1934) and judgments entered by the US Court of Claims. In 1950 the federal court decided in favor of the Utes in four land claim suits. The US government was ordered to pay nearly $32 million in compensation for land taken from the Ute bands. The Southern Utes and Ute Mountain Utes received over $12 million to split.[35] Before the federal government would appropriate the funds, however, each tribe had to submit a "rehabilitation plan" outlining how the money would be spent. The Ute Mountain Utes quickly developed and submitted a plan that was accepted. The process was much more divisive for the Southern Utes. The Planning Committee, led by John Baker, proposed a plan in which only a portion of the total amount would be distributed to tribal members. Each member would receive $3,500.

Sunshine Cloud Smith, a fairly new tribal council member but no stranger to Ute leadership, strongly opposed Baker's plan. Smith was a well-educated World War II veteran when she and her husband, Thurman Smith, returned to the reservation. Sunshine Cloud's father was Edwin Cloud, a medicine man, Sun Dance chief, and former sub-chief under Buckskin Charlie. She attended Ignacio High School for two years before continuing her education at Haskell Institute (Kansas). After graduation she continued her studies at Haskell and at the University of New Mexico, majoring in business. During World War II she and her husband moved to Indiana, where she produced land mines before enlisting in the Women's Army Corps. She worked as a surgical technician in New York before being mustered out of the army at the end of the war. In 1946 she took care of her dying father on the reservation. She and her husband returned "for good" in 1950.[36] She was appointed to complete the council term of a deceased member. A strong advocate of individual tribal members, Smith argued that all the money should be distributed, giving each member approximately $8,000. After considerable debate and discussion, the general council approved the original plan's distribution of $3,500 to each member.[37]

Smith was elected to three-year terms on the Southern Ute Tribal Council on and off over the next several years. She remained fiercely loyal to individual Indians, regularly advocating for greater tribal assistance for the Ute people. During the cultural revival of the 1950s, she and fellow council member Eddie Box actively promoted a return to the cultural life of the tribe—including the Sun Dance, the sweat ceremony, and use of the Ute language.[38]

Through the years, the Southern Ute Tribal Council continued to have a number of female members, notably Martha B. Evensen who served in 1963 and again from 1965 to 1973, Lillian W. Siebel (1980–1995), Vida B. Peabody (1985–2004 and chair of the council in 2011), and Pearl Casias (1995–2005). Other American Indian women, such as Helen White Peterson, found leadership roles at the national level with the National Congress of American Indians.

In 1972 many women in the United States were feeling particularly optimistic. America's divisive participation in the Vietnam War was apparently coming to a close. In domestic affairs, Congress passed the Equal Rights Amendment, a measure promoted by American feminists since 1923. At the time, few thought it would not meet its original deadline (1979) of acceptance by thirty-five states. Congress also passed Title IX of the Civil Rights Act. Minority students were being integrated into public schools, the economy was strong, and there were signs of improvement in economics, health care, and political participation for Colorado's female citizens.

MARILYN VAN DERBUR ATLER: BEAUTY QUEEN AND CHILD ADVOCATE

Marilyn Van Derbur fulfilled her Miss America duties and graduated from the University of Colorado (CU). Her marriage to Gary Nady, a CU football player, was short-lived. The couple separated after three months and later divorced. She was hired by AT&T to be the spokeswoman for commercials on the Bell Telephone Hour. By nature a shy person, Van Derbur overcame her innate reluctance toward public speaking through hard work and preparation. The effort paid off, as she spent sixteen years as General Motor's only female guest lecturer.

In the early 1960s Van Derbur told a former youth minister that her father, Francis Van Derbur, had sexually molested her when she was ages five to eighteen. She also confided in Larry Atler, whom she later married. She credited Atler for helping her pull her life together. For the next ten years Van Derbur Atler was the "Queen of Motivation," the country's highest-paid female speaker. She founded the Marilyn Van Derbur Motivational Institute in Denver. The institute's films were highly acclaimed by corporate leaders and high school counselors. After the birth of her daughter, Jennifer, in 1971, Van Derbur cut back on her demanding travel and speaking tours.

In 1985 she finally confronted her father about the molestation after learning from her older sister, Gwen, that he had also molested her. Her father died later that year. His death propelled her to drastically cut back on her talks: "I am not feeling positively productive right now. I want to be with my family without anything distracting me. My goal right now is not to have one."[39]

But the public speaker could not continue to hide the past when she knew there were other male and female adult survivors of child abuse as well as children who were being molested every day she remained silent. Van Derbur approached the Kempe National Center for the Treatment and Prevention of Child Abuse and Neglect, a Denver-based operation that grew out of Dr. Henry Kempe's research at the University of Colorado's Health Sciences Center, about establishing a network for incest survivors. She went public with her story and announced the formation of the Adult Incest Survivors Program at the Kempe Center. The Van Derbur family gave nearly a quarter-million dollars to establish the program. Over the next few years, thousands of people from all over the world contacted Van Derbur with their stories. Before the network closed for lack of funding, it boasted thirty-five national chapters.[40]

Van Derbur's cause received another blow in the early 1990s when reports of "false memory syndrome" cases flared in the nation's newspapers. Lawsuits filed by accused family members contended that "sinister, incompetent, or misguided" therapists planted false memories of childhood sexual abuse in patients' minds. As the debate played out in the media and more Americans expressed doubt about sexual abuse incidents, incest victims were devastated. Van Derbur Atler explained, "We feel like we aren't being believed again, and as adults it convinces us that we wouldn't have been believed or protected or heard if we had come forward earlier."[41] She continues her work with sexual abuse victims. She has written a book, *Miss America by Day: Lessons Learned from Ultimate Betrayals and Unconditional Love,* and is still a powerful advocate for victims and survivors.

A WOMAN OF STATURE IN STATUARY HALL: FLORENCE R. SABIN

In a drive to reform Colorado's health laws, Dr. Florence Rena Sabin coined the phrase "Health to Match Our Mountains." One could say that this notable scientist was an equal match to the state's Rocky Mountains. Born in Central City in 1871, Sabin received her early education at Denver's prestigious Wolfe Hall. After the death of her mother, her father was the sole caretaker of two young daughters. Unable to care for seven-year-old Florence and nine-year-old Mary, George Sabin sent his two daughters to the boardinghouse school. Later, they lived with his brother in Chicago, who then sent them to live with their grandfather in Vermont.

After graduating from Vermont Academy, Sabin enrolled at Smith College. A freshman course in zoology spurred her interest in science. She was not attracted to teaching, so she approached Dr. Grace Preston, Smith's resident physician, about pursuing medicine. Dr. Preston encouraged her and told her about a promising situation. Three wealthy Baltimore women had offered to help finance a proposed medical school at Johns Hopkins provided women were accepted. Dr. Preston told Sabin to apply as soon as the school was founded, but her father and sister told her there was no money for medical school. Rather, they urged her to follow her older sister into teaching. After graduating from Smith in 1893, Sabin did teach but only for two years until she had saved enough money for her first year of medical school. While teaching at Wolfe Hall, she became acquainted with Ella Strong Denison, who was so impressed with her teaching that she hired her as a summer tutor for her children. The wealthy matron also took a maternal interest in Florence. She sent household gifts and spending money during Sabin's student years.[42]

In 1896 Sabin became one of the first sixteen women accepted to the Johns Hopkins School of Medicine. Captivated by the world that existed under a microscope, she became a fixture in the laboratory. Her model of a newborn baby's brain stem was so accurate that it has been used by gen-

FIGURE 11.4 *Central City native Florence R. Sabin won acclaim as a researcher and public health advocate. Her health laws revolutionized the state's health regulations. Courtesy, History Colorado (Scan #10031083), Denver.*

erations of neurology classes. In 1900 she graduated with high honors and spent her internship at Johns Hopkins. With a fellowship from the Baltimore Association for the Promotion of University Education for Women, Sabin financed her research on the lymphatic system. Her *Atlas of the Midbrain and Medulla* (1901) became a valued medical text.

Recognizing her research and teaching abilities, Johns Hopkins promoted her to anatomy assistant in 1902 and made her the university's first full professor in 1917. After nearly thirty years at Johns Hopkins, Sabin moved to New York to head the Department of Cellular Studies at the Rockefeller Institute for Medical Research, becoming the institute's first female full member.

Sabin garnered even more "firsts." She was the first woman elected president of the American Association of Anatomists and the first female member of the National Academy of Sciences. In addition to her work and honors in medicine, Sabin was a valued member of the National Woman's Party and rose to the office of chairwoman. She participated in the organization's letter-writing campaign and edited a weekly suffrage newspaper. Although she did not march in suffrage parades, tangible proof of her commitment to equal rights for women was displayed in the name she chose for her automobile. In 1923 Denison surprised her with a substantial check to buy an automobile. Sabin bought a Franklin and named it "Susan B. Anthony" after the famous suffrage leader.[43]

In 1938, at age sixty-seven, Sabin retired and joined her sister in Denver. The retirement lasted a mere six years, at which time Governor John Vivian selected her to head the state committee on health. Sabin visited each of Colorado's sixty-three counties and was appalled by what she discovered. For a state that prided itself on its many days of sunshine and clear skies, it was one of the sickest states in the Union. It had one of the highest infant mortality rates in the nation, ranked fifth in diphtheria incidence, and was third in scarlet fever cases. There were no uniform milk pasteurization regulations. She proposed eight health laws: (1) control of sewage, (2) removal of the health department from politics, (3) pasteurization of all milk, (4) inspection of milk cows, (5) provision of health education, (6) establishment of local boards of health, (7) money for CU's medical school, and (8) a new wing for Colorado General Hospital. The legislature passed her program in 1946. The new governor, Lee Knous, selected her to become the head of his new State Board of Health. The mayor appointed her manager of the Denver Department of Health and Charities. In that capacity she began a citywide X-ray program to diagnose tuberculosis. Between 1948 and 1950 the TB rate was cut in half, and the syphilis rate decreased by 90 percent.[44]

Sabin finally retired in 1951. She died from a heart attack on October 3, 1953. Even in death, honors were accorded Dr. Sabin. Colorado's first representative in Statuary Hall in the US Capitol has a college at Johns Hopkins University named after her, as is the Research in Cellular Biology Building at the University of Colorado School of Medicine.

LEADING THE FIGHT: RACHEL LOUISE BASSETTE NOEL

Few individuals are more closely linked to equal educational opportunities in Denver than Rachel Louise Bassette Noel. Born to an attorney and a teacher in Virginia in 1918, Noel received a BS in education from Hampton Institute (now Hampton University) and an MA in sociology from Fisk University. In 1950 she, her husband, Dr. Edmond F. Noel, and their young son, Buddy (Edmond Jr.), moved to Denver where Dr. Noel opened a medical practice in the Five Points neighborhood. The family soon had an addition, daughter Angela.

As a parent of schoolchildren, Noel kept busy in the Parent Teacher Association and Girl Scouts. While the children were still young, Mayor Will Nicholson appointed her to the Denver Commission on Community Relations, where she worked with Helen Peterson on education and human relations in Denver, especially in the area of minority needs. After several years she became a senior consultant, producing reports and pamphlets and conducting training sessions.[45]

In 1960 Denver Public Schools built Barrett Elementary School. When the boundaries were drawn, Noel felt they were done with the intent that the school would be small and would educate only African American children. Angela was enrolled in the new school, and her mother believed her education was inferior to her previous experience at Park Hill School. Determined to make a difference, Noel won a seat on the Denver School Board in 1965, the first minority woman elected to that body. In her position on the seven-member board, she wrote the Noel Resolution, which called for the school district to provide equal educational opportunity for all children. After the school board approved her resolution, the backlash was immediate. Parents wrote angry, hateful letters to her and the other board members who had voted in favor of the resolution. At the next school board election, citizens elected candidates who were opposed to the resolution. They quickly overturned desegregation measures that had been passed in the previous twelve months. A group of parents countered with a suit against the board. US District Court judge William E. Doyle reinstated and broadened the original desegregation implementation measures. Later, the US Supreme Court upheld its decision and ordered busing to achieve integration. Judge Doyle's decision established a Community Education Council to oversee the district's progress toward integration. Noel was one of the committee members who visited schools, wrote reports, and led discussions.[46]

Already an active volunteer for the US Civil Rights Commission, Metro Denver Urban Coalition, Colorado Advisory Committee, and Denver Housing Authority, Noel added another role when she became an assistant professor of sociology at Metro State College in Denver in 1969. She chaired the new Afro-American Studies Department until she retired in 1980.[47]

In 1976 Governor Dick Lamm appointed her to the University of Colorado's Board of Regents to fulfill the term of Jim R. Carrigan, who had been appointed to the Colorado Supreme Court. She ran for reelection in 1978, the first minority to be elected. She served until 1984.

Rachel Louise Bassette Noel died at age ninety on February 4, 2008, in California, but not before she was able to enjoy the many honors and testi-

FIGURE 11.5 *The Noel Resolution, crafted by Rachel B. Noel, required Denver Public Schools, of which she was a board member, to provide equal educational opportunity for all. Courtesy, Denver Public Library Western History Collection, X-28759.*

monials in her name. In 1981 Metro State College established the Rachel B. Noel Distinguished Visiting Professorship to honor her work in civil rights and to foster multiculturalism and academic excellence at the college. Denver Public Schools honored her work in education with the Rachel B. Noel Middle School. Noel was inducted into the Colorado Women's Hall of Fame in 1996; two years later, Shorter A.M.E. Church dedicated a stained-glass window honoring her.[48] Like Emily Griffith before her, Noel's unshakable belief in the power of education drove her to ensure that each child had the opportunity to receive the best possible education.

AN ADVOCATE FOR AMERICAN INDIANS: HELEN LOUISE WHITE PETERSON

Although born in 1915 on the Pine Ridge Reservation in South Dakota of Lakota and Cheyenne heritage, Helen Louise White grew up in Chadron, Nebraska, learning ancient tribal lore from Lucille Mae White, her grandmother. She attended Chadron State Teachers College, married, and had one son before getting divorced. With a young child to support, Peterson and her mother moved to Denver, where she accepted a position as executive director of the Rocky Mountain Council on Inter-American Affairs under Dr. Ben Cherrington of the University of Denver.

After World War II, Peterson worked with Bernie Valdez through the Chicano Rights Movement of the Commission on Community Relations and Denver's Department of Health and Welfare. Focusing on convincing minority people to work together to pass state laws on fair employment and housing, she went door-to-door through twenty-seven precincts, registering minority voters by affidavit. As a result of her efforts, more minorities voted and ran for offices. Her leadership skills were rewarded when she was named the director of Denver's Commission on Community Relations.

In 1953 Peterson found a new home as executive director of the National Congress of American Indians (NCAI), founded in 1944 in response to termination and assimilation policies of the federal government. From the beginning, women were active in the NCAI. When she became the first female American Indian director, Peterson found the organization in disarray and on the verge of collapse. She set to work to unite the tribes and bolster their efforts against federal Indian policies. Members of the US Congress were intent on dissolving the structures that allowed tribes to exercise their sovereignty and right to self-government. Mentored by American Indian leaders, Peterson crammed facts and figures into her head daily before attending congressional hearings, where members of Congress met her with bullying condescension. Without the funds to hire legal specialists, the NCAI depended on her knowledge and diplomacy.

By converting legislators to supporters and rallying the nation's tribes, Peterson was able to save the NCAI. Her summer workshop series for American Indian students at Colorado College became a model for other ethnic studies programs in the United States. She also developed mentor programs to help women in Indian communities enter professions.

In 1962 Peterson returned to Denver as executive director of the city's Commission on Community Relations. For eight years she helped American Indians who had moved to the metropolis with employment, job training, and social services before she joined the Bureau of Indian Affairs as a field liaison officer and coordinator in the Denver US Customs Office. In this capacity, she assisted tribal government members. After her transfer to Washington, DC, as assistant to the commissioner of Indian affairs, she supervised the creation of international forums and Native American exhibits. Her last position was in Portland, Oregon, as tribal government services officer, developing links among federal departments, tribes, local and state governments, churches, and local leaders.[49]

TWELVE

THE MODERN ERA

(1961–PRESENT)

In the economic boom years of the 1970s, construction sites were filled with workers wearing Carhartt jeans, denim work shirts, leather boots, hard hats, and safety vests. Large cranes glinted in the bright Colorado sun. Front-loaders packed clay between the treads of their large wheels as they hauled materials. Workers strode from one end of the site to the other like busy ants. Some workers carried items, some left for a break, and others wiggled into neon orange safety vests as they entered the worksite. At one site a sign on the enclosing fence read "Alvarado Construction." An astute passerby might have noted the Spanish surname but would have been stunned to learn that the owner of the company was a Hispanic female. In 1980 only 161 Hispanic women worked in the construction industry.[1] One of those women—Linda Alvarado—owned her own company.

After graduating from Pomona College with a degree in economics, Alvarado took a position with a California development company. In the

DOI: 10.5876/9781607322078.c12

port-a-johns at job sites, she encountered drawings of herself in various stages of undress. The graphic, crude drawings unsettled her but did not lessen her passion for construction work. If anything, they stiffened her resolve to make it in "a man's job." Her parents had prepared her well for such uncomfortable situations. Alvarado was born in 1951. She and her five brothers were raised in a three-room adobe house in Albuquerque, New Mexico, with no indoor plumbing. During Alvarado's childhood and school years, her mother took in ironing to make ends meet, and both parents stressed education and hard work. They also encouraged her to try things, even if they were not traditional activities for girls. Her mother did all the housework rather than have her only daughter help out. Instead, she told her to concentrate on her studies. Her dad also supported her and allowed her to work on his car. When she decided to form her own construction company, her parents took out a loan for her startup costs. Knowing they would lose $2,500 if she failed, Alvarado made sure their loan was a good investment. Over thirty years later her company had successfully built commercial, housing, government, industrial, institutional, environmental, and technology projects throughout the United States. Her Denver projects include the Colorado Convention Center Expansion, Invesco Field (now Sports Authority Field at Mile High), the Hispanic Heritage Center, Botanic Gardens, and Colorado Ocean Journey. She is noted for the loyalty of her workforce and subcontractors and the awards she proudly displayed in her office: Sara Lee Forerunner Award for exemplary achievement and leadership, United States Hispanic Chamber of Commerce Business Woman of the Year (twice), Revlon Business Woman of the Year, and member of the Colorado Women's Hall of Fame.[2]

Success had not come easily or quickly. But she had broken through the concrete barrier to become the first female head of a major construction company. In addition, in the early 1990s Alvarado was asked to join six other Denver entrepreneurs in a bid to buy a major league baseball team. Sitting in the Colorado Rockies owners' box on opening day in 1993, she recorded two other firsts—she was the first woman and the first Hispanic to buy a major sports team. Suddenly, she was reading the sports pages just as intently as the business pages.

HISPANIC ACTIVISTS

Linda Alvarado is a testament to the opportunities women have found in Colorado and to the changes that have affected women since the 1970s. In 2000 she was one of 735,601 Hispanic or Latino residents in Colorado.

FIGURE 12.1 *Linda Alvarado broke through the concrete barrier of the construction industry and strode through the posh doors of professional sports owners. She owns her own construction company and is the first woman and the first Hispanic to buy a major sports team (the Colorado Rockies baseball team). Courtesy, Alvarado Construction.*

Although Hispanics made up more than 50 percent of the residents in Conejos and Costilla Counties, since 1940 the largest numbers of Hispanics have been located in the large metropolitan counties of Arapahoe, Denver, El Paso, Jefferson, and Pueblo. Totaling 17 percent of the state's population in 2000, 46 percent of Hispanics lived in those five counties.[3] As their numbers grew, so did Latinos' frustration with the status quo of shoddy housing, job discrimination, and inadequate education. Stymied by educators who relegated their children to special education classes or ignored them entirely, Hispanic families pushed for bilingual classes, attention to Hispanic heritage, and seats on school boards. During the 1960s Corky Gonzales established the Crusade for Justice to attack problems facing Denver's Hispanic community. He demanded that neighborhood school boards be created and that schools teach Chicano heritage. A three-day student walkout at West High School led to riots and his arrest. In 1970 Gonzales formed La Raza Unida, a political group of men and women who called for land reform and condemned the Vietnam War. More aggressive rhetoric and individual militance within the group upset moderates in both Hispanic and Anglo quarters.

Moving from the streets and classrooms to the Denver City Council and state offices, Hispanic men and women gradually affected change. In 1970 the Denver City Council increased the number of council districts from nine to eleven. It also redrew a district, creating more opportunities for Hispanic representation. By the mid-1970s, two Hispanics were sitting on the council.

Hispanics also gained representation in the state legislature as they became adept at precinct-level networking. Roger Cisneros and "Paco" Sanchez were followed by Betty Benevidez, Reuben Valdez, Richard Castro, and Pauline (Polly) Baca-Barragán. By 1977 there were two Hispanic state senators and four Hispanic representatives. In 1983 Federico Peña, after serving in the state legislature, rode into the mayor's office on the front end of a snowplow, figuratively speaking. The failure of the incumbent mayor William H. McNichols Jr. to quickly clean up a two-foot snowfall that had dropped on Denver the previous December buried his reelection campaign. If Denverites felt trapped in December 1982, American women understood that feeling all too well.

THE WOMEN'S MOVEMENT

Women of color are no strangers to prejudice and discrimination. No one expected Anglo women, least of all those in the middle class, to experience anything less than security and comfort. But the "complacency, conformity, and comfort" mind-set of the 1950s was challenged by the feminist movement.[4] Betty Friedan's *The Feminine Mystique* put into words the discontent felt by middle-class educated white women. Stating that women felt trapped within the four walls of their homes, Friedan stressed that women, like men, should be free to explore careers and lifestyles in accordance with their intellectual abilities and skills. Through the 1960s her words resonated with other women—and at least some men. President John F. Kennedy, fulfilling a campaign promise, formed the Presidential Commission on the Status of Women and appointed Eleanor Roosevelt its honorary chair. The commission's 1963 report exposed a litany of problems in women's lives. It emphasized the importance of child-care facilities, recommended paid maternity leave, and supported unemployment and minimum wage benefits for large numbers of women not previously covered. Focusing attention on pervasive inequities, the report paved the way for the 1963 Equal Pay Act. By mandating equal pay for equal work, the act was a starting point for working women. One of its long-lasting effects was the establishing and fostering of a network of women and a series of state commissions. Colorado's governor John Love formed a Commission on the Status of Women in 1964. Its diverse work has included a survey of children's literature and a study on how to establish a craft business venture in the San Luis Valley for rural low-income citizens.

The National Organization for Women (NOW) provided an organization for women much as the National Association for the Advancement of Colored People (NAACP) did for African Americans. Like the NAACP, some constituents disagreed with various stances or felt ignored by the organization. Women of color and women of low socioeconomic backgrounds found NOW more focused on the concerns of white, middle-class women. Radical feminists were pushed aside or hidden from view. Friedan denounced radical feminists' "sexual shock tactics and man-hating" and rejected the "lavender menace" of lesbian feminists whom she believed would alienate other potential supporters of women's issues.[5] Later, she admitted that she had made a mistake. Colorado women formed local chapters, which adopted NOW's top-priority issues of abortion and reproductive rights, economic justice, lesbian rights, ending sex discrimination, stopping violence against women, and promoting diversity and ending racism.

As various civil rights movements gained ground and attracted more attention, a backlash was inevitable. For the African American Civil Rights Movement, the backlash began in the late 1960s as militant blacks increasingly threatened white security. For feminists, the backlash hit a crescendo over the Equal Rights Amendment (ERA). This amendment, for which woman suffragists and feminists had lobbied for decades, was passed by the US Congress before being forwarded to the states for necessary ratification. For the ultra-conservative Phyllis Schlafly and other "traditionalists," the ERA was the symbol of everything that was going haywire in the United States. When feminists questioned women's traditional role, they threatened the very foundation of American society. Adoption of the ERA stalled when southern states refused to ratify it, and it ran out of time in 1982. Although most Colorado voters supported the state ERA (the state constitution was amended in the 1970s with language nearly identical to the federal Equal Rights Amendment), the state remained fairly conservative overall.

The 1970 census continued to show women's dominance in clerical fields. Among Anglo women, the top three employment categories were clerical, professional, and service work. For black women, one-third were employed in service work, with clerical and professional fields numbers two and three, respectively. For Spanish-heritage or Spanish-speaking women, the top three categories were service, clerical, and operative work.[6] By the mid-1970s, however, a change could be seen. Nationwide, the number of women planning to enter the traditional feminine occupations of elementary school teaching or nursing plummeted from 31 percent to 10 percent. At the same time, the percentages of female physicians, surgeons, and attorneys had soared, from less than 10 percent to over 30 percent. In 2010, women accounted for 34 percent of the nation's physicians and surgeons and 31.5 percent of lawyers.[7]

NEW OPPORTUNITIES

Political leaders, agencies, and institutions have both affected and been affected by social changes. In the 1970s the Equal Economic Opportunity Commission began monitoring and taking action against complaints about gender discrimination. Title IX of the 1972 Educational Amendments Act prohibited any college or university that received federal aid from discriminating against women. Among other things, it required that college athletic programs allocate scholarships to female athletes on the same basis as male athletes. Its impact was significant, not only for females as a group but also for individuals. Many who grew up in the 1970s and 1980s point to their participation in organized school sports as a monumental influence. Like their male counterparts, female athletes have stated that school athletics kept them in high school, while others gained self-confidence through their participation. Some young women have been able to attend college on athletic scholarships.

Although farm girls and small-town girls in pigtails and ponytails have played on school softball and basketball teams since the 1900s, historically, girls who lived in cities had fewer athletic opportunities. Title IX changed that, however. The number of girls' sports teams blossomed after 1972. Individual and team sports were established in high schools and colleges, resulting in athletic dynasties in some cases. Sports programs offered playing opportunities and also provided opportunities for athletic-minded women to become coaches, athletic trainers, and sports reporters. However, women seldom had a shot at positions in sports administration. For women, athletic director jobs remained behind the schoolyard fence throughout much of the twentieth century. The explosion of female athletics eventually led to equal pay for coaches. Ironically, this also meant that men began applying and being hired for coaching positions with female teams, resulting in proportionately fewer jobs for women. The playing field, which had seemed to be leveling, tilted back in the direction of more men in key positions.

At the collegiate level in Colorado, several sports teams and individuals attained success at the national level. In 1983 Ceal Barry was hired as coach of the University of Colorado (CU) women's basketball team. During her twenty-two years at CU, Barry and her teams accumulated a 427–242 record, twelve NCAA tournament appearances, thirteen twenty-win seasons, and four conference championships. Barry was selected Big Eight Coach of the Year four times and District V Coach of the Year once. In the thirteen seasons CU competed in the Big 8, Barry won more regular season games, league titles, tournament titles, and coach of the year honors than any other league coach. She was named National Coach of the Year in 1994, inducted into the Colorado Sportswomen Hall of Fame, presented with the CU Alumni Association's Robert Stearns Award for extraordinary contributions to the university, and selected as an assistant coach for the US Olympic basketball team that won gold in 1996. Following the 2004–2005 season, Barry retired as CU's coach. She is the first woman at CU to hold her present position as associate athletic director/senior woman administrator.[8]

Women's cross-country teams at Adams State College (Alamosa) and Western State College (Gunnison) are nationally known for the high caliber of both their teams and individual runners. The schools' women's teams have dominated Division II, winning every national title between 1992 and 2009 (Western State in 2000–2002 and Adams State from 1992 to 1999 and 2003 to 2009). In 2010 and 2011, Western State placed second in the nation.

FIGURE 12.2 *Coach of the women's basketball team at the University of Colorado for twenty-two years, Ceal Barry was noted for her defensive-minded teams and commitment to the student athlete. Courtesy, University of Colorado Sports Information, Boulder.*

As women's sports proliferated in the United States, numerous attempts were made to form professional women's teams. The Colorado Xplosion was a Denver-based member of the American Basketball League that opened in nine cities for the 1996–1997 season. The league struggled to draw crowds as it competed against men's and women's basketball seasons at the collegiate and secondary levels. It folded in the middle of the 1998–1999 season. Some of the players moved on to play with the Women's National Basketball Association, which is allied with the men's National Basketball Association; others went to Europe to play professionally.

Although not a direct result of Title IX, women's running has shown an increase in the number of participants. After decades of not allowing women to run races of over 880 yards (800 meters), sports' ruling bodies added longer distances to women's running events. The marathon was added for the 1984 Olympic Games in Los Angeles. Joan Benoit, who won the gold medal for the United States, inspired a countless number of females to challenge themselves. Colorado native Maureen Custy Roben is one of the few women who have qualified for the US Olympic Marathon trials four consecutive times. As a distance runner, she was the top-ranked female marathoner in 1987 and set the US women's record in 1988 at the San Diego Marathon. After her racing career ended, Roben co-founded (with Diane Palmason) women's running camps, spent years as a Team in Training coach, and presently trains and coaches runners of all ages. She was inducted into the Colorado Running Hall of Fame in 2009.[9] Her sister was instrumental in establishing a Denver running tradition, the Susan G. Komen Race for the Cure, a yearly 5k race to benefit the Komen Foundation. After reading an article about the first Race for the Cure, Colleen Custy Lorenz wrote to the organization's Dallas office and inquired about holding a race in Denver to aid in the fight against breast cancer. Lorenz chaired the race for its first two years. Its popularity as a well-managed, fun, and worthy race has exploded over the years. Over 3,000 women ran the inaugural event in 1992. The following year, 4,600 women ran the race.[10] The event, which has expanded to include coed races, is held in other cities throughout Colorado, the nation, and the world. Since 1993 the Denver affiliate of Susan G. Komen for the Cure has invested more than $30 million in local breast health and breast cancer programs in the twelve-county service area.[11]

Nestled at the foot of the Rocky Mountains, the United States Air Force Academy underwent a monumental change in June 1976. The first class of women cadets sat for military haircuts, was measured for uniforms, and was processed as new cadets of the class of 1980. That first year, 157 women reported to the academy to begin basic cadet training amid feelings of anger and betrayal among the previously all-male cadet corps. Most women faced a hostile environment that did not change for several years. Women made up 10 percent of the class of 1980. At present, approximately 20 percent of each graduating class is female. Along the way, the academy dropped its slogan "Bring Me Men" and replaced it on its concrete archway with "Integrity First, Service Self, Excellence in All We Do" following a sexual assault scandal in 2003.

ELECTED AND APPOINTED OFFICIALS

Changes within the two major political parties also resulted in additional opportunities for American women. Female participation in Democratic and Republican state and national primaries and conventions rose. Patricia Scott Schroeder, a Denver attorney, was the first woman from Colorado elected to the US House of Representatives. She earned a BA from the University of Minnesota in 1961, majoring in philosophy, history, and political science.

The following year she married James Schroeder, a law school classmate. With law degrees in hand, they moved to Denver, where she worked as a field attorney for the National Labor Relations Board until 1966. Schroeder then moved into private practice, taught law, and volunteered for Planned Parenthood. In 1972 her husband recruited her to run for the representative seat from Colorado's District One. Running on an anti-Vietnam and pro–women's rights platform, Schroeder beat her Democratic opponent in the primary. She defeated incumbent Republican Mike McKevitt in the general election with 52 percent of the vote. Schroeder was reelected eleven times, rarely receiving less than 60 percent of the vote.[12]

In Congress, Schroeder faced even more blatant sexism than she had as one of fifteen female Harvard Law School graduates eight years earlier. She was one of only fourteen women in the House of Representatives. Schroeder was once asked by a male colleague how she could be a mother of two small children (ages six and two at the time she was sworn in) and a member of Congress at the same time. Her reply became one of many of her notable quotes: "I have a brain and a uterus and I use both."[13] She might also have mentioned her tenacity. As a member of the previously all-male Armed Services Committee, Schroeder butted heads with the committee's conservative chairman, F. Edward Hebert of Louisiana, a thirty-year veteran of Congress. The Dixiecrat forced her and Ron Dellums, an African American Democrat from California, to physically share a chair during the committee's organizational meeting because "women and blacks were worth only half of one regular Member."[14] Hebert also denied her a coveted seat at a Strategic Arms Limitation Treaty disarmament conference on chemical warfare. Schroeder, though, had the last word when she and her Democratic Caucus members ousted Hebert in 1975.

As a member of the Armed Forces Committee, Schroeder pushed for curbing defense appropriations, which put her in conflict with Hebert and other members of the conservative committee. But her desire to curb military spending did not include ignoring the needs of servicemen and women and their families. Schroeder worked to improve benefits, health care, and living conditions for military personnel; crafted the Military Family Act (1985); and chaired the Subcommittee on Military Installations. She was also a strong advocate of women in the military. She convinced the Armed Services Committee to recommend that women be allowed to fly combat missions and demanded military reforms after the "Tailhook" scandal rocked the navy.[15]

As adamant as she was about military reform, Schroeder was even more passionate about the rights of women and families. The first piece of legislation Schroeder sponsored was the Child Abuse and Protection Act at the request of Senator Walter Mondale, chair of the Senate Committee on Children. Familiar with the work of Denver's National Training Center for Child Abuse and Neglect, Schroeder readily agreed to sponsor the bill. The act, which passed in 1974, funded counseling programs on child abuse and tied funding to a state's ability to meet specific reporting and treatment requirements. It established a National Center on Child Abuse and Neglect within the federal government to encourage and coordinate research and training on the problem. In a similar vein, Schroeder spent five years working for passage of the Domestic Violence Prevention and Services Act that granted millions of dollars in federal monies to states to fund shelters and direct services for battered women and their children.[16]

Women's health care, expansion of Social Security benefits, and gender equity in the workplace were other issues Schroeder promoted. To strengthen the pension rights of homemakers and working women who were in and out of the workplace because of family considerations, she worked for passage of the Retirement Equity Act. Passed in 1984, it assured that survivor benefits would be paid to the spouse of any vested participant who died before retirement age, lowered the age of participation, and liberalized rules for working women who stayed out of the workforce to have children.[17]

Schroeder vigorously supported the Equal Rights Amendment and helped pass the Pregnancy Discrimination Act in 1978, which mandated that employers could not dismiss female employees simply because they were pregnant or deny them disability and maternity benefits. The act was a stepping stone to Schroeder's legislative jewel. After nearly ten years, her work was rewarded with passage of the Family and Medical Leave Act in 1993. The law provides job protection of up to eighteen weeks of unpaid leave for the care of a newborn, sick child, or parent.

A staunch Democrat, Schroeder was a presidential primary candidate until she withdrew from the race in the fall of 1987. Her tearful announcement was lampooned by comedians and criticized by some feminists, who feared it set back women's progress in eliminating the stereotype of women as too emotional to rule. After deciding that she had neither the money nor the time to make a proper run, Schroeder announced that she was discontinuing her campaign even as the crowd clamored "Run, Pat, Run."[18] Instead, Schroeder returned to Congress, where she continued to battle her conservative colleagues—particularly House Speaker Newt Gingrich and President Ronald Reagan, whom she nicknamed the "Teflon President" because, despite scandals during his administration, "nothing stuck" to him.[19]

FIGURE 12.3 *Patricia Scott Schroeder was the first Colorado woman elected to the US House of Representatives. She served twelve two-year terms in the US Congress. Courtesy, Thomas J. Noel Collection.*

After twenty-four years in Congress, Schroeder chose not to run a thirteenth time. Diana DeGette succeeded her as District 1 US representative in 1996, keeping the seat in the hands of a liberal Democrat. Schroeder taught at the Woodrow Wilson School of Public and International Affairs at Princeton University before being appointed president and CEO of the Association of American Publishers in 1997. She left that position in 2009.

At the opposite end of the political spectrum from Pat Schroeder was Anne McGill Gorsuch, appointed by President Reagan to head the Environmental Protection Agency (EPA) in 1981. Both her appointment and her term in office were rocked with controversy. McGill received a law degree in 1964. After receiving a Fulbright Scholarship, she and her new husband, David Gorsuch, traveled together to India. When Gorsuch returned to Colorado she served as a deputy district attorney and lawyer for the regional Mountain Bell Company.

In 1981 Gorsuch was thrilled when Ronald Reagan, her political hero, appointed her head of the EPA. Her twenty-two months in office were marred by controversy. A firm believer that the EPA was "too big, too wasteful, and too restrictive of business," she slashed the agency's budget by nearly a quarter. This led to charges from both political parties that she was dismantling the agency rather than using it to clean up the environment. Equally galling to her critics was the fact that a substantial number of her subordinates in the EPA came from the industries they were charged with overseeing. Gorsuch was forced to resign in 1983 after she was cited for contempt of Congress when she refused to turn over Superfund records. She argued that she was following Reagan's orders and the advice of the Department of Justice.[20]

Although Reagan distanced himself from her fight with Congress, he later tried to reward her loyalty by appointing her chair of the National Advisory Committee on Oceans and Atmosphere. That move caused such an uproar, however, that Anne Gorsuch Burford (she and David Gorsuch had divorced, and she had married Robert Burford shortly before her resignation from the EPA) withdrew from the advisory panel. She returned to private law practice in Colorado, concentrating on child advocacy law.[21]

Another high-level federal appointee from Colorado was Gale Norton, who served as the first female secretary of the interior from January 2001 to March 2006. Prior to her cabinet appointment by President George W. Bush, Norton was Colorado's attorney general from 1991 to 1999. During that time she vigorously defended Colorado's Amendment 2, which defined marriage as an institution only between a man and a woman.

Although Colorado women gained the right to vote in 1893, female candidates have struggled to win certain political offices. No woman has been elected to the US Senate from Colorado. No woman has been elected Colorado's governor. Not until the late 1970s, when Richard Lamm selected Nancy Dick as his running mate, was a woman elected lieutenant governor (1979–1987). The second female lieutenant governor was Gail Schoettler

(1996–1999), a former state treasurer. Jane E. Norton (2003–2007) and Barbara O'Brien (2007–2011) were also elected lieutenant governor. Women have been more successful running for state representative and state senator. Ruth Stockton served in the state legislature from 1961 to 1985, was the first woman to chair the Joint Budget Committee, and served as president pro tem of the senate. Her image graces a stained glass window in the senate chamber. Polly Baca-Barragán also served several terms in the Colorado legislature. She was first elected to the state house in 1974. Four years later she was elected to the Colorado senate, the first Hispanic woman senator. In her twelve years as a legislator, Baca-Barragán advocated for the rights of women, minorities, and property taxpayers. Gloria Travis Tanner, a former administrative assistant for the Office of Hearings and Appeals (US Department of the Interior) and a reporter for the *Denver Weekly News,* was elected to the Colorado House of Representatives in 1985. As the house minority caucus leader (1987–1990), Tanner was the second African American elected to a leadership position in the Colorado house. In 1994 she was appointed to the Colorado State Senate, another first for an African American woman, to replace Regis Groff who had resigned. She served as state senator until 2000. Indicative of the political changes in Colorado, three women also held leadership positions in the state assembly. Republican Norma Anderson served as co–majority leader of the senate (2003–2004), Democrat Joan Fitz-Gerald as president of the senate (2005–2007), and Democrat Jennifer Veiga as house minority leader (2003). The first woman to serve as speaker of the house, Lola Spradley, was sworn into office in 2003 by Colorado's first female state supreme court chief justice, Mary Mullarkey.[22]

In 1987 Governor Roy Romer appointed Mullarkey to Colorado's highest court. Prior to her appointment, she had practiced law privately, worked for the Department of the Interior and the Equal Employment Opportunity Commission, headed the Appellate Section of the Colorado Attorney General's Office, and served as the state's solicitor general. In 1998 her fellow justices selected Mullarkey to serve as the court's presiding justice, a position she held until her retirement in 2010.[23] Her tenure as Colorado's chief justice earned her a number of awards: the Mary Lathrop Award from the Colorado Women's Bar Association (2002), the 2003 Judicial Excellence Award from the Denver Bar Association, and the Herbert Haley Award from the American Judicature Society (2010).[24]

Mullarkey's resignation gave Governor Bill Ritter the opportunity to appoint forty-one-year-old Monica Marquez as the newest member of the Colorado Supreme Court. A Grand Junction native and Yale Law School graduate, Marquez is the first Latina and openly gay woman appointed to the state supreme bench. Prior to her appointment, she served as Colorado's deputy state attorney general.[25]

A number of Colorado women have served as mayors of various cities. First among the female mayors of a city with more than 60,000 residents was Norma Walker, mayor of Aurora from 1965 to 1967. The list also includes Cara Russell (Buena Vista), Ada Evans, Colorado's first female African American mayor (Fairplay), Ann Azari (Fort Collins), Treva Edwards (Loveland), Linda Stepien (Longmont), and Mary Lou Makepeace (Colorado Springs).[26] Prior to her election in 1997, Makepeace was a caseworker and the executive director of the Community Council of the Pikes Peak Region, and she led a child placement agency for troubled adolescents. After serving six years as mayor, she joined the Gill Foundation as executive director of the Gay and Lesbian Fund for Colorado. The foundation advocates for lesbian, gay, bisexual, and transgender equality. Makepeace is currently the foundation's vice president. She oversees programs, builds alliances with other nonprofits, and directs the fund's staff and policy.[27]

APPEALS TO THE JUDICIAL SYSTEM

The judicial system was not immune to the attitudinal and behavioral changes of the late twentieth century. The US Supreme Court ruling in *Roe v. Wade* upheld a woman's right to a medically safe abortion until the third trimester of pregnancy. On other social issues, the courts forced or upheld desegregation and increased opportunities for women in nontraditional jobs. Affirmative action policies passed by Congress and upheld by the courts opened previously locked doors to women and people of color. They allowed women- and minority-owned businesses like Linda Alvarado's construction firm to successfully compete for contracts. Once allowed on the playing field, the quality businesses women and minorities developed proved their expertise. Police and fire departments' physical requirements were challenged by female applicants, and some were found discriminatory. The first female members of the Colorado State Patrol (CSP) were hired in 1977. In 1986 Rosiland Johnson made history when she was hired as the CSP's first African American female.[28] In 2011, 52 women—7 percent of the force—were uniformed CSP officers. As of September 2011, there were 164 female officers (11.5 percent of the force) in the Denver Police Department. In April 2012 the city's fire department employed only 39 female firefighters (approximately 3 percent of its force).[29]

PHILANTHROPY

From Clara Brown to Elizabeth Byers to the Bonfils sisters, women have made a difference in their communities through their philanthropic work. Helen Bonfils and her sister May Bonfils Stanton, heirs of *Denver Post* publisher Frederick G. Bonfils, enriched Coloradans through several charities and foundations. Helen, the youngest of Bonfils's daughters, supported artistic organizations with generous donations to the Denver (now Colorado) Symphony and Central City Opera. She was also a valuable benefactor of the Belle Bonfils Memorial Blood Center, the University of Denver, Dumb Friends League, and the Denver Zoo. May Stanton established the library and auditorium at Loretto Heights College, the Bonfils Wing at the Denver Museum of Natural History, and the Clinic of Ophthalmology at the University of Colorado Medical Center.[30]

Mary Dean Reed, widow of Verner Z. Reed, supported a University of Denver library and a day-care center in Denver's Five Points neighborhood. An early benefactor of Colorado Springs art and educational facilities was Alice Bemis Taylor. Dubbed "Lady Bountiful" by the press, she created the Colorado Springs Day Nursery and the Colorado Springs Fine Arts Center (FAC). She also fiscally supported Colorado College and was often the largest individual contributor to the Community Chest. Her friends, socialite and philanthropist Julie Penrose and art maven Betty Hare, first persuaded Taylor to create an art center that would eventually include a museum, a theater, a studio, and a research library for her 6,000 volumes. Taylor consented, on the condition that the center would be free and would welcome everyone. The FAC opened in 1936.[31] The next year Taylor gave FAC $400,000 to create an endowment.[32] Julie Penrose continued her support of the FAC by contributing much of her late husband's millions to it and other charities.

Philanthropic work of a different kind was Carolyn Jaffe's expertise. While working as a nurse in an intensive care unit, Jaffe was dismayed to see dying patients with no hope of recovery hooked to machines and continually resuscitated by doctors trying to stave off the inevitable. With help from other hospice organizations and a small grant from the American Cancer Society, Jaffe co-founded the Hospice of Metro Denver (now the Denver Hospice). Over the next twenty-plus years, Jaffe cared for over 600 terminally ill patients, earning her the prestigious Nightingale Award—one of the highest honors in nursing—and an honorary doctorate of humane letters from the University of Denver.[33]

CONSERVATION AND PRESERVATION

While some Colorado women spent their lives helping other people, others had a passion for natural or manmade landscapes. Beginning with their early support of Mesa Verde National Monument, women were instrumental in convincing the US Congress to set aside significant natural sites. Mary King Sherman, president of the Colorado Federation of Women's Clubs, was known as the "National Park Lady" for her efforts that led to the founding of six national parks. Thirty years after the Alamosa Philanthropic Education Organization (whose mission is to promote educational opportunities for women) lobbied for the establishment of Great Sand Dunes National Monument (established in 1932 and designated Great Sand Dunes National Park and Preserve in 2004), Bettie Willard and Estella Leopold joined with the Sierra Club and the Colorado Mountain Club to lead the fight for the Florissant Fossil Beds National Monument.[34] Gudrun (Gudy) Gaskill, a lifelong outdoor adventurist, was the driving force behind the Colorado Trail—a 470-mile string of hiking trails, paths, and campsites stretching across the mountains from Waterton Canyon, southwest of Denver near Chatfield Reservoir, to Durango. She initiated the project in 1974 by recruiting thousands of volunteers to cut the trail through some of the state's most rugged and beautiful areas. Completed in 1988, the trail passes through seven national forests, traverses five major river systems, and visits six wilderness areas.[35]

In the urban environment, the preservation movement "was sparked by women."[36] In the late 1920s Margaret Tobin Brown, the infamous survivor of the *Titanic* disaster, led a successful drive to rescue the home of Denver poet Eugene Field. Saved from demolition, the home, originally at 315 West Colfax, was moved to Washington Park, where it still resides.[37] Nearly forty years later Maggie's own "House of Lions" on Pennsylvania Street was saved and restored by an equally determined group of preservation-minded Denverites. In 1970 Ann Love—the wife of Governor John Love—and others formed Historic Denver, Inc., to save the Molly Brown House from destruction. Restored as a house museum owned and maintained by Historic Denver, Inc., it is a popular tourist attraction. The organization followed that successful effort with others to help restore houses in the Curtis Park neighborhood.

Just as the patriotic Daughters of the American Revolution had commemorated the overland trails with markers placed in the 1930s, the National Society of the Colonial Dames took over Georgetown's abandoned Hotel de Paris in 1954 and transformed it into a historic hotel-museum run by its Colorado branch.[38]

One of the most significant revivals accomplished during the postwar period was the town of Aspen. Originally a mining town that experienced its heyday in the late nineteenth century, Aspen was just becoming a skiing destination when World War II intervened. In the late 1940s Walter and Elizabeth Paepcke fueled the town's growth as both a ski resort and a cultural mecca. The successful Goethe Centennial Celebration gave birth to the Aspen Music Festival and School and the Aspen Music Institute. In 1968 Elizabeth Paepcke founded the Aspen Center for Environmental Studies, a place she envisioned would offer a bridge back to nature for an increasingly urbanized society and provide a wildlife sanctuary in the heart of Aspen.[39]

Dana Crawford, involved in the salvation of the Molly Brown House, became known as the Dragon Lady of Larimer Street for her work in the redevelopment of historic Larimer Square, creating an attractive shopping area from what had been the neglected and abandoned buildings of Denver's original main street.[40] Old structures on the block were renovated into economically viable uses, a process known as adaptive reuse. Crawford followed that effort with renovations of the historic Oxford Hotel, the Hungarian Flour Mill into residential lofts, and a planned village in Denver's Central Platte Valley.[41]

CONTRIBUTIONS TO THE ARTS

In the twentieth century, more women obtained college degrees and pushed open the doors of institutions of higher learning, the fine arts, and the professions. Hannah Marie Wormington's *Ancient Man in North America* (1939) and *Prehistoric Indians of the Southwest* (1947) are classics. Ruth Underhill, an anthropologist who taught at the University of Denver, wrote the highly readable *Red Man's America: A History of Indians in the United States* (1954). Author Caroline Bancroft is best known for her many booklets on Colorado history. Although Bancroft was never accused of taking the truth too seriously in her books, her tales entertained thousands of readers with stories about Colorado's colorful history of adulterous love affairs (*Silver Queen: The Fabulous Story of Baby Doe Tabor* [1955]), ghost towns (*Unique Ghost Towns and Mountain Spots* [1961]), and a Titanic survivor (*The Unsinkable Mrs. Brown* [1963]).[42]

Preservationists, historians, and ghost town enthusiasts owe a debt to one particular female artist. Muriel Sibell Wolle, a teacher of fine arts and applied art, vacationed in Colorado in 1926 and visited Central City. Aesthetically and emotionally moved by the quickly disappearing town, she sought a teaching position in the West. Within a few months she was appointed to the art faculty at the University of Colorado–Boulder (CU) and was named chair of the art department, a position she held for twenty-one years. From the moment she arrived in Boulder, Wolle spent thousands of hours sketching mining and ghost towns. Reaching isolated sites required a variety of transportation means. She drove a car, rode in wagons and on horses, and hiked into the backcountry. Once there, she quickly sketched the crumbling scenes and took photographs. In her Boulder home, which she shared with her husband, Francis, Wolle finalized her drawings using lithographic crayons. Her collection of sketches of over 200 mining towns was published in pamphlets ("Ghost Cities of Colorado" and "Cloud Cities of Colorado") and her classic book, *Stampede to Timberline: The Ghost Towns and Mining Camps of Colorado* (1949). Her visual documentation is often the sole surviving record of the old camps and has helped preservationists restore individual buildings. In 1966 Wolle retired and donated her Kachina doll collection to CU. Most of her art, photographs, and diaries went to the Western History Collection of the Denver Public Library. When the CU Fine Arts Department moved to another building, it was renamed the Muriel Sibell Wolle Fine Arts Building in her honor.[43] The building was razed in 2008 and replaced with the new Visual Arts Complex.

In the field of music, Judy Collins, trained in classical piano by Antonio Brico, made her name as a folk singer during the 1960s before branching out to include music from other genres. Her renditions of "Amazing Grace," "Both Sides Now," and "Send in the Clowns" are classics. By the mid-1970s, her own compositions were being well-received. A social activist, Collins is involved with UNICEF and campaigns against land mines. Since her son's suicide in 1992, she has become a strong advocate of suicide prevention. Another well-known artist is Cleo Parker Robinson. Born to an interracial couple who raised her in Denver, Robinson witnessed ugly racism. Her company, Cleo Parker Robinson Dance, has celebrated over forty years of bringing dance to all people from her converted church studio.

WOMEN'S CLUBS FACE NEW CHALLENGES

Another sign of the changes in women's lives in the past half century is the decline of women's clubs. In the mid-1950s, nearly 10,000 women belonged to one of Colorado's 250 federated women's clubs. By 2009 the Colorado Federation of Women's Clubs had only 21 member clubs and 350 members. The decline can be attributed to the clubs themselves and to the changes in American society. Although responsible for 75 percent of the nation's public libraries and the instigators of many social welfare programs, clubs are unknown to the general populace today.[44] Local newspapers no longer report club news, and members do not publicize their activities. Women now constitute a large proportion of the labor force and often do not have the time or the energy to actively participate in philanthropic activities, even if they have the desire to do so. For many Americans, dropping a tax-deductible check in the mail for a favorite charity is far less time-consuming than doing the actual work needed to keep the organization moving forward.[45]

Americans are also more mobile than they were in the past. People who move often do not tie themselves to one place by joining an organization as readily as they might have done in the past.

There is at present a great proliferation of organizations and volunteer groups women can join. There are literally hundreds of organizations, ranging from A (alumnae and the arts) to C (church and charitable) to P (professional) to Z (Zonta). If a woman has a particular interest and is pressed for time, an organization that deals specifically with that interest—whether religious, civic, feminist, artistic, historical, or ethnic—is more likely to attract her membership and support.

Many of the roles clubs have played to protect, educate, investigate, and develop American citizens have been adopted by other volunteer organizations and by government departments and agencies. The skills of self-confidence, research, public speaking, and politics that early clubwomen developed in their literary study and philanthropic work are now being developed in colleges and universities, in networking groups, in civic organizations, and on the job.

GAYS AND LESBIANS

Historically, popular culture has taken note of societal changes and helped spread ideas and attitudes. *Time* and *Newsweek* magazines, newspapers, and television programming have reported on, reflected, and advanced that evolution. *Ms* magazine provided a forum for feminist news and views on issues relating to women's status, rights, and points of view. *Big Mama Rag* (*BMR*) was a highly regarded monthly feminist news and cultural journal published by women in Denver. Over the course of eleven years (1973 to 1984), *BMR* reported on women's status in articles that were local, national, and international in scope. In addition to reporting on the gender inequality of women throughout the world, *BMR* was committed to exposing and countering racism, poverty, and classism. Widely distributed in the Denver area, its issues were found in the Book Garden: A Women's Store, as well as at lesbian bars.

The gay and lesbian movement that had its "coming-out" party at the 1969 Stonewall Riot in New York City led to the increased visibility of lesbian communities in Colorado cities. Feminists and lesbians opened bookstores and hosted statewide lesbian conferences. Nationally popular singers such as Meg Christian, Holly Near, and Cris Williamson (who grew up in Colorado) sang to sell-out crowds. Lesbians filed from concert halls to lesbian bars such as Three Sisters and the Globe. For lesbians who had spent their lifetimes—for some, that was fifty to sixty years—"closeted" and fearful of retribution at the hands of family members or employers, it was a heady, unifying time. Common outcasts from society, lesbians and gay men formed friendships and a sense of camaraderie as they socialized in gay bars and at community gatherings. In the early 1980s their lives took a sobering turn when Colorado's first case of Acquired Immune Deficiency Syndrome (AIDS) was diagnosed. Lesbians joined gay men in caring for victims, raising funds, and advocating for alternative medical treatments. They formed the Colorado AIDS Project to help those infected with the disease. The strength and sense of solidarity they derived from their work were severely tested in 1994.

Activist gays and lesbians lobbied Colorado businesses and municipal governments for equal hiring practices and legal protection. More often than not, their demands went unanswered. There were a few successes, however. Coors Brewery issued policies of nondiscrimination based on sexual orientation. Boulder City Council led the way in 1987 with an ordinance prohibiting discrimination based on sexual orientation in housing, employment, and public accommodations. Denver followed suit in 1990, but not before Fort Collins rejected a similar ordinance. Colorado Springs—the home of many military installations, retired military personnel, and conservative religious groups—was known in gay circles as the least gay-friendly city in Colorado. It validated that moniker when Colorado for Family Values, a Colorado Springs group founded in 1991 to oppose gays' attempts to secure protection from discrimination, gathered enough signatures to place Amendment 2 on the ballot. In November 1992, Colorado voters passed the amendment by a nearly 54 percent majority.[46] The amendment read: "Neither the state of Colorado, through any of its branches or departments, nor any of its agencies, political subdivisions, municipalities or school districts, shall enact, adopt or enforce any statute, regulation, ordinance or policy whereby homosexual, lesbian or bisexual orientation, conduct, practices or relationships shall constitute or otherwise be the basis of, or entitle any person or class of persons to have or claim any minority status, quota preferences, protected status or claim of discrimination. This Section of the Constitution shall be in all respects self-executing."

Colorado gay rights activists quickly launched a legal challenge. The lead attorney was Jean Dubofsky, the first woman appointed to the Colorado Supreme Court (1979). At the Second District Court in January 1993, Judge Jeffrey Bayless prevented the amendment from becoming part of the state constitution on the grounds of its possible unconstitutionality and the potential irreparable harm it would cause. A trial was set to decide the case. Before the trial could begin, however, the state appealed to the Colorado Supreme Court, which on July 19, 1993, upheld the original injunction on the grounds that Amendment 2 violated the equal protection clause of the Fourteenth Amendment to the Constitution insofar as Amendment 2 denied gays equal rights to normal political processes. The case was returned to the district court in October 1993, where Judge Bayless ruled Amendment 2 unconstitutional. In November 1993 the state of Colorado appealed to the Colorado Supreme Court, which affirmed the district court's decision. The final appeal was heard by the US Supreme Court. In May 1996, by a 6–3 vote, it ruled that the amendment was unconstitutional, though with different reasoning than the lower courts. Although the amendment was struck down, its initial passage shook the gay and lesbian community.[47]

More challenges were on the horizon. Other states—either through their legislature or by popular vote—passed measures designed to promote or limit the rights of gays and lesbians. As these measures are passed, Coloradans are reacting with their own initiatives: laws defining marriage as an institution between only a man and a woman and policies that disallow domestic partnerships and civil unions. Although the bitterest battles occur between those who support and those who oppose gays and lesbians, some battle lines are murky at best. Within each camp, there are disagreements. Some lesbians believe the drive for civil unions and domestic partnerships weakens the battle for full civil rights, akin to "settling for half a loaf." Not all Coloradans who oppose gay marriage have joined in the clamor to restrict health and survivor benefits to gays.

INTO THE TWENTY-FIRST CENTURY

Just as women living openly as lesbians are changing the face of Colorado, the state's demographics are also changing. Between 1990 and 2000 Colorado's population grew from 3.3 million to 4.3 million people. Females were the majority by less than half of 1 percent in 1990. That difference was reversed in the 2000 census. The greatest percentage increase for females between 1990 and 2000 was among those identified as white/Hispanic (from 12 percent to 16 percent of the total female population). Black females remained at 4 percent of that population, while Asians increased by 1 percent and American Indians showed less than a 1 percent gain. White/non-Hispanic females dropped from 80 percent to 75 percent of the total number of females between 1990 and 2000.[48]

Whatever their heritage, Colorado women are facing many challenges similar to those confronted by their predecessors. In the state's second millennium, a woman raising children without a male provider in the household is just as likely to live in poverty as a mother did in the 1860s when her gold-seeking husband deserted her or was killed in a mining accident. Although women have made inroads into traditionally male-dominated professions such as law and medicine, they continue to make up over 80 percent of workers in "pink-collar" jobs, such as clerical and sales work. Women have penetrated the formerly all-male bastions of police and fire departments, although few sit at the captain's desk. Mothers are still seen as the primary caretakers of children; as the nation's population ages, women are also the primary caretakers of elderly relatives. Elementary school teaching remains a female-dominated profession at a time when the number of women teaching science in universities has risen.

Similarly, women continue to impact the physical environment and dictate the manmade landscape. As historian Virginia Scharff points out, the soccer mom "is an engine of social, economic, political, and indeed geographical change."[49] Like her predecessor whose arrival in mining towns dictated the building of schools, churches, and hospitals, the twenty-first-century mother influences today's communities. Over 100 years ago, well-known women and thousands of anonymous women founded aid societies, supported church auxiliaries, and donated their unpaid labor to community activities. Today, women make up the volunteer labor force that staffs youth sports groups, hospitals, and public schools. Their travels to and from work, schools, children's sporting events, music lessons, and shopping forays have altered our manmade landscapes. Gigantic shopping centers, drive-through fast food and coffee establishments, and day-care centers dominate the physical landscapes that once were home to mule deer, buffalo, elk, coyotes, and Native Americans. Instead of balancing a baby on one arm and a basket of laundry in the other and being surrounded by other children and the family's livestock, today's woman is juggling a cell phone, her work schedule with her husband's and children's schedules, and volunteer obligations. She has weathered natural and manmade catastrophes, endured the loss of ancestral lands, persevered through economic booms and busts, and forged her own history in the state. Then—and now—she probably would have agreed with Margaret Duncan Brown that the years "put iron" into her soul but that it had all been worthwhile.[50]

NOTES

PREFACE

1. Joyce Goodfriend, "Women in Colorado before the First World War," *Colorado Magazine* 53, 3 (Summer 1976): 201–228.

CHAPTER 1

1. Carl Abbott, Stephen J. Leonard, and Thomas J. Noel, *Colorado: A History of the Centennial State*, 4th ed. (Boulder: University Press of Colorado, 2005), 232–233. The prehistoric ruins were explored by Richard Wetherill and his brothers in the late 1880s.

2. "Ancient Voices: Stories of Colorado's Distant Past," *Colorado Heritage* (Denver: History Colorado, Spring 2007), 9–10.

3. Ibid., 16–18.

4. Koshare Indian Museum, La Junta, Colorado. Traditionally, potters were women. In present-day American Indian culture, both men and women create pottery pieces.

5. Abbott, Leonard, and Noel, *Colorado*, 12.

6. "Ancient Voices," 13.

7. Abbott, Leonard, and Noel, *Colorado*, 12.

8. Hannah Marie Wormington, *Prehistoric Indians of the Southwest* (Denver: Colorado Museum of Natural History, 1947), 35.

9. Ibid.

10. Donald J. Hughes, *American Indians in Colorado*, 2nd ed. (Boulder: Pruett, 1987). Ancient Puebloans did not "disappear"; rather, they moved to another place in the Southwest. Archaeological evidence and oral histories indicate that the ancestors of many modern-day Pueblo communities in New Mexico and Arizona migrated from Colorado long centuries ago.

11. Sandy Dexter, *Owl Woman: Her Life with William Bent* (Canon City, CO: Wolf River Productions, 2008), 21.

12. *Bent's Old Fort* (Denver: State Historical Society of Colorado, 1979), 20.

13. Susan Shelby Magoffin, *Down the Santa Fe Trail and into Mexico, 1846–1847* (Lincoln: University of Nebraska Press, 1982), 10.

14. Ibid., 38–39.

15. Ibid., 34.

16. Ibid., 47.

17. Ibid., 51–53 (emphasis added).

18. Ibid., 60–63.

19. Ibid., 67–68.

20. Ibid., 71–72.

21. Ibid., 112.

22. Janet Lecompte, *Pueblo, Hardscrabble, Greenhorn: The Upper Arkansas, 1832–1856* (Norman: University of Oklahoma Press, 1978), 119.

CHAPTER 2

1. Julia Archibald Holmes, "Letter Written on Top of Pike's Peak, July, 1858," *Colorado Magazine* (September 1936): 197.

2. Hattie Gould, "Pioneering Experiences: As Told by Emma Doud Gould to Halie Gould," *Colorado Magazine* (November 1937): 221.

3. Hattie L. Hedges Trout, "Reminiscences of the Early Years in Colorado" (October 10, 1933), Old Colorado City Archives, Colorado Springs, CO; Susan Riley Ashley, "Reminiscences of Colorado in the Early 'Sixties," *Colorado Magazine* (November 1936): 219.

4. Trout, "Reminiscences," 1.

5. Quoted in Nancy F. Cott, ed., *No Small Courage: A History of Women in the United States* (Oxford: Oxford University Press, 2000), 253.

6. Sharon Niederman, *A Quilt of Words: Women's Diaries, Letters and Original Accounts of Life in the Southwest, 1860–1960* (Boulder: Johnson Books, 1988), 6.

7. Sarah Hively Diary, April 29, 1863, M-356, Western History Collection, Denver Public Library.

8. Ibid., April 28, 1863.

9. Ibid., May 11, 1863.

10. Elliott West, "Family Life on the Trail West," *History Today* 42 (December 1992): 33–39 (electronic version).

11. Mrs. A. C. Hunt, "Diary of Mrs. A. C. Hunt, 1859," *Colorado Magazine* (September 1944): 161.

12. West, "Family Life," 33–39.

13. Lillian Schlissel, *Women's Diaries of the Westward Journey* (New York: Schocken Books, 1982), 154. Schlissel found that only 7 percent of the women's overland diaries recorded Indian attacks.

14. Hively Diary, April 22 and May 4, 1863.

15. Albert B. Sanford, ed., "Life at Camp Weld and Fort Lyon in 1861–1862: An Extract from the Diary of Mrs. Byron N. Sanford," *Colorado Magazine* (July 1930): 134.

16. Ibid., 135.

17. Ibid., 138. Elizabeth Sopris was the wife of Captain Richard Sopris, one of the first shareholders in the town of Auraria. In 1860 his wife and children joined him in Denver. Daughters Indiana and Irene were schoolteachers there.

18. Emilio Gallegos Smith, "Reminiscences of Early San Luis," *Colorado Magazine* (January 1947): 24.

19. Sarah Deutsch, *No Separate Refuge: Culture, Class, and Gender on an Anglo-Hispanic Frontier in the American Southwest, 1880–1940* (New York: Oxford University Press, 1987), 14.

20. Ibid., 51.

21. Louise Croft Boyd, "Katrina Wolf Murat, the Pioneer," *Colorado Magazine* (September 1939): 180.

22. Mrs. Samuel Dalman letter, 1924, "Our Earley Setelment in Denver," Dalman Collection, Mini-MSS 1373, History Colorado, Denver.

23. Hunt, "Diary of Mrs. A. C. Hunt," 167–168. Alexander Cameron Hunt was appointed the fourth territorial governor of Colorado (1867–1869).

24. Ashley, "Reminiscences of Colorado," 219.

25. Hively Diary, May 16, 1863.

26. Mrs. Samuel Dalman letter, 1924.

27. Ashley, "Reminiscences of Colorado," 219.

28. "Stratton, Elizabeth Parks Keays, Fort Collins First School Teacher," Local History Archives, Fort Collins Museum, Fort Collins, CO.

29. Mrs. Samuel Dalman letter, 1924.

30. Ashley, "Reminiscences of Colorado," 222–223.

31. Hunt, "Diary of Mrs. A. C. Hunt, 1859," 169.

32. Niederman, *Quilt of Words*, 8.

33. D. W. Working, "History of the Four Mile House," *Colorado Magazine* (November 1941): 209.

34. Gould, "Pioneering Experiences," 221.

35. Ibid.

36. Carl Abbott, Stephen J. Leonard, and Thomas J. Noel, *Colorado: A History of the Centennial State*, 4th ed. (Boulder: University Press of Colorado, 2005), 213.

37. Thomas Dawson, "Colorado's First Woman School Teacher," *Colorado Magazine* (July 1929): 127–128.

38. Nell Brown Propst, *Those Strenuous Dames of the Colorado Prairie* (Boise, ID: Tamarack Books, 1994), 24.

39. United States Department of Commerce, Bureau of the Census, *Eighth Census of the United States 1860: Population* (Washington, DC: US Census Bureau, 1860), table 1: Population by Age and Sex Territory of Colorado; table 2: Population by Color and Condition; table 4: Population, Native and Foreign.

40. United States Department of Commerce, Bureau of the Census, *Ninth Census of the United States 1870: Population by Counties—1790–1870, Territory of Colorado* (Washington, DC: Government Printing Office, 1872); *Tenth Census of the United States 1880: Population Part I* (Washington, DC: Government Printing Office, 1883); Suzanne Schulze, *A Century of Colorado Census* (revised 1977 with microfilm collection by Robert Markham) (Greeley, CO: Michener Library, University of Northern Colorado, 1977).

41. United States Department of Commerce, Bureau of the Census, *Eighth Census of the United States 1860*, table 6: Occupations.

42. United States Department of Commerce, Bureau of the Census, *Ninth Census of the United States 1870*, table XXX: Territory of Colorado Selected Occupations, with Age and Sex, and Nativity.

43. United States Department of Commerce, Bureau of the Census, *Tenth Census of the United States 1880: Occupations*, table C1: Number and Sex of Persons Engaged in Each Class, by States and Territories: 1880.

44. Modupe Labode, "Colorado Colonies," *Colorado History Now* (November-December 2006): 4.

45. Ibid.

46. Ibid., 5.

47. Ruth Moynihan, Susan Armitage, and Christine Fisher DiChamp, eds., *So Much to Be Done: Women Settlers on the Mining and Ranching Frontier*, chapter 9: "I Resolved to Try and Be Cheerful," by Mrs. A. M. Green (Lincoln: University of Nebraska Press, 1990), 124.

48. Ibid., 125.

49. Ella Bailey Diary 1869, January 1, 1869, MS 28, Colorado Historical Society, Denver.

50. Ibid., March 2–13, 1869.

51. Ibid., March 20, 1869.

52. Ibid.

53. Ibid., September 28, 1869.

54. Ibid., July 8, 1869.

55. Ibid., December 13, 1869.

56. Carl Ubbeholde, Maxine Benson, and Duane A. Smith, *A Colorado History* (Boulder: Pruett, 1976), 134–135.

57. Jeanne Varnell, *Women of Consequence: The Colorado Women's Hall of Fame* (Boulder: Johnson Books, 1999), 6–7.

58. "Across the Plains in a Prairie Schooner," from the diary of Elizabeth Keyes, *Colorado Magazine* (March 1933): 78.

59. Ronald W. Walker, "A Mormon 'Widow' in Colorado: The Exile of Emily Wells Grant," *Arizona and the West* 25, 1 (Spring 1983): 5.

60. Ibid., 9.

61. Ibid., 18–19.

62. Ibid., 21.

63. Hively Diary, June 14, 1864.

64. Ibid., November 26, 1864.

65. Abbott, Leonard, and Noel, *Colorado*, 70–72.

66. Hively Diary, December 22, 1864.

67. Abbott, Leonard, and Noel, *Colorado*, 71–72.

68. Ibid., 115.

69. Ibid., 115–117.

70. Cynthia S. Becker and P. David Smith, *Chipeta: Queen of the Utes* (Montrose, CO: Western Reflections, 2003), 18.

71. Ibid.

72. John S. Hough, "Early Day Colorado Election," MS 232, FF16 Manuscript Collection, History Colorado, Denver.

73. Text by Bonnie J. Clark. For more information about Boggsville and historic Bent County, contact the Boggsville Historic Site (P.O. Box 68, Las Animas, CO 81054) or the Las Animas/Bent County Chamber of Commerce.

74. *Clayton Citizen,* June 16, 1906.

75. Ava Betz, *A Prowers County History* (Lamar, CO: Prowers County Historical Society, 1986), 68.

76. "Women of Boggsville, Colorado," 3. In November 2011, runners from the Cheyenne and Arapaho tribes completed the thirteenth annual Sand Creek Spiritual Healing Run. The run, which memorializes those who lost their lives to the Colorado Cavalry, begins near the massacre site and ends in Denver.

77. Mary Prowers Hudnall, "Early History of Bent County," *Colorado Magazine* 22, 6 (1945): 241.

78. Ibid.

79. Ibid., 245.

80. Betz, *Prowers County History*, 68.

81. Bonnie Clark, "Understanding Amache: The Archaeobiography of a Victorian-Era Cheyenne Woman," *Colorado Heritage* (Autumn 2006): 15.

82. Mrs. A. M. Green, *Sixteen Years on the Great American Desert: Or, the Trials and Triumphs of a Frontier Life* (Titusville, PA: Frank W. Truesdell, 1887; reprinted, Windsor, CO: Coren, 1980 and 1983), 1.

83. Ibid., 4.

84. Moynihan, Armitage, and DiChamp, *So Much to Be Done*, 126.

85. Green, *Sixteen Years*, 11.

86. Moynihan, Armitage, and DiChamp, *So Much to Be Done*, 133.

87. Ibid., 137.

88. Ibid., 140.

89. Ibid., 141.

90. Ibid., 145.

91. Green, *Sixteen Years*, 36.

92. Ibid., 42.

93. Ibid.

94. Ibid., 72.

95. Ibid., 74.

96. Ibid., 80.

97. Theodore Roosevelt, stated on Santa Fe Trail Scenic and Historic Byway Marker, Lamar, Colorado, Welcome Center.

CHAPTER 3

1. Sister Mary Joanna Walsh, "Pioneering to Denver, Opening of the School St. Mary's Academy June 1864," 1938, 6, Sister Mary Joanna Walsh Papers C MSS-M815, Western History Collection, Denver Public Library.

2. Ibid., 2–3. Sister Beatriz Maes's name is spelled "Beatrice" in other publications; however, Walsh and Sister Lilliana Owens ("Coming of the Sisters of Loretto to Denver and the Founding of St. Mary's Academy," *Colorado Magazine* [November 1939]: 231–235), spell her name with a *z*.

3. Ibid., 4.

4. Ibid., 6.

5. Sister M. Celestine Casey, S.L., A.M., and Sister M. Edmond Fern, S.L., A.M., *Loretto in the Rockies* (Denver: Loretto Heights, 1943), xv. Sister Mary Pancratia Bonfils is known as the founder of Loretto Heights College.

6. Thomas F. Dawson, "Colorado's First Woman School Teacher," *Colorado Magazine* (July 1929): 127–128.

7. Guy E. Macy, "Organization and Early Development of Pueblo County," *Colorado Magazine* (March 1939): 41.

8. "Elizabeth Parks Keays Stratton, Fort Collins First School Teacher," Fort Collins Public History/Local History Archive, Fort Collins Museum, Fort Collins, CO.

9. In 1876 the Colorado legislature passed an amendment to the state constitution that provided money for the establishment of the University of Colorado in Boulder, the Colorado School of Mines (Golden), and Colorado Agricultural College in Fort Collins (today, Colorado State University). The cornerstone of Old Main was laid on September 20, 1875. The University of Colorado opened on September 5, 1877. At the time, few high schools in the state could adequately prepare students for university work, so a preparatory school was formed on campus. Rippon taught those students also.

10. Sylvia Pettem, *Separate Lives: The Story of Mary Rippon* (Longmont, CO: Book Lode, 1999).

11. Ibid., 2.

12. Ibid.

13. Drawing on Charles Darwin's work on natural selection, Herbert Spencer (Great Britain) and William Graham Sumner (United States) developed the theory of social Darwinism. Social Darwinists believed progress came as a result of the strong surviving and the weak dying off. They equated wealth and power with fitness and the poor as unfit and immoral. They believed the poor should be allowed to die off to advance the human race rather than being helped to survive. James L. Roark, Michael P. Johnson, Patricia Cline Cohen, Sarah Stage, Alan Lawson, and Susan M. Hartmann, *The American Promise: A History of the United States*, vol. 2: *From 1865*, 3rd ed. (Boston: Bedford/St. Martin's, 2005), 618.

14. Thomas J. Noel, with Stephen J. Leonard and Kevin E. Rucker, *Colorado Givers: A History of Philanthropic Heroes* (Boulder: University Press of Colorado, 1998), 10–12.

15. www.denverchildrenshome.org.

16. Denver Area Welfare Council, *A Study of Old Ladies Home Maintained by the Ladies Relief Society of Denver* (Denver: Denver Area Welfare Council, prepared at the request of the Budget Committee of the Denver Community Chest, 1948), 8.

17. "Ladies' Relief Home: A Glance at the Worthy Institution Which Ornaments the Arlington Heights," *Denver Republican*, October 21, 1881.

18. Denver Area Welfare Council, *Study of Old Ladies Home*, 10.

19. Jeanne Varnell, *Women of Consequence: The Colorado Women's Hall of Fame* (Boulder: Johnson Books, 1999), 39.

20. Denver Area Welfare Council, *Study of Old Ladies Home*, 12.

21. Ibid.

22. Billie Barnes Jensen, "Colorado Woman Suffrage Campaigns of the 1870s," *Journal of the West* (April 1973): 257.

23. Ibid., 259–260.

24. Henry Albers, ed., *Maria Mitchell: Life in Journals and Letters* (New York: College Avenue Press, 2001), 200. Available at vcencyclopedia.vassar.edu/index.php/Original_Faculty. Avery's work as resident physician and one of the original faculty members at Vassar is commemorated by Avery Hall. Over the years the 1866 red brick building has been a proud example of "adaptive reuse." Originally the Calisthe-

nium and Riding Academy, it subsequently became "The Museum," Vassar's hall of casts (plaster casts of works of art), and home to the college's Experimental Theatre and Drama, Classics, and English Department. It was named Avery Hall in 1931.

25. Jensen, "Colorado Woman Suffrage," 265–266.

26. Territory of Colorado, *Proceedings of the Constitutional Convention Held in Denver, December 20, 1875, to Frame a Constitution for the State of Colorado* (Denver: Smith-Brooks, 1907), 265, cited in ibid., 261.

27. Quoted in Jensen, "Colorado Woman Suffrage," 267.

28. Editorial, *Lake City Silver World*, January 13, 1877.

29. Jensen, "Colorado Woman Suffrage," 266.

30. "The Election," *Lake City Silver World,* October 6, 1877.

31. St. Mary's Academy, 1940, MSS 553 FF #6, History Colorado, Denver.

32. Varnell, *Women of Consequence*, 2.

33. "Insulted on Street," *Daily Miners' Register* [Central City], April 26, 1865.

34. "A Woman in a Thousand," *Rocky Mountain News*, August 7, 1866.

35. Exodusters were African Americans who fled the southern United States after the end of Reconstruction. Racial oppression and rumors of the reinstitution of slavery led many freedmen to seek a new place to live.

36. Varnell, *Women of Consequence,* 3–4.

37. "A Historical Heroine, Old Aunty Brown, a Well-Known Pioneer, Dying in Denver," *Rocky Mountain News,* October 23, 1885.

38. "Clara Brown's Funeral," *Denver Tribune-Republican*, October 29, 1885.

39. Maxine Benson, *Martha Maxwell, Rocky Mountain Naturalist* (Lincoln, NE: Bison Books, 1999), 5–10.

40. Ibid., 17, 28, 33.

41. Ibid., 35, 41–45.

42. Ibid., 52, 68–70.

43. Ibid., 82; "Third Annual Fair of the Colorado Agricultural Society," *Daily Rocky Mountain News*, October 2, 1868.

44. Mary Dartt, *On the Plains and among the Peaks; or How Mrs. Maxwell Made Her Natural History Collection* (Philadelphia: Claxton, Remsen and Haffelfinger, 1879), 117–118; Benson, *Martha Maxwell*, 89.

45. Dartt, *On the Plains*, 109.

46. Benson, *Martha Maxwell*, 107–108. Hunt's column was published in the *New York Independent*. Hunt, later famous for her book *A Century of Dishonor*, had moved to Colorado Springs in 1873 for her health. She married her second husband, William S. Jackson, a Colorado Springs banker, in 1875.

47. Ibid., 133.

48. Ibid., 134.

49. Ibid., 135.

50. Varnell, *Women of Consequence*, 15.

51. Benson, *Martha Maxwell*, 191.

52. Ibid., 170–171.

CHAPTER 4

1. Roma K. Simons, compiler, *Historical Research for the Walker Ranch: A Living Historical Museum* (Boulder: Boulder County Parks and Open Space, Boulder Historical Society, 1981), 18.

2. Ibid., 16.

3. Ibid., 14. A homestead relinquishment occurred when the original filer did not fulfill the Homestead Act requirements and gave up his or her land. It was then available for someone else.

4. Ibid., 25.

5. Byers was the publisher and owner of the *Rocky Mountain News,* the first newspaper in the region. Evans was a successful railroad promoter in Chicago. In 1862 he was appointed territorial governor of Colorado. He organized the Denver Tramway Company and founded the Colorado Seminary (forerunner of the University of Denver). Moffat was president of the First National Bank in Denver in the 1880s. Evans, Moffat, and others were instrumental in getting the first railroad from Denver to Cheyenne, Wyoming, connecting Colorado to the transcontinental railroad.

6. Frances Bollacker Keck, *Conquistadors to the 21st Century: A History of Otero and Crowley Counties Colorado* (La Junta, CO: Otero, 1999), 168.

7. Lesley Poling-Kempe, *The Harvey Girls: Women Who Opened the West* (New York: Paragon House, 1989), appendix B.

8. Mary Lee Spence, "Waitresses in the Trans-Mississippi West: 'Pretty Waiter Girls,' Harvey Girls, and Union Maids," in Susan Armitage and Elizabeth Jameson, eds., *The Women's West* (Norman: University of Oklahoma Press, 1987), 225–228.

9. Ibid., 228.

10. Janet Compton, ed., *Emily: The Diary of a Hard-Worked Woman* (Lincoln: University of Nebraska Press, 1987), 2–4.

11. Ibid., 120.

12. Ibid., 71, 139.

13. Ibid., 14.

14. Cheryl Siebert Waite, "Denver's Disorderly Ladies: Prostitution in Denver, 1858–1935" (MA thesis, University of Colorado–Denver, 2006), 81.

15. Elizabeth Jameson, *All That Glitters: Class, Conflict, and Community in Cripple Creek* (Urbana: University of Illinois Press, 1998), 128.

16. Cheryl Siebert Waite, "Denver's Disorderly Women," History Colorado lecture, Denver, February 28, 2009.

17. Prostitutes were referred to by various euphemisms: fallen angels, soiled doves, ladies of the night, streetwalkers, ladies of the lamplight, and working girls.

18. Clark Secrest, "Escapade beneath the Cottonwoods," *Colorado Heritage* (Summer 2006): 2–27.

19. William Wei, "Representations of Nineteenth-Century Chinese Prostitutes and Chinese Sexuality in the American West," in Arturo J. Aldama, Elisa Facio, Daryl Maeda, and Reiland Rabaka, eds., *Enduring Legacies: Ethnic Histories and Cultures of Colorado* (Boulder: University Press of Colorado, 2011), 69–86.

20. Waite, "Denver's Disorderly Women."

21. Ibid.

22. Mary Prowers Hudnall, "Early History of Bent County," *Colorado Magazine* 21, 6 (1944): 233–237. After over fifty years of educating the children of Colorado's leaders, the school was torn down and replaced by Morey Junior High School in 1920.

23. *The Wolcott School,* number 12 (Denver, 1909). In 1913, at age forty-five, Anna married Joel F. Vaile, an attorney for the Denver and Rio Grande Railroad. After her marriage, she resigned as principal of her school but continued to work behind the scenes. The school closed in 1924, but Mary Kent Wallace, Mary Louise Rathvon, and Mary Austin Bogue, teachers at Miss Wolcott's, founded the Kent School for Girls (which later merged with Denver Country Day School to become the Kent Denver School).

24. Michael B. Robinson, ed., "The Recollections of a Schoolteacher in the Disappointment Creek Valley," *Colorado Magazine* (Spring 1974): 149.

25. Quoted in Carl Abbott, Stephen J. Leonard, and David McComb, *Colorado: A History of the Centennial State*, 3rd ed. (Niwot: University Press of Colorado, 1994), 229–230.

26. Ibid., 92.

27. Ibid., 97.

28. Foote wrote *The Let-Horse Claim: A Romance of a Mining Camp* (1883), *The Last Assembly Bell* (1889), and *The Chosen Valley* (1892), among others.

29. Sally Zanjani, *A Mine of Her Own: Women Prospectors in the American West, 1850–1950* (Lincoln: University of Nebraska Press, 1997), 116.

30. Ibid., 107.

31. Ibid., 109.

32. Ibid.

33. The mine is one of the few to operate continually from 1890 to modern times. At present, the Mollie Kathleen offers the nation's only historic gold mine tour to visitors, who are taken through the four phases of mining gold.

34. Sarah Deutsch, *No Separate Refuge: Culture, Class, and Gender on an Anglo-Hispanic Frontier in the American Southwest, 1880–1940* (New York: Oxford University Press, 1989), 32.

35. Ibid., 60.

36. Quoted in Abbott, Leonard, and McComb, *Colorado*, 2.

37. Katherine Harris, *Long Vistas: Women and Families on Colorado Homesteads* (Niwot: University Press of Colorado, 1993), 110.

38. Ava Betz, *A Prowers County History* (Lamar, CO: Prowers County Historical Society, 1986), 74.

39. Alice Reich and Thomas J. Steele, S.J., eds., *Fraser Haps and Mishaps: The Diary of Mary E. Cozens* (Denver: Regis College Press, 1990), 17.

40. Ibid., 35.

41. Ibid., 40.

42. Ibid., 64.

43. El Paso County—Office of the Clerk and Recorder, Homestead Claim Notices MSS 0063, Penrose Library, Colorado Springs, CO, November 5, 1908, 1.

44. www.nps.gov. At present, her homestead is within the Florissant Fossil Beds National Monument. The homestead itself is the only original building still standing on the ranch. Support from the Colorado Federation of Women's Clubs was important in securing the area as a national monument.

45. www.heritageaspen.org/womrnch.html.

46. Harris, *Long Vistas*, 84.

47. Mrs. C. P. Hill. "The Beginnings of Rangely and How the First School Teacher Came to Town," *Colorado Magazine* (May 1934): 115.

48. Ibid., 116.

49. United States Department of Commerce, Bureau of the Census, *Ninth Census of the United States 1870: Population* (Washington, DC: Government Printing Office, 1872), table 30: Territory of Colorado Selected Occupations, with Age and Sex, and Nativity; *Tenth Census of the United States 1880: Occupations* (Washington, DC: Government Printing Office, 1883), table C1: Number and Sex of Persons Engaged in Each Class, by States and Territories: 1880. The 1880 census recorded seventy-seven women engaged in agriculture. *Eleventh Census of the United States 1890* (Washington, DC: Government Printing Office, 1897).

50. United States Department of Commerce, Bureau of the Census, *Ninth Census of the United States 1870: Population*, table 30: Territory of Colorado Selected Occupations, with Age and Sex, and Nativity; *Tenth Census of the United States 1880: Occupations*, table C1: Number and Sex of Persons Engaged in Each Class, by States and Territories: 1880.

51. Seletha A. Brown, "Mrs. Mate Smith Hottel, a Pioneer Community Leader," *Colorado Magazine* (September 1948): 219.

52. Ibid., 214.

53. Jessie Yoakum, "The First School in Paonia," *Colorado Magazine* (March 1939): 69, 71.

54. Marilyn Cox, "Education in Montrose County," *Montrose Press*, July 6, 2008.

55. United States Department of Commerce, Bureau of the Census, *Ninth Census of the United States 1870: Population*, table 30: Territory of Colorado Selected Occupations, with Age and Sex, and Nativity; *Twelfth Census of the United States 1900* (Washington, DC: Government Printing Office, 1901), vol. 2: *Population,* part 2: Occupation (in Detail), Classified by Sex, by States and Territories.

56. "A Typhoon's Victims," *Denver Republican*, October 10, 1892. Some of Helen's oil and watercolor paintings are displayed at the University of Denver, History Colorado, the University of Colorado Law School (*Source of the Platte*), and the Denver Public Library (*Pikes Peak*).

57. Cherry remained active in Denver's art circle until she and her husband moved to Houston, where she is credited with being one of the first professional artists to make Houston her home. Patricia Trenton, ed., with essays by Sandra D'Emilio,

Independent Spirits: Women Painters of the American West (Berkeley: Autry Museum of Western Heritage, in association with University of California Press, 1995), 212.

58. United States Department of Commerce, Bureau of the Census, *Eleventh Census of the United States 1890*.

59. Ibid.

60. United States Department of Commerce, Bureau of the Census, *Ninth Census of the United States 1870*; *Tenth Census of the United States 1880*; *Eleventh Census of the United States 1890: Miscellaneous Statistics Compendium*, part 3, 380; *Twelfth Census of the United States 1990: Population*.

61. Nola G. Kirkpatrick Kasten, "Early Days in Southeastern Colorado," *Colorado Magazine* (April 1960): 122.

62. Keck, *Conquistadors to the 21st Century*, 314.

63. Nancy F. Cott, ed., *No Small Courage: A History of Women in the United States* (Oxford: Oxford University Press, 2000), 262, 323.

64. Joanne West Dodd, *Pueblo: A Pictorial History* (Norfolk, VA: Donning, 1982), 59.

65. Gail M. Beaton, "The Widening Sphere of Women's Lives: The Literary and Philanthropic Study of Six Women's Clubs in Denver, 1881–1945," *Essays in Colorado History* 12 (Denver: History Colorado, 1992), 10.

66. Rebecca Hunt, "Denver's Pioneer Medical History: The First Fifty Years, 1858–1908," History Colorado lecture, Denver, February 27, 2009.

67. Carol Green Wilson, *Alice Eastwood's Wonderland: The Adventures of a Botanist* (San Francisco: California Academy of Sciences, 1955), 135, 201, 213.

68. Marcia Myers Bonta, ed., *American Women Afield: Writings by Pioneer Women Naturalists* (College Station: Texas A&M Press, 1995), 86.

69. Leta Walker Daniels, interview with Tony Boone, February 23, 1989.

70. Ibid.

71. Ibid.

72. "District #30 Pine Grove," II-14 (in possession of Stella Daniels Rodgers, Boulder, CO).

73. Ruth Dunn Helert Oral History, OH 0239A, recorded 1978–1979, Boulder Carnegie Library, Boulder, CO.

74. Leta Walker Daniels, interview with Judy Krukoff, February 18, 1989 (in possession of Stella Daniels Rodgers, Boulder, CO).

75. Ibid.

76. "Brief Ancestor Chart of the Walkers," II-1 (in possession of Stella Daniels Rodgers, Boulder, CO).

77. Ibid. Ruth Walker, the second daughter, married Thomas Dunn, the brother of Ruth Dunn, the fourth teacher at Walker Ranch. Delia married Julius Peterson; Esther married Jack Waller; Helen married Richard Pierce; Veronica and William Walker's only son, James F. Walker, married Margaret Daniels, the sister of Carl Daniels, reinforcing the ties between the Daniels and Walker families.

78. Debra Rodgers, interview with author, November 15, 2009.

79. They moved to Boulder, where William died in 1966 and Veronica in 1973. Stella Daniels Rodgers, interview by Jo Grasso, Boulder, CO, November 4, 2009.

80. David Lively, "The Harbisons: An Ordinary Family Who Led an Extraordinary Life," Rocky Mountain National Park presentation, Grand Lake, CO, July 11, 2007.

81. Ibid.

82. Ibid.

83. The Kauffman Hotel was completed in 1892 and operated by Ezra Kauffman until his death in 1920. His widow and daughters then ran it as a summer tourist hotel until 1946. It is now a house museum listed in the National Register of Historic Places because of its log architecture.

84. Lively, "The Harbisons."

85. Ibid.

86. Ibid.

87. Ibid.

88. Ibid.

89. United States Department of Commerce, Bureau of the Census, *Twelfth Census of the United States 1900: Population.*

90. Faye E. Dudden, *Serving Women: Household Service in Nineteenth-Century America* (Middletown, CT: Wesleyan University Press, 1983), 106.

91. Daniel E. Sutherland, *Americans and Their Servants: Domestic Service in the United States from 1800 to 1920* (Baton Rouge: Louisiana State University Press, 1981), 34.

92. Kristine Rutter, "Domestic Servants in Denver, 1900–1910" (unpublished student paper submitted to Dr. Thomas J. Noel for the course History 4840, University of Colorado–Denver, July 24, 1990), 6.

CHAPTER 5

1. Photographs by Jacob Riis, in *How the Other Half Lives: Studies among the Tenements of New York* (New York: C. Scribner's Sons, 1890), eloquently portray the lives of immigrants and the working poor in New York City's tenement districts.

2. Thomas J. Noel, with Stephen J. Leonard and Kevin E. Rucker, *Colorado Givers: A History of Philanthropic Heroes* (Boulder: University Press of Colorado, 1998), 39–41.

3. Ibid., 41.

4. Jane Cunningham Croly, *The History of the Women's Club Movement in America, 1868–1898* (New York: Henry G. Allen, 1898), 98.

5. Edward T. James, ed., *Notable American Women* (Cambridge, MA: Belknap, 1971), 410.

6. Mary Caroline Bancroft, "A Retrospective Sketch of the Fortnightly Club, 1881–1888," Denver, 1888. Denver Fortnightly Club Records, MSS WH741, Western History Collection, Denver Public Library.

7. Mabel Mann Runnette, "In a Changing World, Volume I," Denver, 1935. Monday Literary Club Records, MSS WH317, Western History Collection, Denver Public Library.

8. "Minutes of the Round Table Club, 1891," Round Table Club Records, 1889–1980, MSS WH362, Western History Collection, Denver Public Library.

9. Mary E. Hiatt, "History of the Twenty-Second Avenue Study Club, 1893–1934," Twenty-Second Avenue Study Club Collection: 1893–1965, MSS 965, History Colorado, Denver.

10. Jeanette Bain, ed., *History and Chronology of the Colorado State Federation of Women's Clubs* (Denver: Colorado Federation of Women's Clubs, 1955), 15.

11. Cora V. Collett and Lisbeth G. Fish, *History of the Woman's Club of Denver, 1894–1930* (Denver: Woman's Club of Denver, 1930).

12. A short list for the DFC includes Ella Denison's husband, Charles (a well-known tuberculosis physician); Susan R. Ashley's husband, Eli M. (secretary of state under Territorial Governor John Evans); Lavinia Spalding's husband, John F. (bishop of Wyoming and Colorado); Margaret Gray Evans's husband, John (Colorado's second territorial governor); and Mary Kountze's husband, Charles (co-founder of Colorado National Bank). Of the twenty-three MLC members listed in the 1893–1894 yearbook, seventeen were married to businessmen and one each to a lawyer, a teacher, and a physician. In 1898 the twenty-five members of the Twenty-Second Avenue Study Club were wives of businessmen, lawyers, and a pastor. Like the other two clubs, the Round Table Club consisted of the wives or daughters of businessmen.

13. Among the 200 charter members of the WCD were 26 working women, including several professionals. The 1894–1895 Denver City Directory lists 80 women physicians, 2 newspaper reporters, 1 writer, 1 lecturer, 1 milliner, 3 county clerks, 2 college professors, and 8 public schoolteachers.

14. Byers founded the Ladies Union Aid Society and the Working Boys' Home. Campbell, Routt, and Warren helped form the Denver Orphans' Home. Hill founded the Denver Free Kindergarten Association. Denison served as director of the Denver Orphans' Home and president of the Old Ladies' Home. She assisted in the founding of the Denver YWCA and the establishment of the Civil Service Reform League and the City Improvement Society. Evans organized the Ladies' Relief Society and served as president of the Denver Orphans' Home.

15. Carla Swan Coleman, "The Turn of the Century," Denver, 1971. Denver Fortnightly Club Records, MSS WH741, Western History Collection, Denver Public Library.

16. Amelia Eddy, Thalia P. Rhoads, Minerva C. Welch, and Ione T. Hanna served on the Board of Control of the State Home and Industrial School for Girls. Susan Ashley, Frances K. Thatcher, and Laura P. Coleman served on the Board of Lady Managers of the World's Fair from 1891 to 1895. Helen Wixson served as assistant state librarian from 1894 to 1896. Dr. Minnie C.T. Love (1893–1895), Sarah Platt Decker (1895–1901), Dr. Eleanor Lawney (1901–1907), Nettie C. Caspar (1905–1907), Ella S. Williams (1907–1915), and Anna G. Williams (1907–1915)

served on the State Board of Charities and Corrections. Non-charter members of the WCD who held public office prior to 1900 were Angenette J. Peavey (state superintendent of public instruction, 1893–1895), Louise L. Arkins and Sarah O'Bryan (Board of Control of the State Home and Industrial School for Girls), and Dora E. Reynolds, Louise Arkins, Anna Cochran, and Luna Thatcher (Board of the State Home for Dependent and Neglected Children).

17. Runnette, "In a Changing World," 39.

18. Minnie Hall Krauser, "The Denver Woman's Press Club," *Colorado Magazine* (Spring 1972): 63.

19. Cle Cervi and Nancy M. Peterson, coauthors and editors, *The Women Who Made the Headlines* (Lakewood, CO: Western Guideways, 1998), 5.

20. Stephen J. Leonard, "Bristling for Their Rights: Colorado's Women and the Mandate of 1893," *Colorado Heritage* (Spring 1993): 11.

21. "Colorado Suffrage Centennial, 1893–1993" (Denver: Colorado Coalition for Women's History, 1993), 17. Ensley and Ida DePriest formed the Colored Woman's Republican Club in 1894 after Colorado women won the right to vote. Ensley also founded the Colorado Association of Colored Women's Clubs in 1904.

22. Modupe Labode, "Caroline Churchill: Colorado's Queen Bee," *Colorado History NOW* (History Colorado, November 2003): 3.

23. Leonard, "Bristling for Their Rights," 13.

24. Joseph G. Brown, *History of Equal Suffrage in Colorado, 1868–1898* (Denver: News Job, 1898), 24.

25. Katherine Harris, "Feminism and Temperance Reform in the Boulder WCTU," *Frontiers* 4, 2 (1979): 20.

26. Jerritt Frank, "Women, Politics, and Booze: Prohibition in Mesa County, 1908–1933," *Journal of the Western Slope* 14, 4 (Fall 1999): 40.

27. Peggy Pascoe, *Relations of Rescue: The Search for Female Moral Authority in the American West, 1874–1939* (New York: Oxford University Press, 1990), 20.

28. Ibid., 77.

29. Ibid., 91, 179.

30. Ibid., 180.

31. Ibid., 93.

32. Ibid., 90.

33. Ibid., 59–61.

34. Ibid., 108.

35. Ibid., 202.

36. Otto Wilson, *Fifty Years' Work with Girls, 1883–1933: A Story of the Florence Crittenton Home* (New York: Arno, 1974), 265.

37. Letter to Ellis Meredith from Judge Benjamin Lindsey and George Creel, Denver, October 16, 1915, Ellis Meredith Collection: 1881–1917, MSS 427, History Colorado, Denver.

38. "Florence Crittenton Home," Clipping File, Western History Collection, Denver Public Library, 3.

39. Ibid.

40. Ibid., 3, 5.

41. Joanne West Dodd, *Pueblo: A Pictorial History* (Norfolk, VA: Donning, 1982), 87.

42. Maud Howe Elliott, *Art and Handicraft in the Woman's Building of the World's Columbian Exposition* (Chicago: Goupil, 1893), 48, 68.

43. Noel, Leonard, and Rucker, *Colorado Givers*, 39.

44. www.uw-mc.org/2010-frances-wisebart-jacobs-award.

45. Jeanne Varnell, *Women of Consequence: The Colorado Women's Hall of Fame* (Boulder: Johnson, 1999), 41–42.

46. Duane Vandenbusche and Duane A. Smith, *Land Alone: Colorado's Western Slope* (Boulder: Pruett, 1981), 71–73.

47. Caroline Nichols Churchill, "Women at School Elections," *Colorado Antelope* 2 (March 1881): 28.

48. Caroline Nichols Churchill, "Suffrage Enthusiasm: Western Women Wild with Joy over Colorado's Election," *Queen Bee*, November 29, 1893.

49. Cle Cervi Symons, *100 Moore Years, 1890–1990: A History of Dora Moore School* (Denver: s.n., 1990), 8.

50. Ibid., 9.

51. Mary Lathrop, "The Children's Lesson," *Christian-at-Work*, June 19, 1884.

52. Mary Lathrop Diary, 1890, Mary Lathrop Papers, MSS WH377, Western History Collection, Denver Public Library.

53. George W. Clayton willed $2.5 million to found a college for orphaned boys. The will was contested by T. S. Clayton. Lathrop researched relevant cases and wrote the briefs in the case. Clayton's will was finally supported in the lower and district courts. Lathrop then argued the case before the Colorado Supreme Court and won the decision.

54. "Mary Lathrop, Pioneer-at-Law," *Denver Post Rocky Mountain Empire Magazine* [a Sunday publication of the *Denver Post*], October 9, 1949, 2.

55. Roanne Kuenzler, "Biography of Mary Florence Lathrop," unpublished 1977 typescript in Mary Lathrop Manuscript Collection, MSS 376, History Colorado, Denver.

CHAPTER 6

1. United States Department of Commerce, Bureau of the Census, *Tenth Census of the United States 1880: Population* (Washington, DC: Government Printing Office, 1883), part I; *Thirteenth Census of the United States 1910: Population* (Washington, DC: Government Printing Office, 1913).

2. United States Department of Commerce, Bureau of the Census, *Fourteenth Census of the United States 1920: Population Composition and Characteristics* (Washington, DC: Government Printing Office, 1924).

3. Nell Brown Propst, *Those Strenuous Dames of the Colorado Prairies* (Boulder: Pruett, 1982), 102.

4. Ibid., 98.

5. In the city, Kosuge wrote articles and poems and a daily column, "Women's World," for the *Colorado Times*, a Japanese-language newspaper published from 1918 to 1969. Her column reflected on her personal experiences and philosophy. Ibid., 103.

6. United States Department of Commerce, Bureau of the Census, *Thirteenth Census of the United States 1910: Population*; *Fifteenth Census of the United States 1930: Population* (Washington, DC: Government Printing Office, 1933), table 11: Color or Race and Nativity, by Divisions and States: 1930.

7. George S. McGovern and Leonard F. Guttridge, *The Great Coalfield War* (Boston: Houghton Mifflin, 1972), 66.

8. Emma Langdon, *The Cripple Creek Strike, 1903–1904* (Victor, CO: Press of Victor Daily Record, 1904), 150.

9. Ibid., 151.

10. Ibid., 230. The following month, a women's auxiliary of the Western Federation of Miners was formed in the Cripple Creek District. Among the elected officers was Emma Langdon, recording secretary. For her "bravery in defeating military suppression of the press," she was honored with a party and a gold medal. In 1905 Langdon attended the founding convention of the Industrial Workers of the World in Chicago and was elected assistant secretary under General Secretary-Treasurer William Trautmann. Elizabeth Jameson, *All That Glitters: Class, Conflict, and Community in Cripple Creek* (Urbana: University of Illinois Press, 1998), 240.

11. Mary Wiener, "The Resolve of Three Women," *Images of Boulder County Parks and Open Space* 27, 4 (Winter 2005–2006): 6.

12. Jennie L. Jackson Harris, Spirit of Pioneer Women Collection, Box 2, folder 86, Loyd Files, Research Library, Museum of Western Colorado, Grand Junction [hereafter Spirit of Pioneer Women Collection]. After World War I, Jennie and her youngest daughter, Julia, opened and operated the Harris Ranch Inn until the flight of men leaving to serve in World War II made it too difficult to find help. In 1943 they sold the establishment and moved to Palisade.

13. Maude May Griffith Russell, Spirit of Pioneer Women Collection, Box 1, folder 44.

14. Marietta Martucci Mancuso, Spirit of Pioneer Women Collection, Box 3, folder 92.

15. Mabelle Delight Gardner Clymer, Spirit of Pioneer Women Collection, Box 1, folder 86.

16. Hattie Pearson Murr, Spirit of Pioneer Women Collection, Box 4, folder 36. See also, Laurena Mayne Davis, *125 People, 125 Years: Grand Junction's Story* (Grand Junction: Museum of Western Colorado, 2007), 30–31.

17. Natasha Boyd, *Ola Anfenson: Pioneer Photographer* (Albuquerque: Horizon Communications, 1997), 7, 9–10.

18. Ibid., 71.

19. Carmen J. Johnson, "The Hupps in Estes Park: Part Two 1900–1930," *Rocky Mountain Nature Association Quarterly* (Estes Park) (Winter 2003): 6–7.

20. Wilbur Fisk Stone, *History of Colorado*, vol. 1 (Chicago: S. J. Clarke, 1918), 389.

21. Howard T. Vaille, "History of the Telephone in Colorado," unpublished typescript in the Howard T. Vaille Manuscript Collection, MSS 754, History Colorado, Denver, n.p.

22. "Heard in the Hall of 'Hello,'" *Denver Times*, December 1, 1901.

23. Ava Betz, *A Prowers County History* (Lamar, CO: Prowers Historical Society, 1986), 248–249.

24. Nancy F. Cott, ed., *No Small Courage: A History of Women in the United States* (Oxford: Oxford University Press, 2000), 384. By the 1930 census, only 13 of the 2,656 saleswomen in the state were not white (United States Department of Commerce, Bureau of the Census, *Fifteenth Census of the United States: 1930 Occupation Statistics*); Elyce J. Rotella, *From Home to Office: US Women at Work, 1870–1930* (Ann Arbor: University of Michigan Research Press, 1981), 193.

25. United States Department of Commerce, Bureau of the Census, *Fifteenth Census of the United States: 1930 Occupation Statistics*.

26. Ibid.

27. Cle Cervi Symons, *100 Moore Years, 1890–1990: A History of Dora Moore School* (Denver: s.n., 1990), 11.

28. Arlene Ahlbrandt and Mary Hagen, *Women to Remember of Northern Colorado* (Fort Collins, CO: Azure, 2000), 48–49.

29. Alice C. Newberry Collection: 1893–1965, MSS 1202, History Colorado, Denver.

30. Josephine Dyekman McNey, Oral Interview Transcript, June 11, 1974, call number 921 McNey, J., Fort Collins Public Library, Fort Collins, CO, 16.

31. Ibid., 4, 11.

32. Dorothy Wickenden, "Roughing It," *New Yorker* (April 20, 2009): 56–67.

33. United States Department of Commerce, Bureau of the Census, *Thirteenth Census of the United States 1910: Occupations*; *Fourteenth Census of the United States 1920: Occupations*.

34. http://www.cde.state.co.us/cdelib/History/HistoryA.htm.

35. Ibid.

36. The New York State Library School was founded in 1887 at Columbia College before moving to New York State Library in Albany two years later. A succession of library schools soon followed: at Pratt Institute (1890), Drexel Institute (1892), University of Illinois (1893), Pittsburgh's Training School for Children's Librarians (1901), Simmons College (1902), Western Reserve University (1904), Indiana (1905), and Wisconsin (1906).

37. Joanne E. Passet, *Cultural Crusaders: Women Librarians in the American West, 1900–1917* (Albuquerque: University of New Mexico Press, 1994), 144.

38. Helen F. Ingersoll, "I Remember . . . the Reminiscences of My Years in the Denver Public Library," ed. May Wood Wigginton unpublished document, call number q023In4i, History Colorado, Denver, 12.

39. Passet, *Cultural Crusaders*, 62.

40. Ibid., 109.

41. Letter from Charlotte Baker to Helen Ingersoll, January 17, 1916, cited in ibid., 45.

42. Frances Bollacker Keck, *Conquistadors to the 21st Century: A History of Otero and Crowley Counties Colorado* (La Junta, CO: Otero, 1999), 40.

43. Quoted in Donald A. MacKendrick, "Splendid Public Temples: The Development of Libraries in Mesa County, Colorado, 1892–1977," *Journal of the Western Slope* 12, 2 (Spring 1997): 1–17. See also, Alice Wright, "Mesa County Library Has Come a Long Way since Founding in 1896," *Colorado West Sunday Magazine of the Sentinel*, June 26, 1975.

44. Ingersoll, "I Remember," 12.

45. Susan M. Reverby, *Ordered to Care: The Dilemma of American Nursing, 1850–1945* (Cambridge: Cambridge University Press, 1987), 41.

46. Keck, *Conquistadors to the 21st Century*, 84–86. Nurses underwent similar "training" at Pueblo's Minnequa Hospital, whose patients were men suffering from industrial accidents at CF&I sites. Their injuries ranged from fractures to puncture wounds to loss of limbs from explosions. In 1897, CF&I adopted a policy of hiring only female nurses. The following year the Training School for Nurses was founded, with a three-year curriculum. Hospital physicians lectured nurses on massage, hospital etiquette, nervous diseases, oral surgery, dietetics, anatomy, pathology, gynecology, and care of the insane.

47. In the 1930s she was one of three county school nurses in Colorado and helped found District Nurses Association 9. At age sixty-nine in 1952, she was hailed as the oldest public health nurse in Colorado. Cheryl Miller, "Early Women in Medicine," unpublished and undated biographical sketch, Local History Archives, Fort Collins Public Library, Fort Collins, CO.

48. Anna Fender, Spirit of Pioneer Women, Box 2, folder 32.

49. Janet Cunningham, "Women in Colorado: A Profile of Oca Cushman," *Colorado Coalition for Women's History News* (Fall 1999); 1. Three years after her retirement, Children's Hospital honored her by naming its new wing the Oca Cushman Wing.

50. Cott, *No Small Courage*, 323.

51. Virginia Cornell, *Doc Susie: The True Story of a Country Physician in the Colorado Rockies* (Carpinteria, CA: Manifest, 1991), 221.

52. Stanley W. Henson Jr., MD, *Touching Lives: A History of Medicine in Fort Collins* (S.I.: the author, 2004), 21.

53. "Harriette Collins Lingham, 1873–1961," Spirit of Pioneer Women Collection, the Calendar, Box 3, folder 78, Lingham, 2001, 37.

54. *A Kiowa County Album: Biographies of Pioneer Women, 1887–1920* (Eads, CO: Kiowa County Public Library, 1984), 47.

55. United States Department of Commerce, Bureau of the Census, *Eighth Census of the United States 1860: Population* (Washington, DC: Government Printing Office, 1864); *Tenth Census of the United States 1880; Eleventh Census of the United States 1890* (Washington, DC: Government Printing Office, 1897).

56. Susan Armitage, Theresa Banfield, and Sarah Jacobus, "Black Women and Their Communities in Colorado," *Frontiers* 2, 2 (1977): 46.

57. Ibid.

58. Ibid., 47.

59. A'Lelia Bundles, *On Her Own Ground: The Life and Times of Madam C. J. Walker* (New York: Scribner, 2001), 85.

60. Ibid.

61. "Highest Honor Ever Paid to Dead Laic Here Goes to Negress," *Denver Catholic Register,* June 13, 1918, St. Mary's Academy Collection, MSS 553, History Colorado, Denver.

62. This was not only a belief of white Catholics. In Gretchen M. Bataille's *Native American Women: A Biographical Dictionary* (New York: Garland, 1993), Rhoda Carroll wrote the entry on Laura Tohe. Tohe, born in Arizona to a Navajo father and a Navajo-Laguna mother, was baptized into the Mormon religion. She became disillusioned when "a Mormon church member told her that if she kept Mormon law, when she died, she would become white" (262).

63. St. Mary's Academy Collection: 1867–1941, MSS 553, Box 166-223, folder 214, History Colorado, Denver. This secular order was founded by St. Francis of Assisi over 800 years ago and is an international religious institution of the Catholic Church. Each fraternity meets in local groups made up of Catholics who profess a lifelong commitment to living a Gospel-based life following the rule of St. Francis of Assisi for laypeople. Orders of the Catholic Church: a First Order Sister is neither "of the world" nor "in the world." These nuns are cloistered in convents and cannot marry. A Second Order Sister is not "of the world" but "is in the world." These nuns also cannot marry, but they teach or serve in other areas of public life. A Third Order Sister is both "of the world" and "in the world" and can marry (because she is "of the world"). Third Order Sisters still have vows of "chastity, simplicity, and obedience to God." Chastity in this case means sexual virtue, not abstinence.

64. Cited in George H. Wayne, "Negro Migration and Colonization in Colorado—1870–1930," *Journal of the West* 15, 1 (January 1976): 115.

65. Armitage, Banfield, and Jacobus, "Black Women and Their Communities," 48–50. In 1969 Jennie, age eighty-five, was living in the Weld County Nursing Home. She died the following year.

66. Keck, *Conquistadors to the 21st Century*, 351–352.

67. Propst, *Those Strenuous Dames*, 106.

68. In 1910, of the 2,300 persons of Japanese descent in Colorado, all but 108 were males. In 1920, as the US government was shutting the door on any more Japanese picture brides, the state's numbers reflected the successful efforts of the "mar-

riage brokers." Of the state's 2,464 Japanese, 863 were female, a significant increase from the previous census count. These numbers reflect the arrival of picture brides as well as the formation of Japanese American families and the births of daughters to those families. In 1930, Japanese totals in the census were 1,847 males and 1,366 females, once again a large increase in the number of females. United States Department of Commerce, Bureau of the Census, *Thirteenth, Fourteenth, and Fifteenth Censuses of the United States: Population.*

69. Propst, *Those Strenuous Dames*, 106.

70. Ibid., 104–105.

71. Keck, *Conquistadors to the 21st Century*, 353.

72. Rick J. Clyne, *Coal People: Life in Southern Colorado's Company Towns, 1890–1930* (Denver: History Colorado, no. 3, 1999), 79.

73. Ibid., 80.

74. Ibid., 82.

75. Ibid., 84.

76. Priscilla Long, "The Women of the Colorado Fuel and Iron Strike, 1913–1914," in Ruth Milkman, ed., *Women, Work, and Protest: A Century of Women's Labor History* (Boston: Routledge and Kegan Paul, 1985), 66.

77. Ibid., 84.

78. Clyne, *Coal People*, 85.

79. Ibid., 86.

80. Long, "Women of the Colorado Fuel and Iron Strike," 79.

81. Todd Laugen, *The Gospel of Progressivism: Moral Reform and Labor War in Colorado, 1900–1930* (Boulder: University Press of Colorado, 2010), 56.

82. Long, "Women of the Colorado Fuel and Iron Strike," 79.

83. Ibid., 80–81. The UMW bought forty acres surrounding the Ludlow site. In 1918 a monument was erected and dedicated to the striking miners and victims.

84. Sally Mier, producer of the Storytellers Project, *Dearfield: A Videotaped Interview with Erma Downey Ingram* (Boulder: Storytellers Project, May 23, 1998), citation pages from Denver Public Library typescript copy. Blair-Caldwell African-American Research Library, MS-ARL-58, Denver Public Library.

85. Ibid., 6.

86. Ibid.

87. Ibid., 16.

88. Ibid., 15.

89. Ibid., 17.

90. Ibid., 18.

91. Sarah Deutsch, *No Separate Refuge: Culture, Class, and Gender on an Anglo-Hispanic Frontier in the American Southwest, 1880–1940* (New York: Oxford University Press, 1989), 48.

92. Ibid., 51.

93. Ibid., 48.

94. Ibid., 49.

95. Ibid., 47. For a discussion of the incorporation of *curanderismo* by contemporary Chicanos, see Ramon Del Castillo, "Institutionalizing Curanderismo in Colorado's Community Health System," in Arturo Aldama, Elisa Facio, Daryl Maeda, and Reiland Rabaka, eds., *Enduring Legacies: Ethnic Histories and Cultures in Colorado* (Boulder: University Press of Colorado, 2011), 291–308.

96. Ibid., 50–51.

97. Ibid., 75.

98. Katherine B. Osburn, *Southern Ute Women: Autonomy and Assimilation on the Reservation, 1887–1934* (Albuquerque: University Press of New Mexico, 1998), 4, 27, 72; Deutsch, *No Separate Refuge*, 82.

99. Deutsch, *No Separate Refuge*, 75–76.

100. Ibid., 78.

CHAPTER 7

1. Women in Wyoming (1890), Colorado (1893), Utah (1896), Idaho (1896), Washington (1910), California (1911), Oregon (1912), Kansas (1912), Arizona (1912), Montana (1914), and Nevada (1914) had full voting rights. In addition, the Territory of Alaska (1913) had granted women full voting rights.

2. "Helen Ring Robinson First Lady Senator," *Denver Republican*, November 8, 1912.

3. "Women Legislators Should Be Womanly," *New York Times*, November 23, 1913.

4. Nancy F. Cott, ed., *No Small Courage: A History of Women in the United States* (Oxford: Oxford University Press, 2000), 418.

5. "Woman Senator on Stump," *New York Times*, September 22, 1915.

6. "State's Woman Senator Returns," *Denver Republican*, July 10, 1913.

7. US accounts put the number of those who died at 1,517, while British reports said the disaster claimed 1,490 lives. Kristen Iversen, *Molly Brown: Unraveling the Myth* (Boulder: Johnson Books, 1999), 56–57.

8. Letter to Ellis Meredith from Judge Benjamin Lindsey and George Creel, Denver, October 16, 1915, Ellis Meredith Papers, MSS 427, History Colorado, Denver.

9. Gail M. Beaton, "The Widening Sphere of Women's Lives: The Literary Study and Philanthropic Work of Six Women's Clubs in Denver, 1881–1945," *Essays in Colorado History* 13 (Denver: History Colorado, 1992), 14.

10. Edward T. James, ed., *Notable American Women, 1607–1950: A Biographical Dictionary* (Cambridge, MA: Belknap Press of Harvard University Press, 1971), 451–452.

11. Ibid., 452.

12. Shafroth was a four-term US representative, Colorado governor (1908–1912), and US senator (1913–1919). As governor, he pushed for passage of the direct primary law and the direct election of senators. Lindsey founded Denver's

juvenile court and tried to abolish child labor. Patterson was elected to the US House of Representatives in 1877. He purchased the *Rocky Mountain News* and the *Denver Times,* which gave him a forum to support organized labor and fight corruption in state and city governments. The reform-minded Mayor Henry Arnold of Denver appointed Creel, of the *Rocky Mountain News* and the *Denver Post,* police commissioner. Creel ordered the police to methodically raid brothels and cribs to destroy the city's red light district and ordered them to give up their nightsticks and clubs.

13. Cott, *No Small Courage,* 389.

14. Lynda F. Dickson, "Lifting as We Climb: African-American Women's Clubs of Denver, 1890–1925," *Essays in Colorado History* 13 (Denver: History Colorado, 1992), 71–72.

15. Ibid., 73.

16. Jeanne Abrams, *Jewish Women Pioneering the Frontier Trail: A History in the American West* (New York: New York University Press, 2006), 76.

17. Ibid., 61.

18. Ibid., 82.

19. Ibid., 78.

20. Ibid., 64.

21. Robert G. Athearn, *The Coloradans* (Albuquerque: University of New Mexico Press, 1976), 235.

22. "Governor Names Advisory Council with Sixty-Eight Women," *Denver Post,* May 13, 1917.

23. Susan Riley Ashley, "A Very Brief Chronicle of the Denver Fortnightly's First Thirty-Five Years," November 1916, Denver Fortnightly Club Collection, MSS WH741, Western History Collection, Denver Public Library.

24. "Rich Women of Denver Will Save Food through Voluntary Rationing," *Rocky Mountain News,* January 30, 1918.

25. Seletha A. Brown, "Mrs. Mate Smith Hottel, a Pioneer Community Leader," *Colorado Magazine* 25, 5 (September 1948): 219.

26. Mary E. Hiatt, "Fortieth Anniversary of the Twenty-Second Avenue Study Club," October 18, 1933, in the possession of Zimmie Rupp, Denver.

27. Harriet Campbell, "There Were Giants in Those Irreclaimable Days," February 2, 1937, Denver Fortnightly Club Collection, MSS WH741, Western History Collection, Denver Public Library, 10.

28. Ibid.

29. "Woman's War Motor Service Here Has Been Reorganized," *Rocky Mountain News,* March 24, 1918.

30. "Minutes of the Twenty-Second Avenue Study Club, 6 February 1918," in the possession of Zimmie Rupp, Denver; *Yearbook of the Woman's Club of Denver, 1918–1919* (Denver: Woman's Club of Denver, 1918), Western History Collection, Denver Public Library.

31. Sister M. Celestine Casey, S.L., A.M., and Sister M. Edmond Fern, S.L., A.M., *Loretto in the Rockies* (Denver: Loretto Heights, 1943), 136.

32. Ibid., 137.

33. Ibid., 138.

34. Ibid.

35. "Women Help Solve Problems Peace Will Call before Nation," *Rocky Mountain News,* February 2, 1919.

36. Frances Bollacker Keck, *Conquistadors to the 21st Century: A History of Otero and Crowley Counties, Colorado* (La Junta, CO: Otero, 1999), 87.

37. Ashley, "Very Brief Chronicle," 221.

38. Cle Cervi and Nancy M. Peterson, coauthors and eds., *The Women Who Made the Headlines: Denver Woman's Press Club, the First Hundred Years* (Lakewood, CO: Western Guideways, 1998), 16.

39. "Women Legislators Should Be Womanly," *New York Times*, November 23, 1913.

40. Cervi and Peterson, *Women Who Made Headlines*, 17.

41. Helen Ring Robinson, *Preparing Women for Citizenship* (New York: Macmillan, 1918).

42. Ibid., 1.

43. "Mrs. Helen Ring Robinson Dies of Ailment Incurred by Overwork during the War," *Denver Post*, July 10, 1923.

44. Janet Robertson, *The Magnificent Mountain Women: Adventures in the Colorado Rockies* (Lincoln: University of Nebraska Press, 1990), 62–63.

45. Ibid., 64.

46. Ibid., 65.

47. A mustard plaster is made by combining dry mustard plaster with flour and either water or egg whites to form a paste that is applied to a cotton or flannel cloth. This is placed on a person's abdomen or chest to treat the common cold, runny nose, rheumatism, and respiratory problems.

48. Robertson, *Magnificent Mountain Women*, 68–70.

49. Ibid., 71.

50. Ibid., 71–72.

51. In 1900, 52 percent of African Americans were men and 48 percent were women. Ten years later, black women outnumbered black men in Denver. Lyle W. Dorsett, *The Queen City: A History of Denver* (Boulder: Pruett, 1977), 104.

52. Dickson, "Lifting as We Climb," 73.

53. Ibid., 82.

54. Ibid., 85.

55. Ibid., 86.

56. Ibid., 87.

57. Ibid., 87–88.

58. Ibid., 92.

CHAPTER 8

1. Tricia Henry, "Perry-Mansfield School of Dance and Theater Dance Research," *Journal of the Society for Dance Research* 8, 2 (Autumn 1990): 52–53.

2. Ibid., 55–56.

3. Jody Lopez and Gabriel Lopez, with Peggy A. Ford, *White Gold Laborers: The Story of Greeley's Spanish Colony* (Bloomington, IN: Author House), 165.

4. "Women KKK File Papers for State Charter," *Denver Post*, December 8, 1924.

5. Phil Goodstein, *In the Shadow of the Klan: When the KKK Ruled Denver, 1920–1926* (Denver: New Social Publications, 2006), 252.

6. "Invisible Empire, Women of the KKK," Women of the Klan (Limon) Collection 1925–1926, Box 1, MSS 1817, History Colorado, Denver.

7. Ibid., folder 4.

8. Ibid., folder 2.

9. Ibid., folder 6.

10. Betty Jo Brenner, "The Colorado Women of the Ku Klux Klan," presentation at History Colorado, Denver, February 28, 2009.

11. James L. Roark, Michael P. Johnson, Patricia Cline Cohen, Sarah Stage, Alan Lawson, and Susan M. Hartmann, eds., *The American Promise: A History of the United States,* 3rd ed., vol. 2: *From 1865* (Boston: Bedford/St. Martin's, 2005), 838.

12. Mary Jane Elizabeth Herrera, "Hispanic People of Grand Junction," *Journal of the Western Slope* 6, 3 (Fall 1991): 12.

13. José Aguayo, "Los Betabeleros (the Beetworkers)," in Vincent C. DeBaca, ed., *La Gente: Hispano History and Life in Colorado* (Denver: History Colorado, 1998), 107.

14. Ibid., 110.

15. Ibid., 115.

16. Ibid., 114, 119.

17. United States Department of Commerce, Bureau of the Census, *Fourteenth Census of the United States 1920: Population* (Washington, DC: Government Printing Office, 1924); *Fifteenth Census of the United States 1930* (Washington, DC: Government Printing Office, 1933).

18. United States Department of Commerce, Bureau of the Census, *Fifteenth Census of the United States 1930.*

19. Susan Armitage, "'The Mountains Were Free and We Loved Them': Dr. Ruth Flowers of Boulder, CO," in Quintard Taylor and Shirley Ann Wilson Moore, eds., *African American Women Confront the West, 1600–2000* (Norman: University of Oklahoma Press, 2003), 165–177.

20. United States Department of Commerce, Bureau of the Census, *Twelfth Census of the United States 1900: Population* (Washington, DC: Government Printing Office, 1901); *Fifteenth Census of the United States 1930.*

21. Nancy F. Cott, ed., *No Small Courage: A History of Women in the United States* (Oxford: Oxford University Press, 2000), 494.

22. United States Department of Commerce, Bureau of the Census, *Ninth Census of the United States 1870* (Washington, DC: Government Printing Office, 1872); *Eleventh Census of the United States 1890* (Washington, DC: Government Printing Office, 1897); *Fourteenth Census of the United States 1920*.

23. United States Department of Commerce, Bureau of the Census, *Fifteenth Census of the United States 1930: Population Colorado*, table 17: Women 15 years and over in selected occupations, by marital condition, with a distribution of the single and unknown and of the married by age, for the state, 1930; Joseph A. Hill, *Women in Gainful Occupations, 1870–1920* (Washington, DC: Government Printing Office, 1929), 36.

24. United States Department of Commerce, Bureau of the Census, *Fourteenth Census of the United States 1920: Population*; *Fifteenth Census of the United States 1930*.

25. United States Department of Commerce, Bureau of the Census, *Fifteenth Census of the United States 1930*; *Sixteenth Census of the United States 1940* (Washington, DC: Government Printing Office, 1941).

26. United States Department of Commerce, Bureau of the Census, *Sixteenth Census of the United States 1940*.

27. United States Department of Commerce, Bureau of the Census, *Fifteenth Census of the United States 1930*, table 11: Males and females, 10 years old and over in selected occupations, by color, nativity, and age, for the state, 1930.

28. Clark Secrest, "Calling by Dial: And to the Operator Goodbye," *Colorado Heritage* (Winter 1993): 29.

29. "Models Are to Be Awarded Phone Co. Employes [*sic*] at Pueblo," *Denver Post*, November 27, 1921.

30. United States Department of Commerce, Bureau of the Census, *Fifteenth Census of the United States 1930*.

31. Ibid., table 11: Males and females 10 years old and over in selected occupations, by color, nativity, and age, for the state: 1930.

32. Laura Gilpin, *The Pueblos: A Camera Chronicle* (New York: Hastings House, 1941); Gilpin, *The Rio Grande: River of Destiny* (New York: Duell, Sloan and Pearce, 1949).

33. Cle Cervi Symons and Nancy M. Peterson, coauthors and editors, *The Women Who Made the Headlines* (Lakewood, CO: Western Guideways, 1998), 31–32.

34. Elizabeth M. Safanda and Molly L. Mead, "The Ladies of French Street in Breckenridge," *Colorado Magazine* (Winter-Spring 1979): 24–25.

35. Ibid., 25.

36. United States Department of Commerce, Bureau of the Census, *Fourteenth Census of the United States 1920*.

37. Jill Boice, oral interview of Dr. Helen Fickel, Berthoud, CO, July 24, 1974, Fort Collins Public Library Oral History Project, Fort Collins, CO.

38. Ibid.

39. United States Department of Commerce, Bureau of the Census, *Fourteenth Census of the United States 1920*.

40. "Gertrude Vaile Chosen for Most Important Work," *Denver Republican*, October 8, 1912; "Miss Vaile Named to State Charities Board by Governor," *Rocky Mountain News*, January 23, 1924.

41. "Florence Huntsinpillar" [obituary], *Denver Post*, March 7, 1968.

42. Brenda Morrison, "Their Hats in the Ring: Colorado's Pioneer Female Politicians, 1890–1920," *Colorado History* 10 (2004): 3.

43. Ibid., 10.

44. Ibid., 8.

45. Joanne West Dodds, *Pueblo: A Pictorial History* (Norfolk, VA: Donning, 1982), 144.

46. Nell Brown Propst, *Those Strenuous Dames of the Colorado Prairies* (Boulder: Pruett, 1982), 80.

47. Myra Rich, *History of Planned Parenthood of the Rocky Mountains* (Denver: Planned Parenthood, 1994), 4.

48. Ibid., 13. The Denver Birth Control League became Planned Parenthood of Colorado in 1944. In 1972 it took the name Rocky Mountain Planned Parenthood before becoming Planned Parenthood of the Rocky Mountains in 1984.

49. "Honors Awarded 2 Women Medics" and "Greeley Physician Receives Florence Sabin Award," *Denver Post*, September 20, 1947, and May 16, 1958.

50. Mary Lou LeCompte, *Cowgirls of the Rodeo: Pioneer Professional Athletes* (Urbana: University of Illinois Press, 1993), 40–41, 55, 75.

51. Ibid., 85, 132, 223.

52. "She Packed a Punch . . . and Vital Goods," *Durango Herald*, February 11, 2012.

53. Janet Robertson, *The Magnificent Mountain Women: Adventures in the Colorado Rockies* (Lincoln: University of Nebraska Press, 1990), 44–46.

54. Ibid., 48.

55. Ibid., 50–51.

56. Ibid., 51–56.

57. Marjorie Perry, "The Saga of a Social Outlaw," April 7, 1964, 1, Perry Family Collection, C MSS WH 629, Box 3, folder #26, Western History Collection, Denver Public Library.

58. Ibid., 7, 9.

59. Ibid., 25.

60. Ibid., 28.

61. Bliss, 30, "Personal—Manuscripts—Text of Speech on Marjorie Perry," C MSS WH 628, Box 1, folder #29, Western History Collection, Denver Public Library. Eleanor Bliss continued to live in Steamboat Springs. She was so respected and loved by the community for her work in saving the railroad depot that its art center is named the Eleanor Bliss Center for the Arts.

62. http://divinescience.com/beliefs/ds_history.htm],

63. Henry, "Perry-Mansfield School," 51.

64. Ibid., 52–53.

65. "Charlotte Perry Honored," *Steamboat Pilot*, September 24, 1970.

66. Ibid.

67. "Vaudeville at Faurot," *Lima* [Ohio] *News*, November 2, 1923.

68. Henry, "Perry-Mansfield School," 60.

69. In 1961 Stephens College (Columbia, Missouri) began offering college credit to dance and theater students enrolled in Perry-Mansfield courses. In the mid-1960s the camp became an official part of Stephens College.

70. Letter from Julie Harris to the State Historical Fund, July 30, 1994, quoted in "Close to Creatures and Mountains," Ben Fogelberg, ed., *Colorado News* (June 2005): 9.

71. Henry, "Perry-Mansfield School," 65–66.

72. "Brief History Covering 1916–1940," YWCA of Metropolitan Denver Collection, #1254, Box 19, folder #461, History Colorado, Denver.

73. Ibid., Box 11, folder #234.

74. Ibid., Box 15, "Misc. 1927–1930."

75. Marcia Tremmel Goldstein, "Breaking down Barriers: The Denver YWCA and the Phyllis Wheatley Branch, 1940–1949," *Historical Studies Journal* 12, 1 (Spring 1995): 41.

76. Ibid. Camp Nizhoni closed in 1945 when black girls were allowed to participate in integrated camps at the YWCA's Camp Lookout.

77. Marcia Tremmel Goldstein, "Breaking down Barriers: Black and White Women's Visions of Integration: The Young Woman's Christian Association in Denver and the Phyllis Wheatley Branch, 1915–1964" (MA thesis, University of Colorado–Denver, 1995), 50–51.

78. Goldstein, "Denver YWCA," 49.

79. Goldstein, "Black and White Women's Visions," 127–128.

80. Goldstein, "Denver YWCA," 57.

81. Jeanne Varnell, *Women of Consequence: The Colorado Women's Hall of Fame* (Boulder: Johnson Books, 1999), 90.

82. Debra Faulkner, *Touching Tomorrow: The Emily Griffith Story* (Palmer Lake, CO: Filter, 2005), 132.

CHAPTER 9

1. Gertrude Rader, "The New Deal Program as Seen from Loma," *Journal of the Western Slope* 2, 4 (Fall 1987): 16–20.

2. Ibid., 16–17, 19.

3. Ibid., 19–20.

4. Ibid., 17–18.

5. Ibid., 18.

6. Modupe Labode, "Border Blockade," *Colorado History Now* (September-October 2007): 4.

7. Ibid.

8. Ibid., 4–5.

9. Judy Lopez and Gabriel Lopez, with Peggy A. Ford, *White Gold Laborers: The Story of Greeley's Spanish Colony* (Bloomington, IN: Author House, 2007), 150, 155–157, 165.

10. Sarah Deutsch, *No Separate Refuge: Culture, Class, and Gender on an Anglo-Hispanic Frontier in the American Southwest, 1880–1940* (New York: Oxford University Press, 1989), 88–89.

11. "Some Statistics of Employment Department," Phyllis Wheatley Branch YWCA, Fiscal Year 1930, YWCA of Metropolitan Denver Collection, CHS #1254, Box 11, folder #235, Misc. 1927–1930, History Colorado, Denver.

12. Ibid., "Statistics of Phyllis Wheatley Branch, 1931–1932," Box 15, folder #381, Phyllis Wheatley Administration 1930–1935.

13. Ibid.

14. Katherine B. Osburn, *Southern Ute Women: Autonomy and Assimilation on the Reservation, 1887–1934* (Albuquerque: University of New Mexico Press, 1998), 23.

15. Ibid., 4.

16. Richard K. Young, *The Ute Indians of Colorado in the Twentieth Century* (Norman: University of Oklahoma Press, 1997), 108.

17. Ibid., 86.

18. Lois Scharf, " 'The Forgotten Woman': Working Women, the New Deal, and Women's Organizations," in Lois Scharf and Joan M. Jensen, eds., *Decades of Discontent: The Women's Movement 1920–1940* (Westport, CT: Greenwood, 1983), 245.

19. Ibid., 246.

20. Ibid., 247.

21. Deutsch, *No Separate Refuge*, 176.

22. Ellen S. Woodward, "Hot Lunches for a Million School Children," speech by the assistant administrator of the Works Progress Administration, 1939, WPA Papers, Record Group 69, Series 737, Box 8, National Archives, Washington, DC.

23. James F. Wickens, *Colorado in the Great Depression* (New York: Garland, 1979), 289.

24. Ibid., 289–290.

25. Ibid., 290–291.

26. Stephen J. Leonard and Thomas J. Noel, *Denver: Mining Camp to Metropolis* (Niwot: University Press of Colorado, 1990), 214–215.

27. Louise W. Brand, interview with Jo Campbell, July 5, 1979, Denver, C MSS OH2-5, Western History Collection, Denver Public Library.

28. This building later housed the Department of Health, Education, and Welfare. Patricia Trenton, ed., *Independent Spirits: Women Painters of the American West*,

1890–1945 (Berkeley: Autry Museum of Western Heritage in association with University of California Press, 1995), 230–231.

29. Ibid.

30. Letter to her parents, June 6, 1934, Elizabeth Schroeder Kletzsch Manuscript Collection 732: 1934, History Colorado, Denver [hereafter Kletzsch Collection].

31. "50,000 Cattle Need to Be Removed from Bent, Prowers, and Baca Counties," *Rocky Mountain News*, March 25, 1935.

32. Ibid.

33. "US Sends 20,000 Men to Fight Dust as Worst Storm of Year Hits West," *Denver Post*, April 15, 1935.

34. Rader, "New Deal Program," 9.

35. Wickens, *Colorado in the Great Depression*, 238–242.

36. Carl Abbott, Stephen J. Leonard, and Thomas J. Noel, *Colorado: A History of the Centennial State*, 4th ed. (Boulder: University Press of Colorado, 2005), 285.

37. Paul Reddin, "Hard Times but Good Times: Grand Junction Women during the Great Depression," *Journal of the Western Slope* 1, 1 (Winter 1986): 4.

38. Ibid., 6, 17.

39. Ibid., 17.

40. Stephen J. Leonard, *Trials and Triumphs: A Colorado Portrait of the Great Depression, with FSA Photographs* (Boulder: University Press of Colorado, 1993), 38.

41. Julie Jones-Eddy, *Homesteading Women: An Oral History of Colorado, 1890–1950* (New York: Twayne [Oral History Series], 1992), 176, 179, 183.

42. Scharf, "Forgotten Woman," 253.

43. Judy Nolte Temple, *Baby Doe Tabor: The Madwoman in the Cabin* (Norman: University of Oklahoma Press, 2007), x.

44. Ibid., xvii–xviii.

45. Kletzsch, letter to her parents, April 12, 1934, Kletzsch Collection.

46. Ibid., March 16, 1934, Kletzsch Collection.

47. Ibid., March 18, 1934, Kletzsch Collection.

48. Ibid., letter to Carl [her son], April 22, 1934, Kletzsch Collection.

49. Ibid., letter to her parents, May 5, 1934, Kletzsch Collection.

50. "Milwaukee Woman Takes over Denver Relief Administration," *Denver Post*, March 12, 1934.

51. Kletzsch, letter to her parents, March 26, 1934, Kletzsch Collection.

52. Ibid.

53. Ibid., April 19, 1934, Kletzsch Collection.

54. Ibid., April 21, 1934, Kletzsch Collection.

55. Ibid., May 10, 1934, Kletzsch Collection.

56. In 1938 Robinson was a lecturer in social work in the School of Social Service Administration at the University of Chicago before returning to Denver in 1941 to care for her ailing mother. After her mother's death, she applied to the Denver chapter of the Red Cross as a caseworker. Instead, she was named its director

of home services, a position she held until her retirement in 1956. During World War II, Esther Sudler served as a vice-chairwoman of the Denver Red Cross and was active in its motor corps division. In 1936 Alice van Diest was invited to re-join Colorado College's Sociology Department, where she taught until ill health forced her retirement in 1954. A state founder of the Business and Professional Women's Clubs and the Colorado State League of Women Voters, as well as branches of both organizations in Colorado Springs, van Diest helped formulate Colorado state laws on Social Security.

57. Jeanne Varnell, *Women of Consequence: The Colorado Women's Hall of Fame* (Boulder: Johnson Books, 1999), 100.

58. Abbott, Leonard, and Noel, *Colorado*, 137.

59. Varnell, *Women of Consequence*, 103.

60. Elinor Myers McGinn, *A Wide-Awake Woman: Josephine Roche in the Age of Reform* (Denver: Colorado Historical Society, 2002), 76.

61. Abbott, Leonard, and Noel, *Colorado*, 211–212.

62. Varnell, *Women of Consequence,* 105–106.

63. Eudochia Bell Smith, *They Ask Me Why* (Denver: World Press, 1945), 20.

64. "Denver Woman Is Threatened in Probe of Un-American Activities," *Denver Post*, February 28, 1939.

CHAPTER 10

1. Oleta Crain, oral interview for *Colorado Reflections* (Denver: University of Colorado at Denver, Office of Public Information [1984]).

2. Marcia Goldstein, "We Can Wear the Pants, Too! Denver's Women Ordnance Workers, 1941–1945," unpublished paper, 1996, in author's possession.

3. Christine Pfaff, "Celebrating 50 Years of GSA: From the Denver Ordnance Plant to the Denver Federal Center" (Denver: General Services Administration, 1999), n.p.

4. Oleta Crain interview.

5. Christine Pfaff, "Bullets for the Yanks: Colorado's World War II Ammunition Factory," *Colorado Heritage* (1992): 37.

6. Nancy Cott, ed., *No Small Courage: A History of Women in the United States* (Oxford: Oxford University Press, 2000), 476.

7. Goldstein, "We Can Wear the Pants, Too," 11.

8. Moya Hansen, " 'Try Being a Black Woman!' Jobs in Denver, 1900–1970," in Quintard Taylor and Shirley Ann Wilson Moore, eds., *African American Women Confront the West* (Norman: University of Oklahoma Press, 2003), 207–227. After the war she was hired as a cook in a special diet kitchen at Fitzsimons Army Hospital, finally using her Opportunity School training.

9. Ibid., 212.

10. Ibid., 218. Later, Jennie graduated from the University of Denver's Library School, finally fulfilling her mother's wish for her—a college education.

11. Cott, *No Small Courage*, 479.

12. Goldstein, "We Can Wear the Pants, Too," 17.

13. "On the DOP Home Front," *Denver Ordnance Bulletin,* May 15, 1943, 8.

14. Cott, *No Small Courage*, 479.

15. Goldstein, "We Can Wear the Pants, Too," 16.

16. Lee H. Scamehorn, *Mill and Mine: The CF&I in the 20th Century* (Lincoln: University of Nebraska Press, 1992), 154.

17. Stephen J. Leonard, "Denver at War: The Home Front in World War II," *Colorado Heritage* (1987): 34.

18. *Transportation,* July 1943, quoted in the *Gazette-Telegraph* (Colorado Springs), April 29, 2001.

19. In 1947 the federal government converted the site to the Denver Federal Center. Pfaff, "Bullets for the Yanks," 47. It is now home to myriad federal agencies, including the Veterans Administration, Bureau of Reclamation, and General Services Administration.

20. Clark Secrest, "Vitamins for Victory," *Colorado Heritage* (1995): 27.

21. Ibid., 28.

22. Letter from May Wilkins to Don Wilkins, October 17, 1942, May Wilkins Collection, Box 3, folder 51, Fort Collins Library, Fort Collins, CO [hereafter May Wilkins Collection].

23. Letter from J. M. Lloyd, MD, to May Wilkins, October 27, 1943, May Wilkins Collection, Box 5, folder 63.

24. Letter from Don Wilkins to May Wilkins, November 12, 1943, May Wilkins Collection, Box 3, folder 51.

25. Letter from May Wilkins to Don Wilkins, October 17, 1942, May Wilkins Collection, Box 7, folder 90.

26. "Italians in Colorado" exhibit at History Colorado, Denver.

27. Cott, *No Small Courage*, 485.

28. "Two Denverites Are Chosen for WAAC Training," *Denver Post*, July 6, 1942.

29. "Denver Office Swears in 31 WAAC Recruits," *Denver Post*, November 11, 1942.

30. William Wei, "The Strangest City in Colorado: The Amache Concentration Camp," *Colorado Heritage* (2005): 12.

31. Letter from May Wilkins to Don Wilkins, October 17, 1942.

32. "Coloradan Broke Navy Barriers," *Denver Post*, June 7, 2009.

33. Virginia Moore interview, 1995, World War II Oral History Project, Fort Collins Public History, Local History Archive, Fort Collins Library, Fort Collins, CO.

34. "Woman Marines Faithful to the Core," *Denver Post*, April 8, 2002.

35. "50 WAACs Arrive at Lowry Field," *Rocky Mountain News*, January 1, 1943.

36. "Lowry Graduates Class of WAACs in Photography," *Rocky Mountain News*, April 25, 1943.

37. "Army Nurses at Lowry Field Are Typical Members of Corps," *Denver Post*, December 10, 1942.

38. Michael H. Levy and Staff Sgt. Patrick M. Scanlan, "Mrs. Dewey Takes Lowry Social Post," in *Pursuit of Excellence: A History of Lowry Air Force Base, 1937–1987* (Denver: History Office, Lowry Technical Training Center, Air Training Command, 1987), 34.

39. Thomas J. Noel and Chuck Woodward, *The Lowry Neighborhood: A Historic Denver Guide* (Denver: Historic Denver, 2002).

40. "Lowry's Women's Club First of Its Kind in US," *Rocky Mountain News*, December 13, 1942.

41. "Camp Hale's Forgotten Veterans," *Denver Post*, November 11, 2004.

42. Letter from May Wilkins to her mother, March 25, 1944, May Wilkins Collection, Box 4, folder 53.

43. "Denver Woman Serves Negro Troops in Britain," *Rocky Mountain News*, January 31, 1943.

44. Quoted in ibid. Jarrett had a number of aunts and uncles in Denver to whom she regularly wrote.

45. Virginia Moore interview.

46. Carl Abbott, Stephen J. Leonard, and Thomas J. Noel, *Colorado: A History of the Centennial State*, 4th ed. (Boulder: University Press of Colorado, 2005), 304.

47. Melyn Johnson, "At Home in Amache," *Colorado Heritage* (1989): 7.

48. Amache Collection, MSS 1269, Box 1, folder 86, History Colorado, Denver.

49. Ibid., Box 1, folder 85, and Box 3.

50. "Japanese See Their Evacuation as Part of America's War Effort," *Lamar Daily News*, September 19, 1942, in ibid., Box 1, folder 27.

51. Ibid., Box 1, folders 27, 29.

52. Ibid., "Amache Directory January 1943."

53. Wei, "Strangest City in Colorado," 14–15.

54. Goldstein, "We Can Wear the Pants, Too," 12.

55. Ibid.

56. Oleta Crain interview.

57. "Oleta Crain: A Major Achiever," *Rocky Mountain News*, February 9, 1995.

58. "Carr Creates State Defense Organization," *Denver Post*, June 8, 1941.

59. Zimmie Rupp, Twenty-Second Avenue Study Club, interview by author, Denver, CO, May 20, 1987.

60. Lucile Kling, "History of the Twenty-Second Avenue Study Club, 1943–44," Twenty-Second Avenue Study Club Collection, MSS 965, History Colorado, Denver.

61. Ibid.

62. *Yearbooks of the North Side Woman's Club, 1942–1944*, Western History Collection, Denver Public Library.

63. Kling, "History, 1943–44."

64. Ibid.; Dorothy Fallon, "History of the Twenty-Second Avenue Study Club, 1945–46," Twenty-Second Avenue Study Club Collection, MSS 965, History Colorado, Denver.

65. Kling, "History of the Twenty-Second Avenue Study Club, 1944–1945," Twenty-Second Avenue Study Club Collection, MSS 965, History Colorado, Denver.

66. Fallon, "History, 1945–46."

67. *Yearbook of the Woman's Club of Denver, 1942–1943.*

68. Kling, "History, 1944–1945"; Fallon, "History, 1945–1946."

69. Jeanette Bain, *History and Chronology of the Colorado State Federation of Women's Clubs, 1895–1955* (Denver: Colorado Federation of Women's Clubs, 1955), 81.

70. *Yearbook of the North Side Woman's Club, 1942–1943.*

71. Bain, *History and Chronology,* 81–82.

72. "World War II 'Angels' Get Their Due," *Rocky Mountain News,* May 14, 2008.

73. Ibid.

74. Althea Williams, oral interview, November 30, 1994, Local History Archive, Fort Collins Public Library, Fort Collins, CO.

75. Ibid.

76. Ibid.

77. Cle Cervi Symons and Nancy M. Peterson, coauthors and eds., *The Women Who Made the Headlines* (Lakewood, CO: Western Guideways, 1998), 55.

78. Ibid., 53, 55.

79. Jeanne Varnell, *Women of Consequence: The Colorado Women's Hall of Fame* (Boulder: Johnson Books, 1999), 153.

80. Ibid., 154.f

CHAPTER 11

1. "Marilyn Is Miss America! Denver's Blonde Chosen," *Denver Post,* September 18, 1957. Colorado's first Miss America was Sharon Kay Ritchie (1955).

2. Ibid.

3. "Ex–Miss America Reveals Horror," *Rocky Mountain News,* May 10, 1991.

4. United States Department of Commerce, Bureau of the Census, *Seventeenth Census of the United States 1950: Population* (Washington, DC: Government Printing Office, 1953); *Eighteenth Census of the United States 1960: Detailed Characteristics* (Washington, DC: Government Printing Office, 1963).

5. Carl Abbott, Stephen J. Leonard, and Thomas J. Noel, *Colorado: A History of the Centennial State,* 4th ed. (Boulder: University Press of Colorado, 2005), 185.

6. Quoted in Jeanne Varnell, *Women of Consequence: The Colorado Women's Hall of Fame* (Boulder: Johnson Books, 1999), 79–80.

7. Ibid., 80.

8. United States Department of Commerce, Bureau of the Census, *Eighteenth Census of the United States 1960: Colorado General Population Characteristics*, table 18: Marital status, by color and sex, for the state, by size and place, 1960, and for the state, 1950 and 1940.

9. Ibid; Nancy F. Cott, ed., *No Small Courage: A History of Women in the United States* (Oxford: Oxford University Press, 2000), 576.

10. Ibid., 496.

11. Ibid., 497.

12. Ibid.

13. Cle Cervi and Nancy M. Peterson, *The Women Who Made the Headlines: Denver Woman's Press Club, the First 100 Years* (Lakewood, CO: Western Guideways, 1998), 75–76.

14. "Antonio Brico, 87, a Conductor, Fought Barriers to Women in 30's," *New York Times*, August 5, 1989.

15. "1985 NEA National Heritage Fellow: Eppie Archuleta," at http://www. nea.gov/heritage/fellows.

16. Cott, *No Small Courage*, 501.

17. Ibid., 492.

18. "How to Be a Good Wife," excerpted from a 1950s high school home economics textbook, quoted in Clark Secrest, "The 50s: Shake, Rattle and Roll," *Colorado Heritage* (1996): 3.

19. Alice K. Beaton, interview by author , Denver, CO, November 26, 1999.

20. Cott, *No Small Courage*, 517.

21. "Colorado Abortion Rights Got Start 40 Years Ago Today," *Denver Post*, April 25, 2007.

22. Abbott, Leonard, and Noel, *Colorado*, 422; Cott, *No Small Courage*, 563.

23. "Comfort, Aid Offered at Crittenton" and "A Building Need," *Rocky Mountain News*, April 8 and 14, 1962.

24. "Home Helped 600 Unwed Mothers in '63," *Rocky Mountain News*, November 5, 1964.

25. "Florence Crittenton Association of America to Observe 75th Anniversary," *Denver Post*, April 18, 1968. The Florence Crittenton Home and School survives in the twenty-first century as an alternative school for teen mothers and fathers.

26. Stephen J. Leonard and Thomas J. Noel, *Denver: Mining Camp to Metropolis* (Niwot: University Press of Colorado, 1990), 372.

27. Quoted in ibid., 373.

28. Ibid. A similar hub for black society was the Kapre Lounge in Denver's Five Points, owned and operated by Delores Cousins Williams Webster ("Her Kapre Lounge Was a Hub of Black Society," *Denver Post*, December 23, 2005).

29. Moya Hansen, "Try Being a Black Woman! Jobs in Denver, 1900–1970," in Quintard Taylor and Shirley Ann Wilson Moore, eds., *African American Women Confront the West* (Norman: University of Oklahoma Press, 2003), 222.

30. Leonard and Noel, *Denver*, 381–382.

31. Ibid., 392; also see Bernadette Garcia-Galvez, "Latin Education and Life in Rural Southern Colorado, 1920–1945," in Arturo J. Aldama, Elisa Facio, Daryl Maeda, and Reiland Rabaka, eds., *Enduring Legacies: Ethnic Histories and Cultures in Colorado* (Boulder: University Press of Colorado, 2011), 219–236.

32. Leonard and Noel, *Denver*, 394.

33. Richard K. Young, *The Ute Indians of Colorado in the Twentieth Century* (Norman: University of Oklahoma Press, 1997), 265–266.

34. Ibid., 266–267.

35. Ibid., 141–143.

36. Ibid., 144–145. Nationwide, 800 Native American women joined the armed forces during World War II.

37. Ibid., 148. In 1952 the people voted to increase the distribution amount to $4,000 per member.

38. Ibid.

39. "Queen of Motivation," *Rocky Mountain News*, July 6, 1985.

40. "Devastated," *Rocky Mountain News*, July 7, 1994.

41. Ibid.

42. Elinor Bluemel, *Florence Sabin: Colorado Woman of the Century* (Boulder: University of Colorado Press, 1959), 28–32. Ella Denison was founder of the Denver Fortnightly Club and the Woman's Club of Denver. She served on the boards of the Denver YWCA, Civil Service Reform League, City Improvement Society, and Old Ladies' Home.

43. Ibid.

44. Abbott, Leonard, and Noel, *Colorado*, 328.

45. Ibid., 195.

46. Ibid.

47. "Trailblazer's Leadership Honored," *Denver Post*, February 2, 2007.

48. Ibid.

49. Varnell, *Women of Consequence*, 181–183.

CHAPTER 12

1. United States Department of Commerce, Bureau of the Census, *Twentieth Census of the United States 1980: Colorado: General Social and Economic Characteristics* (Washington, DC: Government Printing Office, 1984). Over twenty years later, females made up only 2.4 percent of the total number of persons employed in the construction trade in Colorado.

2. www.alvaradoconstruction.com.

3. United States Department of Commerce, Bureau of the Census, *Twenty-Second Census of Population and Housing 2000: Summary Social, Economic, and Housing Characteristics, Colorado* (Washington, DC: Government Printing Office, 2003).

4. Nancy F. Cott, ed., *No Small Courage: A History of Women in the United States* (Oxford: Oxford University Press, 2000), 537.

5. Ibid., 561.

6. United States Department of Commerce, Bureau of the Census, *1970 Census of Population and Housing, Detailed Characteristics, Colorado* (Washington, DC: Government Printing Office, 1973).

7. Bureau of Labor Statistics, *Current Population Survey* (Washington, DC: Government Printing Office, 2011), table 11: Employed persons by detailed occupation, sex, race, and Hispanic or Latino ethnicity, 3–4.

8. www.cubuffs.com.

9. Maureen Custy Roben, interview by author, Denver, CO, September 9, 2009.

10. Colleen Custy Lorenz, interview by author, Denver, CO, September 22, 2009.

11. www.komendenver.org.

12. Marcy Kaptur, *Women in Congress: A Twentieth-Century Odyssey* (Washington, DC: Congressional Quarterly Press, 1996), 174.

13. Pat Schroeder, with Andrea Camp and Robyn Lipner, *Champion of the Great American Family* (New York: Random House, 1989), 18.

14. Quoted in Ronald V. Dellums and H. Lee Halterman, *Lying down with the Lions: A Public Life from the Streets of Oakland to the Halls of Power* (Boston: Beacon, 2000), 149–150.

15. http://womenincongress.house.gov/member-profiles.

16. Schroeder, *Champion of the Great American Family*, 149, 158.

17. Ibid., 107–108.

18. Ibid., 108.

19. Ibid., 162.

20. "Anne Gorsuch Burford, 62, Dies; Reagan EPA Director," *Washington Post*, July 22, 2004.

21. Ibid.

22. Stephen J. Leonard, "Afterword," in *Helen Ring Robinson: Colorado Senator and Suffragist* by Pat Pascoe (Boulder: University Press of Colorado, 2011), 160–161.

23. "Chief Justice Mary J. Mullarkey Honored for 20 Years of Service on Colorado Supreme Court," Colorado State Judicial Branch news release, July 2, 2007, Denver.

24. http://www.courts.state.co.us/Bio.cfm.

25. "Milestone a Family Affair," *Denver Post*, December 11, 2010.

26. Vivian Sheldon Epstein, *History of Colorado's Women for Young People* (Denver: Vivian Sheldon Epstein, 1998), 44.

27. http://www.cogreatwomen.org/makepeace.

28. "Women's History," Colorado State Patrol Women's Resource Network, at http://www.colorado.gov.

29. E-mails from Detective Sheri Duran, DPD recruiter, April 16, 2012, and Wendi Smith, engineer, Denver Women Firefighters, April 16, 2012.

30. Thomas J. Noel, with Stephen J. Leonard and Kevin E. Rucker, *Colorado Givers: A History of Philanthropic Heroes* (Niwot: University Press of Colorado, 1998), 91–92.

31. Ibid., 83–86.

32. "Dream City Vision 2012: Alice Bemis Taylor," *Gazette* (Colorado Springs), April 26, 2010.

33. "Dying as She Lived, with Grace," *Denver Post,* October 21, 2011.

34. Janet Robertson, *The Magnificent Mountain Women: Adventures in the Colorado Rockies* (Lincoln: University of Nebraska Press, 1990), 179–180.

35. Ibid., 170–178.

36. Stephen J. Leonard and Thomas J. Noel, *Denver: Mining Camp to Metropolis* (Niwot: University Press of Colorado, 1990), 451.

37. Ibid., 164.

38. Stephen J. Leonard, "Women and Historic Preservation," *Colorado Magazine* (March-April 2009): 25.

39. Robertson, *Magnificent Mountain Women,* 180–181.

40. Leonard and Noel, *Denver,* 164.

41. Leonard, "Women and Historic Preservation," 26.

42. Ibid.

43. Ibid.

44. Jeannette Bain, ed., *History and Chronology: Colorado State Federation of Women's Clubs, 1895–1955* (Denver: Colorado Federation of Women's Clubs, 1955), 99.

45. General Federation of Women's Clubs, *GFWC Volunteers* (Washington, DC: General Federation of Women's Clubs, 1986), n.p.

46. Carl Abbott, Stephen J. Leonard, and Thomas J. Noel, *Colorado: A History of the Centennial State,* 4th ed. (Boulder: University Press of Colorado, 2005), 425.

47. Stephen Zamansky, "Colorado's Amendment 2 and Homosexuals' Right to Equal Protection of the Law," *Boston College Review* 35 (1993): 221–222.

48. United States Department of Commerce, Bureau of the Census, *Twenty-First Census of the United States 1990: Population* (Washington, DC: Government Printing Office, 1993); *Census of the United States: Colorado: 2000 Vital Statistics Population* (Washington, DC: Government Printing Office, 2002).

49. Virginia Scharff, *Twenty Thousand Roads: Women, Movement, and the West* (Berkeley: University of California Press, 2003), 188.

50. Margaret Duncan Brown, *Shepherdess of the Elk River Valley* (Denver: Golden Bell, 1967), 108.

FURTHER READING

Colorado libraries, historical societies, and museums have archival collections that offer a trove of information on the state's women and women's organizations. A listing can be found in Victor J. Danilow's *Colorado Museums and Historic Sites* (University Press of Colorado, 2000). Federal and state census records, the Colorado State Archives, and the National Archives contain valuable information for researchers. Susan Armitage's *Women in the West: A Guide to Manuscript Sources* (New York: Garland Publishing, 1991) and *History of Women, Guide to the Microfilm Collection* (Woodbridge, Connecticut: Research Publications, 1983) are excellent guides to primary sources by and about women.

Since the 1970s, many outstanding history books on American women have been published and many Colorado history books include chapters or sections on the state's women. Colorado History's *Colorado Heritage,*

Colorado Essays and Monographs, and *Colorado Now* newsletter publish a variety of articles for those interested in women's history.

The following is a list of suggested books that are not cited in *Colorado Women.*

AMERICAN WOMEN

Armitage, Susan, and Elizabeth Jameson, eds. *The Women's West.* Norman: University of Oklahoma Press, 1987.

Bataille, Gretchen M., and Kathleen Mullen Sands. *American Indian Women, Telling Their Lives.* Lincoln: University of Nebraska Press, 1984.

Benson, Susan Porter. *Counter Cultures: Saleswomen, Managers, and Customers in American Department Stores, 1890–1940.* Urbana: University of Illinois Press, 1986.

Blair, Karen J. *The Clubwoman as Feminist: True Womanhood Redefined, 1868–1914.* New York: Holmes and Meier Publishers, 1980.

Bruhns, Karen. *Women in Ancient America.* Norman: University of Oklahoma Press, 1999.

Butler, Anne M. *Daughters of Joy, Sisters of Misery: Prostitutes in the American West, 1865–90.* Urbana: University of Illinois Press, 1985.

Foote, Cheryl. *Women of the New Mexico Frontier, 1846–1912.* Boulder: University Press of Colorado, 1995.

Hartmann, Susan M. *The Home Front and Beyond: American Women in the 1940s.* Boston: Twayne Publishers, 1982.

Jameson, Elizabeth, and Susan Armitage, eds. *Writing the Range: Race, Class, and Culture in the Women's West.* Norman: University of Oklahoma Press, 1997.

Jeffery, Julie Roy. *Frontier Women: The Trans-Mississippi West, 1840–1880.* New York: Hill and Wang, 1979.

Jensen, Joan M., and Lois Scharf, eds. *Decades of Discontent: The Women's Movement 1920–1940.* Westport, CT: Greenwood Press, 1983.

Kaufman, Polly Welts. *National Parks and the Woman's Voice: A History.* Albuquerque: University of New Mexico Press, 2006.

Kerber, Linda, and Janet Sherron DeHart, eds. *Women's America: Refocusing the Past.* New York: Oxford University Press, 2000.

Moore, Marat. *Women in the Mines: Stories of Life and Work.* New York: Twayne Publishers, 1996.

Myres, Sandra L. *Westering Women and the Frontier Experience: 1800–1915.* Albuquerque: University of New Mexico Press, 1982.

Polk, Milbry, and Mary Tiegren. *Women of Discovery: A Celebration of Intrepid Women Who Explored the World.* New York: Clarkson Potter / Crown Publishers, 2001.

Riley, Glenda. *Confronting Race: Women and Indians on the Frontier, 1815–1915.* Albuquerque: University of New Mexico, 2004.

Riley, Glenda. *The Female Frontier: A Comparative View of Women on the Prairie and Plains*. Lawrence: University Press of Kansas, 1989.

Riley, Glenda. *A Place to Grow: Women in the American West*. Arlington Heights, IL: Harlan Davison, 1992.

Riley, Glenda. *Women and Indians on the Frontier, 1825–1915*. Albuquerque: University of New Mexico, 2004.

Rossiter, Margaret W. *Women Scientists in America: Struggles and Strategies to 1940*. Baltimore: Johns Hopkins University Press, 1987.

Ruiz, Vicki L., and Ellen Carol DuBois, eds. *Unequal Sisters: A Multicultural Reader in U.S. Women's History*. 2nd ed. New York: Routledge, 1994.

Schackel, Sandra K., ed. *Western Women's Lives: Continuity and Change in the Twentieth Century*. Albuquerque: University of New Mexico Press, 2003.

Scharf, Lois. *To Work and to Wed: Female Employment, Feminism, and the Great Depression*. Westport, CT: Greenwood Press, 1980.

Scharff, Virginia. *Taking the Wheel: Women and the Coming of the Motor Age*. Albuquerque: University of New Mexico Press, 1999.

Schlissel, Lillian, Vickie L. Ruiz, and Janice Monk. *Westering Women: Their Land, Their Lives*. Albuquerque: University of New Mexico Press, 1988.

Stratton, Joanna L. *Pioneer Women: Voices from the Kansas Frontier*. New York: Simon and Schuster, 1981.

Ware, Susan. *Beyond Suffrage: Women in the New Deal*. Cambridge, MA: Harvard University Press, 1981.

COLORADO BOOKS

General History

Abrams, Jeanne, Betty Jo Brenner, Michael Childers, Eric L. Clements, B. Erin Cole, Marcia Tremmel Goldstein, Rebecca A. Hunt, Azusa Ono, Melanie Shellenbarger, Shawn Snow, and Cheryl Siebert Waite. *Denver Inside and Out*. Boulder: University Press of Colorado, 2011.

Davis, Laurena Mayne. *125 People, 125 Years: Grand Junction's Story*. Grand Junction: Museum of Western Colorado, 2007.

De Onis, José, ed. *The Hispanic Contribution to the State of Colorado*. Boulder: University of Colorado Centennial Commission, 1976.

Pettit, Jan. *Utes: The Mountain People*. Boulder, CO: Johnson Printing, 1990.

Simmons, Virginia McConnell. *The San Luis Valley: Land of the Six-Armed Cross*. 2nd ed. Niwot: University Press of Colorado, 1999.

Simmons, Virginia McConnell. *The Ute Indians of Utah, Colorado, and New Mexico*. Niwot: University Press of Colorado, 2000.

Stephens, Robert J., La Wanna M. Larson, and the Black American West Museum. *African Americans of Denver*. Charleston, SC: Arcadia Publishing, 2008.

West, Elliott. *The Contested Plains: Indians, Goldseekers and the Rush to Colorado*. Lawrence: University Press of Kansas, 1998.

Wolle, Muriel Sibell. *Stampede to Timberline: The Ghost Towns and Mining Camps of Colorado*. Boulder, CO: 1949. Rev. ed., Chicago: Swallow Press, 1974.

Wroth, William, ed. *Ute Indian Arts and Culture: From Prehistory to the New Millennium*. Colorado Springs: Colorado Springs Fine Arts Center, 2000.

Women

Bluemel, Elinor. *One Hundred Years of Colorado Women*. Denver: Author, 1973.

Faulkner, Debra B. *Ladies of the Brown: A Women's History of Denver's Most Elegant Hotel*. Charleston, SC: The History Press, 2010.

McGinn, Elinor M. *Female Felons: Colorado's Nineteenth Century Inmates*. Cañon City, CO: Fremont-Custer Historical Society, 2001.

Mefford, Jack, Janet Sanders-Richter, and Jan Weir. *Hardship and Hope: Fascinating Women of Northern Colorado*. Denver: Midland Federal Savings, 1977.

Riley, Marilyn Griggs. *High Altitude Attitudes: Six Savvy Colorado Women*. Boulder, CO: Johnson Books, 2006.

Schnellman, Sue-Ann. *Colorado Women's History: A Multi-cultural Treasury*. Denver: Author, 1985.

Schweninger, Lee, ed. *The First We Can Remember: Colorado Pioneer Women Tell Their Stories*. Lincoln: University of Nebraska Press, 2011.

Semple, James Alexander, comp. *Representative Women of Colorado: A Pictorial Collection of Women Who Have Attained Prominence in Social, Political, Professional, Pioneer and Club Life in the State*. Denver: Alexander Art Publishing Company, 1911.

Shirley, Gayle G. *More Than Petticoats: Remarkable Colorado Women*. Guilford, CT: The Globe Pequot Press, 2002.

Smith, Duane A. *Town Building on the Colorado Frontier*. Albuquerque: University of New Mexico Press, 1987.

Underwood, Kathleen. *Women to the Rescue: Creating Mesa Verde National Park*. Mesa Verde Centennial Series. Durango, CO: Durango Herald Small Press, 2005.

The Fine Arts

Bogue, Lucile. *Dancers on Horseback: The Perry-Mansfield Story*. San Francisco: Strawberry Hill Press, 1984.

Kovinick, Phil, and Marian Yoshiki-Kovinick. *An Encyclopedia of Women Artists of the American West*. Austin: University of Texas Press, 1998.

Sternberg, Barbara Edwards, with Jennifer Boone and Evelyn Waldron. *Anne Evans—A Pioneer in Colorado's Cultural History: The Things That Last When Gold Is Gone*. Denver: Buffalo Park Press and Center for Colorado and the West at Auraria Library, 2011.

Watt, Eva Hodges. *A Woman for All Seasons: Helen Marie Black, Heart of the Denver Symphony Orchestra*. Denver: Helen Marie Black Music Education Fund, 2001.

Autobiographies and Biographies

Babb, Sonora. *An Owl on Every Post*. New York: McCall, 1970.

Backus, Harriet Fish. *Tomboy Bride: A Woman's Personal Account of Life in Mining Camps of the West*. Boulder, CO: Pruett Publishing, 2001.

Baker, Roger. *Clara: An Ex-Slave in Gold Rush Colorado*. Central City, CO: Black Hawk Publishing, 2003.

Barker, Jane Valentine, and Sybil Downing. *Martha Maxwell: Pioneer Naturalist*. Boulder, CO: Pruett Publishing, 1982.

Bird, Isabella Lucy. *A Lady's Life in the Rocky Mountains*. New York: G. P. Putnam's Sons, 1879–1880.

Black, Celeste. *Queen of Glen Eyrie: The Story of Mary Lincoln Mellen Palmer, Wife of General William Palmer*. Colorado Springs: BlackBear Publishing, 1999.

Bluemel, Elinor. *Opportunity School and Emily Griffith, Its Founder*. Denver: Green Mountain Press, 1970.

Brown, Margaret Duncan. *Shepherdess of the Elk River Valley*. Denver: Golden Bell Press, 1967.

Bruyn, Kathleen. *Aunt Clara Brown: Story of a Black Pioneer*. Boulder, CO: Pruett Publishing, 1970.

Burke, John. *The Legend of Baby Doe: The Life and Times of the Silver Queen of the West*. New York: G. P. Putnam's Sons, 1974.

Ellis, Anne. *The Life of an Ordinary Woman*. Boston: Houghton Mifflin, 1990.

Ellis, Anne. *Plain Anne Ellis: More about the Life of an Ordinary Woman*. Lincoln: University of Nebraska Press, 1997.

Furman, Evelyn E. Livingston. *My Search for Augusta Pierce Tabor: Leadville's First Lady*. Denver: Quality Press, 1993.

Hall, Ruth Schooley. *Soddie Bride: Reminiscences of a Homesteader's Wife Who Lived on the High Plains of Northeast Colorado in the Early Years of This Century*. Fort Collins, CO: Robinson Press, 1973.

Lowery, Linda. *One More Valley, One More Hill: The Story of Aunt Clara Brown*. New York: Random House, 2002.

Mathes, Valerie Sherer. *Helen Hunt Jackson and Her Indian Reform Legacy*. Austin: University of Texas Press, 1990.

McClure, Grace. *The Bassett Women*. Athens: Swallow Press/Ohio University Press, 1985.

Metz, Myrtle D. *Of Haviland and Honey: A Colorado Girlhood, 1924–1947*. Boulder: Pruett Publishing, 1992.

Moynihan, Betty. *Augusta Tabor: A Pioneering Woman*. Evergreen, CO: Cordillera Press, 1988.

Mumey, Nolie. *The Saga of "Auntie" Stone and Her Cabin*. Boulder, CO: Johnson Publishing Company, 1964.

Phillips, Kate. *Helen Hunt Jackson: A Literary Life*. Berkeley: University of California Press, 2003.

Richards, Clarice E. *A Tenderfoot Bride: Tales from the Old Ranch*. Lincoln: University of Nebraska Press, 1988.

Shaw, Edith Taylor. *Edith Taylor Shaw's Letters from a Weminuche Homestead, 1902*. Durango, CO: Durango Herald Press and Center of Southwest Studies at Fort Lewis College, 2003.

Stewart, Elinore Pruitt. *Letters of a Woman Homesteader*. Boston: Houghton Mifflin Company, 1914.

West, Mark I., ed. *Westward to a High Mountain: The Colorado Writings of Helen Hunt Jackson*. Denver: Colorado Historical Society, 1994.

Whitacre, Christine. *Molly Brown: Denver's Unsinkable Lady*. Denver: Historic Denver, 1984.

Education

Bluemel, Elinor. *The Golden Opportunity: The Story of the Unique Emily Griffith Opportunity School of Denver*. Boulder, CO: Johnson Publishing, 1965.

Bluemel, Elinor. *Opportunity School and Emily Griffith, Its Founder*. Denver: Green Mountain Press, 1970.

Delta Kappa Gamma Society. *Up the Hemline: Being a True Account of One Hundred Years of Classroom Experience in Colorado*. Colorado Springs: Delta Kappa Gamma Society, 1975.

Symons, Cle Cervi. *100 Moore Years, 1890–1990: A History of Dora Moore School*. Denver: s.n., 1990.

Westermeier, Therese Stengel. *Women Too at CU*. Boulder: University of Colorado Centennial Commission, 1976.

Prostitution

Agnew, Jeremy. *Brides of the Multitude: Prostitution in the Old West*. Lake City, CO: Western Reflections Publishing, 2008.

Black, Celeste. *The Pearl of Cripple Creek: The Story of Cripple Creek's Most Famous Madam, Pearl Devere*. Colorado Springs: BlackBear Publishing, 1997.

Blair, Kay Reynolds. *Ladies of the Lamplight*. Ouray, CO: Western Reflections Publishing, 2000.

Dodds, Joanne West. *What's a Nice Girl Like You Doing in a Place Like This? Prostitution in Southern Colorado, 1860–1911*. Pueblo, CO: Focal Plain, 1996.

MacKell, Jan. *Brothels, Bordellos, and Bad Girls: Prostitution in Colorado, 1860–1930*. Albuquerque: University of New Mexico Press, 2004.

Secrest, Clark. *Hell's Belles: Denver's Brides of the Multitudes with Attention to Various Gamblers, Scoundrels, and Mountebanks and a Biography of Sam Howe, Frontier Lawman*. Aurora, CO: Hindsight Historical Publications, 1996.

Wommack, Linda R. *Our Ladies of the Tenderloin: Colorado's Legends in Lace*. Caldwell, ID: Caxton Press, 2005.

Ranching and Farming

Cirbo, Fran. *Working the Land: Building a Life*. Denver: Kimco Printers, 2009.

Hensley, Marcia Meredith. *Staking Her Claim: Women Homesteading the West*. Glendo, WY: High Plains Press, 2008.

Jones-Eddy, Julie. *Homesteading Women: An Oral History of Colorado, 1890–1950*. Oral History Series. New York: Twayne Publishers, 1992.

Sammons, Judy Buffington. *Riding, Roping, and Roses: Colorado's Women Ranchers*. Montrose, CO: Western Reflections Publishing, 2006.

Schackel, Sandra K. *Working the Land: The Stories of Ranch and Farm Women in the Modern American West*. Lawrence: University Press of Kansas, 2011.

Science and Medicine

Barker, Jane Valentine, and Sybil Downing. *Martha Maxwell: Pioneer Naturalist*. Boulder, CO: Pruett Publishing, 1982.

DeMund, Mary. *Women Physicians of Colorado*. Denver: Range Press, 1976.

Downing, Sybil, and Jane Valentine Barker. *Florence Rena Sabin: Pioneer Scientist*. Boulder: Pruett Publishing, 1981.

Women's Organizations

Buren, Dorothy, comp. *History: Daughters of the American Revolution in Colorado, 1894–1953*. Colorado Springs: Dentan Printing Co., 1952.

Fisher, Ellen Kingman. *Junior League of Denver: Leaders in Community Service, 1918–1993*. Denver: Colorado Historical Society, 1993.

Iona, Nancy Mossman. *Brief History of the Denver, Colorado Branch American Association of University Women*. Denver: Author, 1998.

Tarbell, Grace Elizabeth [Butler]. *History of the Daughters of the American Revolution of Colorado, 1894–1941*. Denver: s.n., 1941.

Woman's Suffrage and Politics

Beeton, Beverly. *Women Vote in the West: The Woman Suffrage Movement, 1869–1896*. New York: Garland, 1986.

Lowy, Joan A. *Pat Schroeder: A Woman of the House*. Albuquerque: University of New Mexico Press, 2003.

Pascoe, Pat. *Helen Ring Robinson: Senator and Suffragist*. Boulder: University Press of Colorado, 2011.

Pellet, Betty, with Alexander Klein. *"That Pellet Woman!"* New York: Stein and Day, 1965.

Schroeder, Pat. *Twenty-four Years of Housework—And the Place Is Still a Mess: My Life in Politics*. Kansas City: Andrews McMeel, 1999.

INDEX

Page numbers in italics indicate illustrations.